THE ARDEN SHAKESPEARE

GENERAL EDITORS:
RICHARD PROUDFOOT, ANN THOMPSON
and DAVID SCOTT KASTAN

KING RICHARD II

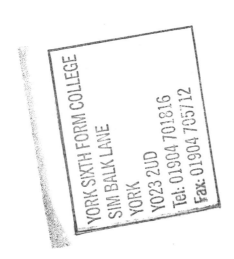

THE ARDEN SHAKESPEARE

* Third Series

THE ARDEN EDITION OF THE WORKS OF WILLIAM SHAKESPEARE

KING RICHARD II

Edited by
PETER URE

The general editors of the Arden Shakespeare have been
W. J. Craig and R. H. Case (first series 1899-1944),
Una Ellis-Fermor, Harold F. Brooks, Harold Jenkins
and Brian Morris (second series 1946-1982)

Present general editors (third series)
Richard Proudfoot, Ann Thompson and David Scott Kastan

This edition of *Richard II,* by Peter Ure,
first published in 1956 by Methuen & Co. Ltd
Reprinted 22 times

Reprinted 1998 by Thomas Nelson & Sons Ltd

Thomas Nelson & Sons Ltd
Nelson House Mayfield Road
Walton-on-Thames Surrey
KT12 5PL UK

I(T)P® Thomas Nelson is an International
Thomson Publishing Company
I(T)P® is used under licence

Editorial matter © 1956 Methuen & Co. Ltd

Printed in Italy

ISBN 0-17-443577-0 (hardback)
ISBN 0-17-443576-2 (paperback)
NPN 9 8 7 6 5 4 3

CONTENTS

PREFACE

THIS EDITION is not based upon the previous Arden edition by
Ivor B. John, although it has of course been consulted. Amongst
editions of the play, I am chiefly indebted to that by Professor
J. Dover Wilson (Cambridge University Press, 1939, second edition 1951). Although I have ventured to disagree from time to time
with his findings, the debt which all modern students of Shakespeare owe to Dover Wilson is perhaps even greater than usual in
the case of an editor of this play. I have also made especially continuous use of the editions by C. H. Herford (Warwick Shakespeare), W. A. Wright (Cambridge Shakespeare), and J. C. Smith
and Henry Newbolt (Clarendon Press), and of the studies of various
aspects of the play by A. W. Pollard, A. P. Rossiter, Richmond
Noble, and Paul Reyher, and of M. P. Tilley's magnificent *A Dictionary of the Proverbs in England*.

I have been helped in various ways by the General Editor, Professor R. H. Bowers, Dr A. S. Cairncross, Dr N. A. Furness, Professor A. R. Humphreys, and Dr A. Macdonald and, especially, by
Mr J. C. Maxwell, who gave me much valuable advice and saved
me from numerous errors. I am grateful to the staff of the University Library, Newcastle upon Tyne, in particular to Miss
Winifred Donkin and Mr G. M. Budge, for their efficient aid, and
to the Council of King's College for granting me a term's leave of
absence in which to complete my work. My biggest debt is to the
Advisory Editor, Dr Harold F. Brooks: there are few pages in this
volume which are not the better for his tireless scrutiny and
generous criticism.

P. U.

18 January 1955.

vii

PREFACE TO THE FIFTH EDITION
(1961)

SINCE the fourth edition went to press the chief publications bearing on the play have included the New Variorum edition by M. W. Black (Philadelphia and London, 1955), the article by Josephine Waters Bennett, 'Britain among the Fortunate Isles', in *Studies in Philology* (1956), the chapter in M. M. Mahood's *Shakespeare's Wordplay* (London, 1957), a chapter on King Richard in E. H. Kantorowicz's *The King's Two Bodies* (Princeton, 1957), and the third volume of Geoffrey Bullough's *Narrative and Dramatic Sources of Shakespeare* (London, 1960). In this edition some mistakes are corrected, and some additional notes presented. Readings have been altered in four places (I. iv. 20, II. i. 70, III. ii. 30, III. iii. 119).

P. U.

ABBREVIATIONS

The abbreviated titles of Shakespeare's works are those of Onions, *A Shakespeare Glossary* (2nd edn, 1919); line numbers and texts of passages cited or quoted as in *Complete Works*, ed. P. Alexander (London, 1951). Quotations from the Bible, unless otherwise stated, are from the Bishops' Bible, 1569 edn. The usual abbreviations are used for titles of periodicals.

Abbott	E. A. Abbott, *A Shakespearian Grammar* (3rd edn), London, 1870.
Alexander	William Shakespeare, *The Complete Works*, ed. Peter Alexander, London and Glasgow, 1951.
Apperson	G. L. Apperson, *A Dictionary of English Proverbs and Proverbial Sayings*, London, 1929.
Bond	*Complete Works of John Lyly*, ed. R. W. Bond, Oxford, 1892.
Brereton	'Some Notes on *Richard II*' in *Writings on Elizabethan Drama* by J. Le Gay Brereton, collected by R. G. Howarth, Melbourne, 1948.
Coleridge	*Coleridge's Shakespearian Criticism*, ed. T. M. Raysor, London, 1930.
Craig	*The Tragedy of Richard II*, ed. Hardin Craig (Tudor Shakespeare), New York, 1912.
Créton	Jean Créton, *Histoire du Roy d'Angleterre Richard*, ed. and trans. by J. Webb in *Archaeologia*, vol. xx, London, 1824.
Daniel, *C. W.*	Samuel Daniel, *The First Fowre Bookes of the ciuile warres between the two houses of Lancaster and Yorke*, London, 1595.
Deighton	*The Tragedy of King Richard II*, ed. K. Deighton, London, 1898.
Edward II	Marlowe, *Edward II*, ed. H. B. Charlton and R. D. Waller, London, 1933.
England's Parnassus	*England's Parnassus*, compiled by Robert Allot, 1600, ed C. Crawford, Oxford, 1913.
Frijlinck	*The First Part of the Reign of King Richard the Second*, or *Thomas of Woodstock*, ed. W. P. Frijlinck, Malone Society Reprint, 1929.
Froissart	*The Chronicle of Froissart translated out of French by Sir John Bourchier Lord Berners*, with an introduction by W. P. Ker, London, 1903.
Hall	Edward Hall, *The vnion of the two noble and illustre famelies of Lancastre & Yorke*, London, 1809 edn.
Hart	Alfred Hart, *Shakespeare and the Homilies*, Melbourne, 1934.

Hayward   Sir John Hayward, *The First Part of the Raigne of King Henrie IIII*, London, 1599.

Hazlitt's Dodsley *A Select Collection of Old English Plays*, ed. W. C. Hazlitt, London, 1874–6.

Herford   *The Tragedy of King Richard II*, ed. C. H. Herford (Warwick Shakespeare), London, 1893.

Hol.   Raphael Holinshed, *The Historie of England*, London, 1586–7. (References are normally to the page, the column, and the first line of the passage cited.)

Homilies   *Certain Sermons or Homilies . . .*, London, 1844 edn.

John   *The Tragedy of King Richard II*, ed. I. B. John (Arden Shakespeare), London, 1912.

Kittredge   *The Tragedy of King Richard II*, ed. G. L. Kittredge, Boston, 1941.

Kökeritz   H. Kökeritz, *Shakespeare's Pronunciation*, New Haven, 1953.

Mirror   *The Mirror for Magistrates*, ed. L. B. Campbell, Cambridge, 1938.

M.S.R.   Malone Society Reprint.

Nares   Robert Nares, *A Glossary, or Collection of Words, Phrases and Names . . .* London, 1822.

Newbolt   *Shakespeare's Richard the Second*, ed. H. Newbolt [and J. C. Smith], Oxford, 1912.

Noble   Richmond Noble, *Shakespeare's Use of the Bible*, London, 1935.

O.E.D.   *Oxford English Dictionary*.

Onions   C. T. Onions, *A Shakespeare Glossary* (2nd edn), Oxford, 1919 (last corrected impression, 1946).

Pollard   *King Richard II. A New Quarto*. With an Introduction by A. W. Pollard, London, 1916.

Reyher   P. Reyher, 'Notes sur les Sources de Richard II', *Revue de l'Enseignement des Langues Vivantes* (1924), pp. 1 ff, 54 ff, 106 ff, 158 ff, Paris, 1924.

Rossiter   A. P. Rossiter, ed. of *Woodstock* [q.v.].

Schmidt   A. Schmidt, *Shakespeare-Lexicon* (3rd edn), Berlin, 1902.

Scott-Giles   C. W. Scott-Giles, *Shakespeare's Heraldry*, London, 1950.

Shakespeare's England *Shakespeare's England: an Account of the Life and Manners of his Age*, Oxford, 1916.

R. M. Smith   R. M. Smith, *Froissart and the English Chronicle Play*, New York, 1915.

Steel   A. Steel, *Richard II*, Cambridge, 1941.

Tilley   M. P. Tilley, *A Dictionary of the Proverbs in England . . .*, Ann Arbor, 1950. (The references are to the proverbs as alphabetically arranged according to the initial letters of significant words.)

Traïson   *Chronicque de la Traïson et Mort de Richart Deux Roy Dengleterre*, ed. B. Williams, English Historical Society Publications, London, 1846.

Wilson   *Richard II*, ed. J. Dover Wilson (2nd edn), Cambridge, 1951.

Woodstock	*Woodstock, a Moral History*, ed. A. P. Rossiter, London, 1946.
Wright	Edition of *Richard II* in *The Works of . . . Shakespeare*, ed. W. A. Wright (The Cambridge Shakespeare), vol. IV, London, 1891.
Zeeveld	W. G. Zeeveld, 'The Influence of Hall on Shakespeare's English History Plays', *ELH, A Journal of English Literary History*, vol. III, 1936.

A dagger indicates that an additional note will be found at the end of the Introduction (p. lxxxiv) or of the text (pp. 208 ff.)

INTRODUCTION

I. TEXT

There are five Quarto editions of the play before the First Folio, one in 1597, two in 1598, and one each in 1608 and 1615.[1] The relation of these Quartos to one another has been thoroughly investigated by A. W. Pollard, whose findings are set down here. The first Quarto derives either directly or through intermediate transcriptions from Shakespeare's manuscript, and each of the other Quartos is a reprint of its immediate predecessor.

First Quarto (Q1), title-page:

THE / Tragedie of King Ri / chard the se- / cond. / *As it hath beene publikely acted / by the right Honourable the / Lorde Chamberlaine his Ser- / uants.* [Device] / LONDON / Printed by Valentine Simmes for Androw [*sic*] Wise, and / are to be sold at his shop in Paules church yard at / the signe of the Angel. / 1597

Running title: *The Tragedie of / King Richard the second*
Collation: A–I⁴, K².

Q1 was entered in the Stationers' Register by Andrew Wise on 29 August 1597, Wise having presumably purchased his copy from Shakespeare's company, the Lord Chamberlain's Men. Three copies of Q1 are known: in the Capell collection at Trinity College, Cambridge, in the British Museum (formerly the property of Alfred Huth), and in the Huntington Library, California (formerly the property of the Duke of Devonshire).† Some errors on certain sheets were detected in the printing-house in the course of the printing of this edition. Because these were corrected in some copies of these sheets only, and the corrected and uncorrected sheets bound up at random into the volumes in accordance with the usual practice, the three extant copies of Q1 chance to differ from one another in their proportion of corrected and uncorrected sheets.[2] This Quarto, like the two which immediately follow it,

---

1. For a full bibliographical description of these, see W. W. Greg, *A Bibliography of the English Printed Drama to the Restoration*, 1 (1939), no. 141.
2. The sheets affected are A, B, C, D, and I. Of these Q1 (Hunt.) has two (A and D) in the uncorrected state, and three in the corrected (B, C, and I);

omits the passage in IV. i. 154–318 on Richard's abdication (the "deposition scene"). This is likely to have been performed on the stage, but was cut out of the manuscript as sent to the printer,[1] probably because political conditions towards the end of the century made the dethronement of an English monarch a dangerous subject for public discussion.

In 1598 Wise brought out two more editions (Q2 and Q3), the only instance except that of *Pericles* of a Shakespearian Quarto going into two editions in the same year. Pollard has shown that the second Quarto was set up from the first: it repeats most of the errors of Q1, and, on Pollard's count, introduced a hundred and twenty-three new ones.[2] The third Quarto, a copy of which, now in the Folger Shakespeare Library at Washington, was identified by Miss Henrietta C. Bartlett in 1913, reproduces most of this "mass of new errors", apart from a few obvious corrections, as well as some corrections of Q1 made by Q2. Pollard has shown that Q3 must be the later of the two Quartos of 1598 because it attempts to mend two passages corrupted by Q2 and also makes a significant typographical error at II. iii. 116.[3]

The Stationers' Register records that on 25 June 1603 Wise transferred his rights in *Richard II*, *Richard III*, *1 Henry IV*, and two other items to Matthew Law. Law, when he came to print the play in 1608 from Wise's last Quarto (Q3), added the scene of Richard's abdication for the first time. The title-page of Q4 is found in two states, of which the second and later advertises the additional material:

THE / Tragedie of King / Richard the Second: / With new additions of the Parlia- / ment Sceane, and the deposing / of King Richard, / As it hath been lately acted by the Kinges / Maiesties seruantes, at the Globe. / By *William Shake-speare*. / [Device.] / AT LONDON, / Printed by W. W, for *Mathew Law*, and are to / be sold at his shop in Paules Church-yard, / at the signe of the Foxe / 1608.

We can only conjecture how Law obtained his copy for the;

Q1 (Huth) has the corrected sheets A, C, and D and the uncorrected B and I; Q1 (Cap.) has only one corrected sheet (I).

1. Pollard, p. 97.   2. *Ibid.*, p. 46.

3. See Pollard, p. 17: "In [Q1] this reads quite clearly
        You are my father, for me thinkes in you
        I see old Gaunt aliue.
In [Q2] the f in 'for' is so broken away that only a thin ridge representing part of the back is visible. In [Q3] the f is omitted, 'or' taking the place of 'for'. The omission of the f in [Q3] is thus explained by the compositor having overlooked the small fragment of one in [Q2]."

"additions".[1] These, as they appear in Q4 and again in Q5, seem to be a memorial reconstruction, as certain omissions and mislineations show. Law's Quarto of 1615 is derived from Q4.

Q1 is likely to be fairly close to Shakespeare's autograph. Pollard argued that in some of the set speeches (for example, III. iii. 142–59) the Quarto preserves what looks like authorial dramatic pointing; the rest of the Quarto is "patently underpunctuated", perhaps because Shakespeare composed much of the play very rapidly—"the words often coming to him as fast as he could set them down"—so that the compositor had to supply most of the punctuation, which he did in rather meagre measure. Pollard concluded from this combination of inadequate punctuation and dramatic pointing, though not, apparently, with a great deal of confidence, that it is simpler to suppose that the compositor had before him Shakespeare's foul papers rather than any intervening transcription of these.[2] Another sign of closeness to autograph is a certain type of mislineation and wrong division of verse which occasionally occurs in the Quarto. In some places a half-line or a metrically detached phrase is printed as part of the line that follows or precedes it:

IV. i. 65–6:
    Dishonorable boy, / that lie shall lie so heauie on my
      sword,

II. ii. 60–1:
    And al the houshold seruants fled with him / to
      Bullingbrook

I. iv. 11–12:
    Farewel, / & for my hart disdained that my tongue

III. iii. 35:
    H. Bull. / on both his knees doth kisse king Richards hand,

The Quarto here probably represents correctly what was in its copy and the errors are not to be blamed on the compositor; if so, the copy reflects what is suspected to be a habit of Shakespeare's own.[3] In other places the lineation and verse-division are more radically affected by the compositor's attempt to rectify the disturbance

---

1. Pollard (p. 64) suggested that they were obtained from "some subordinate person employed about the theatre", or from shorthand writers sent there for the purpose. The latter is unlikely, since none of the three known Elizabethan systems of stenography could have produced a text so comparatively "good" as these Quartos' versions of the scene: see G. I. Duthie, *Elizabethan Shorthand and the First Quarto of King Lear* (Oxford, 1949), *passim*.

2. Pollard, pp. 96–8.

3. Dover Wilson, *The Manuscript of Shakespeare's Hamlet* (Cambridge, 1934), p. 221.

caused by mistaking the original one-and-a-half lines for one:

II. i. 186–8:

> Oh my liege, / pardone me if you please,
> If not I pleasd / not to be pardoned, am content with all,

Here Shakespeare probably wrote: "Oh my liege, pardone me if you please, if not I pleasd / Not to be pardoned. . .' (For discussion of similar cases, see the notes to III. iii. 11, III. iv. 57, IV. i. 181–3.) Other errors in lineation and verse-division are to be attributed to the compositor rather than to his copy.[1] Other signs of closeness to autograph include the "graphic and informal" stage directions such as those at v. ii. 71, 84 and v. v. 104, 107, which are "clearly the author's", as well as inconsistency in the designation of characters. (E.g., "Bolingbroke" is occasionally "Hereford" and later "King").[2]

None of this rules out the possibility of an intervening transcript; some other features of QI tend to show that there may have been one.[3] A fairly clear example is provided in the last scene of the play: at v. vi. 7–8 the Quarto reads:

> The next newes is, I haue to London sent
> The heades of Oxford, Salisbury, Blunt and Kent,

"Oxford" is here a bad mistake; it implies quite wrongly that Aubrey de Vere, Earl of Oxford, was implicated in the Abbot of Westminster's conspiracy against Henry IV. The Folio emends the line to "The heads of *Salsbury, Spencer, Blunt,* and *Kent:*" (Spencer is Hugh, or Thomas, Spenser, whose execution at Bristol is recorded by Holinshed).[4] The obvious source of QI's error occurs four lines and an intervening stage direction later:

> My Lord, I haue from Oxford sent to London
> The heads of Broccas, and sir Benet Seely,

That the Quarto should have anticipated the "Oxford" of this line cannot well be explained by normal catching on the part of a compositor. It is very unlikely that a compositor, accustomed to carry not more than a few words in his composing stick and his memory,

---

1. E.g. I. iii. 123–4, II. iii. 28–9, IV. i. 17–19, v. i. 27–8, v. ii. 99–100.

2. On these last two points, see W. W. Greg, *The Shakespeare First Folio* (Oxford, 1955), p. 236.

3. The hypothesis of memorial contamination was, so far as I know, first suggested by Dr A. S. Cairncross. Dr H. F. Brooks has since developed it independently in notes for a projected article; to him I am indebted for generous permission to consult these notes and to make use of the theory and the examples with which he supports it.

4. Hol., 516/2/16.

would anticipate a word so far ahead of the line he is setting.[1] But a scribe, who knew how the scene went already, engaged on copying a fair text from Shakespeare's foul papers, might allow his memory, confused by the similarity in general import and phrasing of the two passages, to play him the trick of substituting the wrong name for the right one.

Wilson has shown, in the case of the transcript of the promptbook which he thinks was the copy for the Folio text of *Hamlet*, how a scribe who is familiar with the text of the play that he is copying may be led astray by his confidence that his memory of the text is accurate and make thereby errors of omission, transposition of words, anticipation, and understanding which have a wider range and a different character from the mistakes that can be made by a compositor, who merely follows the lines of his copy and has no general knowledge of the text. The kind of trick that memory can play with a dramatic text has been further investigated by D. L. Patrick in his study of the textual history of *Richard III*.[2] Patrick shows that the First Quarto of *Richard III* is an abridgement and adaptation of the play for simplified production with a more limited number of actors, and that this text was orally transmitted to a scribe. The First Quarto of *Richard II* is, of course, not like this; but the kind of mistake made in the transmission of *Richard III* occurred because the persons concerned were familiar with the text of the play as a whole and were sometimes deceived by their memories of one part of the play into allowing such memories to corrupt their versions of other parts. Such corruptions are especially likely to occur when the different parts are similar or identical in sense and wording, and where exclamations, titles and forms of address, because these are so readily interchangeable in the memory, are concerned. What we know can happen to the memory of actors engaged in recording a dramatic text may have analogies to the behaviour of the memory of a transcriber of such a text, provided he is already familiar with it. If he has heard the play fairly often on the stage—if, for example, he is someone such as the bookholder—his memory may be affected by what he has heard from the stage,[3] and he might in this way duplicate in his transcript memorial errors perpetrated by the actors during performance.

In such a play as *Richard II*, as in *Richard III*, disturbance of metre is often a sign that something has gone wrong with the text, since there is good reason to believe that Shakespeare was generally con-

1. Dover Wilson, op. cit., pp. 54 ff.
2. *The Textual History of Richard III* (Stanford University, California, 1936); cf. W. W. Greg, *The Editorial Problem in Shakespeare* (Oxford, 1951), pp. 79–85.
3. Wilson, op. cit., pp. 78–9.

tent at this period to write fairly regular verse. I give here some examples of probable errors in the First Quarto; they are accompanied by disturbance of the metre and may be of a memorial character. The passages fall into some of the categories that D. L. Patrick found were especially susceptible to memorial contamination, namely titles, exclamatory phrases and synonymous variants.

(i) I. i. 204:

Lord Marshal, commaund our Officers at Armes

Lord here is extrametrical; Richard on other occasions (I. iii. 7, 26, 99) uses plain *Marshal*. It may therefore be an anticipation of I. iii. 46, a line spoken by Bolingbroke: "Lord Martiall let me kisse my Souereignes hand".

(ii) v. iii. 40–5:

King. Vilain Ile make thee safe.   (feare
Aum. Stay thy reuengefull hand, thou hast no cause to
York. Open the dore, secure foole, hardie King,
Shall I for loue speake treason to thy face,
Open the dore, or I will breake it open.
King. What is the matter vncle, speake, recouer breath,
Tell vs, how neare is daunger,

Here the cause of the metrical disturbances may be the two exclamatory phrases *Vilain* and *What is the matter vncle*. Aumerle is twice called "villain" elsewhere in the play (v. ii. 72, 79), also by York, and again at v. iii. 52; and at v. ii. 86 York's serving-man is called "villain" by the Duchess of York. These instances may have intruded into the transcriber's or actor's memory here. *What is the matter* is used thrice in v. ii. (73, 79, 81), by the Duchess of York, who addresses York on two of the occasions and Aumerle on the other, and is also used by Bolingbroke himself at v. iii. 28. Earlier in the play the same query is addressed to York by Richard at the memorable moment when the king's uncle breaks down in his presence: "Why Vnckle whats the matter?" (II. i. 186). There seems to be a strong link between York, uncle to both the king and the usurper, and the phrase *What is the matter*, established elsewhere in the play, and therefore perhaps intruded here through the memory of scribe or actor. It is very significant that if we eliminate these two exclamatory phrases we can restore the verse to regularity:

King. Ile make thee safe.
Aum.   Stay thy reuengefull hand,
Thou hast no cause to feare
York.   Open the dore,
Secure foole, hardie King, shall I for loue

Speak treason to thy face, open the dore,
Or I will breake it open.
King.   Vncle, speake,
Recouer breath, tell us, how neare is daunger,

(iii) I. iii. 26:

Marshall aske yonder Knight in armes

The metre here may have been damaged because the synonymous variant *ask* was substituted for *demand of* as this is found in the very similar formula some twenty lines earlier in the scene:

Marshall demaunde of yonder Champion,
The cause of his arriuall here in armes,
Aske him his name,

Here, it may appear, a transcriber's memory, especially liable to blunder because of the similarity of the two passages, was influenced by his recollection of *Aske* in the earlier one, and, prompted by its association with *in armes*, which occurs in both, transferred it to the later.

The examples which I have quoted, and some others,[1] seem to warrant emendation of the text at the points where they occur. There are other places where an editor may suspect that similar faults have crept in owing to memorial errors by a transcriber.[2] I have discussed these in the notes. It is, I think, no longer possible to overlook the evidence for memorial elements in the Quarto and hence the probability that a transcript intervened between it and the foul papers. It may be significant that the errors, so far as they have been detected, tend to accumulate in two scenes in which York plays a prominent part (II. ii, v. ii), although they are by no means found exclusively there.[3]

1. See notes on II. i. 254, v. ii. 28, 55.
2. See notes on I. iii. 83; II. ii. 53, 59, 98–121; II. iii. 86; v. i. 25; v. ii. 65, 70, 101; v. v. 13–14, 69.
3. One important aspect of Dr Brooks's investigation, which I have not touched on here, is his suggestion that the memory of the transcriber was affected by his memory of *Richard III*, the Q1 text of which was issued in the same year as *R2* (1597), by the same printer and for the same bookseller; that his errors are occasionally comparable with the errors apparently made by the transcriber of Q1 *Richard III*, and that the two transcribers may in fact have been the same person, perhaps the book-holder. Dr Brooks informs me that this possibility may also have occurred to Pollard, as is shown by a note in Pollard's copy of the Griggs facsimile of Q1 *R2* now at Birkbeck College. It has also been suggested, in connexion with a different general theory of the character of both Quartos, by Dr Cairncross in an unpublished study of the *R3* text. The way in which Dr Brooks's further investigations into the matter aid conjecture about the cause and character of some of the suspect passages can be seen from the notes on II. ii. 98–121, III. ii. 203, v. ii. 55, v. v. 69.

If the text of Q1 is thus corrupted, there is additional reason to try to establish the nature of the copy for the First Folio version of *Richard II*, 1623, because, according to the current theory, this text, set up from one of the Quartos, also benefited from corrections derived from the prompt-book. Such corrections might enable us to detect, and perhaps emend, further memorial errors in Q1; the prompt-book could be brought in to redress the balance upset by the hypothetical transcript.

According to Pollard,[1] the copy for the Folio text was a printed Quarto which had been rather carelessly collated with a copy of Q1 that had been in use as a prompt-book at the theatre—"a play-house copy which the prompter had kept up to date in accordance with the changing needs of the theatre". Wilson holds that the printed Quarto used as copy by F was collated with an independent manuscript prompt-book, itself deriving from the foul papers.[2] There is reason to believe, as the result of a recent study by Richard E. Hasker,[3] that the printed Quarto in question was a copy of Q3, which was used by the Folio editors for all but the last three columns of their text; these columns were set up from the last two leaves of a copy of Q5. It is difficult to believe that the Folio editors and printer would in the normal way be reduced to making up their text from two mutilated Quartos. Accident or failure to notice, before work began, that the last leaves of the copy of Q3 were damaged or missing, might account for it, but Hasker suggests that the copy of Q3 had itself been in use as the prompt-book at the theatre, replacing, at some time before the publication of Q4 in 1608, an earlier prompt-book that had become worn out, and being at that time collated with it. This Q3 prompt-book had suffered subsequent damage. Since the prompt-book, duly annotated for use as such, was a valuable thing, not to be lightly abandoned even when somewhat defective, the missing (three) leaves were replaced by the corresponding (two) leaves of Q5. This was done when the copy of Q3 in question was still in use at the theatre. (Since it was Q5 [1615] which was used to supplement the damaged copy, it is likely, incidentally, that the play was still being revived after 1615.[4])

There are thus three theories as to the character of the prompt-

1. Pollard, pp. 88–99. For the use of printed Quartos as prompt-books, see C. J. Sisson, 'Shakespeare Quartos as Prompt Copies', *R.E.S.*, xviii (1942), 129–43.

2. Wilson, pp. 109–13; cf. Greg, *Editorial Problem*, pp. 15 and 121 and *The Shakespeare First Folio*, p. 238.

3. 'The Copy for the First Folio *Richard II*', *Studies in Bibliography*, v (1952–3), 58–68.

4. *Ibid.*, pp. 69–72.

book which the Folio is believed to have used: that it was a manuscript directly derived from the foul papers, that it was a copy of Q1
"kept up to date", or that it was a copy of Q3, minus some damaged
leaves and supplemented by Q5. By the first of these theories, the
manuscript in the possession of the company was consulted, and
collated with whichever Quarto was being used as copy for the
Folio; by the second, the Quarto prompt-book, not available in
Jaggard's printing-house, was made use of in much the same way.
The third theory commits itself to stating not only which Quarto or
combination of two Quartos was used as copy, but also to the view
that this made-up Quarto was itself the prompt-book. Before we
attempt to decide between these views, it would be as well to try to
estimate the extent to which the Folio made corrections and alterations of a character that indicates prompt-book provenance.

It may be argued with fair confidence that there are two places
where the Folio corrects the Quarto, both of which entail historical
knowledge and seem to presuppose the use of an external authority, such as the prompt-book, because they lie beyond the range of
editorial or compositors' ingenuity. One of these is the correction
Spencer for *Oxford* at v. vi. 8, which has already been mentioned.
The second is the correction of what appears to be the Quarto's
misprinting of the name *Coines* at II. i. 284 to *Quoint*, which is closer
to Holinshed's *Coint*. It is possible of course that the Folio editors
knew more history than we suppose or even that they consulted
Holinshed.[1] Such an explanation will hardly fit the case of the
Folio line at I. iv. 23: "Our selfe, and *Bushy*: heere *Bagot* and
Greene". By far the best explanation of this, which is Wilson's,
argues, as the note at that point attempts to show, that the Folio
consulted the prompt-book.

It is also hard to explain, except as proceeding from the prompt-
book, the tendency, which appears spasmodically in the Folio, to
substitute, for some words in the Quarto, words of nearly equivalent meaning in the Folio. Perhaps the majority of these are simply
unauthorized editorial replacements of the harder by the easier,
supposedly more elegant, or more usual word.[2] But there are some,
at least, which do not fall very easily into this category,[3] and Pollard

1. Wilson, p. 234; see also P. A. Daniel, Introduction to his facsimile of Q1
(1890), pp. xvii–xviii and cf. Greg, *The Shakespeare First Folio*, p. 236.

2. E.g., the historically motivated change *Woodstocks/Gloucesters* at I. ii. 1, and
changes like *vp/downe* at I. i. 186, *furbish/furnish* at I. iii. 76, *life/death* at I. iii. 140,
grieuous/verie at I. iv. 54, *forfend/forbid* at IV. i. 129.

3. E.g., *moneth/time* at I. i. 157, *right/iust* at I. iii. 55, *power/friends* at III. ii. 35,
coward/sluggard at III. ii. 84, *twenty/fortie* at III. ii. 85, *and/losse* at III. ii. 102, *laugh/
mocke* at III. iii. 171, *raise/reare* at IV. i. 145, *men/friends* at v. i. 66, *wife/Queene* at

explained them as systematic variations from the original by the actors, with which the prompt-book had eventually been brought into agreement.[1]

In regard to the other places where F varies from Q1, the general character of the changes has been discussed by Pollard. From amongst the mass of "careless blunders", "unimportant alternatives", and "petty tinkerings", to use his phrases, there emerge some which have to be considered on their merits as conjectural emendations. A number of these are, rightly or wrongly, rejected in this edition, but I do not think that we need entertain the possibility of prompt-book provenance for any of them.[2] In other places the Folio succeeds in mending broken metre by the restoration or elimination of a word and in curing obvious misprints in Q1, but did not exercise more than elementary editorial ingenuity in doing so.[3] There are three cases where such ingenuity may be by some (and was by Pollard) regarded as a not entirely adequate explanation for F's restoration of what appears to be the correct text. These are the reading *incaged* for Q1's *inraged* at II. i. 102, the insertion of *with you* at III. iii. 13 and the consequent repair of the lineation in this passage, and the emendation of Q1's *This sweares he, as he is princesse iust* at l. 119 of the same scene to *This sweares he, as he is a Prince, is iust*. If, however, Hasker is right in claiming that Q3 was the printing source for the Folio, then half the work had already been done by that Quarto, which reads *This sweares he, as he is a Prince iust*.

In lineation and verse-division—excluding the special case of the deposition scene—the Folio has succeeded in mending the Quartos (which do not differ amongst themselves in this respect) only in five places.[4] The Quarto errors arise from Q1's habit of printing as one line what Shakespeare originally intended as one and a half, or from misdivision of one and a half lines, and it was not difficult to correct them. Folio lineation differs from that of the Quartos in some fourteen other places; in only three of these are the Quartos themselves likely to be wrong. The Folio has failed to deal with a number of other places where the Quartos give evidence of mislineation.

So far then as the evidence of the Q1/F variants goes, the Folio

---

v. i. 78, *years/dayes* at v. iii. 22. The possibility that these are the errors of a careless compositor is not, so far as I can judge, supported by the evidence of the errors made by the compositors in setting the F text of *1 Henry IV* as described by Alice Walker, *Studies in Bibliography*, VI (1954), 45–59.

1. Pollard, p. 99.

2. See notes on II. i. 232, II. iii. 65, III. ii. 55, v. iii. 1, v. iii. 135.

3. E.g., at I. i. 118, I. iii. 172, II. ii. 31, III. iv. 34, v. ii. 2.

4. II. iii. 28–9, III. iii. 11–12, IV. i. 65–6, v. ii. 99–100, v. iii. 11–12.

used the prompt-book somewhat sparingly. The question is, however, not finally separable from speculation about the character of this prompt-book, and hence about the nature of the copy for the Folio, which was entered upon a couple of pages ago. This may be continued a little way if we assume for the present that Hasker is correct in claiming that the printing source of the Folio was a made-up copy of Q3 and Q5, and examine on the basis of that assumption the places where the Folio, in departing from Q3(5), restores the Q1 reading. There are some eighty such Q3/F variants,[1] and only one of these have editors found it necessary to reject as an error in both Q1 and Folio.[2] Some of these restorations of Q1 may be ascribed to chance or the operation of Folio habits which can also be detected at work amongst the Q1/F variants (e.g. *thy/thine* at I. ii. 35, *our/your* at I. iv. 10, *this/his* at IV. i. 138) without the intervention of any intention on F's part; at v. v. 17, by eliminating "small" altogether from Q3's line "To threed the small posterne of a small needles eye", F restores the first half of Q1's line by reading "To thred the posterne of a Needles eye", but this is due to F's attempt to regularize the metre of the line on the assumption that *needle* is pronounced as a disyllable. A majority of the other restorations may be ascribed to the unaided editorial acumen of the Folio, but the acumen required was in many instances not very great. Q3, by defective metre or grammar or some other obvious sign, betrays the fact that something fairly simple has gone wrong, and here the Folio apparently succeeds in mending some of the errors introduced into the text since Q1.[3] Less easy than these are such successful emendations as *sparks* for *sparkles* (v. iii. 21), *lives* for *lies* (I. iii. 86), *eare* for Q5's *care* (v. v. 45),[4] until we come to cases where it is at least arguable whether the Folio had external assistance. It is usu-

1. The figure is computed on the basis of the selective apparatus in this edition. For the purposes of this description it excludes changes in punctuation and hyphening, changes in the form of speech prefixes (such as *Rich* for *King*) and stage directions, and the alterations of *God* to *heauen* (in one case of *Pray God* to *I would*) made in deference to the Act against Oaths. It also excludes any consideration of the deposition scene, absent from Q3.

2. II. i. 124: "Oh spare me not my brother⟨s⟩ Edwards sonne".

3. Thus we observe regularizations of metre by restoration of a missing word (e.g., II. iii. 3, III. iii. 205, IV. i. 117) or by elimination of an unwanted one (e.g., II. i. 171, v. iii. 100, v. v. 32) or by adjustments like *'twixt* (v. i. 72, 74) and *'gainst* (II. i. 243, 245), the restoration of a rhyme (II. i. 210) and the easy elimination of grammatical anomalies (I. iii. 237, II. iii. 101, II. iii. 116, III. i. 18, III. ii. 53, v. i. 46).

4. Especially when we remember Dr Walker's enunciation of the principle behind some F proof-reading "that a combination of letters should make a word, but that a combination of words . . . need not necessarily make sense" (*Studies in Bibliography*, VI [1954], 58).

ally fairly plain that there is something wrong with Q3 in the following examples, but the Folio emendations, which successfully restore Q1, are not absolutely dictated by the character of the error in Q3:

   I. iv. 25–7:
> How he did seeme to diue into their hearts,
> With humble and familiar curtesie,
> With [What F] reuerence he did throw away on slaues,

   II. i. 145–6:
> Right, you say true, as Herfords loue, so his,
> As theirs, so mine, ⟨all F⟩ be as it is.

   III. iii. 164–6:
> Or shall we play the wantons with our woes,
> And make some pretty match with sheading teares,
> And [As F] thus to drop them still vpon one place,

Perhaps more difficult are the following achievements:

   I. i. 188–9:
> Shall I seem Crest-fallen in my fathers sight?
> Or with pale begger-face [beggar-feare F] impeach my
>   hight

   I. iii. 187:
> This louing [lowring F] tempest of your home-bred hate

   V. v. 34–7 (Q5):
>   then crushing Penurie
> Perswades me I was better when a King;
> Then am I *a King* [king'd F] againe, and by and by,
> Thinke that I am vnkingd by *Bullingbrooke*

In this last, we might have expected F, for the sake of regularizing the metre, to strike out "a" but not to produce the unusual word *king'd*, which Shakespeare himself does not use often, unless *vnkingd* in the line following gave the hint. In these five examples, there is nothing very obviously wrong with Q3's version; yet the Folio has restored Q1:

   I. i. 146:
> And enterchangeably hurle downe the [my F] gage

   I. iii. 72:
> To reach a [at F] victorie aboue my head

   III. ii. 116–17:
> Thy very beadsmen learne to bend their browes,
>   [Bowes F]
> Of double fatale wo [Eugh: F] against thy state

   IV. i. 96–8:
> And toild with workes of warre, retir'd himselfe

To *Italy*, and there at *Venice* gaue
His body to a [that F] pleasant countries earth

v. i. 95:
One kisse shall stoppe our mouthes, and doubly
[dumbely F] part

These successes—some of which seem at least comparable for
ingenuity to those Q1/F variants which Pollard felt uneasy about
attributing to the unaided editorial acumen of the Folio—can be
easily accounted for by the rest of Hasker's theory, by which the
copy of Q3(5) used was itself the prompt-book, collated with the
worn-out manuscript prompt-book. As such, it would naturally be
the source of corrections like these. Another strong argument for
the view that the printing source of F was the prompt-book itself is
the fact that the Folio omits fifty lines (from eight different places)
found in the Quarto; some of these were probably dropped by accident, but Pollard thought that the rest represented theatrical cuts:
it is easier to imagine that these cuts appear in the Folio because the
compositor found them in his copy than to suppose that the Folio
editors, faced with a choice between a full-length Quarto text and
a shortened prompt-book, deliberately selected the latter.[1]

Yet there are, in the case of *Richard II*, cogent objections to the
view that a printed Quarto was used as a prompt-book, which were
originally advanced by Wilson against Pollard's view that the
prompt-book was an altered copy of Q1.[2] Somehow the Folio editors had available a better source for the text of the deposition scene
than that represented by the memorial and probably surreptitious
version of the scene in Q4 and Q5. There seems no reason to suppose, though it was censored out of the earlier Quartos, that the
scene was not being played in the theatre, or had not, at least,
originally been "allowed" by the censor of plays. It is difficult to
believe that the manuscript prompt-book, "worn-out" or not,
would be other than tenaciously preserved by the players because
of the existence of this scene in it; and, if the scene was being performed or if such performance was contemplated as a future possibility, the prompter was not likely to choose as a prompt-book a
Quarto (Q1 or Q3) which inconveniently omits it. Pollard suggested
that the Folio editors reconstructed the scene from actors' parts;
Hasker, that a transcript of it was made at the time when the
change from manuscript prompt-book to Q3 was effected. But it is
simpler to suppose the continued existence of the manuscript
prompt-book, directly derived from foul papers, and complete
with deposition scene and censor's allowance.

1. Pollard, pp. 91–6; Hasker, art. cit., p. 70.   2. Wilson, p. 113.

If this argument is sound, and if it is indeed true that a copy of Q3(5) was the printing source of the Folio, and if the Folio editors had no access to a copy of Q1, one conclusion follows: the extent to which the Folio consulted the prompt-book, collating the manuscript of it with the Quarto, is increased by the measure of such of the Q3/F variants which restore the readings of Q1 as can hardly be attributed to the unaided ingenuity of the Folio editors.

The refinement of Hasker's theory, namely that the made-up Q3(5), used as copy by the Folio, was itself the prompt-book, is not, therefore, necessary to explain the Q3/F variants which restore the readings of Q1. Nor was it arrived at for that purpose, but in order to explain the use of a made-up copy. We can, as I have suggested, think of other reasons for this—accident, or unnoticed defect in the copy of Q3 before the work was begun. There is a further objection to the view that the Folio was using an actual prompt-book as its copy. If it was, then, where Folio and Quarto duplicate suspected memorial errors (for example, in York's speech at II. ii. 98–121), this must be because these were left uncorrected in the Quarto when it was adopted as prompt-book. This could only happen if, when the change-over from the original manuscript prompt-book to Q3 was effected, the passages in Q3 were left untouched because they corresponded to stage-practice, and had survived untouched ever since. While we can imagine that some of the putative transcriber's errors of memory would be the same as those incorporated into the original manuscript prompt-book, because some of them would have a common source in sounds heard on the stage, it is impossible to suppose that they would coincide so exactly as to make Q3(5), when adopted as a prompt-book, entirely accurate as such over the whole range of suspected memorial errors common to the Quarto and the Folio. It is easier to believe that where the Folio and the Quarto share this type of error it is due simply to naive reprinting from the Quarto and that where a suspected memorial error has apparently been corrected by the Folio (as at V. vi. 8) the Quarto had at those points been collated with the manuscript prompt-book in the theatre.

Some such hypothesis is, I think, the one which best fits the facts as they can be discerned at present. The range of collation of the supposed manuscript prompt-book in the theatre with the printed Quarto used as copy by the Folio must be presumed to include the Folio's theatrical cuts and some of the Folio's synonymous variants and a very small number of places where we may suspect external aid rather than editorial ingenuity in the process of conjectural emendation; if the Quarto in question was a copy of Q3(5), the range of emendations in the Folio which derive, as far as the Folio is concerned, from the prompt-book, is greater. It is disappointing that the Folio does not help us to identify and perhaps emend more of the suspected memorial errors in Q1, but this may be a tribute to the general soundness of Q1.

Ever since the identification of Q3 in 1913 and Pollard's investigations into the sequence of the Quartos in 1916, it has not been disputed that the text closest to Shakespeare's manuscript, and therefore the basic text for a critical edition of the play, is that of the first Quarto. The first edition to take account of the discovery of Q3 was that by Dover Wilson (1939). In the case only of the deposition scene, lacking in Q1, and obviously bad as it is found in Q4 and Q5, the Folio provides the basic text. No variant in Quartos later than Q1, or Folios later than the First, has more authority than attaches to any other conjectural emendation.

The present edition is based on Q1. The apparatus is selective in accordance with the principles of the Arden series. I have omitted mere spelling variants of no interest in themselves and have recorded punctuation variants only where there could be serious dispute about their effect on meaning; nonsense-words resulting from misprints have not been recorded, nor have the more obvious mistakes and corrections, especially when they occur in the later Quartos (e.g. Q5's *gorgde* for the previous Quartos' *gorde* at I. iii. 60; Q4's *breach* at I. iii. 215 corrected to *breath* by Q5). I have expanded contracted proper names (Ric:, H. Percie; H. Bull; Brist. [for Bristow] etc.) without recording. I have returned in general to the stage-directions of Q1, but speech-prefixes have been normalized. Stage-directions which derive from editions later than the Folio are enclosed in square brackets. This has not been done in cases where directions proceeding substantially from Quartos or Folio have merely been regularized in the matter of titles or proper names (e.g., "Bishop of Carlisle" for "Carlisle", "Bolingbroke" for "Duke of Hereford"). Stage-directions at the side of the text have the usual single square bracket preceding; where they are enclosed in square brackets this again indicates that they derive from editions later than the Folio. Spelling is modernized, but I have retained such archaic forms as may reasonably be believed to be more than mere spelling variants: thus readers will find Q1's *caitive* (I. ii. 53), *president* (II. i. 130), *bankrout* (II. i. 151, and elsewhere), *murthered* for the Cambridge Editors' *murder'd* (III. ii. 160), and *tottered* for the Cambridge Editors' *tatter'd* (III. iii. 52). In the matter of proper names absolute consistency is not desirable: thus Q1's *Bullingbrooke* becomes *Bolingbroke* throughout; but I have retained Q1's common, though by no means invariable, *Herford*, instead of using the form *Hereford*, because the modern pronunciation that goes with this spelling is, I think, more often metrically wrong than right. For the sake of pronunciation or metre or both I have also retained Q1's archaic forms which are of interest such as *Glendor* (Glendower), *Callice* (Calais), and *Bristow* (Bristol). In regard to elisions in present participles and of past participial endings in -ed, I have adhered to Q1,[1] although I have used apostrophes to mark the elided letters which Q1 does not do. Thus

> In suff'ring thus thy brother to be slaught'red

replaces the Cambridge Editors'

> In suffering thus thy brother to be slaughter'd;

the Cambridge Editors'

> Transform'd and weaken'd? hath Bolingbroke deposed

gives way to

> Transform'd and weak'ned? hath Bolingbroke depos'd;

and their

> He that hath suffer'd this disorder'd spring

is replaced by

> He that hath suffered this disordered spring.

There is some reason to suppose that the compositor of Q1, like the compositor of the second Quarto of *Hamlet*,[2] was in the habit of expanding some of what may have been Shakespeare's colloquial contractions in phrases like *I'll*, *he's*, *that's* and words like *o'er* and *e'en*. The disturbance of metre caused by the full form in the following lines would almost certainly be repaired by an actor, who would use the colloquial contractions:

II. ii. 105:
> Come sister, cousin I would [I'd] say, pray pardon me:

II. ii. 134:
> Well I will [I'll] for refuge straight to Bristow castle,

v. iii. 80:
> I know she is [she's] come to pray for your foule sinne.

---

1. Except for some instances where Q1 seems obviously at fault in not eliding: e.g. restored (III. iii. 41), lodged (v. i. 14), well-graced (v. ii. 24), prayed (v. iii. 143), awed (v. v. 91), consumed (v. vi. 2).

2. Wilson, *The Manuscript of Shakespeare's Hamlet*, p. 232.

In about fourteen of these instances—a large majority—the Folio prints the colloquial and contracted forms and may well be returning to what Shakespeare originally wrote, although there is no reason to suppose that it had any authority for doing so other than its own ear and its understanding of the practice of its time. I have followed the not entirely defensible practice of printing the accepted modern equivalents of the Folio's contracted forms in all these cases, but where the Folio does not contract, I have left the Q1 readings as they stand. Copying the Folio here at least has the merit of lessening the number of occasions on which the reader of a modernized text will be held up by what seems defective, and may well be non-Shakespearian, metre. The exceptions to this are the need for expanding what the Folio has mistakenly contracted at IV. i. 333, and the ignoring a group of Folio contractions at v. ii. 73, 74, and 76, the first of which damages the metre, and the other two, occurring in three-foot "lines" which are really loud cries of anxiety, seem to have no metrical implications. (The Folio reading *King's* [first occurring in Q3] at II. i. 257 for Q1's *King* is an emendation justified by the sense of the line and so in a somewhat different class from the other Folio contracted forms.)

Punctuation is, of course, modernized. In view of the possibility, which has been discussed on a previous page, that Q1 preserves a degree of Shakespeare's own dramatic pointing, it behoves an editor to be especially careful, even when modernizing, to try to avoid more than the inevitable degree of falsification which this entails. I have found the edition of the play in Peter Alexander's *William Shakespeare: The Complete Works* (1951) to be much the most faithful and sensitive in this respect.

2. DATE

The earliest definite date for *Richard II* is its publication in 1597 after the Stationers' Register entry on 29 August. The play's probable indebtedness to Daniel's poem *The First Fowre Bookes of the ciuile warres* (1595) allows us to suppose that 1595 may have been the year of composition.[1] Chambers suggested that Sir Edward Hoby's letter of 7 December 1595 to Sir Robert Cecil refers to a private performance:[2]

1. See below, pp. xlii–xliv.
2. For some records of performances of plays in private houses between 1598 and 1613, see Chambers, *Elizabethan Stage*, I. 219–20. An Act of the Common Council of London (6 Dec. 1574), given by Chambers, op. cit., IV. 276, mentions plays in private houses as though they were fairly customary.

Sir, findinge that you wer not convenientlie to be at London to morrow night I am bold to send to knowe whether Teusdaie ⟨9 Dec.⟩ may be anie more in your grace to visit poore Channon rowe where as late as it shal please you a gate for your supper shal be open: & K. Richard present him selfe to your vewe. Pardon my boldnes that ever love to be honored with your presence nether do I importune more then your occasions may willingly assent unto, in the meanetime & ever restinge At your command Edw. Hoby. [*Endorsed*] 7 Dec. 1595 [*and*] readile.[1]

But I. A. Shapiro (*S.Q.*, IX [1958], 204–6) has shown that this letter constitutes no proof of performance of our play. "K. Richard shall present him selfe to your vewe" may mean only that Hoby (who was interested in history and collected historical portraits) was offering to show Cecil a portrait of a King Richard or a book about him. Even if a play is meant, it might as easily have been *Richard III*, *Woodstock*, *Jack Straw*, or some other play in which a King Richard appeared.

3. SOURCES

I. FOREWORD

It has been suggested that Shakespeare drew upon not less than seven principal sources: (1) Holinshed's *Chronicles of England, Scotland and Ireland* (1586–7); (2) Samuel Daniel's *The First Fowre Bookes of the ciuile warres* (1595); (3) the anonymous play *Woodstock*, also known as *1 Richard II*, found in British Museum MS Egerton 1994; (4) Lord Berners' translation of Froissart's *Chronicle* (1523–5); (5) Edward Hall's *The vnion of the two noble and illustre famelies of Lancastre & Yorke* (first extant edition, 1548); (6) a version of an anonymous French manuscript chronicle of about 1400 entitled *La Chronicque de la Traïson et Mort de Richart Deux Roy Dengleterre*; (7) Jean Créton's metrical history of about the same date, the *Histoire du Roy d'Angleterre Richard*.

If Shakespeare made use of all these, he read exceptionally widely for the purpose of creating this play. That he did use them all is a hypothesis, which, as I attempt to show in the following pages, rests on somewhat insecure foundations.

It is difficult to establish beyond doubt that Shakespeare read and remembered a particular book, and that it affected in decisive ways his handling of a subject. Even when the first is proved, the second may remain uncertain. Sometimes it may be dangerous to confuse the two processes. We ought not, on the one hand, to assume, although it may have been proved on other grounds that Shakespeare was acquainted with a particular book, that therefore

1. Chambers, *William Shakespeare*, II. 320–1.

its influence manifests itself at points in the play where material and treatment may reasonably be ascribed to Shakespeare's unaided invention or to the evolution of the play's internal design. Nor, on the other hand, is it always safe, in cases where a critic or editor has perceived parallels in conception and design between play and putative source, to use these parallels themselves as proof of Shakespearian indebtedness to the work in question—especially when firmer links (such as unmistakable verbal echoes) are missing. Parallels which proceed from editorial acumen or ingenuity may have little to do with Shakespeare's way of seeing his subject. Especially is this so when we are offered "hints", "germs", and "suggestions" (the terms are various and obscure) in the supposed source and informed that what we see in Shakespeare's play evolved from these. The theory on which such methods flourish is boldly stated by H. N. Paul:

> ... the mind of William Shakespeare was subject to a notable idiosyncrasy. His creative mind could have created the characters and events of his plays solely from his imagination, but it was his inveterate habit to seek for suggestions from other minds on which to build. So highly developed was this trait that at every point it is well to look for, and if possible find, the external suggestions which started the building process.[1]

This suggests that, like Chaucer's alchemist, commentators may occasionally be under suspicion of having put into the furnace beforehand the golden nugget which is to be the issue of the experiment. At present the thoroughness with which external suggestions are sought for is matched only by the confidence with which the "building process" is described.

II. HOLINSHED

The primary source is Holinshed's account of the last two years of Richard's reign in his *Chronicles*, which Shakespeare used in the edition of 1586-7.[2] The action of the play opens on 29 April 1398, when Richard arrived at Windsor and assigned to Mowbray and Bolingbroke a day for their trial by combat; it closes with the exhibition of Richard's corpse in London in March 1400. From Holinshed's account of the events that occurred between these two dates Shakespeare took most of his historical matter; he also used information and suggestions from some places in Holinshed lying outside these limits.[3] The extent of his reliance on Holinshed, and the

---

1. H. N. Paul, *The Royal Play of Macbeth* (1951), p. 201.
2. See note to II. iv. 8.
3. For example, information about Gloucester's death (I. i. 132-4, III. iii. 176),

way in which he transformed Holinshed's prose into dramatic poetry can be judged from the Appendix and from the notes on material at the head of each scene.

Shakespeare's deviations from Holinshed include omissions and added material. The main omissions are of the whole of Holinshed's long account of Richard's campaign in Ireland, and of his story of how Northumberland led Richard into an ambush between Conway and Flint. Holinshed also printed full texts of various documents, including a sermon by the Archbishop of Canterbury, issued at the time of the deposition. These Shakespeare did not make use of, although the instrument of abdication has left a trace at IV. i. 204 ff. Shakespeare once or twice alters the chronological sequence of the events recorded by Holinshed,[1] or abridges it, and there are innumerable minor deviations as well as invented factual touches.[2]

Shakespeare's additions to the material are harder to describe. By taking the single speech as a unit, we can observe one stage of the process. Thus, if we compare I. i. 87 ff with Holinshed 494/1/27 ff (Appendix, p. 182), we can see the quite recognizable original of a speech full of a colour and life entirely absent from the source. It is the speech which supplies a sense of place, a sense of occasion, and a feeling that the words are issuing from the mouth of a vigorous personality at a crisis in his career. This kind of energy was frequently, though not invariably, at work in Shakespeare's use of Holinshed.

There are times, however, when it is much more difficult to identify the original which Shakespeare, like Henry James, induced to "grow as tall as possible"; when, indeed, we may reasonably conclude that Shakespeare worked entirely without such seminal aid, at any rate from Holinshed. Such seems to be the case with some of the more famous of Richard's and John of Gaunt's speeches.

Some of Shakespeare's departures from Holinshed are on a much larger scale than the single speech. In this kind, the main deviations centre upon: (1) the character and behaviour of John of Gaunt; (2) the Duchess of Gloucester's meeting with Gaunt in I. ii; (3) nearly all Isabel's part, her grief, her parting with Richard, and her womanly behaviour (in Holinshed, as in history, she was a child of eleven); (4) the character and behaviour of the Duchess of York in Act v; (5) the Garden scene, III. iv; (6) much of the character and

---

about "benevolences" (II. i. 250), about York's character (II. i. 221) and about Isabel's marriage (V. i. 79): see notes on the lines mentioned.

1. Most strikingly in IV. i: see note on material to this scene.

2. For example, Hotspur Percy's youthfulness, his meeting with Bolingbroke and what follows (II. iii. 33–6), York's reason for failing to resist the invasion (II. iii. 153), Bolingbroke's apparent surprise at IV. i. 101, Isabel's presence at York's house (III. i. 36): see notes on the passages mentioned.

behaviour of Richard, especially in the last two Acts; (7) the part played in the tragedy by Northumberland.

By these departures, and without any serious modification of Holinshed's facts so far as they affect the historical sequence that may be called "Richard's fall and Bolingbroke's rise", the dramatist has, as Samuel Daniel put it, "beautified" his history, or, in Marston's phrase, "enlarged every thing as a Poet". He has developed character and motivation, made women prominent in the narrative, ranged protagonist against antagonist, and developed a type of action by means of symbolic objects (the Crown, the mirror, roan Barbary) which is alien to Holinshed.[1] One of Shakespeare's motives for some of his deviations may have been that he was already planning the continuation of the story into the reigns of Henry IV and Henry V.[2] The difference between playwright and historian may be summed up by saying that it is only Shakespeare who obliges us to undertake a fresh activity of the imagination every time we read his account.

It is natural to look for the sources and external suggestions that may have originated the new elements. So far as I know, no important conjectures have been offered as to specific sources for (4),(5),or (7). The Garden scene, indeed, like the episode with the looking-glass in IV. i, raises a rather different set of questions which must be tackled separately. The other elements have been ascribed to so various a range of originals, and so many different problems attach to each, that the trail grows long and confused. In what follows I have confined the discussion to salient matters, although it ranges from minute verbal echoes to wider analogies in theme and conception. Amongst the notes to the text will be found an accumulation of auxiliary evidence.

1. For discussion, see R. A. Law, 'Deviations from Holinshed in "Richard II" ', *Texas Studies in English*, XXIX (1950). Law also provides (pp. 92–3) a convenient table, not quite accurate, showing the relation between Holinshed's text and Shakespeare's.

2. There are of course several retrospective passages in *1* and *2 Henry IV* which establish a connection with *Richard II* (see note on II. iii. 45–50, and cf. *2 Henry IV*, IV. i. 115 ff). There are also elements in *Richard II* which show that Shakespeare may already have had a sequel in mind when writing this play (e.g., the references to Hal in v. iii. 1–12, Bolingbroke's change of mood at the end of v. vi). The prominence of Northumberland in IV. i and v. i may also indicate that he was developing the character with an eye on his future importance in *1 Henry IV*. For discussion, see S. C. Dodson, 'The Northumberland of Shakespeare and Holinshed', *Studies in English* (Texas, 1939), pp. 74–81. It is impossible to agree with Dodson that Shakespeare's main motive for deviating from Holinshed's portrayal of Northumberland was the desire to blacken the latter's character, because Shakespeare omits the blackest of all Northumberland's acts, his perjury at Conway (see note on material, III. iii).

III. JOHN OF GAUNT, BERNERS' FROISSART, AND "WOODSTOCK"

The character and behaviour of Richard's uncle, John of Gaunt Duke of Lancaster, father of the future Henry IV, constitute one of the most marked departures from Holinshed, and one of the greatest things in the play. The question of its provenance also introduces two of the more important suggested sources, Berners' translation of Froissart and the anonymous *Woodstock*.

Shakespeare had no authority in Holinshed for the Gaunt of the play. Holinshed's Gaunt is a turbulent and self-seeking magnate, whose death in 1398, although its aftermath—Richard's seizure of his property—had grave consequences for king and kingdom, is very simply noted by the chronicler. The Gaunt of Shakespeare is a father and patriot of grandiose stature, a prophet whose dying speech on England attracted the attention of the anthologist (for *England's Parnassus*) as early as 1600. Where did Shakespeare get this utterly unhistorical Duke of Lancaster?

Two important suggestions have been made. The first, strongly urged by Dr Dover Wilson, is that Shakespeare derived his conception of the character from Berners' translation of Froissart. It is only Froissart who reports that Gaunt "had on hym a paryllous sicknesse, which shulde be his dethe", and who gives some details about his gloomy last days:

> So it fell that aboute the feest of Crystmasse, duke Johan of Lancastre, who lyved in great dyspleasure, what bycause the kynge had banysshed his sonne out of the realme for so litell a cause, and also bycause of the yvell governynge of the realme by his nephewe kynge Rycharde: for he sawe well that if he longe perceyvered and were suffred to contynewe, the realme was lykely to be utterly loste: with these ymagynacyons and other, the duke fell sycke, wheron he dyed, whose dethe was greatly sorowed of all his frendes and lovers. The kynge, by that he shewed, toke no great care for his dethe, but sone he was forgotten.[1]

It is only Froissart who speaks about the "maner of joye" in which Richard wrote to the French king about Gaunt's death;[2] Richard shows no "joy" in the play, but he plainly gapes for Gaunt's death:

> Now put it, God, in the physician's mind
> To help him to his grave immediately! (I. iv. 59–60)

Similarly, the following passage in Froissart has been cited by Wilson as a close anticipation of the Gaunt of Shakespeare:

> The duke of Lancastre was sore dyspleased in his mynde to se the kynge his nephewe mysse use hymselfe in dyvers thynges as

1. Froissart, VI. 335–6.   2. *Ibid.*, p. 337.

he dyd. He consydred the tyme to come lyke a sage prince, and somtyme sayd to suche as he trusted best: Our nephue the kynge of Englande wyll shame all or he cease: he beleveth to lyghtly yvell counsayle who shall distroy hym; and symply, if he lyve longe, he wyll lese his realme, and that hath been goten with moche coste and travayle by our predecessours and by us; he suffreth to engendre in this realme bytwene the noble men hate and dyscorde, by whom he shulde be served and honoured, and this lande kept and douted... The Frenchemen are right subtyle; for one myschiefe that falleth amonge us, they wolde it were ten, for otherwyse they canne nat recover their dommages, nor come to their ententes, but by our owne meanes and dyscorde betwene ourselfe. And we se dayly that all realmes devyded are dystroyed; it hath been sene by the realme of Fraunce, Spayne, Naples ... in lykewise amonge ourselfe, without God provyde for us, we shall dystroy ourselfe; the apparaunce therof sheweth greatly.[1]

So also we are told by Froissart that Gaunt did not attempt to avenge the murder of his brother the Duke of Gloucester, but "wisely and amiably he apeased all these matters":[2] this is a Gaunt who has some resemblance to the Gaunt who dares not lift his arm against God's minister (I. ii. 40–1).

The case is not overwhelming. Shakespeare did not need to consult Froissart in order to learn that princes are often sick before they die, and Richard's attitude at Gaunt's death could have been imagined from Holinshed's account of Richard's "hard dealing" with Gaunt's property (Hol. 496/1/40 ff). Many of Gaunt's sentiments, as occasioned, in Froissart's account, by reflection on Richard's unwisdom in permitting Mowbray and Bolingbroke to quarrel, and not, as in Shakespeare's, by the bitter stimulus of his own approaching end, are, in so far as they are paralleled by Gaunt's speeches in II. i, commonplaces with plentiful analogies elsewhere.[3] In Shakespeare, it is the farming of the realm in particular for which Gaunt reproaches Richard, a topic which forms no part of Gaunt's anxious meditations in Froissart. There are no verbal echoes at all.

Some of these points have been made by Mr A. P. Rossiter in his edition of *Woodstock*. Rossiter's candidate is Thomas of Woodstock, Duke of Gloucester, hero of his play, whom Rossiter rightly sees as belonging to a tradition of patriotic counsellors and king's servants long active in the drama. *Woodstock* dramatizes various events of Richard's reign between 1382 and 1397; it is heavily biased against the king, and is essentially the story of how his uncle Woodstock

1. Froissart, VI. 311.   2. *Ibid.*, p. 338.
3. See especially notes on II. i. 40–68, 65–6.

fails in his attempt to restrain a degenerate monarch surrounded by minions and machiavels. The play ends with Woodstock's arrest, his conveyance to Calais and his assassination there on Richard's orders. Throughout, Woodstock is unhistorically presented as a plain, elderly, well-meaning patriot and good counsellor, and Richard as a headstrong, passionate youth absorbed in desperate expedients to get money for riot and finery.

The unknown playwright has transformed the Duke of Gloucester, the "man of high mind and stout stomach", the "sore and a right severe man" of the chronicler,[1] into what Rossiter describes as a "type of virtuous Englishry", much as Shakespeare transformed the Gaunt of Holinshed into Gaunt the prophet of England. One verbal detail at least in Gaunt's tremendous last speeches as well as much in their general sentiments and those of the scene in which they occur (II. i) have parallels in *Woodstock*.

Woodstock has, therefore, rival claims to be considered as a source of Shakespeare's idea of Gaunt. Before leaving Berners' Froissart and examining these, it is well to ask what supporting evidence there is elsewhere in the play, outside the Gaunt episodes, that the dramatist knew Froissart.

The quality of this evidence varies. The most convincing bit depends upon the possibility that Shakespeare had somewhere heard the story[2] (not recorded by Holinshed), which was spread abroad by Lancastrian propagandists, that Richard was not the son of the Black Prince but of a priest of Bordeaux (whence his name of "Jehan" in *Traïson*). Froissart is the only source which gives a full and self-explanatory account of this, the words being put into Bolingbroke's own mouth as he reproaches the captured Richard in the Tower:

> ... the common renome rynneth through Englande, and in other places, that ye were never sonne to the prince of Wales, but rather sonne to a preest or to a chanon; for I have herde of certayne knightes that were in the princes howse, myne uncle, howe that he knew well that his wyfe had nat truely kepte her maryage. Your mother was cosyn germayne to kynge Edwarde, and the kynge beganne to hate her, bycause she coulde have no generacion; also she was the kynges gossyp of two chyldren at the fonte; and she that coulde well kepe the prince in her bandon by crafte and subtylte, she made the prince to be her husbande, and by-

1. Hol., 486/1/20, 464/1/37. But for the fainter tradition of Gloucester's virtuousness and the injustice of his end, hinted at in Holinshed and emphasized by *The Mirror for Magistrates*, see note to II. i. 128.

2. See note on IV. i. 256-7.

cause she coulde have no chylde, she douted that the prince shulde be devorsed fro her; she dyd so moch that she was with chyld with you, and with another before you. As of the fyrst I can nat tell what to judge, but as for you bycause your condycions have ben sene contrary fro all nobles and prowes of the prince, therfore it is sayd that ye be rather sonne to a prest or to a chanon; for whan ye were gotten and borne at Burdeaux, there were many yonge preestes in the princes house.[1]

Unfortunately, the value of this parallel is somewhat lessened by our uncertainty as to whether the phrases used by Richard at iv. i. 256-7 do indeed refer to this story. Other suggested connexions between the play and Froissart have, I think, been inferred on inadequate grounds. These bear on the reasons given by the king for his sentence on Bolingbroke and Mowbray (i. iii. 123-38), the behaviour of Northumberland in ii. i and iii. iii (see the notes on material to these scenes) and ii. ii. 56-61, the popularity of Bolingbroke with the crowds of citizens (i. iv. 24-36, v. ii. 18-20), the rendering of the act of abdication (iv. i. 181) and York's part in it (iv. i. 106),[2] and some minor matters.[3] From amongst all these passages, only two verbal parallels have been offered, neither of them of the kind that are exclusive of coincidence.[4] That Froissart acted as a source of continuous inspiration to Shakespeare in the manner suggested by Dover Wilson has not, I think, been satisfactorily proved.

The case for *Woodstock* is different. There is a very large number of verbal echoes; but we do not really know whether or not the writing of *Woodstock* preceded that of *Richard II*. Since it was first printed by Halliwell from MS Egerton 1994 in 1870, *Woodstock* has had three different editors.[5] The manuscript of the play "bears marks of having been in long and constant use as a prompt copy, while the marginal entries in different hands suggest that it underwent several revivals".[6] As to the date of composition and first per-

1. Froissart, vi. 377.   2. See notes on the places mentioned.

3. See, for example, notes on i. iii. 140, ii. i. 165-8, iii. iii. 53, v. i. 54, v. ii. 15-16, v. v. 77-80.

4. See notes on i. iii. 140, v. ii. 18. *At the fonte* in the quotation from Froissart above may be echoed in Richard's line "No, not that name was given me at the font" (iv. i. 256).

5. W. Keller in *Shakespeare-Jahrbuch*, xxxv; W. Frijlinck, Malone Society Reprint, as *First Part of the Reign of King Richard the Second*; Rossiter, edn cit. F. A. Marshall, who edited *R 2* for the Henry Irving Shakespeare (1888) seems to have been the first, apart from Halliwell, to note connexions between *R 2* and *Woodstock*; see also his paper in *New Shakespeare Soc. Proc.*, *1880-6*, meeting of 10 April 1885.

6. Frijlinck, edn cit., p. xxiv.

formance, the evidence of the manuscript itself points in conflicting directions.[1]

It is clear that there is a relation of some kind between *Woodstock* and *Richard II*—the number and nature of the verbal echoes make that as indisputable as such things ever can be. But that Shakespeare borrowed from *Woodstock*, rather than the other way about, is remarkably difficult to prove.

One detail helps to make it look as though Shakespeare might have been the borrower. In *Richard II* Gaunt reproaches the king:

> Landlord of England art thou now, not king,
> Thy state of law is bondslave to the law   (II. i. 113–14)

In *Woodstock* Richard is on several occasions referred to as his country's "landlord". The passage closest to that in *Richard II* is Woodstock's own reproach:

> And thou no king, but landlord now become
> To this great state that terrored christendom.[2]

In four other places in *Woodstock* Richard is described as a landlord, twice by himself, once by Greene, and once by the Ghost of Edward III.[3] There is no parallel in Holinshed or elsewhere[4] to this five-times-repeated reproach. It is of course more likely that Shakespeare remembered the word because it is repeated so often in the other play than that the author of *Woodstock* expanded the single reference in *Richard II* into so abundant a treatment in his own work.

Other arguments for the priority of *Woodstock* and consequently for Shakespeare's indebtedness to it have been advanced by Boas, and by Rossiter. They can be summarized as follows: (i) there are some passages in the first two Acts of *Richard II* which are only fully intelligible when we know the story in *Woodstock*. I have discussed these in the notes.[5] Few of them are, I think, of much force as proofs of Shakespeare's indebtedness. This is because it is more probable that Shakespeare was assuming knowledge of events as recorded by Holinshed, *The Mirror for Magistrates*, or by tradition,[6] not neces-

1. See F. S. Boas, 'Thomas of Woodstock: a non-Shakespearian Richard II', in *Shakespeare and the Universities* (Oxford, 1923); Chambers, *Elizabethan Stage*, IV. 43; Frijlinck, edn cit.; W. W. Greg, *Dramatic Documents from the Elizabethan Playhouse* (Oxford, 1931), II. 251 ff. Greg dates the manuscript 1592–5.

2. Rossiter's edn, v. iii. 106–7.   3. *Ibid.*, IV. i. 146, 210, 243–4, v. i. 90.

4. Except in Hayward's *First Part of the Raigne of Henry IIII* (1599), p. 55. On the significance of this, see below, pp. lxii, and note to II. i. 113.

5. See especially notes to I. i. 100, I. i. 104–5, I. i. 132–4, I. ii. 38–41, I. iv. 45 (and cf. II. i. 256), II. i. 64, II. i. 114, II. i. 128, II. i. 168.

6. See especially note on II. i. 128.

sarily the *Woodstock* author's version of them; or because Shakespeare was simply transcribing the words in question from Holinshed; or because the references explain themselves quite adequately in the theatre, and only require a gloss when we begin to wonder about them in the study. At II. i. 202–4 Shakespeare uses Holinshed himself in this way. There is certainly no warrant for thinking that our play was deliberately designed as a sequel to *Woodstock*: it contradicts and overlaps in a way that no sequel would. (ii) The supposed Shakespearian borrowings from scattered places in *Woodstock* tend to accumulate in a single scene of *Richard II* (II. i). "The writer who uses the *general idea* or a *recurrent theme* in an earlier play tends unwittingly to collect his 'echoes' into the place or places where that idea or theme is treated."[1] (The recurrent theme in question is Richard's relation with his favourites, his financial exactions, and the attitude of graver persons, such as Thomas of Woodstock and John of Gaunt, to his behaviour.) This second argument seems a good one.

It is in the light of such arguments, various though their quality is, for the precedence of *Woodstock* that the great majority of the verbal echoes, which I have indicated in the commentary,[2] must be surveyed. In itself, this last type of relatedness proves nothing about who was the borrower. But if the case for *Woodstock* as a source is in general a valid one, such often trivial parallels as these show us Shakespeare regularly taking hints from *Woodstock*, especially during the composition of the first and second Acts.

We may now return to the original subject of this section, the provenance of Shakespeare's Gaunt.[3] As the case stands at present, there are links between the play and both Froissart and *Woodstock* for which the easiest explanation is that Shakespeare had read and remembered both works. Even if these links were established with all the firmness that we could desire, the relation between Thomas of Woodstock, or Froissart's Gaunt, or both, and the John of Gaunt of Shakespeare remains a conjectural one. It is the relation of the "germ" to the finished work, not of fact to fact, or word to word. I do not think, therefore, that we need rule out the possibility that Shakespeare simply "enlarged" his history by inventing a good counsellor, whose most important moral and dramatic function is

1. Rossiter, p. 50.
2. See, for example, notes on I. i. 1, 24, 57; I. ii. 11, 47–52; I. iii. 150; II. i. 60, 67–8, 69, 77, 104, 124–5, 172–83, 242–3, 246, 247, 258, 262; II. ii. 10, 100, 141–2; III. iii. 106.
3. S. C. Dodson (*Studies in English*, Texas, 1934) advances, in Holinshed's account of Thomas of Woodstock, Duke of Gloucester, yet another candidate for the original of Shakespeare's Gaunt. I do not find the argument convincing.

to be rejected by the wanton king, who must indeed be so rejected if the causes of Richard's fall are to be laid open to the audience.[1] Certainly, the fact that Shakespeare may have known both Froissart and *Woodstock* should not encourage us to be other than cautious about the supposition that he was also "inspired" by them in the fashion suggested by some commentators. We are, in the end, forced back upon somebody's literary invention—for we cannot assume that all the traits of character of Froissart's Gaunt and the Gloucester of *Woodstock* are owing to lost historical traditions; why should that faculty of invention not have been Shakespeare's?[2]

IV. "THE MIRROR FOR MAGISTRATES"

This massive composite collection of exemplary stories which relate the falls chiefly of princes and noblemen was collected and issued in various editions by William Baldwin between 1555 and 1587; it was in 1587 that the similar series of John Higgins (1574) and Thomas Blennerhasset (1578) were incorporated in it. Amongst the tragic princes are Thomas of Woodstock, Duke of Gloucester, Thomas Mowbray, Duke of Norfolk, Henry Percy,

---

1. See below, pp. lxvi–lxvii.

2. We may legitimately wonder why Shakespeare bestowed the patriots' mantle on Gaunt, of all people. There is some evidence that during this period John of Gaunt had acquired repute as a popular hero because of his exploits in Spain. (He was already well known for his part in the Tudor family tree: see the pageant at Leadenhall described by Hall, *Union* . . . [1809 edn, p. 638] and cf. R. Withington, *English Pageantry* [Cambridge, Mass., 1918], i. 177). In *The Spanish Tragedy*, ed. Boas, I. v. 48–52, he is remembered as one of the three English warriors who were victorious in the Peninsula; in *3 Henry VI*, III. iii. 81–2, he is described as "great John of Gaunt / Which did subdue the greatest part of Spain", and in Heywood's *Wise-Woman of Hogsdon* (?1604) an old warrior boasts of having been "once in Spain, / With John a Gaunt" (Mermaid edn of Heywood, p. 304). In May 1594 a Stationers' Register entry reads: "A booke entituled the famous historye of John of Gaunte sonne to Kinge Edward the Third with his Conquest of Spain and marriage of his Twoo daughters to the Kinges of Castile and Portingale &c". This, Chambers (*Elizabethan Stage*, IV. 401) thinks, was not a play but the chapbook source of a lost (and never completed) play, begun in 1601 by William Rankins and Richard Hathway, called *The Conquest of Spain by John of Gaunt*. H. F. Brooks refers me to a passage (sts 479–80) in Hoccleve's *Regiment of Princes* (ca. 1410; Hoccleve, *Works*, III, E.E.T.S., e.s., LXXII) where Prince Hal is advised to take heed of the example of "your graunt-syre" who was merciful: "He neuere was, in al his lyf, vengeable / But ay foryaf the gylty and coupable". A surviving tradition of John of Gaunt's aversion from vengeance might partly account for the attitude of Shakespeare's Gaunt at I. ii. 40. If Gaunt had a latent reputation as a loyal, merciful, and anti-Spanish hero, which, by 1594 at least, was being found convenient by the literary interpreters of Tudor patriotism, it is less surprising that Shakespeare cast him for the role of Good Counsellor.

Earl of Northumberland, and Richard II—three of Shakespeare's main characters in this play and a fourth whose shadow lies over it.

As a popular collection of metrical moral tales, *The Mirror for Magistrates* may be taken as a fair indication of some of the historical issues of Richard's reign the outline of which any audience witnessing *Richard II* for the first time might be expected to know.[1] *The Mirror* tells of the shocking affair of the Duke of Gloucester's murder (which lies at the back of Act I and the first part of IV. i), relates the story of Mowbray as a warning example of the harm done by a flattering counsellor, and shows how Richard's overthrow was hastened by his injustice to Northumberland. Its characterization of Richard himself is almost entirely black:

> I am a Kyng that ruled all by lust,
> That forced not of vertue, ryght or lawe,
> But alway put false Flatterers most in trust,
> Ensuing such as could my vices clawe:
> By fayithful counsayle passing not a strawe.
> When pleasure pryckt, that thought I to be iust.
> I set my minde, to feede, to spoyle, to lust,
> Three meales a day could skarce content my mawe,
> And all to augment my lecherous minde that must
> To Venus pleasures alway be in awe.[2]

Shakespeare's view of Richard is of course a good deal more subtle and sympathetic than this grotesque rubbish, as I have attempted to show in a later section, and any of his audience who was thinking on the lines laid down in *The Mirror* may have had a surprise. There is not, I think, much indication that Shakespeare supplemented his other sources with any material facts from the very eclectic histories in *The Mirror*.[3] But there are one or two places where verbal echoes may be detected,[4] and, more importantly, Shakespeare, in his own task of selecting his material from Holinshed, may well have been influenced here and there by the emphases already pitched upon by *The Mirror*. A line in the quotation I have just given, for example—"By fayithful counsayle passing not a strawe"—might have helped him towards his own insistence on one very important element in his protagonist's conduct: his disregard of the sage advice of his uncles York and Gaunt. Other instances in which *The Mirror* seems to complement Shakespeare's

1. For this and many other points connected with *The Mirror* I am again indebted to Dr H. F. Brooks, who first made me realize the full importance of this work to a student of the play.

2. *Mirror*, p. 113. 3. But see notes on I. iii. 125–6, II. i. 128, II. i. 246–7.
4. See notes on I. ii. 38, II. i. 209–10, III. iii. 194–5, IV. i. 112.

choice of incident and allusion from Holinshed are collected in the commentary.[1]

V. DANIEL'S "CIVIL WARS"

Charles Knight in his Pictorial Edition of Shakespeare (1838–45) was the first to suggest that Shakespeare borrowed material from Samuel Daniel's poem on the Wars of the Roses.[2] The first instalment of this—the only one on which Shakespeare could have drawn—was entered in the Stationers' Register on 11 October 1594, and published as *The First Fowre Bookes of the ciuile warres between the two houses of Lancaster and Yorke*, with the date 1595 on the title-page. Daniel's poem, which is a courageous attempt to write a historical epic in the manner of Lucan, is heavily charged with a sense of the disastrousness of civil conflict and the threat to the country's future entailed by the deposition of a lawful monarch. Richard emerges finally as a lamenting figure wailing his fall, a figure akin to, but refined upon, the dreary ghosts of *The Mirror for Magistrates*.

There are about thirty places where the language and ideas of the poem resemble those of the play. Not all these can confidently be ascribed to borrowing by one writer from the other. Thus, when both Daniel and Shakespeare make the Bishop of Carlisle, unlike Holinshed's Bishop, exclaim against the wickedness of the subjects who presume to judge their king, both may be drawing independently upon the standard official thought of their time as represented by the Homilies.[3] The connexion, much emphasized by Dover Wilson, between v. iv and a passage in Daniel, proves, so far as I can judge, to be of the slenderest kind, from which coincidence may

1. See notes on I. iii. 1–2, I. iv. 48, II. i. 156, II. i. 242–3, II. i. 250, II. i. 253, II. ii. 56–61, III. i. 12–15, IV. i. 98, V. iii. 134, V. vi. 34.

2. *Histories*, I. 82–3. Knight's chief successors in the investigation of the matter were F. W. Moorman, 'Shakespeare's History Plays and Daniel's Civil Wars', *Shakespeare-Jahrbuch*, XL (1904)—Moorman concluded. after a markedly superficial examination, that there was no connexion between the works; Hardin Craig, *Richard II* (Tudor Shakespeare, New York, 1912); R. M. Smith, Reyher, and Wilson (see list of Abbreviations for full titles). In addition to the many parallels which he cited, R. M. Smith also noted that Shakespeare and Daniel both use the spellings "Bullingbrooke" and "Herford": the former is not used by other writers, but "Herford" is found in Hardyng's Chronicle, and in Hall (see on this point B. Williams in his edition of *Traison*, p. 139, note 1). By Holinshed and by the other chroniclers, we may add, the king's uncle is called "the Duke of Lancaster", but Daniel twice refers to him as "John of Gaunt" without other addition, and it is as "John of Gaunt" that Shakespeare thinks of him. This was an appellation that had probably become already established in popular usage—see note 2, p. xl above.

3. See note on IV. i. 121–9.

not be excluded. The heavenly portents of another very short scene (II. iv) could have been suggested to Shakespeare by a reference in Holinshed.[1] None the less, there are enough places left to make the connexion a probability, if not a certainty. There is a group of echoes in II. i, as well as in the deposition scene, which, if the individual examples are weak enough, have some persuasive force in the aggregate.[2]

But it is especially in the fifth Act of the play that Shakespeare and Daniel come closest together. The treatment of the processional ride of Richard and Bolingbroke into London; the grief of Queen Isabel, looking on from a window at her lord's disgrace; and the final meeting of Richard and Isabel—these are episodes which in their general mood resemble a passage in Daniel's second Book, stanzas 66–98.[3] Although Daniel's and Shakespeare's treatments differ,[4] they have a grand design in common, which rests on the unhistorical conception of Isabel as a mature woman, not a girl of eleven: "her passions [are] not suited to her years", apologized Daniel in the preface to the 1609 edition of his poem, with a newly acquired allegiance to the "bare *Was*" of history.[5] There are, in addition, at least three passages in V. i which are verbally very close to passages in the relevant section of Daniel's second Book.[6] Provided with this link, which seems fairly firm, we can feel more confident that the resemblances which have been perceived between other parts of the play and the poem may be genuine, and not the outcome of accident or editorial ingenuity. Of these, the one with the most interesting implications is the suggestion that there is a link between what Shakespeare probably thought Bolingbroke's policy was when he first began his campaign after Ravenspurgh and Daniel's meditations on the same theme.[7]

Who was the borrower? If it was Daniel, we must suppose that he carried away from some performance, or performances, of *Richard II*, presumably in or before 1594, a number of verbal

1. See notes on V. iv and II. iv.
2. See notes on II. i. 44, 47–9, 65–6, 221, 263–9; IV. i. 121–9, 141, 208, 210, 214–15, 216, 328.
3. See Appendix, pp. 198–206
4. For details, see notes on material, V. i and ii.
5. Daniel, *Complete Works in Verse and Prose*, ed. Grosart (1885), II. 7.
6. See notes on V. i. 7, 13, 40–50. The last is particularly clear.
7. Cf. below, pp. lxxiii–lxxiv, and see Wilson, p. lxii. The suggestion that there is a connection between Richard's soliloquy in Daniel (*C. W.*, III, sts 64–71) and the soliloquy in prison (V. v. 1–66) is less convincing. If taken into account, it points rather at Daniel as the borrower, since a soliloquy for the fallen monarch follows almost inevitably from Shakespeare's dramatization of his theme, and the example of *Edward II*, where the fallen Edward similarly bewails his fate.

echoes, as well as an impression of Shakespeare's Queen and her last meeting with Richard, which eventually left their traces all over his four Books (but especially Book II) and may have inspired him to compose the stanzas on Isabel and Richard in that Book. This passage is one of the most moving and dramatic things in his whole poem. This supposition is by no means an impossible one. Daniel's epical project may well have led him to take an exceptionally lively interest in anything that bore upon it.[1] But, since Daniel's poem was published probably early in 1595 and Shakespeare's play was not in print until 1597, it is simpler and easier to believe that Shakespeare was the borrower; that he read the poem soon after its publication, seized on its grandest dramatic idea and absorbed some other and slighter material.[2] It is worth stressing that it is largely upon this reasonable guess that we may assume Shakespeare's indebtedness to Daniel, and, as its consequence, a date for the composition of *Richard II* in 1595. But it is not much more than a guess.[3]

VI. "TRAÏSON" AND CRÉTON

Two French eye-witness accounts of Richard's fall are the anonymous *Chronicque de la Traïson et Mort de Richart Deux* and Jean Créton's metrical *Histoire du Roy d'Angleterre Richard*. The former may have been written by a member of Queen Isabel's household.[4] His account begins about the middle of the year 1397 and continues until the death and burial of Richard. Créton came to England about 1398; his account begins a year later than that of *Traïson* with Richard's departure for the Irish campaign. Créton,

---

1. Daniel did incorporate hints from Shakespeare in later editions of *C.W.* (an example is given in note to v. v. 108–12). Such alteration of work in progress might have been his response to the appearance of a new model; it could also be argued that he had so responded from the start and was merely extending his borrowing.

2. Some evidence that Daniel may have been at work on his epic by 1594 or earlier is provided by the undated manuscript of the first two Books in the British Museum; see C. C. Seronsy, 'Daniel's Manuscript *Civil Wars* . . .', *J.E.G.P.*, LII (1953).

3. Wilson's argument (p. 157) that Shakespeare's line "Against infection and the hand of war" (II. i. 44) is explicable only by reference to Daniel's allusions to the contagion of foreign iniquities (*C.W.*, IV, sts 43 and 90: see note on II. i. 44), and that Shakespeare therefore *must* have been the borrower, is unfortunately weakened by the fact that Shakespeare could have meant several things by *infection*, that he refers to foreign iniquities himself earlier in the scene, and by the parallel in Eliot's Du Bartas translation (see Appendix, p. 206, and note on II. i. 40–68). Eliot has the line "Thy soile is fertile-temperate-sweet, no plague thy air doth trouble".

4. Steel, p. 299.

unlike the author of *Traïson*, accompanied Richard to Ireland and was with him when he was captured by Bolingbroke in Wales. Soon after Richard's surrender Créton went back home to France,[1] and the rest of his narrative, which continues up to Isabel's own return to France, relies on information sent to him from England Both Créton and the author of *Traïson* are friendly to Richard, Créton especially so. His poem is full of shocked asides, and diatribes against Bolingbroke and his followers. Both *Traïson* and Créton report long formal lamentations over his fate as from Richard's own mouth.

In Shakespeare's time both these accounts existed only in manuscript. Créton was, however, accessible to Shakespeare's contemporaries: Stow made considerable use of his poem in his *Chronicles of England from Brute vnto this present yeare of Christ* (1580), repeating the material in later recensions of the work, which was re-titled *Annals* in editions from 1592.[2] Holinshed refers to it three times in his margin as "a French pamphlet that belongeth to master Iohn Dee" or "master Dees French booke". Dee's copy, bearing his signature and the date 1575, is extant in the Library of Lambeth Palace. Hall made use of *Traïson* in his *Union* (1548),[3] but it is not quite certain that a complete version of *Traïson* was available in Shakespeare's own time.[4] Holinshed cites "an old French pamphlet belonging to Iohn Stow" four times in his margin, but Stow himself does not seem to have made use of *Traïson*, and the document that Holinshed refers to may be only the fragmentary draft of a translation into English of the first one-fifth of *Traïson*, which breaks off at a point corresponding to I. iii. 122 in Shakespeare's play.[5]

The suggestion that Shakespeare was acquainted with *Traïson* was first advanced to explain what is possibly an allusion in the play to the Lancastrian tale of Richard's illegitimacy.[6] On the assumption that Shakespeare could have followed up Holinshed's marginal references and consulted the French manuscripts that the historian cites (or claims, perhaps not quite accurately in the case of *Traïson*, to be citing), the argument has been greatly forwarded

1. Créton, p. 182/378.
2. E.g., in his accounts of the Irish campaign and of Richard's capture in Wales, *Chronicles* . . . (1580), pp. 531, 538–9.
3. E.g., in his account of Richard's murder, which Holinshed copied from Hall, and Shakespeare from Holinshed; cf. C. L. Kingsford, *Prejudice and Promise in the Fifteenth Century* (Oxford, 1925), pp. 4–5.
4. For discussion, see P. Ure, 'Shakespeare's Play and the French Sources of Holinshed . . .' *Notes and Queries*, CXCVII (1953), 426–9.
5. This is Harl. MS 6219, folios 9–12b (British Museum).
6. See note on IV. i. 256–7 and p. xxxvi above.

by Paul Reyher[1] and Dover Wilson. It is based on verbal echoes, the transmission of certain historical details not otherwise available to Shakespeare, and on supposed general resemblances in theme. These last bear especially on the treatment of Richard's character in the last two Acts of the play.

Behind this argument lies the view that, if it is satisfactorily proved that Shakespeare read the manuscripts, it is fair to conclude that he also found in them a source of creative inspiration or "invention". Thus, it is believed, Shakespeare's rendering of Richard's character, as he found it in Holinshed, was profoundly modified by the friendly and pitying attitude towards him expressed by Créton and the author of *Traïson*. This belief itself is given colour by the view that some of Shakespeare's phrases and facts are derived from the French accounts, and it can thus be used in its turn as additional evidence that Shakespeare knew them. In the case of these French sources, there is a second argument, not so obviously needed for the identification of such sources as Daniel, *Woodstock*, or Froissart. This is, that Shakespeare (or, in Wilson's theory, the unknown author of the lost play which Shakespeare was adapting) had such an exigent interest in the historical background of *Richard II* that he worked on the material rather in the manner of an historian; that he searched well below the surface of Holinshed for primary sources which took the form of privately-owned manuscripts in fifteenth-century French. We may not refuse to believe this, unlikely as it seems at first, provided that the links between the manuscripts and the play are demonstrably firm. In this case, at least, a mere chain of ingenious probabilities will not serve, although one verbal echo which cannot be ascribed to coincidence or the intervention of another source, or to the internal logic of the drama,[2] or one historical fact of the same kind, will be quite sufficient. I do not think that this has been forthcoming so far.[3]

There remain for discussion the suggestions and hints which Shakespeare may have found in the pages of Créton and *Traïson*. That in a remark of Bolingbroke's reported by *Traïson* Shakespeare found the "germ" of the Garden scene is, I think, unlikely, for

1. For the full reference see list of Abbreviations.

2. By this phrase I refer to the kind of development discussed in the notes to III. ii. 64 or IV. i. 106.

3. For discussion, see commentary: (i) *Traïson*: (a) suggested verbal echoes: I. iii. 11–13, I. iii. 43, III. iii. 176, IV. i. 55; (b) shared historical data : I. i. 103, II. iv. 11, III. ii. 64, IV. i, material, IV. i. 92–100, IV. i. 152–3, IV. i. 256–7; (ii) Créton: (a) suggested verbal echoes: V. ii. 32, V. ii. 34–6; (b) shared historical data: II. ii. 10, II. ii. 106, II. iv. 11, III, ii. 60–3, III. ii. 119, IV. i. 319, V. v. 77–80.

Bolingbroke's images arise from a common stock;[1] that the unhistorical maturity in years of Queen Isabel and her parting scene with Richard were suggested by scenes between Isabel and Richard depicted in *Traïson* and Créton must be balanced against Shakespeare's debt to Daniel[2]—a sufficient one, if admitted, to make the hypothesis of another source unnecessary. At IV. i. 235, where Richard reproaches Northumberland for his perjury and treachery, it is possible that Shakespeare means his audience to understand that the character is referring not specifically to Northumberland's perjured promise of safe-conduct at Conway, but generally to the heinousness of a subject's breaking his oath of fealty to his king—a crime sufficiently present to the Elizabethan consciousness without its needing to be derived from a particular source.[3] Even if Shakespeare had the Conway perjury in mind when he made Richard speak thus, the parallel between Richard's warning to Northumberland and a passage in *Traïson* is not convincing,[4] while Richard's subsequent remarks to Northumberland at V. i. 55-6 may well be echoed from Daniel.[5]

It is true that *Traïson* and Créton, in their anti-Lancastrian way, make a great deal of this betrayal (the fact of it is, of course, amply reported by Holinshed), and that Créton is especially shocked, as others have been since, at the way the English behave to their anointed kings. So, naturally enough, is Shakespeare's Richard, and certainly his creator was drawing upon similar, if more generalized, ideas current about kingship in his own time in order to use them in the dramatic portrayal of Richard. The deepening atmosphere of shock in the last two Acts, the pity for Richard that his abasement induces in himself and the audience, thus have a family resemblance to the consternation and pity aroused by the whole affair which finds expression in the pages of *Traïson* and Créton. But to suggest that the one is the cause of the other is a conjecture which is not supported by those evidences of verbal correspondence between the three accounts which, in similar cases of doubt, can carry conviction. The evidence in this kind which has been offered centres on the fact that in *Traïson* and Créton, as in Shake-

1. See below, pp. li–lvii. Bolingbroke says: "I vow to God that I will gather up the weeds and clear my garden of them, and will sow good plants, until my garden shall be all clean within my ditches and walls, unless some of you repent" (*Traïson*, p. 93/247).

2. See above, pp. xlii–xliv.   3. See notes on III. iii, material, and IV. i. 235.

4. Richard says (*Traïson*, p. 50/199): "Northumberland, for God's sake be sure you consider well what you have sworn, for it will be to your damnation if it be untrue."

5. See note on V. i. 55–6.

speare (IV. i. 169–71, 237–42), Richard compares himself or is compared to Christ before Pilate:

> Then spake Duke Henry quite aloud to the commons of the said city, "Fair Sirs, behold your king! consider what you will do with him." And they made answer with a loud voice, "We will have him taken to Westminster." And so he delivered him unto them. At this hour did he remind me of Pilate, who caused our Lord Jesus Christ to be scourged at the stake, and afterwards had him brought before the multitude of the Jews, saying, "Fair Sirs, behold your king!" Then Pilate washed his hands of it, saying, "I am innocent of the just blood". And so he delivered our Lord unto them. Much in like manner did Duke Henry, when he gave up his rightful lord to the rabble of London, in order that, if they should put him to death, he might say, "I am innocent of this deed".[1]

Shakespeare could, however, have evolved his striking comparison without outside assistance, even from Holinshed,[2] where it occurs in another connexion. He had glanced at Pilate before in *Richard III*; the comparison of the fallen monarch with Christ could have developed both from the familiar habit of dubbing any traitor a Judas,[3] and from the view of the king as God's vicar and substitute, the figure of God's majesty, His captain and deputy, for whom the angels fight, which is stressed throughout the play, and which, deriving from the Bible and the contemporary leaders of Protestant thought, is fundamental to Tudor political doctrine. For when this divine royal figure is betrayed, it is at least possible that the poet could see him in the same perspective as another betrayed Divinity.[4] So comparatively clownish a writer as the author of *Edmond*

---

1. Créton, p. 179/377; cf. *Traïson*, p. 52/201: "we are all betrayed . . . for God's sake have patience, and call to mind our Saviour, who was undeservedly sold and given into the hands of his enemies."

2. Hol. 501/1/24 describes the Archbishop of Canterbury, who gave Richard false guarantees about his safety, as prophesying "not as a Prelat but as a Pilate". Shakespeare uses the Pilate comparison in *Richard III*, I. iv. 270, putting it into the mouth of one of Clarence's murderers: "How fain, like Pilate, would I wash my hands / Of this most grievous murder!"

3. See note on III. ii. 132. The first passage under discussion especially (IV. i. 169–71) may spring from the Judas–traitor association, since Richard's thought arises from the enigmatic salutation "all hail". This greeting, H. N. Paul suggests (*Royal Play of Macbeth*, p. 199), was associated in Shakespeare's mind with treachery because of its use by Judas in the Gospel story of Christ's betrayal: cf. its employment by the Witches in *Mac.*, I. iii. 47 ff; *3 H 6*, v. vii. 33–4; *LLL.*, v. ii. 340. There is the same associative link in the passage from *Edmond Ironside* here quoted.

4. The similitude of God and King is well worked: "and as the name of the king is very often attributed and given unto God in the holy scriptures; so doth

Ironside, one of the plays in MS Egerton 1994, could make a similar comparison, when his betrayed monarch reproaches his Machiavellian betrayer Edricus:

> *Edricus.* All haile vnto my gracious soueraigne
> *Edmond. Iudas* thie nexte parte is to kisse my Cheeke
> And then Comitt mee vnto *Cayphas*.[1]

VII. HALL

This is not the place to discuss the view, advanced by Dr Tillyard and others, that Shakespeare was indebted to Edward Hall's *The vnion of the two noble and illustre famelies of Lancastre & Yorke* for much in the planning and doctrine of the history plays. "The most striking parallel between Hall and [*Richard II*]", writes Wilson, "is the fact that both begin at the same point [the 'appeals' of Mowbray and Bolingbroke] and that in a sense Hall furnished the frame and stretched the canvas for the whole Shakespearian cycle, *Richard II* to *Richard III*."[2]

There is very little evidence, however, of any connexion more direct and less generalized than this between our play and the language and historical information peculiar to Hall and not found in Holinshed. Although Shakespeare may well have remembered Hall's general scheme, and perhaps some of his emphases, I cannot feel with any confidence that he actually consulted the text of Hall while his play was being written or planned.[3] It was suggested by the Clarendon editors that the scenes of Aumerle's conspiracy (v. ii, iii) owed something to Hall. The argument was developed in detail by Reyher on the rather doubtful ground that because Hall's version is more vivid than Holinshed's Shakespeare preferred to use it. That there is a specific link between these scenes and Hall's

---

God himself in the same scriptures sometimes vouchsafe to communicate his name with earthly princes, terming them gods . . ." (*Certain Sermons or Homilies* . . . [1844 edn], p. 493). For other material on the sacred status of the prince see Hart, p. 41 *et passim*, and notes to v. iii. 134, I. ii. 38, IV. i. 121–9. V. K. Whittaker, *Shakespeare's Use of Learning* (San Marino, 1953), p. 160, finds the comparison of the Lord's Anointed to Christ to be "a logical inference from the teaching of the Homilies which Shakespeare might easily have made". A. P. Rossiter, 'Prognosis on a Shakespeare Problem' in *Durham University Journal*, xxxiii (1941), p. 136, suggests the influence of the "staged spectacle of a sacrificial king of sorrows before his judges", familiar to the Elizabethans from the mystery cycles that were still being performed at the end of the sixteenth century.

    1. *Edmond Ironside*, M.S.R., ll. 1644–6.   2. Wilson, p. liv.

    3. For discussion see (*a*) suggested verbal echoes: II. i. 263–9, III. iii. 117, and see note below; (*b*) historical information: I. i. 9, I. i. 15–17, II. ii. 53–4, II. iii. 120–1, II. iv. 5–6.

version seems, on the evidence so far offered, to be unlikely.[1]

VIII. SHAKESPEARE AT WORK

An opinion about how Shakespeare approached his subject will depend in some measure on the number of works to which we are prepared to grant the status of sources. If these, besides Holinshed and *The Mirror for Magistrates*, included Daniel and *Woodstock*, we can observe the dramatist turning to two other creative writers of his time, one a playwright and the other an epic poet, to find out what they have made of the theme he has undertaken. Since he is a dramatist with an immediate interest in a particular phase of history, he might well have consulted Froissart and Hall, too, for both impose a significant design on history in a way that Holinshed does not.

If we add to this list of sources *Traïson* and Créton, our estimate of how Shakespeare worked on this play will alter. As Rossiter puts it: "The cumulative effect of such evidence is to compel us . . . to consider that Shakespeare worked like a historical scholar, and made his histories by collating authorities, cross-checking and (in a word) Research."[2] There is no way of escaping from this conclusion, despite Black's demonstration of how little actual time Shakespeare would have needed to spend upon his task of gathering the material.[3]

I have suggested that we are not forced to such a conclusion, because the evidence for Shakespeare's use of the French manuscript chroniclers is not good enough to prove the case. Shakespeare the researcher into the life and times of Richard II, even the rapid reader postulated by Black—these are unnecessary hypotheses.

They are hypotheses which have brought further problems in their train. Wilson found it necessary to suppose the existence of an intermediary, a dramatist "soaked in the history of England", who wrote Shakespeare's original, and so may be said to have done his research for him. This view is partly to be attributed to the difficulty we have in believing that Shakespeare worked on his material like a scholar-chronicler. It does not, however, fall to the ground

1. See notes on material to v. ii and iii and notes on v. ii. 44, 61–2, 111–15; v. iii. 134.

2. 'Prognosis on a Shakespeare Problem', p. 130. This article, which Black's partly supersedes, but which Black does not appear to have known, should be consulted on the points discussed here.

3. M. W. Black, 'The Sources of *Richard II*', *J. Q. Adams Memorial Studies* (Washington, 1948), pp. 210–15. For further discussion of individual instances in which Shakespeare has been seen at work collating historical information, see notes to III. ii. 64, IV. i, material, IV. i. 106, IV. i. 152–3. He was also collating Froissart in I. iii, if we accept Wilson's view: see note on I. iii. 125–38.

simply because the hypothesis which gave rise to it is disallowed. Wilson has adduced in support of it evidence of several kinds: the existence in our present text of *Richard II* of supposed threads left over from the material that went to make up the old play; the presence of the "bones of the old play sticking through" Shakespeare's text in the form of vestigial rhymed couplets in passages of blank verse; and the indifferent quality of some parts of the play, especially in the fifth Act. Readers may be referred to Black's full treatment of these points.[1] He has shown that the supposed threads from the old play are elements which may be explained by the dramatist's own mistakes—or, it may be added, that he is in some cases simply copying a name from the text of Holinshed open before him—and that they are mistakes of the order that is noticed in the study rather than in the theatre; that there is no need to suppose that the traces of derelict couplets mean more than that Shakespeare originally drafted some passages in rhyme, and then changed his mind; and that the genuine badness of some of the writing may be explained, especially when it occurs in the fifth Act, by weariness, haste, and boredom. The most convincing argument[2] against the "old play" hypothesis is this: it is hard to conceive of any play which could be at once the foundation of the play that we have and at the same time could have treated in full the matters— such as Bolingbroke's marriage, or the fates of Gloucester and Richard's brother Huntingdon—which, because they obtain passing mention in *Richard II*, are believed by Wilson to be tell-tale signs of a non-Shakespearian archetype.

4. THE GARDEN SCENE

The Garden scene is located in the Duke of York's garden at Langley. This unexceptionable setting is the ground for a parable. The Gardener's Man wonders why they should keep their garden in order while the whole land falls to ruin for want of such attendance, but the Gardener informs him that Bolingbroke has taken charge now of the kingdom's garden, and, moralizing on Richard's decay, instructs the man to prune the emblematic plants as Richard should have done those of his kingdom.

From amongst the extensive range of secondary meanings attached to the garden in the Middle Ages and the Renaissance, it seems likely that we must look chiefly in three places for the background of this scene, and for its main idea—the comparison of the disordered state and ruler with the neglected garden.

1. Black, art. cit., pp. 204–10.   2. *Ibid.*, p. 208.

(i) Other writers before Shakespeare, especially political satir-ists, had compared the elements of disorder in a state to weeds that must be rooted out and plucked away; so common, indeed, is this figure that it makes for what is almost a subsidiary meaning of the verb *weed*, one that is familiar enough today. Occasionally a writer is able to amplify and bring the metaphor to life by turning it con-sciously to the ends of parable. So, for example, does the sixteenth-century reformer Henry Brinklow (d. 1546) in his *Complaynt of Roderyck Mors*:

> the kyngs grace began wel to wede the garden of Ingland, but yet he left stonding (the more pytye!) the most fowlest and stynkyng wedys, which had most nede to be first pluckyd vp by the rootys; that is to say, the prycking thistels and styngyng nettels; which, styll stondyng, what helpyth the deposyng of the pety membres of the Pope, and to leaue his whole body behynd, which be the pompos bisshops. . .[1]

In the same way, writing after Shakespeare, Traiano Boccalini in his once famous work, the *Ragguagli di Parnaso* (written in 1612) devises an elaborate parable: gardeners from all over the world complain to Apollo that their ground is choked with henbane, nettles, and other useless plants which prevent the growth of their vegetables; these, it turns out, are the vagabonds which infest the commonwealth and which can be removed by the sound of drum and trumpet, that is, by turning them into soldiers.[2]

It is likely that Shakespeare, too, realized the life in the old meta-phor and the long-exploited figurative potency in the fact that:

> The noisome weeds . . . without profit suck
> The soil's fertility from wholesome flowers,

and that he amplified it into a stage parable, with speakers, just as Boccalini and Brinklow independently expanded the metaphor into moralization and fable. We need not suppose any conscious memory on the writers' part of *Matthew* xiii (the parables of the seed and the tares, and the comparison of the kingdom of heaven to growing things), or any source but an old metaphor purified and re-charged.[3]

1. *Roderyck Mors*, ed. Cowper, E.E.T.S., e.s., 1874, p. 55.
2. T. Boccalini, *Advertisements from Parnassus*, trans. Earl of Monmouth (1657), p. 27; referred to by Butler, *Hudibras*, I. ii. 173–81: see note in Z. Grey's edn.
3. How readily the metaphor could be enlivened and amplified for a similar purpose can be seen from a passage in Sir T. Elyot's *Governour* (1531), I. iv, Everyman edn, pp. 18–19: here it is applied to the education of children. Plutarch, too, as Miss R. L. Anderson points out (*North West Missouri State Teachers College Studies*, III (1939), pp. 27–8), uses it in his essay 'Of Delay in Divine Punishment', whence the proverb: 'The fattest soyle without husbandrie,

For some part of the metaphor's growth, however, that represented by the Gardener's order to his man:

> like an executioner
> Cut off the heads of too fast growing sprays,
> That look too lofty in our commonwealth

Shakespeare, as H. J. Leon has shown,[1] may have been indebted to
some passages in classical writers which compare the lopping of
tall plants to the elimination of the unruly great. Because the
analogy of garden and kingdom occurs in a number of early history
plays, as well as in *2* and *3 Henry VI*,[2] it seems likely that this classical
echo did not originate the analogy but only helped to consolidate it.

(ii) Some other parallels may set the Garden scene in a context.
Shakespeare's comparison of the state to a garden is like the comparison of the social order to a garden which was current amongst
the medieval preachers. They derived it from the parable in
Matthew xx about the labourers in the vineyard and compared the
three estates of priests, knights, and labourers to the three orders of
husbandmen whose duty it is to tend the vineyard of the church.[3]
A passage in Dekker's *The Seven Deadly Sinnes of London* (1606) testi-
fies that this comparison was still very much alive in Shakespeare's
day:

> you that are Stewards ouer the Kings house of heauen, and lye
> heere as Embassadors about the greatest State-matters in the
> world: what a dishonour were it to your places, if it should bee
> knowne that you are Sloathfull? you are sworne labourers, to
> worke in a Vineyard, which if you dresse not carefully, if you cut
> it not artificially, if you vnderprop it not wisely whē you see it
> laden, if you gather not the fruites in it, when they bee ripe, but

---

is soone overgrowen with weedes' (L. Wright, *A Display of dutie* [1589], sig.
A4^r): cf. III. iv. 59–63.

1. See note on III. iv. 33–6.

2. See note on III. iv. 37–9, and especially C. Spurgeon's investigation there
cited. Iden's garden in *2 H 6*, IV. x, may reasonably be taken, as by Tillyard, as
specially appropriate to Iden as an upholder of hierarchical order in the state,
although it is not, in its immediate context, more than a convenient location.

3. See G. R. Owst, *Literature and the Pulpit in Medieval England* (Cambridge,
1933), pp. 549–51. In a comment on Bunyan's garden in the House of the Inter-
preter in *Pilgrim's Progress*, given by H. Talon in his *John Bunyan* (London, 1951),
p. 303, Owst adds: "The image of a garden and its various plants was often
used by the theologians and homily-writers of the Middle Ages to illustrate the
Church, or religion, particularly the latter." Cf. also the "garden of the soul,
with its weeds of sin and blossoms of virtue . . . a figure met frequently in
devotional literature", and found in Isaiah lxiii. 11 and elsewhere. On this, see
J. J. Molloy, *A Theological Interpretation of the Moral Play, Wisdom, Who is Christ*
(Washington, 1952), p. 12. (I owe this reference to J. C. Maxwell.)

suffer them to drop down, and bee eaten vp by Swine, O what a
deere account are you to make to him that must giue you your
hire? you are the Beames of the Sun that must ripen the Grapes
of the Vine, & if you shine not cleerely, he will eclipse you for
euer: your tongues are the instruments yᵗ must cut off rancke
& idle Sprigs, to make the bearing-braunches to spred, and
vnlesse you keep them sharpe, and be euer pruning with them,
he will cast you by, and you shall be eaten vp with rust. The
Church is a garden and you must weede it...[1]

Shakespeare's garden, like this one, contains emblematic plants:
herbs swarming with caterpillars (parasites), overpeering sprays,
and apricots bowed down by their own weight. They are not
realized with the sharply pictorial vision of the emblematist, but
seem to grow naturally out of the rhetoric of the whole scene. It is
pointless, therefore, to search for specific counterparts for these
symbolic plants, but we may note one celebrated example of the
garden filled with emblematic objects: that into which Eusebius, in
Erasmus's colloquy "The Religious Feast", leads his friends in order
to show them his speaking statues, symbolic fountain, morally significant plants, and emblematic creatures with labels in their
mouths.[2] Shakespeare's garden has affinities, however distant and
unspecific, with the Renaissance habit of seeing the fields, the
creatures, the trees, and the hedgerows eloquent of higher mysteries—all that method of perception which owed much to Plato
but gave the lie to the Socratic dictum: "Men who dwell in the city
are my teachers, and not the trees or the country." In handling this
type of image, Shakespeare moves further away from the stiff and
arbitrary manner of the emblematists: when he comes to describe
in *Henry V* (v. ii. 36–60) war-torn France, "best garden of the
world", now grown to wildness, the description seems innocent of
emblem, though not of rhetorical point.

"There is no ancient gentlemen but gardeners, ditchers and
grave-makers—they hold up Adam's profession", remarks the
Grave-digger in *Hamlet*. The Gardeners, humble people—no

1. Dekker, *Seven Deadly Sinnes of London*, ed. Brett-Smith (Oxford, 1922),
p. 40. Cf. the world-field metaphor in Bp J. Hall's 'Vpon a Corn field ouer-
growne with weeds' in his *Occasional Meditations* (*Works*, 1634, sig. Nnn2ᵛ):
"Heere were a goodly field of Corne, if it were not over-laid with Weeds; I do
not like these reds, and blewes, and yellowes, amongst these plain stalkes and
eares: This beauty would do well elsewhere, I had rather see a plot less faire and
more yeilding; In this field I see a true picture of the world wherein there is
more glory, then true substance; Wherein the greater part carries it from the
better... Wherein Parasites and vnprofitable hang-byes doe both rob and ouer-
top their Masters..." and so on.
2. *Colloquies*, trans. N. Bailey (1878 edn), I. 57 ff.

better things than earth, as Isabel cries, with an irony of which she is unaware—criticize the court and its great men in language and ideas drawn from their rural discipline. This is the device of pastoral, the contrast between the good and the bad shepherd which allowed Renaissance pastoral much latitude for satirical comment on the great, put into the mouth of the humble and detached shepherd who looked at the court with innocent but perceptive eyes. It is used, for example, by Spenser in the five "moral" eclogues of *The Shepheardes Calender*, where the defects of contemporary religion are under fire, and in *Colin Clouts Come Home Againe*, where the courtier and shepherd are opposed as types of the worldly and the incorruptible,[1] and the shepherd, back returned to his flocks, has seen it all. The Gardeners undoubtedly belong to this tradition, and the scene as a whole to that by which conventionalized bucolic rectitude is made the touchstone of urban and courtly life. The Gardeners' wisdom is dignified by it and their perceptions sharpened; when Isabel retires from them back to the disastrous court-world, anxious and weeping, they remain the wise and pitying masters of the scene: the Gardener's skill is not "subject to [her] curse" (III. iv. 103).

(iii) Lastly, we may notice, as part of the background of the scene, the uses of the garden in ceremony and pageant. Gardens were often represented on the Elizabethan stage, and in the Elizabethan and Jacobean masque; but this is one of the few occasions where the setting is endowed, by what the characters are given to say, with a meaning more recondite than spring-time, seclusion, or pleasant relaxation.[2] In the French *tableaux vivants* since the fifteenth century, however, a fenced garden has been used to represent "the city, the nation, or the blessed state of prosperity".[3] This device may have been derived from the *Paradis* of the French mystery plays, scenes of Adam's labour, which the greengrocers furnished out with fruits and vegetables.[4] It was from such a garden, rather

1. ll. 680–730.
2. For discussion of the staging of garden-scenes, see Chambers, *Elizabethan Stage*, III. 55, G. R. Kernodle, *From Art to Theatre* (Chicago, 1944), pp. 143–4, G. F. Reynolds, *Staging of Elizabethan Plays* ... (New York, 1940), pp. 72–7. For gardens in the masque, see A. Nicoll, *Stuart Masques* ... (London, 1937), pp. 81, 91, 112.
3. Kernodle, op. cit., pp. 73–5. It is from this that there perhaps arose the panegyrical description of a particular country as the "world's garden" (as France in *H 5*, v. ii. 36 and see note on II. i. 42); on the other hand, this conceit may originate earlier and have itself helped to make the garden–state comparison easier. The description of a particular part of a country as that country's garden (e.g. Kent) is presumably an extension of the trope.
4. G. Cohen, *Histoire de la mise-en-scène* ... (Paris, 1926), p. 91.

than from the fortress more often mentioned in the English equivalents, that the maidens arose to greet the prince at a royal entry.[1]

There is not much reason to suppose that Shakespeare was conscious of this tradition when he composed the Garden scene, unless the reference to "Adam" (III. iv. 73) proves a connexion. Yet there is some evidence that the garden, with something of the significance of the French *vergier*, was used in English pageantry.[2]

The imaginative process most fundamental to the scene was perhaps the granting of new life to an old metaphor, not the borrowing of devices and sets of meanings from elsewhere. It was a response to a hidden force in language. Caroline Spurgeon describes it as resulting from an "undertone—at first faint, later clear and definite —in the earlier historical plays, [which] here in *Richard II* gathers strength and volume, until it becomes the leading theme"; in the garden-scene, it is "as it were, gathered up, focused and pictorially presented".[3] But it is helpful to realize that the "tendency to think of matters human as of growing plants and trees", of which Caroline Spurgeon speaks, lies at the root of countless common expressions. What distinguishes the garden scene is the rebirth, as a dramatized parable, of a metaphor—the comparison of bad men and things to weeds—which is so widespread that without the amplification given it by the author of *Matthew*, by Brinklow, Shakespeare, or Dekker, it tends to lose its moral efficacy.

This metaphor "gathers strength and volume" from the proverbial wisdom of the Gardener at ll. 55–65. Behind the images which he uses, as behind his commands to his man at ll. 29–32, lies Erasmus's "the better the nature of the soil, the more it is wasted and filled with worthless shrubs if the farmer does not take care. So it is with a man's character. . ." (*Institutio*). This is a pedagogic metaphor with a long history from Plutarch to *Euphues*:[4] "Most

1. Such a garden is illustrated in G. Babst, *Essai sur l'histoire du Théâtre* (Paris, 1893), p. 96; see also Withington, *English Pageantry* (Cambridge, Mass., 1918), I. 171–2, on "le vergier de France", which featured in the entry of Louis XII's Queen into Paris, 1513.

2. Thus, at a City pageant for the visit of Charles V in 1522, a mountain island surrounded with water and full of beasts, trees, and flowers betokened England (see Withington, op. cit., I. 177, quoting from a MS at Corpus Christi College); Hall (*Union . . .*, p. 639) has an account of the same pageant; for the verses (by William Lilly) used on the occasion, see C. R. Baskervill in *H.L.B.*, no. 9 (April 1936), pp. 1–14. At the coronation of Elizabeth the decayed commonwealth was represented on a pageant at the Little Conduit as a barren rocky mountain planted with a withered tree, the flourishing commonwealth as a hill, fair, fresh, green and beautiful, bearing "one tree very fresh and fayre" (Nichols, *Progresses of Queen Elizabeth* [London, 1823], I. 49–50).

3. *Shakespeare's Imagery* (Cambridge, 1935), p. 222.   4. Bond, pp. 251, 263.

subject is the fattest soil to weeds" (*2 Henry IV*). The organization into a scenic whole of the three metaphors I have discussed—weeds must be eradicated, straggling branches "executed", fat soil tilled —is very remarkable and very Shakespearian.

5. THE QUESTION OF POLITICAL ALLEGORY

It has been suggested that Shakespeare's play was deliberately composed as a political allegory, with the purpose of warning Elizabeth I of her possible fate if she encouraged flatterers and permitted unjust taxation and monopolies. By this theory, the play contains hints that the Earl of Essex would make an excellent Bolingbroke, as well as parallels between Richard's and Elizabeth's management of Irish affairs.

There are instances, occurring in 1578, some time before 1588, and in 1597, of certain of Elizabeth's courtiers hinting at an analogy between Richard II and the Queen, although in no disloyal spirit.[1] The fact that when the first Quarto was printed the deposition scene was omitted (and not restored until after Elizabeth's death) suggests that official sensitivity about representing the discrowning of a monarch might have been sharpened by the currency of this analogy. There is nothing here, of course, that tells us about Shakespeare's own purpose in writing the play, and the deposition scene may have been omitted for other reasons.

Indeed, the real starting-points for those who see political allegory in the play are three in number:

(i) On 8 February 1601 the Earl of Essex launched the abortive uprising which led to his execution for treason. The previous day, some of his followers had persuaded the Lord Chamberlain's Men, for a fee of forty shillings, to stage a play at the Globe about the deposing and killing of Richard II. This was later described by the

---

1. The instances are given by Chambers, *William Shakespeare*, 1. 353. L. B. Campbell in *Shakespeare's Histories* (San Marino, 1947), pp. 169–81, cites also (i) discussions on *Leicester's Commonwealth* (1584), a libellous attack on the Earl, which was published abroad and associates him with the favourites who helped to ruin Edward II, Richard II, and Henry VI; (ii) the mention in 1592 of a notice fixed on James VI of Scotland's door warning him to beware of Richard's fate; (iii) *A Conference about the Next Succession to the Crowne of Ingland* (1594), by R. Parsons, S.J., which discusses whether Richard was justly deposed or no, and concludes that he was—a point rebutted by P. Wentworth in his rejoinder of 1598. Miss Campbell implies that this sort of thing was in Shakespeare's mind when he wrote *R 2*, a play which she appears to consider as a mere peg on which he hung a political controversy of his own time; she fails to show, however, that the matter bulked large in the minds of any but a few professional controversialists and politicians, and her over-emphasis on the political elements undoubtedly present in *R 2* has, I think, damaged her reading of the play.

actor Augustine Phillips,[1] one of the Globe shareholders who answered for the Company on this occasion, as "so old and so long out of use that they should have small or no company at it. But at their request [they] were content to play it". Essex's followers appear to have thought that the play would encourage the citizens to support the rebellion, and, although there can be no proof, it seems reasonable to agree with Chambers, that the play was probably Shakespeare's, complete with deposition scene.[2] There is no reason at all to suppose that what Essex's followers hoped would have a seditious effect in 1601 had been composed by Shakespeare some six or seven years earlier with a seditious intention.[3] Further, all the officials concerned seem to have exonerated the players from any treasonable design, and they were playing at court "a few days after the trial of Essex and several times the following winter".[4]

(ii) In February 1599 Sir John Hayward published a small book called *The First Part of the Life and Raigne of King Henrie IIII*, a work which, despite its title, deals with the last years of the reign of King Richard II. The book appeared at a time when Essex was in difficulties with the Queen, and contained a Latin dedication to Essex in the course of which he is addressed: "Magnus siquidem es, et presenti iudicio, et futuri temporis expectatione". Furthermore, there are one or two places in the book where parallels have been drawn between Hayward's phrasing and Shakespeare's in *Richard II*. After some copies had been issued, the dedicatory leaf was removed, and the work was allowed to circulate; but a revised second edition was suppressed, and Essex himself seems to have been one of the first persons to object to the book. Hayward's *Henry IV* was later brought into evidence against Essex, probably first at the private trial of 5 June 1600, when Essex was charged with mishandling affairs in Ireland. There exists in the State Papers a document entitled *Analytical Abstract in support of the charge of treason against the Earl of Essex*, which probably refers to this trial of the summer of 1600. An extract reads:

> Essex's own actions confirm the intent of this treason. His permitting underhand that treasonable book of Henry IV to be

1. On Phillips, see Chambers, *Elizabethan Stage*, II. 205, 333–4; and for a possible connexion with the "informing" actor in *Poetaster* (1601), see *ibid.*, 207, and *Ben Jonson*, ed. Herford and Simpson, IX. 566–7.

2. *William Shakespeare*, I. 354.

3. The same argument applies to G. B. Harrison's suggestion about the readers of Q1 construing certain lines as a reference to the Earl of Essex: see notes on I. iv. 24. 31.

4. R. Heffner, 'Shakespeare, Hayward and Essex', *P.M.L.A.*, XLV (1930), 757; cf. Chambers, *Elizabethan Stage*, I. 325, *William Shakespeare*, I. 355.

printed and published; it being plainly deciphered, not only by the matter, and by the epistle itself [i.e. the dedication], for what end and for whose behalf it was made, but also the Earl himself being so often at the playing thereof, and with great applause giving countenance to it.[1]

Hayward himself was committed to the Tower, and was questioned on the matter at his two trials of 11 July 1600 and 22 January 1601. The notes of the questions put to him, and his answers, abstracted by Sir Edward Coke, survive, and have been printed.[2] Hayward protested his innocence of any attempt to draw analogies between Richard, Elizabeth, and Essex, and gave fairly detailed information about his intentions and historical sources; but he remained in prison apparently until after Elizabeth's death.

(iii) Lastly, the Queen herself had a word to say on the subject. The following memorandum by William Lambarde the antiquary was first printed by Nichols:[3]

That which passed from the Excellent Majestie of Queen ELIZABETH *in her Privie Chamber at East Greenwich, 4° Augusti* 1601, 43° *Reg. sui, towards* WILLIAM LAMBARDE.
He presented her Majestie with his Pandecta of all her rolls, bundells, membranes, and parcells that be reposed in her Majestie's Tower at London; whereof she had given to him the charge 21st January last past ... she proceeded to further pages, and asked where she found cause of stay ... so her Majestie fell upon the reign of King Richard II. saying, "I am Richard II. know ye not that?"
W. L. "Such a wicked imagination was determined and attempted by a most unkind Gent. the most adorned creature that ever your Majestie made."
Her Majestie. "He that will forget God, will also forget his benefactors; this tragedy was played 40tie times in open streets and houses."
... returning to Richard II. she demanded, "Whether I had seen any true picture, or lively representation of his countenance and person?"
W. L. "None but such as be in common hands."
Her Majestie. "The Lord Lumley, a lover of antiquities, discovered it fastened on the backside of a door of a base room; which he presented unto me, praying, with my good leave, that I might put it in order with the Ancestors and Successors; I will command Tho. Kneavet, Keeper of my House and Gallery at Westminster, to show it unto thee."

1. Cal. S. P. Dom., 1598–1601, pp. 453–5.
2. M. Dowling, 'Sir J. Hayward's Troubles . . .', *Library*, 4th ser., XI (1931).
3. Op. cit., iii. 552–3.

The attempt has been made by Miss Albright[1] to make a consecutive story out of these events in order to support her view that Shakespeare wrote his play as a political allegory with an immediate contemporary reference. Her reconstruction of the matter is open to some fatal objections advanced against it by Heffner.

Shakespeare's play was already in print by 1597, and Hayward's book did not appear until 1599. Miss Albright conjectures that Shakespeare saw Hayward's work in manuscript and used it as a source for political analogies and historical information. Even if the great bulk of Miss Albright's parallels between play and book were acceptable—and they are not—there remains the fact that Hayward stated at his first examination (according to Coke's report thereof) that he "Wrote a history of 300 years past, and acquainted none therewith before he brought it to the printer. Began to write the history about a year before it was published, but had intended it a dozen years before, although he acquainted no man therewith." Hayward may have been lying, but it is utterly unlikely, for, as Heffner observes: "If [Hayward] could have proved that he wrote the history as early as 1595 he would certainly have been acquitted, for he was accused of writing an old story to suit present times—1598–9".[2]

Again, Miss Albright attempts to re-date the *Analytical Abstract* referring to the first trial of Essex in 1600 and make it refer to his second and final trial of 1601, in order that she may read the remarks about the Earl's presence at the "playing" of a "treasonable book" as a reference to the behaviour of the Lord Chamberlain's Men in 1601, and to their special performance, on the eve of the Essex rebellion, of a play about Richard II which may have been Shakespeare's. By this reckoning, the play at which the Earl was "so often" present was *Richard II* and appeared to Essex's prosecutor as simply a dramatization of *The Life and Raigne of Henrie IIII*. Even if we accept Miss Albright's re-dating of the *Analytical Abstract* (and it is rejected by Heffner[3]), the argument will not hold. The Globe play of 7 February was not performed in Essex's presence, and the players were not punished. It is really impossible to believe that this happy result would have accrued to the dramatic company if the play had been performed "often", as was the "treasonable book", according to the *Abstract*.

A similar objection applies to the attempt to expand the performance of 7 February 1601 into the forty performances in open

1. In a series of articles in *P.M.L.A.*, XLII (1927), XLVI (1931), XLVII (1932).

2. Art. cit., *P.M.L.A.*, XLV (1930), 767.

3. 'Shakespeare, Hayward and Essex again', *P.M.L.A.*, XLVII (1932), 898–9.

streets and houses of which the Queen complained to Lambarde. The Queen, even in her indignation, is hardly likely to have exaggerated one performance into forty, and it is difficult to believe that the Government would have taken no action about the Lord Chamberlain's Men if they had been guilty of a *series* of performances. To what then was the Queen referring? Chambers suggests,[1] on the supposition that the special performance ordered by Essex's followers was one of Shakespeare's *Richard II*, that the performances complained of by the Queen some six months later included earlier stagings of Shakespeare's play from about 1595, the Queen thus allowing the one Essex-instigated performance of 1601 to blacken with retrospective suspicion the earlier performances of the play. If we could feel certain about this, it would perhaps help to prove that the play performed on the eve of the rebellion was indeed Shakespeare's. Unfortunately, the theory leaves unexplained the "playing" of the treasonable book, at which Essex is said in the *Analytical Abstract* to have been "so often" present. It seems a good deal more plausible to hold, with Heffner, that the "tragedy" referred to by the Queen was the same as the "playing" mentioned in the *Abstract*: some kind of "tragical" recitation or dramatic show, based on Hayward, and full of pointed political analogies. Of course, the Queen may have muddled this kind of thing with the one performance at the Globe in February, and included them both in her anathema—her phraseology is ambiguous enough to apply to one or the other or both;[2] but there is no reason why the commentators should follow her example.

There remains the question of the parallels that can be drawn between *Richard II* and Hayward's treatise. Miss Albright found a large number,[3] but her evidence is of small value because she neg-

1. *William Shakespeare*, i. 354-5. This view is accepted by Wilson, p. ix: "We have it on the authority of Queen Elizabeth herself that it was acted forty times, an unusually long run for an Elizabethan play. . ." One cannot help wondering, though, whether Elizabeth's "forty" is not simply equivalent to "umpteen", or "many more times than I approve of": on the indefinite use of "forty" see K. Elze, *Notes on Elizabethan Dramatists* (1880), pp. 87-92.

2. By "tragedy" the Queen may have meant a tragical narrative recited, like those in the *Mirror*; "open streets and houses" might mean "open streets and [private] houses", i.e. street-corner shows *and* special performances in private houses for the better sort such as the Earl himself; the phrase could also mean "open streets and open houses", where "open houses" can surely refer only to the public playhouses (as distinct from the private playhouses), in which case it would be contradicted by "open streets" if that means street-corner shows. It may be that the phrase is simply the Queen's loose reference to the performances in public playhouses, and that she is making no distinction between "house" and street.

3. *P.M.L.A.*, xlii (1927), 706-18.

lected to examine properly sources that may have been common to both works, and was so eager to prove that Shakespeare borrowed from Hayward that she relied on unremarkable coincidences in phrasing and general treatment. There are still left, however, a number of reasonably good parallels between play and book, which I have set out in my commentary.[1] Some of these may be due to the two writers' drawing on a common stock of ideas,[2] and one or two may be explained by their having a common source.[3] But when all is said, and bearing in mind the evidence for the priority in date of Shakespeare's play—which had enjoyed two reprints in 1598, the year when Hayward, according to Coke's account of what he said, began to compose his *Henry IV*—it seems reasonable to conclude that the play was a source of that troublesome little work. This was the conclusion that Chambers reached, though without going into the details.[4] Hayward and his *cause célèbre* must therefore be regarded, from our point of view, as part of the history of Shakespeare's reputation at the turn of the century.

6. KING RICHARD'S TRAGEDY

When at first examined, the design of *Richard II* may appear un-expected. The play is in four unequal phases:

(i) I. i–II. i. 223. Richard as king; the political crises with which he is faced (shown as derived in part from earlier events), and his lack of wisdom in dealing with them.

(ii) II. i. 224 to the end of III. i. Bolingbroke's invasion, and the transference of real power.

(iii) III. ii to the end of v. i. Richard's deposition, or what can perhaps be called his "passion".

(iv) v. ii to the end. Bolingbroke as king; his mastery in a political crisis.

These phases are not as mechanical or clear-cut as their tabu-

---

1. Both works are imaginative treatments of the same episodes, so one must be cautious; but see notes on II. i. 113, 246, 250, II. iii. 119–21, IV. i. 130, v. ii. 18, v. v. 77–80, v. vi. 34, 38.

2. See notes on II. iii. 119–21 and v. ii. 18.

3. See notes on II. i. 113, 246.

4. *William Shakespeare*, 1. 356. E. P. Kuhl in *S.P.*, xxv (1928), 312–15, holding that Hayward was Shakespeare's debtor, suggests that when Hayward said in 1601 that he had taken certain ideas "from a book written three years since, but cannot remember the author", the forgotten author was Shakespeare, whom Hayward was protecting because Shakespeare was, like himself, connected with the Essex faction. There is, though, nothing in the ideas which Hayward says he borrowed from the unknown author that can be identified with any certainty with anything in the two relevant plays, *R 2* and *1 H 4* (Q. 1598).

lation may suggest; in the first part of IV. i, which echoes the trial by combat scenes of the first Act, Bolingbroke is manifestly ruling, while the most absorbing scene of the last phase develops Richard's suffering to its conclusion in death. Such counterpointing preserves unity and sequence without disorganizing the four-part design; the first two phases seem especially deliberate.

This view of the design serves to show, at least, what Shakespeare was *not* concerned to do, and why our expectations may be baffled. The play, although it touches upon this subject, is not about a struggle for power between two royal houses, nor even between two royal men, despite contrasts in temperament and politics. Shakespeare could have written a play of political intrigue, and made the military action which accompanies it a good deal more uncertain and exciting—the material was there in Holinshed. Instead, he placed the emphasis on Richard's nature and behaviour, and gave his play the order and unity of biography. He did this even at the risk of exaggerating what might be thought to be, by a dramatist chiefly concerned with dynastic and military conflict, a disadvantage of the original story: the fact that Richard was so largely a passive victim of events, and Bolingbroke so easy a victor. Shakespeare gives them even less to do in the fields of conquest and intrigue than his history permitted. He chose to do this, and makes his choice clear to the audience.

The first phase works towards, as its climax, a striking demonstration of Richard's unfitness for his kingly office. He has, first, the legacy of past mistakes to contend with. These mistakes are brought to dramatic life in the dead-and-gone business of Gloucester's murder which has come alive again in the person of the avenging nephew, and his challenge to the murderer's wretched tool, Mowbray; meantime, the Duchess of Gloucester, a lamenting chorus, serves to revivify for the audience the shock and horror, as well as the plangent dynastic issues, attendant upon the tyrant's buried act.

On the whole, Richard deals with this situation creditably enough. Since Coleridge gave the lead, many commentators have read Richard's "insincerity, partiality, arbitrariness and favouritism",[1] as well as Mowbray's bluster and Bolingbroke's tenacity, between the lines of the challenge scenes. John Palmer perhaps has it both ways:

The more vigilant spectator may detect a subtle difference in Richard's addresses to the two men. Surely there is a touch of irony in his words to Bolingbroke:

1. Coleridge, i. 153.

> Cousin of Hereford, as thy cause is right,
> So be thy fortune in this royal fight;

and a touch of affectionate approval in his valediction to Mowbray:

> Farewell, my lord; securely I espy
> Virtue with valour couchèd in thine eye.

But these are hints to the wary. The simple onlooker is absorbed by the knightly courtesy of it all and is as eager for the fight as the champions themselves.[1]

It is possible that the scenes yield these hints to the wary in a measure as great as some commentators have claimed, but they are taken only at the cost of neglecting the broad theatrical effect. Shakespeare gives little sign, as he tries to breathe life into the chivalric forms that he found in Holinshed, that Richard steps out of the part prescribed for a monarch faced with a trial by combat between two of his nobility. The challenge scenes are not, to any of the actors engaged in them, much more, of course, than a political performance staged to the common view, serious enough perhaps, but with the kind of gravity that attends upon the operation of a fairly stereotyped social institution. All this is indicated by the formal arrangement and character of the speeches and gestures, a stiffness which suggests very cleverly that the lines of procedure have been laid down in advance, probably by a committee. Richard plays his appointed part. His attempts to make peace—prescribed as necessary for the validity of what was a strictly legal process—which are rejected by the angry knights, as they had full right within the process to do, are Gaunt's attempts, too; the old man, unlike the young, is not accused of weakness or "levity of tone".[2]

What we are to understand by the stopping of the trial is even more of an open question. Hayward thought that the incident was a contrived anti-climax, thoughtlessly devised by Richard so that he might indulge in irresponsible splendours, and many critics, such as Craig, have agreed with him: "he loves the pomp of his office, else he would hardly have suffered Bolingbroke and Mowbray to meet."[3] Yet Shakespeare does not seem at this stage to be

1. *Political Characters of Shakespeare* (London, 1945), p. 130.

2. Herford, p. 116.

3. H. Craig, *An Interpretation of Shakespeare* (New York, 1948), p. 128. In further discussion of the trial, Craig writes: "If Mowbray had won, Bolingbroke would have been silenced. If Bolingbroke had won, the King would have been rid of a follower who, he feared, would betray him, and he would have been at least no worse off as regards Bolingbroke. Then, too, in the decision of the council, which Richard had dictated, he follows the one course of

exploiting a fact of history, from which he could hardly escape, to the detriment of Richard, nor is there any hint in the sources available to Shakespeare that the trial was a thoughtless display, terminated by an act of royal petulance. Indeed, *if* Shakespeare had read Froissart, he would know that order and public safety made this last act advisable, and, *if* Shakespeare knew anything of the ordinances of the trial by combat, he would know that its termination at any stage was one of the royal umpire's allowed acts of authority. Whatever his sources said or, in the case of Holinshed, left unsaid on the point, Shakespeare was free to make thoughtlessness and petulance a part of Richard's character here. Whether he did, depends not on our estimate of the wisdom or folly of the historical Richard, measured with the foresight of one who knows the rest of the story, nor even on hints to the vigilant spectator, but on unprejudiced theatrical effect, even if this means ranging ourselves with that humble creature, Palmer's simple onlooker. From his point of view, Richard's sudden regaining of the initiative, and the submissions which follow it, can be seen as a ruler's stroke: it deflates the quarrelling magnates, and is explicitly justified by that highest of all Elizabethan arguments, the avoidance of civil tumult. It permits, so clear is the ascendancy Richard has now established, the remission of four years from Bolingbroke's exile: this is an act of mercy whose kingly and politically unforced nature is emphasized by Shakespeare's rendering of it as a free response to Gaunt's pleas rather than (as it is in Froissart) a shrewd calculation by the Council.

It is not difficult for the actor who plays Richard, and who knows what comes next, to "twinkle" with a consciousness of mischievous intentions and to make every one of the few sentences which he speaks in these scenes bristle with hints of the "skipping king [who] ambled up and down".[1] But it is, I think, more correct to believe that Shakespeare intended, with a larger theatrical effect in mind, to show Richard playing the part of majesty with a fair efficiency in these first scenes, the more dramatically to reveal his profounder unfitness for the role in the later ones. In Richard's sudden lapse of tone in the last scene of the first Act, it is unlikely that we see disclosed the "true" motive for the act of state which exiled the two rivals: for there is no indication that Shakespeare's monarch, like

conduct that was sure to do injustice to both appellants; and most cruelly and unnaturally, he inflicts the heavier penalty on Mowbray, who had no ulterior motive and had been honest and faithful." All this is perhaps true, but it is a historian's judgement about the Richard II of history; it does not necessarily apply to the character in Holinshed or in Shakespeare.

1. As Palmer (p. 131) suggests that he should.

Froissart's, knew of Bolingbroke's wooing of the commonalty until it is manifested in his conduct when he departs for exile.[1] But we do see a glittering autocrat when he is no longer concerned to keep up public appearances. The scene has a broken opening, a cheap irony, a naturalistic speech, full of sneers, and some quite sinister frankness and brutality; all this would have been impossible in the public context of the preceding scene, which asks for rehearsed gestures and harmless formulae. A general relaxation occurs when Richard is no longer kinging it. Is there even to be observed, perhaps, an offending gap between the public and the private character? This is one reason why the scenes are juxtaposed.[2]

This shock and disharmony are followed by the scene in which we are directly told for the first time about Richard's mismanagement of himself and his kingdom. Gaunt, our informer, has been shown so far as an orthodoxly loyal subject, a counsellor of patience to the Duchess and to his son. Loyal, time-honoured, and dying, he is to be believed without reservations when he paints *his* picture of a king who "mingled his royalty with cap'ring fools". Richard does not hear the great speech on the ruin of England, perhaps because Shakespeare avoided having to show a lack of response on Richard's part that would have prejudiced the beholder too finally against him. But it is the background to the more strictly technical reproaches of both Gaunt and York that follow, and, reinforced by the dynastic appeal to the great past of Richard's line, help to prepare for the climax towards which this first phase of the play has been moving. For Richard totally fails to raise himself to Gaunt's level, or even to respond to the good sense of York's argument[3] at II. i. 195–9:

> Take Herford's rights away, and take from time
> His charters, and his customary rights;
> Let not to-morrow then ensue to-day:
> Be not thyself. For how art thou a king
> But by fair sequence and succession?

This makes plain that his act of state in this scene, the seizure of Gaunt's property, is to be seen as a paramount folly that matches nothing he has done so far. Our sense of this is induced by the spectacle of the prince, in wilful choler, rejecting the advice of the good

---

1. See note on I. iv. 24–36.

2. For discussion of the juxtaposition of scenes, see W. B. C. Watkins, *shakespeare and Spenser* (Princeton, 1950), p. 78.

3. On this, as a factor leading directly to the rebellion, see G. C. Reese, 'The Question of the Succession in Elizabethan Drama', *Studies in English* (Texas, 1942), p. 79.

counsellors, who speak with a special authority. The good courtier, wrote Castiglione, must

> understand how to behave himselfe readily in all occurrents to drive into his Princes heade what honour and profit shall ensue to him and to his by justice, liberallitie, valiantnesse of courage, meekenesse, and by the other vertues that belong to a good prince, and contrariwise what slander, and damage commeth of the vices contrarie to them.

Richard rejects the good courtiers' persuasions to justice; thereby the scene makes its impact and reveals the defectiveness of this prince.[1] Other inferences from it—such as "Richard should not have gone to Ireland, leaving an unsettled land behind him", or, "Richard should not have appointed York Lord Governor because York's allegiance has been shaken"—are of minor force beside the king's rejection of the good counsellors. For Shakespeare did not expect his audience to exercise the kind of logic that comes more readily to the historian; by watching where Shakespeare places the dramatic emphasis—using invented material to achieve it—we may at least avoid confusing the dramatic character with the historical personage. What the audience is left with is the reflection that a prince who so cavalierly rejects the advice of grave persons must be deficient in the qualities that nourish kingship.

This is allowed to hang in the air of the second phase of the play, which deals with the transference of power. Here, Shakespeare has greatly compressed his scale of time and has omitted all the business of the intrigue culminating in the Archbishop of Canterbury's mission to Bolingbroke in France which might have compromised the swift pace of the action. The struggle for power is of the most perfunctory kind. When we encounter Bolingbroke in II. iii, he is already deep in the country receiving the access of powerful followers, while York's incompetence and the Queen's forebodings in the previous scene have already made plain how little of a fight he is likely to have. All this is designedly contrasted with the defection of Richard's own companies. Power slides from the absent and silent Richard with the speed of an avalanche: this is not a play about how power is gained by *expertise*, nor even about how cunning overcomes stupidity—Richard is simply not there, either to provide the one, or counter the other. The phase ends with an act of quasi-regal authority by Bolingbroke—the execution of the favourites—which indicates how completely he has taken over from

---

1. Our understanding of the rejection is also guided, of course, by Gaunt's previous insistence on Richard's susceptibility to the influence of the bad counsellors, the flatterers.

Richard. Shakespeare so arranges matters that, when Richard re-enters in III. ii to begin the third phase, the phase of his suffering, he is a man whom the audience knows, after this series of bloodless victories and defeats, to be a king without power ready to receive the bad news that he is so. It is by now clear where the centre of interest is to lie: not in an intrigue, nor in the confrontation of tyrant and usurper, but, as Coleridge said, in "a history of the human mind".[1]

This design must control our understanding of how Shakespeare wished us to read Richard's character. The second scene of the third Act is crucial in any interpretation of this. Richard lands in Wales, his mind tense and large with the knowledge that his kingdom has been invaded; he hears, hard upon each other, of the disasters to his cause: that the Welsh have deserted him, the favourites been taken, and the Lord Governor gone over to the enemy; Aumerle tries to keep his spirits up, only to have the comfort dashed away by the next piece of ill news. At the end of the scene there is nothing Richard can do except shut himself up in the neighbouring castle. The audience already knows, before the scene begins, the worst that he is yet to learn; their interest is not in the news itself, but in his reception of it. They also know that Richard cannot now act against Bolingbroke: any expectation of that kind has been stripped from them as efficiently as Bolingbroke has stripped from Richard the apparatus of physical power. The audience is prepared for action only in the field of mind, for, as it turns out, the dizzying alternation of hope and despair.

The situation in which Richard now finds himself is that of a king, deprived of physical power, who retains a circumscribed personal liberty and the sacred name and attributes pertaining to his kingship. Amongst these we must include a Queen. The rest of this phase of the play is to be concerned with how he gives even these things one by one into the hands of the usurper; it is not until the last phase that life itself is required of him. It is sometimes said that Shakespeare shows up Richard's weakness and unfitness for the throne by indicating his preference for words over action, his temperamental inability to implement Carlisle's saying:

> My lord, wise men ne'er sit and wail their woes,
> But presently prevent the ways to wail.

This judgement—which overlooks the fact that even the Bishop falls silent when the final disaster of York's desertion is reported—does not seem to accord with Shakespeare's intention so far as that is apparent in his design. It is in the first phase of the play that Richard's unfitness has been shown, his political misjudgement, the burdensome legacy of past mistakes and brutal disregard of present advice: all defects in the princely character and failures to rise to the level of his function. It is these that are the sufficient causes of the loss of power that has followed upon them in the swift retribution of the second phase. But in this third phase, which this scene initiates, Shakespeare is not now dealing with the causes, already adequately set out in political terms, but with the effects on Richard of the new situation. That part of his fall which was political and entailed the loss of power has been accomplished; there remains that aspect of it which trenches upon a sacred tragedy, the divesting of royalty of its mysterious panoply. It is the wish to set this last in a clear and free light, as a thing that happened to a man who was also a king, which, we may conjecture, shaped the design of the play as a whole. Shakespeare bundled the narrative of causes away into the first two and a half Acts so that he might more fully set forth the drama of the sufferer constrained to reduce himself from king to man by shedding the "great glory" of the Name.

Hence it is that we meet for the first time in this scene the new, the expressive Richard. It is hardly just to read back his loquacity here into one of the causes of a loss of power already adequately accounted for by his political misjudgement and defects as a prince. Richard is a new character here in the sense that the play's design has now developed to the point where it is laid down for him that he must give voice to what is in him; more narrowly, that he must say what he feels all the time about his situation, or many successive situations: his appearance on the walls of Flint Castle, his abdication, his parting with Isabel, his death in the prison; and these are contrived about him by Bolingbroke, nor can he alter them save as Bolingbroke directs. That is to say, to survive at all as the protagonist of a poetic drama designed, as this one is, with a helpless king at its centre, Richard has to use words or, more accurately, poetry.

But the poetry in Richard is there because he is a character in a poetic drama, not because Shakespeare thought that Richard II lost his kingdom through a preference for blank verse over battles, or, as Mark Van Doren puts it, because he loved poetry "more than power and more than any other person".[1]

1. *Shakespeare* (New York, 1939), p. 89. Van Doren's section on the play carries the conception of "Richard as poet" about as far as it will go. A similar conception seems to underlie, though less clearly, the censures of Swinburne (*Three Plays of Shakespeare* [London, 1909], pp. 59 ff) and the sympathies of Yeats in 'At Stratford-on-Avon' in *Ideas of Good and Evil* (in *Collected Works*, vol.

This is not to deny that there is a large element of conscious ex-pressiveness and calculated gesture in the Richard who is drawn for us in the last two and a half acts of the play. These show that Shakespeare wished us to see him as akin in some respects to the poet and the actor. Richard's ability to see his story as story is an aspect of this conscious expressiveness, comparable to that of Thomas Mann's Joseph or of Brutus and Cassius when they reflect, the one on the glory, the other on the pitiableness of their deed:

> How many ages hence
> Shall this our lofty scene be acted over
> In states unborn and accents yet unknown!

So Richard can see his fall as a mirror for princes (III. ii. 155 ff), or compare it to that of "glist'ring Phaeton", or of Christ, or urge Isabel: "Tell thou the lamentable tale of me". It is a part of the drawing of his character, too, that this expressiveness is sometimes shown to fall short of the effect he intends, or to induce self-disgust. In III. iii Aumerle is reduced to tears by the genuine pathos of the first half of Richard's speech (III. iii. 143–59):

> Aumerle, thou weep'st (my tender-hearted cousin!)

But Richard goes too far in the rococo image which follows; tears turn to embarrassment:

> Well, well, I see
> I talk but idly, and you laugh at me.

Another of Richard's miscalculations occurs at the end of the mirror episode, where he needs time to recover from Bolingbroke's curt demolition of the mirror-smashing gesture (IV. i. 292–5) before he can turn Bolingbroke's own quibble upside down. The soliloquy in prison ends with a movement of self-disgust at a too abundant fancy: "I stand fooling here".

Akin to this kind of miscalculation is a strong element of corrupt fantasy in Richard. This is not, I conceive, the same as saying with Van Doren that he is the "great poet of the play", albeit a "minor poet". He is a man, as Yeats remarked,[1] full of capricious fancy; in his sorrow he behaves like a "fantastic", a changeful, restless figure imperfectly governed by the reason to which he should be subject: "how many chimeras, antics, golden mountains and castles in the

---

vi [1908], or *Essays* [1924], pp. 117 ff). Yeats rightly pointed out the pleasure which commentators take in scolding Richard: Hardin Craig's pages in *An Interpretation of Shakespeare* maintain the tradition.

1. *Collected Works* (Stratford-on-Avon, 1908), vi. 123.

air do they build unto themselves!"[1] "Meethinkes", says Phantaste in Jonson's *Cynthia's Revels*:

> I should wish my selfe all manner of creatures. Now, I would bee an empresse; and by and by a dutchesse; then a great ladie of state; then one of your *miscelany* madams; then a waiting-woman; then your cittizens wife; then a course countrey gentle-woman; then a deyrie maide; then a shepheards lasse; then an empresse againe, or the queene of *fayries* . . .[2]

So Richard, too, longs for other roles than that which fate constrains him to play:

> Thus play I in one person many people,
> And none contented.

But it is quite another thing to claim that because Richard "thinks in images",[3] Shakespeare therefore wished us to think of him as a poet, or even as a bad poet because his images sometimes misfire,[4] with the corollary that "Richard's fall is due . . . to his preference for words over deeds".[5] The design of the play, as already exposed, shows that Richard's fall *is* due to a specific deed, a rash act which he was warned to avoid and which springs not from a corrupt fancy but from a failure in duty and the understanding of his function. The poetry which he speaks thereafter is Shakespeare's medium, which he uses to show—and by means of images to show as lustrously as possible—what is going on in Richard's mind and heart. This is why it is legitimate to use the images which Shakespeare puts into his mouth as clues to the way he reacts to his situation and from them to draw conclusions about his nature as a whole. The sun-images, used by him and by others of him, express his and their feeling for the splendour of the royal office;[6] the image of mother and child (III. ii. 8 ff) shows that his intense love of country is touched with a feminine feeling;[7] the images of earth and the grave show

---

1. Burton, *Anatomy of Melancholy*, 1. 2. 3. 2 (London, 1881 edn), p. 166.
2. *Ben Jonson*, ed. Herford and Simpson, IV. 104–5.
3. W. Clemen, *The Development of Shakespeare's Imagery* (London, 1951), p. 60.
4. "A dilettante in poetry as well as in kingship" (Herford, p. 28).
5. R. D. Altick, 'Symphonic Imagery in *Richard II*', *P.M.L.A.*, LXII (1947), p. 351.
6. These have been much studied. Oscar Wilde seems to have been the first to note the connexion between Richard's sun-badge (see note on III. iii. 178) and the sun-imagery, in 'The Truth of Masks' (*Works* [London, n.d.], p. 1241. I owe this reference to J. C. Maxwell). See also Reyher, 'Le Symbole du Soleil . . .', *Rev. de l'Enseignement des Langues Vivantes*, June 1923; C. Spurgeon, op cit., pp. 233–8; Wilson, pp. xii, xiii; S. Kliger in *S.P.*, XLIV (1948), 196–202; Clemen, op. cit., p. 59.   7. Coleridge, 1. 155.

how ready he is to decline into the ultimate of sorrow, and that of the clock how discrowning seems to him to have robbed him of life itself. Richard D. Altick has brilliantly collated these and others to bring out their interrelation and the force they acquire through studied repetition.[1]

In expressiveness Bolingbroke contrasts with Richard. Shakespeare has made use of the fact that his design—"The Tragedy of King Richard the Second"—is shaped to set out as fully as possible the passion of the deposed monarch, rather than the struggle between two rivals, and therefore throws Bolingbroke into a subordinate position. This subordination does not mean that he is simply flatter and obscurer than Richard; his flatness and obscurity become attributes of his character. This is most keenly felt in the deposition scene, where Bolingbroke's silence seems to have a positive quality.

To identify precisely this quality is difficult. Elsewhere in the play, Bolingbroke has at his command the florid and formal language of the politician and patriot; as Tamburlaine "plays the Orator" against Theridamas, so Bolingbroke can use enticing argument to draw York into his camp.[2] His fair discourse has been "as sugar" to Northumberland, and, as Dr Tillyard notes,[3] there is a "plain and understandable passion" in his language when he recounts his wrongs in III. i. Yet, compared with the full and free expression of what is in Richard's mind, Bolingbroke's mind and motives are in shadow.[4] This is why the view, held by some commentators,[5] that the whole play is built on the contrast in character between Richard and Bolingbroke needs to be defined. It is true that the two men are manifestly contrasted in respect of their success as princes. Richard's chief act as prince is, as we have seen, one which makes plain his unfitness to hold the sceptre which inheritance has bestowed upon him; Bolingbroke's mastery in the kingly office is emphasized in the challenge scene of IV. i and throughout

1. Altick, art. cit.

2. Cf. Palmer, op. cit., p. 149. On York's character in general Coleridge's observations (I. 153, 154) are not likely to be bettered; Swinburne (op. cit., pp. 72–3) allows the pleasure of vituperation to carry him too far.

3. *Shakespeare's History Plays* (London, 1944), p. 259.

4. B. Stirling's 'Bolingbroke's "Decision" ' in *Shakespeare Quarterly*, II (1951) is a persuasive attempt at reading them.

5. E. Dowden: "The interest of the play centres . . . in the personal contrast between the falling and rising kings" (*Shakespeare* [1912 edn], p. 88); Herford: "the action is merely a prolonged duel between Richard and Bolingbroke" (*Shakespeare* [1912], p. 28); F. S. Boas: "In the detailed contrast of character between [Richard and Bolingbroke] lies the cardinal interest of the play" (*Shakespeare and his Predecessors* [1918 edn], p. 250).

the fifth Act, where his tempering of mercy with justice shows that he understands the duties classically prescribed for the wise ruler.[1] Thus, when the two men are compared as rulers and magistrates, it is plain that Bolingbroke knows how and what to do:

And with that odds he weighs King Richard down.

But the metaphor of the balance, as a means of discerning the structure of the play, will not work over the whole of it. We do not know about Bolingbroke's sensations as he takes the heavy weight of the crown on his head as we do about Richard's when he puts it off.[2] On all that aspect of the event which touches not simply the transference of executive power, but the divinity which hedges and sanctions it, Bolingbroke is silent. It is a theme of which Richard makes much; if we are to trust the design of the tragedy, which orders the free unfolding of this subject in terms of Richard's suffering, as well as the whole scheme of the history plays, it is one with which Shakespeare and his audience were deeply concerned; yet Bolingbroke evades it. Are his silence and evasion, then, to be interpreted as Shakespeare's method of indicating that Bolingbroke is indifferent to the accredited sanctions of power, so long as he can grasp the reality of it; that he is depicted as the new man whose embryonic "Counter-Renaissance" world is destined to overthrow the medievalism of Richard's?[3] This is a persuasive view, and is supported by much in the play, so that some sense that an old order is giving place to a new is present to most of its readers: Richard says

My time
Runs fooling on in Bolingbroke's proud joy

and in the "new spring of time" of the fifth Act, York appears as a pathetic survival of an old winter of discontent. Yet we cannot be perfectly confident that Shakespeare could have felt the contrast between old pageantry and new principles in so contemporary a fashion as Dr Tillyard suggests. It may have been that Shakespeare created a Bolingbroke partially inarticulate because the usurper's springs of action puzzled him, as they did Daniel:

Doubtfull at first, he warie doth proceed

---

1. See E. T. Sehrt, *Vergebung und Gnade bei Shakespeare* (Stuttgart, 1952), pp. 111–16.

2. In later plays both Henry IV and Henry V are shown as fully conscious of the burden of the diadem: see especially 2 H 4, IV. v. 23 ff and 158 ff.

3. See Tillyard, op. cit., pp. 257 ff. For Shakespeare's literary use of such countervailing themes, see some suggestive remarks by H. Haydn, *The Counter-Renaissance* (New York, 1950), pp. 652–3.

Seemes not t'affect, that which he did effect,
Or els perhaps seemes as he ment indeed,
Sought but his owne, and did no more expect:
Then fortune thou art guilty of his deed,
That didst his state aboue his hopes erect,
And thou must beare some blame of his great sin
That left'st him worse then when he did begin.[1]

Hazlitt, by contrast, held that Shakespeare portrayed him as "seeing his advantage afar off, but only seizing it when he has it within reach, humble, crafty, bold, and aspiring, encroaching by regular but slow degrees".[2] Bolingbroke, certainly, though he may have inherited Gaunt's lands, does not inherit his moral role. Shakespeare seems almost ostentatiously to avoid pressing it upon him by omitting the scene of his first landing in England: here we might have expected some declaration of policy and some affirmation of his country's good to countervail Richard's landing at Harlech and his own patriotic slogan when we last saw him. It is difficult to be as confident as Hazlitt that we can read a policy so circumscribed with shadow as this. Right up to the deposition scene he is not represented as seeking more than his hereditary rights as Gaunt's son and the punishment of those who have wronged him. Yet the pursuit of those rights involves him in defiance of the anointed king's authority; though York himself weakens, there is no answer, except denial of the premises on which it is based, to York's rebuke at II. iii. 107–11:

> *Bol.* My gracious uncle, let me know my fault:
>   On what condition stands it and wherein?
> *York.* Even in condition of the worst degree—
>   In gross rebellion and detested treason;
>   Thou art a banish'd man, and here art come,
>   Before the expiration of thy time,
>   In braving arms against thy sovereign.

Bolingbroke's reply:

>   As I was banish'd, I was banish'd Herford;
>   But as I come, I come for Lancaster

(which Shakespeare did not find in Holinshed) sounds suspiciously like a piece of chicanery hastily run up for the occasion. Bolingbroke's appeal to his father's shade (II. iii. 116 ff) may remind us that Gaunt himself, if his advice to the Duchess of Gloucester (I. ii.

---

1. Daniel, *C.W.*, I. st. 94; Daniel continues his speculations for a further six stanzas.
2. *Characters of Shakespeare's Plays* (*Complete Works*, ed. Howe, IV. 275).

36–41) is any guide, would have rejected it, and Bolingbroke is certainly ready to lift an angry arm against God's minister (III. iii. 42 ff) although the threat becomes characteristically ambiguous a moment later (III. iii. 58–60) and when Northumberland rephrases it (III. iii. 101 ff). It may be fair to conclude from all this that indifference to what Richard feels so deeply about is the positive quality of Bolingbroke's silence during the deposition scene, but Shakespeare does not seem to have provided enough evidence about Bolingbroke's state of mind for us to conclude with Hazlitt that we are to see him as plotting for supreme power from the first. The contrast between Bolingbroke as an efficient ruler and Richard as an unwise one contributes to the play's structure and helps to balance the last phase against the first. But a similar balance is not found in that region where deeper motives and sanctions greater than that of physical power are exposed; it is Richard who brings these to life and awareness; against his exposition of them we cannot set the outward man who is Bolingbroke—his impulses are hidden from us;† his conduct is ambiguous, partly because such ambiguity is for him an instrument of policy and partly, perhaps, because of his creator's irresolution. "To find out right with wrong —it may not be", says York: Bolingbroke's apparent total unawareness of the dilemma may be due to a settled determination to get what he wants at the cost of ignoring it or merely to Shakespeare's unwillingness to sound his motives too deeply. Whatever the reason, the effect—and this perhaps is the calculation that lies behind the whole unbalance—is to throw all the light upon Richard: his "right" is the burden of his thoughts, and he is the uninterrupted expositor of it.

He introduces the theme in the central scenes of the third Act. His inability to resist Bolingbroke or his demands sets him free, as it were, both to fall back upon the divinity of his kingship as a last resource and to bring it to our awareness, not as a mere theory of sovereignty, but as an active component in the situation as a whole and in his own suffering. In its former relation, York had begun to propound the theme in the preceding Act: Bolingbroke and his company are rebels, *nemine contradicente*; neither their power, nor York's inability to resist it, cancels out the fact of their treason:

> I cannot mend it, I must needs confess,
> Because my power is weak and all ill left.
> But if I could, by Him that gave me life,
> I would attach you all, and make you stoop
> Unto the sovereign mercy of the king;

York speaks as a subject, as Carlisle is later to do. When this theme

of powerless, but divinely ordained, right overcome by powerful
wrong is transferred from the subject, who infers from it the future
punishment of the sinners, to the king himself, who incarnates the
right, and is transmuted by his personality, it becomes at once a
spring of faith and a cause of suffering. By its nature, since it supposes that the rightful king is a deputy appointed by God and not by
the election of power, it is a faith which supports Richard when
power is diminished or gone:

> show us the hand of God
> That hath dismiss'd us from our stewardship;
> For well we know no hand of blood and bone
> Can gripe the sacred handle of our sceptre,
> Unless he do profane, steal, or usurp.
> And though you think that all, as you have done,
> Have torn their souls by turning them from us,
> And we are barren and bereft of friends,
> Yet know, my master, God omnipotent,
> Is mustering in his clouds, on our behalf,
> Armies of pestilence, and they shall strike
> Your children yet unborn, and unbegot,
> That lift your vassal hands against my head,
> And threat the glory of my precious crown.

But it is a faith which is, as faiths generally are, at times held with
this kind of sublime and richly figured confidence, but at other
times has to struggle in Richard's mind with the facts that seem to
contradict it: in this case, the paradox of the rightful king who is
without power to substantiate his right. Thus arises Richard's suffering. There is a kind of denial of his faith which springs from the
difficulty of holding it when the startling fact of the *king's* helplessness seems to mock at its truth or efficacy:

> Cover your heads, and mock not flesh and blood
> With solemn reverence; throw away respect,
> Tradition, form, and ceremonious duty;
> For you have but mistook me all this while.
> I live with bread like you, feel want,
> Taste grief, need friends—subjected thus,
> How can you say to me, I am a king?

Richard suffers, too, in performing the acts which his dilemma en-
forces upon him because they make him conscious of their contradiction of his claims:

> O God! O God! that e'er this tongue of mine,
> That laid the sentence of dread banishment
> On yon proud man, should take it off again
> With words of sooth!

and this leads to the striving to escape from the dilemma, the wish
to be no longer the "god on earth" who is so manifestly at the mercy
of his subjects:

> O that I were as great
> As is my grief, or lesser than my name!
> Or that I could forget what I have been!
> Or not remember what I must be now!

Yet Richard can recover from this mood enough to affirm the con-
fidences of the next scene, to collapse again, and in the end, even
after his resignation, to feel that his own act has betrayed his faith
and to suffer because he seems to have committed a kind of
voluntary apostasy:

> Mine eyes are full of tears, I cannot see.
> And yet salt water blinds them not so much
> But they can see a sort of traitors here.
> Nay, if I turn mine eyes upon myself,
> I find myself a traitor with the rest.
> For I have given here my soul's consent
> T'undeck the pompous body of a king;
> Made glory base, and sovereignty a slave;
> Proud majesty a subject, state a peasant.

These alternating states, this personal accent and hypertension
of grief surely result from Shakespeare's attempt to give us a man
who is really suffering. The kind of attention, or the degree of
respect, we pay to this suffering will partly depend on our estimate
of how far Shakespeare established Bolingbroke's ascendancy in
physical power and Richard's weakness as a ruler early in the play.
I have suggested that the design is in fact of this kind, leaving the
last half of the play largely occupied with the fate of a king deprived
of power through his own defects (which are measured against
their absence in Bolingbroke) yet hedged about with divinity. If
this issue seemed important enough to Shakespeare for it to shape
his design and be built into the fabric of his protagonist, Richard's
agonies over it are evidently amongst the things which the dramatist wanted us to contemplate at length and in detail. The very fact
that we have been encouraged early and firmly to decide that
Richard is deficient in the qualities that nourish kingship suggests
that we are now to see him as a king who is tragic because this
deficiency, and its consequence in loss of power, has not freed him,
for himself at least, from the burden of majesty.

It is to make us pay attention to this that Shakespeare at first
takes sides between Bolingbroke and Richard, making the latter
quickly and deservedly lose power and even underlining the suc-

cess of the former as ruler. He does this not for the sake of making a political point but in order to create the conditions of outer and inner turbulence proper to a protagonist of stature. Through them the protagonist's sufferings become not merely those of a prince who falls pathetically from high place into darkness, like the heroes of the old *casus* stories, but also those of one in whom belief strives with weakness within while enemies without affront it by their power to force him, as they eventually do, to seem to deny it by his own acts. Similarly, the purpose of Richard's speeches on the inviolability of his right, delivered against the background of Bolingbroke's advancing army and of total loss of power, is not to proclaim the Tudor doctrine of majesty in the teeth of the odds, nor even, as Irving Ribner suggests,[1] to make it sound silly, but to tell us what Richard is feeling and move us with the spectacle. This also is the purpose of Richard's collapses into despair and repudiations under stress. The alternating moods go to make up a man rather than to expose the relativity of a doctrine. It is the design that makes all this life in the character possible by bringing about at an early stage the condition: unarmed and deficient majesty versus armed and able usurpation. It is doubtful if we can even ask about this play Ribner's question "What is the precise political position taken by Shakespeare in the conflict between Richard II and Bolingbroke?",[2] because this is a question about the condition artificially detached from the character which is its reason for being.

But just as Richard's miscalculations and capricious fancy give us an insight into his weakness, so the kind of attention we pay to his sufferings will be to some extent determined by what commentators have diagnosed as the theatricality with which he expresses them. "He throws himself into the part of the deposed monarch", says Pater, "[and] falls gracefully as on the world's stage."[3] Here again we are in danger of confusing Shakespeare's medium, which is a play designed to cast light above all others on to Richard, with the dramatic character. The gracefulness, the enthusiasm, the loquacity, the taking of the centre of the stage and the consciousness of onlookers are Shakespeare's own powers and the means which he uses to give us Richard as fully and centrally as he can; they are not attributes of the character, for Richard is no more an actor than he

---

1. 'The Political Problem in Shakespeare's Lancastrian Tetralogy', *S.P.*, XLIX (1952), 179–81.

2. *Ibid.*, p. 171.

3. 'Shakespeare's English Kings' in *Appreciations* (1944 edn), p. 206; Chambers thinks that Richard is "himself a born actor", and Craig (op. cit., p. 128) that he "spent his life not living, but playing parts".

is a poet.[1] We are not to suppose that because a character in a play speaks a great deal, he is necessarily fond of the sound of his own voice, or because he continually takes the centre of the stage, that he necessarily enjoys playing a part. The Richard who luxuriates in his own destruction is a product of some such suppositions; it also springs from an unwillingness to recognize the appeal of the tradition of the "complaint" and *The Mirror for Magistrates*, from which Richard's lamentations and reproaches in part descend.[2] It is not Richard who stages the impressive and symbolical scenes in which he appears, as G. A. Bonnard claims,[3] but Shakespeare, who desired to set before us the honoured spectacle of the fallen king.

There is another way in which play-acting or theatricality may be said to be an element in the character. The scenes, including the deposition scene, in which Richard appears in the last half of the play are stage-managed by Bolingbroke in the sense that his power and decisions prescribe the scope of Richard's actions. Richard must play the part set down for him, and he shows from time to time a weary and baffled consciousness of this: "What must the king do now?" (III. iii. 143 ff).† The bitter irony is manifest if we remember Queen Elizabeth's remark on her death-bed about "must" not being a word which may be used to princes.

> What says King Bolingbroke? Will his Majesty
> Give Richard leave to live till Richard die?
> You make a leg, and Bolingbroke says "ay".

Here Richard caricatures the set nature of the characters' behaviour. That actions previously planned are now being performed is emphasized, especially in the deposition scene, by the way in which they are represented as done for the benefit of an audience within the play:

> Fetch hither Richard, that in common view
> He may surrender;

1. No more—and no less—than Brutus or Cassius. All are conscious of "bearing a part", their role in life. There is an element of theatricality in Richard just as there is an element of corrupt fancy: but to describe Richard as an actor is to allow a useful metaphor to get out of control. The same thing happens when we describe him as a poet. It is not helpful to say that he is playing the part of a fallen king when he *is* a fallen king, even though we may consider that his behaviour in that condition is unmanly or consciously overdone; he does not bleed in sport; cf. Clemen, op. cit., p. 55; and for a similar point about Macbeth, K. Muir's Arden edn of *Mac.*, p. lx.

2. See W. Farnham, *Medieval Heritage of Elizabethan Tragedy* (Berkeley, 1936), pp. 416 ff.

3. 'The actor in Richard II', *Shakespeare-Jahrbuch*, lxxxvii–lxxxviii (1952), 99.

Richard is to confess his crimes in order that men may "deem" that he is "worthily deposed" (IV. i. 227) or "the commons will not then be satisfied" (IV. i. 272). Bolingbroke is the silent *régisseur*, who intervenes only occasionally to modify the course of the piece. And we learn from York how marked is this element of staging in Richard's humiliation (V. ii. 23 ff). The device emphasizes the helpless yet central position of Richard, the man with the pistol at his ribs.

Bolingbroke, as Leonard F. Dean expresses it,[1] has in this way turned the state itself into a theatre; he has assigned his part to Northumberland, and, in the deposition scene, he has set down a part for Richard, too, to play. From Bolingbroke's point of view, if it is true that the seizure of power is all that matters to him, Richard has become, indeed, a mere actor in his play, since, in resigning his crown before the assembled parliament and placing it in the usurper's hands, he passively does what is expected of him. If it is true that Bolingbroke cares nothing about the divine sanctions of power, the way in which Richard performs the act—emphasizing his own grief (IV. i. 191 ff) and shame (IV. i. 245 ff) and betrayal (IV. i. 233 ff) —hardly amounts to more than a nuisance, an indulgence in sorrow springing from the weakness of temper that made Richard a bad king; it is sentimentalizing, and confirms Bolingbroke in what we may suppose to be his view that the Name without the reality is a shadow without substance: let Richard be king of sorrows if he will, Bolingbroke will be king in England. But Bolingbroke's "play" is not Shakespeare's, and it is a mistake, made by some commentators, to suppose that the two coincide. The Bishop's prophecy preceding the act of discrowning (IV. i. 136 ff), the conspiracy that follows it, Richard's warning to Northumberland (V. i. 55 ff), and, of course, Henry IV's own disturbed conscience later on, show something of the woe that has been engendered and make it plain that, if Bolingbroke takes the Name to be only a shadow, disarmed before the untitled holder of power and of no force in politics, Shakespeare does not, and never expected his audiences to do so either.

It is not only this which shows that our point of view is not to be identified with the attempt to reduce Richard's status to that of mere play-actor. For, except on the level of his confirmation in real power through a public act of abdication, the level of his immediate concern, Bolingbroke is actually in very imperfect control of his leading actor. It is the contrast between what Richard has

1. '*Richard II:* the State and the Image of the Theatre', *P.M.L.A.*, LXVII (1952).

to do with the way he does it that brings out the shocking paradox of the *helpless king*, the king who "must". Marlowe's play has
this too:

> They give me bread and water being a king

and it has been Richard's area of suffering ever since he was introduced in his more expressive form in III. ii. But here it is climactic; for
in this scene, by performing what Pater called an "inverted rite",[1]
the king must shed the glory of his name and so, as it were, try to
shatter the paradox that has caused him to suffer and yet, because
one part of it affirmed his right, has allowed him to hope. We can
imagine, perhaps, that Bolingbroke would have liked to run the
deposition as he managed the execution of the favourites, or to contrive some effect akin to that of the challenge scenes of the first Act,
where, as I have suggested, the stiffness of the language and gestures argues that the characters are following obediently a procedure laid down in advance. But Richard, so far as the audience is
concerned, knocks awry Bolingbroke's carefully staged professional spectacle. With all the weaknesses of his feminine sensibility
and capricious fancy upon him, he moves us to pity[2] in verse the
contrast of which with the formal vigour of the verse in the challenge scenes is the measure of Shakespeare's attempt to give him the
voice of a man who is really in pain. And this remains true even
though Shakespeare learnt later on, in *Lear*, to write verse which is
much more expressive of the agonies of fallen majesty.

The episode of the looking-glass towards the end of the deposition
scene is the most remarkable of Richard's departures from the role
set down for him by Bolingbroke. It wrenches attention inwards to
Richard, the more designedly in that it seems to complete a movement apparent throughout the whole scene. This begins in a very
public and external way with the yells and threats of the appellants,
modulates to Carlisle's appeal to God and men's consciences, and
thence to Richard's profoundly personal rendering of the formal act
of abdication, in which the crown becomes an image of his grief
(IV. i. 181–9) and the bystanders not witnesses but participators
in a crime (IV. i. 167–75). Northumberland tries to drag Richard
back towards the public and the formal, towards Bolingbroke's
"theatre"; but the movement, with Richard in command of it, has
gathered too much momentum, and his efforts are in vain. Richard

---

1. "It is as if Shakespeare had had in mind some inverted rite, like those old
ecclesiastical or military ones, by which human hardness, or human justice,
adds the last touch of unkindness to the execution of its sentences", op. cit.,
p. 205.
2. As Dryden thought: see *Essays*, ed. Ker, I. 226–7.

sends for the looking-glass, the double-edged symbol of vanity and truth-telling.[1]

The episode points forward to the solitary and self-communing Richard of the prison soliloquy. There is something deliberately unexplained, something therefore impulsive and compulsive, about his wish to have the mirror at this moment, and something intense and private in his act of looking at it, for this, too, is a kind of soliloquy, his first. It is also thematically linked with the prison soliloquy in that it touches the question whether Richard, in divesting himself of the name of king, has anything at all left by which to live: for the "great glory" was the source of his hopes, even though, conjoined with his helplessness (the *king must*), it was the ground of his suffering. The sending for the mirror is a movement towards asking the question "What am I like now I have given everything away?" (see IV. i. 266–7), but has behind it, perhaps, the question "Am I anything at all?" The first question is a move towards self-knowledge, and even repentance:

> I'll read enough
> When I do see the very book indeed
> Where all my sins are writ, and that's myself.

This is but faintly hinted at (and again at v. v. 47–9).[2] But the thought of the mirror is a close neighbour to the thought of annihilation:

> O that I were a mockery king of snow,
> Standing before the sun of Bolingbroke,
> To melt myself away in water-drops!

1. As iconographers have shown, the mirror is the attribute of *Vanitas*: on this, see G. F. Hartlaub, *Zauber des Spiegels* (Munich, 1951) and H. Schwarz, 'The Mirror in Art', *Art Quarterly* (Detroit), xv (1952), 97–118. The epithet which Richard uses for it, *flattering* (and therefore lying) is very commonly attached to looking-glasses of any kind: e.g. in Lyly, Daniel, Heywood, Webster, and Burton (for references see my article in *P.Q.*, xxxiv (1955), 220); Elizabeth I on her death-bed rejected a "flattering" glass and called for a "true" one (see Nichols, op. cit., iii. 614). The mirror also has the property of reflecting the true state of things: hence its use as a book-title for works (*specula*) of moral instruction (*Mirror for Magistrates* etc.), which is also very common; on this see E. Curtius, *European Literature and the Latin Middle Ages* (London, 1953), p. 336, L. B. Campbell, op. cit., pp. 107–8, M. Doran, *Endeavors of Art* (Madison, 1954), p. 72, R. Bradley, 'Speculum Backgrounds in Medieval Literature', *Speculum*, xxix (1954), 100–15, and cf. *Cæs.*, i. iii. 55–8. Shakespeare may have been conscious of both these connotations of the mirror here.

2. Cf. v. i. 24–5. Dr Johnson thought that Richard's self-reformation was radical: "In his prosperity we saw him imperious and oppressive, but in his distress he is wise, patient and pious"; cf. Stopford Brooke, *On Ten Plays of Shakespeare* (London, 1905), pp. 97–8.

When the mirror lies to him about his inward condition, he smashes it.[1] He does this, perhaps, simply because of the analogy between its behaviour and that of his flattering followers, and thereby repudiates them and his own folly when he encouraged them in the past. But the smashing is also an act of self-destructive violence, for he has destroyed the image of the face with which he must henceforth live in as manly a fashion as he can:

> A brittle glory shineth in this face;
> As brittle as the glory is the face,
> For there it is, crack'd in an hundred shivers.
> Mark, silent king, the moral of this sport—
> How soon my sorrow hath destroy'd my face.

Repudiation of the past self may also be a mere destruction of the self, unless the penitent has the power to contrive a new being. There is no sign that Richard possesses this power. In the prison soliloquy he can picture himself only as something less than a man, an automaton, the Jack of the clock that moves as Bolingbroke bids (v. v. 50–60), or at best his beast of burden (v. v. 92–3). If Richard did ask himself the question "Am I, unkinged, anything?" the answer came back "Nothing at all":

> Then am I king'd again, and by and by
> Think that I am unking'd by Bolingbroke,
> And straight am nothing.

This is only the confirmation of a truth recognized by sixteenth-century statists: the balm cannot be washed off; the anointed cannot become a man who lives "with bread like you"; for the mark of his divinity is in the bone, and he must either rule or die. Richard's actual death is courageous, or perhaps perfunctory, but it does not alter this.

The play, then, is not simply about a weak but legitimate monarch out-generalled by an able usurper. By showing us this subject in terms of Richard's suffering, Shakespeare adds a further dimension; and extends this beyond the mere pathos of a spectacular fall from glory to dishonour. Shakespeare seems to have used all the skill then at his command to give voice to the inwardness of his protagonist and to show him alive and exciting within the area of his peculiarly exact and individual tragic dilemma: the king who must. As Hazlitt said, "the part of Richard himself gives the chief interest to the play", and with it all the more important problems of its interpretation connect.

1. For a discussion of the light thrown by the references to music in v. v. on Richard's inward condition, see L. Spitzer, 'Classical and Christian Ideas of World Harmony', *Traditio*, III (1945), 335.

NOTES ADDITIONAL TO THE INTRODUCTION

p. xiii

To these must be added the Petworth Castle copy, collated by M. W. Black in his New Variorum edition (1955; see also J. G. McManaway in *Shakespeare Survey*, x [1957], 151). Forme D (i) is found in an uncorrected state earlier than those in the three other copies. There are altogether eight variants, which have been included in the collation of this edition.

p. lxxv

For this view of Bolingbroke compare Leonard Unger, 'Deception and Self-Deception in Henry IV' (in his *The Man and the Name* [Minneapolis, 1956], p. 4): "... the development of Bolingbroke's motivation—from his reasonable determination to have the title and estates of Gaunt to his ambition for the crown, Shakespeare treats vaguely, almost evasively. The development merely happens—off-stage, as it were. It is as if Shakespeare ... were not yet artistically ready to involve fully, exhaustively, in a single play, two such psychologically complex situations as those of Bolingbroke and Richard."

p. lxxix

Compare Marlowe, *Edward II*, IV. ii. 80–2:

K. Edw. And, Leicester, say what shall become of us?
Leices. Your majesty must go to Killingworth.
K. Edw. Must! 'tis somewhat hard, when kings must go.

KING RICHARD II

KING RICHARD THE SECOND.

JOHN OF GAUNT, *Duke of Lancaster, uncle to the King.*

HENRY BOLINGBROKE, *Duke of Hereford, son to John of Gaunt, afterwards King Henry IV.*

THOMAS MOWBRAY, *Duke of Norfolk.*

THE DUCHESS OF GLOUCESTER, *widow to Thomas of Woodstock, Duke of Gloucester.*

THE LORD MARSHAL.

THE DUKE OF AUMERLE, *son to the Duke of York.*

Two Heralds.

SIR HENRY GREENE.

SIR JOHN BUSHY.

SIR JOHN BAGOT.

EDMUND OF LANGLEY, *Duke of York, uncle to the King.*

HENRY PERCY, *Earl of Northumberland.*

LORD ROSS.

LORD WILLOUGHBY.

ISABEL, *Queen to King Richard.*

The Duke of York's Servingman.

HARRY PERCY, *surnamed Hotspur, son to the Earl of Northumberland.*

LORD BERKELEY.

THE EARL OF SALISBURY.

A Welsh Captain.

THE BISHOP OF CARLISLE.

SIR STEPHEN SCROOPE.

Two Ladies attendant upon Queen Isabel.

A Gardener.

His Man.

LORD FITZWATER.

A Lord.

THE DUKE OF SURREY.

THE ABBOT OF WESTMINSTER.

THE DUCHESS OF YORK.

SIR PIERS EXTON.

His Servant.

A Groom of the Stable to King Richard.

The Keeper of the Prison at Pomfret.

Guards, Soldiers and Servants.

SCENE: *England and Wales.*

1. Not in Qq, F.

2

THE TRAGEDY OF
KING RICHARD THE SECOND

ACT I

SCENE I.—[*Windsor Castle.*]

Enter KING RICHARD, JOHN OF GAUNT, *with other* Nobles
and Attendants.

Rich. Old John of Gaunt, time-honoured Lancaster,

Title. The Tragedy] *Qq;* The Life and Death *F.*   Acts and Scenes] *Act and
Scene headings in Latin throughout F; Act and Scene divisions as in F up to V. iv. No
Act or Scene headings in Qq.*

ACT I

Scene 1

Location] *Ed.; not in Qq, F.*

MATERIAL. For historical facts the
scene closely follows Hol., 493/2/56–
494/2/40 (see Appendix, pp. 181–3),
although Holinshed's is not a good
version of what actually happened (see
Steel, pp. 246–7); the spirited language is Shakespeare's. Shakespeare
knew from a previous section in Holinshed that the immediate cause of the
quarrel was Bolingbroke's accusing
Mowbray at a parliament at Shrewsbury of uttering "certaine words . . .
sounding highlie to the King's dishonor" in a private talk as they rode
together near London. Richard's
attempts to make peace are recorded
by Holinshed. In Holinshed, Bolingbroke's speech represented by ll. 87–
108 and part of Mowbray's speech at
ll. 111 f are spoken by unnamed
knights on behalf of the two appellants. The business with the gages at

ll. 69, 146, and 160 f is expanded from
a sentence in Holinshed: "the duke of
Hereford cast downe his gage and the
duke of Norfolke took it up", and
John of Gaunt's behaviour here is
invented by Shakespeare.

Location] After Bolingbroke had
accused Mowbray of treason in January 1398 at Shrewsbury, both men
appeared before a commission at
Oswestry in February, where the
charge was repeated and again
denied; both were then arrested so
that they might be on hand when the
king was ready to hold the inquiry
necessary before the matter could be
allowed to proceed to the last resort—
a chivalric trial by combat. Bolingbroke was permitted to "put in
pledges", of whom Gaunt was one
(see 1. i. 2), but Mowbray was taken
under arrest to Windsor Castle. About

3

Hast thou according to thy oath and band
Brought hither Henry Herford thy bold son,
Here to make good the boist'rous late appeal,
Which then our leisure would not let us hear,   5
Against the Duke of Norfolk, Thomas Mowbray?
Gaunt. I have, my liege.
Rich. Tell me, moreover, hast thou sounded him,
If he appeal the Duke on ancient malice,

5. hear] *Q1–4, F;* here *Q5.*

six weeks after the dissolution of the Shrewsbury Parliament, Richard arrived at Windsor to hear the case.

1. *Old . . . Gaunt*] Gaunt was fifty-eight in 1398 when the play opens; his name comes from his birthplace of Ghent in Flanders. This line (and cf. I. ii. 44, II. i. 72) emphasizes his age. Brereton (pp. 98–9) cites several passages in *Woodstock* which underline the comparative senility of the king's uncles (Gaunt, York, and Thomas of Woodstock) and the youthfulness of the king and his minions.

2. *band*] bond. The forms were interchangeable; cf. II. ii. 71, v. ii. 65 and note.

3. *Herford*] Qq and F prefer this spelling, which has been adopted throughout this edn, to Holinshed's *Hereford*, as did Daniel in *C.W.* It seems to be nearly always scanned as a disyllable.

4. *late appeal*] recent appeal; see note under "Windsor Castle" above. An "appeal" was a "formal challenge based upon a criminal charge which the accuser [or "appellant"—see l. 34] was bound to make good at an appointed time and place, both parties giving security for their appearance" (Herford). See Sir T. Smith, *De Republica Anglorum* (1583), III. 3: "Of that which in England is called appeale, in other places accusation."

5. *our leisure*] i.e. want of leisure. Holinshed gives no such reason for the postponement of the hearing, and Shakespeare seems to have invented it. The real reason for the failure of

the Parliament at Shrewsbury to deal immediately with the matter was probably Richard's wish to avoid scandal (Steel, p. 246).

9–14. *appeal . . . on ancient malice, . . . some known ground of treachery . . . On some apparent danger . . . no inveterate malice*] These phrases should be distinguished from the phrase at l. 27— "appeal each other *of* high treason", which names the crime of which the culprit is accused. These lines deal with the grounds on which he is accused and the motives of the accuser, and may be paraphrased: "Is Bolingbroke bringing Mowbray to the trial actuated by some former hatred of his against Mowbray [not "Is Bolingbroke accusing Mowbray of 'ancient malice'?"] or worthily . . . because he knows some evidence of Mowbray's treachery?" *Gaunt* ". . . Because of something plainly dangerous, aimed at your Highness, which he has detected in Mowbray, not because he always hated Mowbray." Zeeveld (p. 331) relates the passage to Hall's statement (p. 3) that Bolingbroke began to "break his mind to [Mowbray] more for dolour and lamentacioun then for malice or displeasure". There is little but the word *malice* to connect the passages, for Hall refers to the original conversation that caused the quarrel (as does Daniel's similar observation—"what came of good minde [Mowbray] makes it hate", *C.W.*, I. st. 62), but Shakespeare's *malice* refers to Bolingbroke's motives in bringing his accusation.

Or worthily as a good subject should   10
On some known ground of treachery in him?
Gaunt. As near as I could sift him on that argument,
On some apparent danger seen in him,
Aim'd at your Highness, no inveterate malice.
Rich. Then call them to our presence; face to face,   15
And frowning brow to brow, ourselves will hear
The accuser and the accused freely speak.
High-stomach'd are they both and full of ire,
In rage, deaf as the sea, hasty as fire.

Enter BOLINGBROKE *and* MOWBRAY.

Bol. Many years of happy days befall   20
My gracious sovereign, my most loving liege!
Mow. Each day still better other's happiness
Until the heavens, envying earth's good hap,
Add an immortal title to your crown!

---

15. presence;] *Pope;* presence *Qq, F.*   24. an] *Q1, 2, F;* in *Q3–5.*

Richard distinguishes between long-standing hatred of the accused as the accuser's motive and definite evidence ("known ground") possessed by the accuser against the accused. Cf. note on l. 32 below.

12. *sift him*] explore his designs by questioning him.
   argument] theme, subject.

15–17.] This detail is one of the "occasional historical data in Hall but not recorded in Holinshed" which Zeeveld (p. 332) cites as evidence that Shakespeare regularly utilized Hall for this play. Hall, however, provides nothing that is not in Holinshed (cf. the corresponding passages in Hol., 494/1/11 and Hall, p. 3). From Holinshed also Shakespeare learnt (Hol., 494/2/19, 494/2/11) that the council and Gaunt were present.

16. *ourselves*] i.e. we ourselves, royal plural. Shakespeare's practice as between royal *we ourself* and *we ourselves* is not very consistent. Both here and at III. iii. 127 (where F has *our selfe*) Q1 prints *ourseiues*, but at I. iv.

23, 42 both Q1 and F have *Our selfe.* On the whole he seems to have favoured the latter form (see *2 H 6,* III. i. 196; *Mac.,* III. i. 42; *Meas.,* I. i. 44; but contrast *Mac.,* III. iv. 32).

18. *High-stomach'd*] high-spirited, haughty, stubborn. Not found elsewhere in Shakespeare, though figurative use of *stomach,* as the seat of stubborn courage, is common (e.g. *2 H 4,* I. i. 129). Holinshed describes Woodstock as a man of "high mind and stout stomach".

19. S.D. BOLINGBROKE] So called because he was born (1367) at his father's castle of Bolingbroke in Lincolnshire. The name is spelled Bullingbrooke in Q1; R. M. Smith suggests that Shakespeare is following Daniel.

24. *Add . . . crown*] i.e. "add the title of immortality to that of kingship" (Herford). The opposing idea is found in *Woodstock,* I. i. 36–7: "But heaven forestalled his [the Black Prince's] diadem on earth / To place him with a royal crown in heaven"; cf. v. i. 24–5 and note.

Rich. We thank you both, yet one but flatters us,   25
　　　As well appeareth by the cause you come,
　　　Namely, to appeal each other of high treason:
　　　Cousin of Herford, what dost thou object
　　　Against the Duke of Norfolk, Thomas Mowbray?

Bol. First—heaven be the record to my speech!   30
　　　In the devotion of a subject's love,
　　　Tend'ring the precious safety of my prince,
　　　And free from other misbegotten hate,
　　　Come I appellant to this princely presence.
　　　Now Thomas Mowbray do I turn to thee,   35
　　　And mark my greeting well; for what I speak
　　　My body shall make good upon this earth,
　　　Or my divine soul answer it in heaven.
　　　Thou art a traitor and a miscreant,
　　　Too good to be so, and too bad to live,   40
　　　Since the more fair and crystal is the sky,
　　　The uglier seem the clouds that in it fly;
　　　Once more, the more to aggravate the note,
　　　With a foul traitor's name stuff I thy throat,
　　　And wish—so please my sovereign—ere I move,   45
　　　What my tongue speaks my right drawn sword may
　　　　　prove.

26. *the cause . . . come*] the nature of the cause you come for.

28. *what . . . object*] What is the specific charge you bring (Kittredge).

32. *Tend'ring*] watching over. In ll. 31–3 Bolingbroke takes care to explain (in view of Richard's question at ll. 9–14 above) the purity of his motives; such purity was also a recognized obligation for those participating in a chivalric trial: see Dante, *De Monarchia*, II, x (*Latin Works*, Temple Classics edn, p. 211): "the contenders or champions should enter the palaestra, not in hate or love, but in sole zeal for justice, with common consent"; and cf. Amphialus' letter to Phalantus in Sidney's *Arcadia* III. ix: "Prepare therefore your armes to fight, but not your hart to malice; since true valure needes no other whetstone, then desire of honour."

36. *greeting*] address.

38. *divine*] immortal.

40–2. *Too good*] i.e., in rank. "The thought [of ll. 41–2] resembles the saying *corruptio optimi pessima*, 'the greater the excellence, the more ruinous its decay'; but Mowbray's rank is regarded as a permanent *ground* which his treason disfigures, but cannot destroy" (Herford).

43. *note*] mark of disgrace < L. *nota*, official rebuke by the censor. So Tarquin meditates in *Lucr.*, 208: "my posterity, sham'd with the note, / Shall curse my bones".

46. *right drawn*] "Drawn in a right or just Cause" (Johnson). Q1 has *right drawen*. Obsolete past participial *-en* occurs elsewhere in Q1 (*throwen*, I. iii. 118, v. ii. 30; *knowen*, II. ii. 39, II. iii. 157; *drawen*, III. i. 15); but only in one case (I. iii. 118)

Mow. Let not my cold words here accuse my zeal.
'Tis not the trial of a woman's war,
The bitter clamour of two eager tongues,
Can arbitrate this cause betwixt us twain;   50
The blood is hot that must be cool'd for this.
Yet can I not of such tame patience boast
As to be hush'd and nought at all to say.
First, the fair reverence of your Highness curbs me
From giving reins and spurs to my free speech,   55
Which else would post until it had return'd
These terms of treason doubled down his throat;
Setting aside his high blood's royalty,
And let him be no kinsman to my liege,
I do defy him, and I spit at him,   60
Call him a slanderous coward, and a villain,
Which to maintain I would allow him odds,
And meet him were I tied to run afoot
Even to the frozen ridges of the Alps,
Or any other ground inhabitable   65
Where ever Englishman durst set his foot.

57. doubled] *Qq;* doubly *F.*   60. and I] *Q1, F;* and *Q2–5.*

is there reason to suppose that the obsolete disyllabic form might differ in pronunciation from the modern form; see notes on I. iii. 118 and v. i. 24–5.

47. *Let . . . zeal*] i.e. "May the coldness of my words not reflect upon my zeal" or, "cause me to be accused of want of zeal".

48. *trial . . . war*] Mowbray does not want the effeminate kind of "trial" of two women warring with words. Cf. Aeneas to Achilles, *Iliad*, xx. 251–5.

51. *cool'd*] i.e. in death.

56. *post*] To *post* is to travel with relays of horses (originally as a courier) and hence to travel with speed. The word continues the horse-and-rider metaphor of the preceding lines.

57. *doubled*] "increased twofold" and therefore, when applied to spoken words, "reiterated". The verb

has the latter sense at *Woodstock*, v. iii. 122, where Rossiter suggests that it implies "make you eat your own words", an implication which is certainly present in the whole phrase *doubled down his throat* here. Shakespeare does not elsewhere use the verb *double* of spoken words.

63. *tied*] bound, obliged.

65. *inhabitable*] uninhabitable (L. *inhabitabilis*): cf. "the whole lunar world is a Torrid Zone; and . . . may be supposed *inhabitable*, except they are *Salamanders* which dwell in those *fiery Regions*", J. Glanvill, *Scepsis Scientifica* (1665), ed. Owen, p. 151. For Mowbray's sentiment cf. iv. i. 74, and *Mac.*, iii. iv. 104: "And dare me to the desert with thy sword". "The expression . . . implied a fight to the death, since in the desert none could part the fighters or help the wounded" (Wilson).

Meantime, let this defend my loyalty—
By all my hopes most falsely doth he lie.

Bol. Pale trembling coward, there I throw my gage,
Disclaiming here the kindred of the king,   70
And lay aside my high blood's royalty,
Which fear, not reverence, makes thee to except.
If guilty dread have left thee so much strength
As to take up mine honour's pawn, then stoop.
By that, and all the rites of knighthood else,   75
Will I make good against thee, arm to arm,
What I have spoke, or thou canst worse devise.

Mow. I take it up; and by that sword I swear,
Which gently laid my knighthood on my shoulder,
I'll answer thee in any fair degree   80
Or chivalrous design of knightly trial;
And when I mount, alive may I not light,
If I be traitor or unjustly fight!

Rich. What doth our cousin lay to Mowbray's charge?
It must be great that can inherit us   85
So much as of a thought of ill in him.

Bol. Look what I speak, my life shall prove it true:

67. Meantime] *Q1-4*, *F* (Mean time); Meant time *Q5*.   70. the king] *Q1*;
a King *Q2-5*, *F*.   73. have] *Qq*; hath *F*.   77. spoke, or thou canst worse]
Q1; spoke, or thou canst *Q2*; spoke, or what thou canst *Q3-5*; spoken, or
thou canst *F*.   82. mount, alive] *Q1-3*, *F*; mount aliue, aliue *Q4*, *5*.
87. speak] *Q1*; sayd *Q2*, *4*; said *Q3*, *5*, *F*.

67. *this*] i.e., either the statement in
the next line, or perhaps his sword on
which Shakespeare lays his hand.

69. *gage*] literally "pledge", because by throwing an object down the
challenger pledged himself to meet
whoever took it up (Nares). According to Holinshed, "hoods" were used
on this occasion, but Wilson suggests
that Shakespeare may have had
gloves in mind: see note on IV. i. 25.

70. *Disclaiming . . . king*] waiving
the fact of my kinship to the king (and
the privileges attached to it).

72. *except*] set aside. *O.E.D.*, citing
this line, defines *except* as "to take exception to", and cfs. *Sonn.*, CXLVII. 8;
but the object of the verb is "high

blood's royalty" which in l. 58 above
Mowbray has "set aside".

74. *honour's pawn*] Cf. IV. i. 55, 70.

77. *thou . . . devise*] Here *devise* probably means not "plan to perform in
the future", but "name or think of at
this moment"; hence Bolingbroke is
saying that he will be ready to prove
Mowbray the author of any crimes,
even worse than the ones with which
Bolingbroke has already charged him,
that Mowbray likes to name.

80-1. *in any . . . design*] to any fair
measure or in any form of knightly
trial allowed by the laws of chivalry.

85. *inherit us*] "to put us in possession of", literally "to make us heir of".

87. *Look what*] i.e. "that which" or

That Mowbray hath receiv'd eight thousand nobles
In name of lendings for your Highness' soldiers,
The which he hath detain'd for lewd imployments,   90
Like a false traitor, and injurious villain;
Besides I say, and will in battle prove,
Or here, or elsewhere to the furthest verge
That ever was survey'd by English eye,
That all the treasons for these eighteen years   95
Complotted and contrived in this land
Fetch from false Mowbray their first head and spring;
Further I say, and further will maintain
Upon his bad life to make all this good,
That he did plot the Duke of Gloucester's death,   100
Suggest his soon-believing adversaries,
And consequently, like a traitor coward,
Sluic'd out his innocent soul through streams of blood,

97. Fetch] *Q1*; Fetcht *Q2–5*; Fetch'd *F.*

"whatever": a common 16th-century idiom; see M. Eccles, 'Shakespeare's Use of "Look How" and similar Idioms', *J.E.G.P.*, XLII (1943), and cf. I.iii.286.

88. *nobles*] A noble = a gold coin worth 20 groats, or 6s. 8d.

89. *lendings*] i.e. advances made to soldiers when regular pay cannot be given (*O.E.D.*); cf. Jonson's description of Shift in *Every Man out of his Humour* as "A Thred-bare Sharke. One that neuer was Souldier, yet liues upon lendings" (*Ben Jonson*, ed. Herford and Simpson, III. 426).

90. *lewd*] base, improper.

95. *eighteen years*] From Holinshed, and referring to the time elapsed since Wat Tyler's rebellion in 1381.

100. *Gloucester's death*] Modern historians believe that Richard was almost certainly implicated in the murder of his uncle "Thomas of Woodstock", Duke of Gloucester (Steel, p. 239); it occurred at Calais under Mowbray's supervision in September 1397, and is recounted at length by Holinshed (489/1–2). It is also the third "tragedy" in the 1559

edn of *Mirror*. Shakespeare does not necessarily assume that his audience knew, or knew only, the account in the play *Woodstock*, nor is the parallel with *Woodstock*, cited in note on ll. 104–5 below, close enough to show that Shakespeare himself was thinking of *Woodstock*.

101. *Suggest*] prompt, incite; cf. III. iv. 75.

102. *consequently*] subsequently.

103.] The line suggests beheading rather than the smothering with towels in a feather-bed which Holinshed and *Woodstock* report as the manner of Gloucester's end: cf. I. ii. 21 and II. ii. 102. Wilson maintains that the detail shows that Shakespeare knew le Beau's version of *Traïson* which, alone of suggested sources, says that Gloucester was beheaded: "le roi envoya son oncle à Calais, et là fut décollé", Buchon, *Chroniques Nationales Françaises*, vol. xv (1826), Deuxième Supplément, p. 10. It is odd that Shakespeare should bow to le Beau's authority in this minor detail, and I think a simpler explanation may be that Shakespeare automatically

Which blood, like sacrificing Abel's, cries
Even from the tongueless caverns of the earth   105
To me for justice and rough chastisement;
And, by the glorious worth of my descent,
This arm shall do it, or this life be spent.

Rich. How high a pitch his resolution soars!
Thomas of Norfolk, what say'st thou to this?   110

Mow. O, let my sovereign turn away his face,
And bid his ears a little while be deaf,
Till I have told this slander of his blood
How God and good men hate so foul a liar.

Rich. Mowbray, impartial are our eyes and ears.   115
Were he my brother, nay, my kingdom's heir,
As he is but my father's brother's son,
Now by my sceptre's awe I make a vow,
Such neighbour nearness to our sacred blood
Should nothing privilege him nor partialize   120

116. my ... my] *Qq;* my ... our *F.*   118. my] *F; not in Qq.*   119. neighbour
nearness] *Qq; hyphened in F.*

thought of the manner of execution as
conforming to Elizabethan custom
when applied to a victim of Gloucester's rank: Marlowe (*Edward II*, II. v.
21–4) makes Warwick say of Gaveston
"his head shall off" and a moment
later orders him to be "hanged at a
bough". Note also that the mention of
"blood" here and "bloody axe" at
I. ii. 21 is essential for the metaphors
that follow; Shakespeare could not
have gained the effects with Abel's
spilt blood or the cracked vial of
I. ii. 17–21 if he had restricted his
thought to a death by smothering.

104–5.] Cf. Gen., iv. 10. "This is
aimed directly at Richard who was as
closely related to Gloucester as Bolingbroke himself" (Wilson). The point
again pre-supposes the audience's
knowledge of history, but not necessarily that Shakespeare is assuming
that they knew *Woodstock* (cf. note on
l. 100 above): with the lines cf. *Mirror*,
p. 99, "Gloucester's Tragedy": "For
blood axeth blood as guerdon dewe /

And vengeaunce for vengeaunce is
iust rewarde / . . . Blood wyll haue
blood, eyther fyrst or last"; *Woodstock*,
v. iv. 47 f (and Rossiter's note): "O
my dear friends, the fearful wrath of
heaven / Sits heavy on our heads for
Woodstock's death. / Blood cries for
blood; and that almighty hand / Permits not murder unrevenged to
stand." Neither passage need have
been in Shakespeare's mind; the
Genesis reference and the proverb
"blood will have blood" (see Tilley,
B468) are commonplaces.

104. *sacrificing*] Abel is so called because he sacrificed the beasts of the
earth.

109. *pitch*] the height to which a
falcon soared, before she stooped upon
her prey (Nares); cf. I. iii. 61; *Cæs.,*
I. i. 74.

113. *slander*] i.e. "this disgrace to
the royal blood".

118. *sceptre's awe*] the reverence due
to my sceptre (Johnson).

120. *partialize*] render partial; not
found elsewhere in Shakespeare.

The unstooping firmness of my upright soul.
He is our subject, Mowbray; so art thou:
Free speech and fearless I to thee allow.
Mow. Then, Bolingbroke, as low as to thy heart
   Through the false passage of thy throat thou liest.   125
   Three parts of that receipt I had for Callice
   Disburs'd I duly to his Highness' soldiers;
   The other part reserv'd I by consent,
   For that my sovereign liege was in my debt
   Upon remainder of a dear account   130
   Since last I went to France to fetch his queen:
   Now swallow down that lie. For Gloucester's death,
   I slew him not, but to my own disgrace

127. duly] *Q1; not in Q2–5, F.*   133. my] *Q1; mine Q2–5, F.*

124–5. *as low . . . throat*] "a heightened variation on the common formula [see Tilley, T268] 'thou liest in thy throat' " (Herford); cf.l.44 above.

126. *receipt*] sum received.

Callice] Calais.

128. *by consent*] This statement, which apparently means that Richard agreed to Mowbray's retention of some of the money, is not in Holinshed.

130. *Upon . . . account*] on the balance of a heavy debt. *Dear* here means "dire", "heavy", as well as "of great value".

131. *Since . . . France*] Mowbray means that he spent his own money when he went on the embassy to France, and Richard was therefore in debt to him. Mowbray went to France in 1395 to negotiate Richard's marriage with his second queen, Charles VI's daughter, the Isabel of this play; but he cannot be said to have "fetched" her, since Richard himself went to Calais in 1396 for the wedding.

132–4.] "An embarrassed and ambiguous speech" (Wilson), which Rossiter (pp. 48–9) explains by reference to *Woodstock*; but it is based, I think, on information from Holinshed's account of Gloucester's murder, although Shakespeare departs from his

source in making Mowbray rebut this part of Bolingbroke's accusations: in Holinshed, Mowbray's reply is silent on Gloucester's death. What Shakespeare here makes Mowbray say is derived from elsewhere in Holinshed. Mowbray was Richard's agent in the murder at Calais though he did not kill him with his own hands ("I slew him not"); he also "neglected his sworn duty" to his own disgrace by failing to dispatch Gloucester as soon as Richard gave the order: "[Mowbray] prolonged time for the executing of the kings commandement [to make Gloucester secretly away], though the king would haue had it doone with all expedition, wherby the king conceiued no small displeasure, and sware that it should cost the earle his life if he quickly obeied not his commandement" (Hol., 488/1/67). The same points are repeated at more length in Hol., 511/2/60: Bagot reports that Mowbray claimed to have saved Gloucester's life contrary to the king's will "by the space of three weeks", "affirming . . . that [Mowbray] was never in all his life time more affraid of death, than he was at his comming home againe from Calis at that time, to the kings presence, by reason he had not put the duke to death."

Neglected my sworn duty in that case.
For you, my noble lord of Lancaster,   135
The honourable father to my foe,
Once did I lay an ambush for your life,
A trespass that doth vex my grieved soul;
But ere I last receiv'd the sacrament,
I did confess it, and exactly begg'd   140
Your grace's pardon, and I hope I had it.
This is my fault—as for the rest appeal'd,
It issues from the rancour of a villain,
A recreant and most degenerate traitor,
Which in myself I boldly will defend,   145
And interchangeably hurl down my gage
Upon this overweening traitor's foot,
To prove myself a loyal gentleman
Even in the best blood chamber'd in his bosom.
In haste whereof most heartily I pray   150
Your Highness to assign our trial day.
Rich. Wrath-kindled gentlemen, be rul'd by me,
     Let's purge this choler without letting blood—

137. did I] *Qq*; I did *F*.   139. But] *Q1* (*Huth*), *F*; Ah but *Q1* (*Cap. and Hunt.*),
Q2, 3; Ah, but *Q4, 5*.   146. my] *Q1, F*; the *Q2-5*.   149. his] *Q1-4, F*; your
Q5.   152. gentlemen] *F*; gentleman *Qq*.

135-41.] Shakespeare is closely following Holinshed's words, and may
not have known the exact character
of the "ambush" Mowbray refers to.
Its character is discussed by Steel
pp. 244 f), but the whole event is still
obscure. John suggests that there is a
reference to the plot to seize Richard,
Gaunt, and York which Holinshed
(488/2) reports as having been con-
certed in 1397, and which was betrayed to Richard by Mowbray himself; but Shakespeare is probably not
thinking beyond the words on the
page of Holinshed before him.
   140. *exactly*] expressly:
   142. *as . . . appeal'd*] "as for the rest
of the crimes of which I am accused".
   144. *recreant . . . degenerate*] "false to
his religion" and "false to his rank".
   145. *Which . . . defend*] "The truth of
which statement I will in my own per-

son boldly defend." Mowbray has
counter-"appealed" Bolingbroke of
treason.
   146. *interchangeably*] reciprocally.
   149. *chamber'd*] lodged.
   150. *In haste whereof*] "for a speedy
settlement of which" (Newbolt), i.e.,
"so that I may speedily prove myself
loyal in his blood".
   153-7.] The analogy of king with
physician, which Richard is not using
frivolously, is elaborately developed
elsewhere, e.g., Tyndale, *Obedience of a
Christian Man* (1528) who compares
the evil ruler's activities to the surgeon's and physician's searching irons
and bitter drinks (*Doctrinal Treatises*,
Parker Soc. edn, 1848, p. 197); *Woodstock*, I. i. 141-8; James VI and I,
A Counterblaste to Tobacco (1604): ". . .
it is the King's part (as the proper
Phisicion of his Politicke bodie) to

This we prescribe, though no physician;
Deep malice makes too deep incision.   155
Forget, forgive, conclude and be agreed:
Our doctors say this is no month to bleed.
Good uncle, let this end where it begun;
We'll calm the Duke of Norfolk, you your son.
Gaunt. To be a make-peace shall become my age.   160
Throw down, my son, the Duke of Norfolk's gage.
Rich. And, Norfolk, throw down his.
Gaunt.   When, Harry, when?
Obedience bids I should not bid again.
Rich. Norfolk, throw down we bid, there is no boot.
Mow. Myself I throw, dread sovereign, at thy foot;   165
My life thou shalt command, but not my shame:
The one my duty owes, but my fair name,
Despite of death, that lives upon my grave,

---

157. month] *Qq; time F.*   162–3. When ... bids] *Pope* (bids,); When Harry?
when obedience bids, / Obedience bids *Q1;* When Harry, when? obedience
bids, / Obedience bids *Q2–5, F.*

---

purge it of all those diseases by Medi-
cine". The theme is prominent in
Mac. (e.g., v. ii. 27–9) and is discussed
by H. N. Paul, *Royal Play of Macbeth*
(1951), pp. 391–2. Cf. the references
to the "infected" Richard and the
"fevered" commonwealth in *2 H 4,*
IV. i. 54–66.

156. *Forget, forgive*] A proverbial
usage: see Tilley F597, and cf. *Lr.,*
IV. vii. 85.

157.] Physicians were supposed to
know, and others could find out from
almanacks, the favourable seasons for
blood-letting. Deighton cfs. Fletcher,
The Chances, I. viii (*Fifty Comedies and
Tragedies,* 1679, p. 411): "all Physicians / And penny Almanacks allow
the opening / Of veins this moneth."
Kittredge remarks that the month in
the play is April, and that spring was
usually considered a favourable season
for blood-letting.

160. *make-peace*] Cf. Heywood, *If You
Know not Me II* (Sh. Soc. edn, p. 81).

162–3.] *When ... when?* is an exclamation of impatience; cf. *Cæs.,* II. i. 5.

The repetition of *obedience bids* in Q1
may be due to dictation in the printing-house (Wilson, who cfs. I. iii. 136
in Q1 Cap. and Huth). H. F. Brooks,
on the other hand, suggests that in the
MS ll. 162–3 (*When, ... again.*) were
written as one line, and that the compositor began to set it up thus, realized
his mistake, but then failed to cancel
his first *obedience bids.*

164. *no boot*] no help for it.

167. *The one ... owes*] "I am bound
by duty to place my life at your dis-
posal."

168.] i.e. "[My name] that lives,
despite of death, upon my grave", as
most edd. explain, attributing the in-
version to the needs of emphasis or
rhyme. By this interpretation, "live
upon my grave" must mean "continue to live above my grave" (triumphing over death because undis-
honoured) or "continue an honourable existence after my death *like* the
name honourably inscribed upon a
tombstone". For the sentiments and
some of the phraseology cf. *LLL.,*

To dark dishonour's use thou shalt not have.
I am disgrac'd, impeach'd, and baffl'd here,   170
Pierc'd to the soul with slander's venom'd spear,
The which no balm can cure but his heart-blood
Which breath'd this poison.

Rich.   Rage must be withstood:
Give me his gage; lions make leopards tame.

Mow. Yea, but not change his spots. Take but my shame,
And I resign my gage. My dear dear lord,   176
The purest treasure mortal times afford
Is spotless reputation—that away,
Men are but gilded loam, or painted clay.
A jewel in a ten-times barr'd-up chest   180
Is a bold spirit in a loyal breast.
Mine honour is my life, both grow in one,
Take honour from me, and my life is done.
Then, dear my liege, mine honour let me try;
In that I live, and for that will I die.   185

Rich. Cousin, throw up your gage, do you begin.

---

179. or] *Q1–4, F*; and *Q5*.   186.] *As Qq*; . . . gage / . . . begin / *F*.   up] *Qq*; downe *F*.

1. i. 1–3: "Let fame, that all hunt after in their lives, / Live regist'red upon our brazen tombs, / And then grace us in the disgrace of death."

170. *impeach'd and baffl'd*] accused of treason and rendered infamous as a knight. *Baffling* a recreant knight is explained by Hall (p. 559): "He was content that the Scottes should Bafful hym, which is a great reproach among the Scottes, and is used when a man is openly perjured, and then they make of him an Image paynted reverted with his heles upwarde, with hys name . . ." (*O.E.D.*; cf. Nares); cf. *1 H 4*, I. ii. 98; the baffling of Turpin, *Faerie Queene*, VI. vii. 27; Nashe, *Have with You to Saffron Walden* (*Works*, ed. McKerrow, III. 31), 1596: "Bafful and infamize my name".

174. *lions . . . tame*] Perhaps a heraldic reference: the lions are those in Richard's royal arms, the leopard the lion *statant* forming Mowbray's crest,

"the lion in any attitude but rampant having been termed a leopard, or *lion leopardé*, in ancient heraldry" (Scott-Giles, p. 75).

174–5. *leopards . . . spots*] Quibble on the "spots" and stains of shame and the leopard's spots. Noble (p. 61) cites Jer., xiii. 23, but points out that the phrase had become proverbial; Tilley (L206) lists the proverb, but all his examples are later than this of Shakespeare's. F. P. Wilson (*R.E.S.*, N.S., III (1952), 196) gives a yet earlier example from Lyly's *Euphues* (1578).

177–9.] These lines are anthologized in *England's Parnassus* (1600), no. 605, in the section entitled "Good name".

177. *mortal times*] the lives of mortal men.

182. *in one*] undivided from each other.

186. *throw . . . gage*] The "gage" is Mowbray's, picked up by Boling-

Bol. O God defend my soul from such deep sin!
Shall I seem crest-fallen in my father's sight?
Or with pale beggar-fear impeach my height
Before this out-dar'd dastard? Ere my tongue   190
Shall wound my honour with such feeble wrong,
Or sound so base a parle, my teeth shall tear
The slavish motive of recanting fear,
And spit it bleeding in his high disgrace,
Where shame doth harbour, even in Mowbray's face.
Rich. We were not born to sue, but to command;   196
Which since we cannot do to make you friends,
Be ready, as your lives shall answer it,
At Coventry upon Saint Lambert's day.

187. God] *Qq;* heauen *F.*   deep] *Qq;* foule *F.*   189. beggar-fear] *Q1, F;*
begger-face *Q2–5.*   191. my] *Qq;* mine *F.*   192. parle] *F;* parlee *Qq.*
195.] *After this line F has S.D.* Exit Gaunt.   198. lives] *Q1, F;* life *Q2–5.*

broke when Mowbray hurled it down
at l. 146. "Throw up" is equivalent to
"Give me his gage" at l. 174 and
probably means "throw it up to me"
or, as Wilson suggests, "throw it up on
to the scaffold on which Richard is
sitting". "Throw up" might mean
"relinquish", on the other hand, and
might indicate that this new connotation for *throw up* was current before
1678, the earliest date given for its
appearance by *O.E.D.*

189. *impeach my height*] discredit my
high birth (Newbolt).

190. *out-dar'd*] "Excelled in daring" as well as *dared down, cowed* (Herford).

191. *feeble*] An unexpected adj.
here, since it is the magnitude of the
wrong of which Bolingbroke is complaining. The phrase must mean
"wrong [act] characteristic of a weak,
feeble person", or (Herford's suggestion) a wrong "implying feebleness in
the man who submits to it".

192. *sound . . . parle*] "A metaphor
taken from the blowing of a trumpet
for a parley between opposing forces"
(John).

193. *motive*] instrument, organ;
here, the tongue. Bolingbroke's rant

vividly expands the phrase "to bite
one's tongue", meaning "to keep
silence", as used in *2 H 6,* i. i. 225;
3 H 6, i. iv. 47; *Tit.,* iii. i. 131. Bolingbroke likens himself to the tortured
prisoner who bites off his tongue to
avoid confession: in *Euphues* (Bond, i.
279) Lyly translates from Plutarch's
De Garrulitate the story of Zeno who
"bitte of his tongue and spit it in the
face of the Tyraunt"; cf. Hieronimo
in Kyd's *Spanish Tragedy,* iv. iv. 193
(John, and Reyher).

194. *his . . . disgrace*] i.e. the tongue's, not Mowbray's, disgrace, because it is dispatched to the "harbour
of shame", Mowbray's face.

199. *Saint Lambert's day*] 17 September. Holinshed is uncertain of the date
appointed for the trial, but this is one
of his suggestions. Herford considers
that Richard's speech (ll. 196–205) is
unhistorical and intended to demon-
strate Richard's "combination of
arrogance and weakness". It is true
that trials by combat were, according
to custom, only proceeded with for
want of other evidence to settle the
case and not simply on the grounds
given here, viz. the rejection of recon-
ciliation by both appellant and defen-

There shall your swords and lances arbitrate   200
The swelling difference of your settled hate.
Since we cannot atone you, we shall see
Justice design the victor's chivalry.
Marshal, command our officers-at-arms
Be ready to direct these home alarms.   [*Exeunt.*   205

SCENE II.—[*John of Gaunt's house.*]

Enter JOHN OF GAUNT *with the* DUCHESS OF GLOUCESTER.

Gaunt. Alas, the part I had in Woodstock's blood

202. we shall] *Q1;* you shall *Q2–5,* F.   204. Marshal] *Capell;* Lord Marshal
Qq, F.

Scene II

Location.] *Ed.; not in Qq,* F.   S.D.] *Qq;* Enter Gaunt, and Dutchesse of Glou-
cester. F.   1. Woodstock's] *Qq;* Glousters F.

dant; but Shakespeare is here faith-
fully following Holinshed, who shows
no awareness of the historical fact that
it was the absence of evidence that
obliged the historical Richard to use
the method of trial by combat. The
historical Richard's action was quite
proper; neither Holinshed nor Shakespeare seem aware that, as *they* represent it, it has become, measured by
the ordinances of the trial by combat,
improper.

202. *atone*] reconcile: cf. Webster,
White Devil, III. ii. 308: "peace,
t'attone our hatred".

203. *design . . . chivalry*] "designate
the winner in a chivalrous combat".
The theory behind trial by combat
was similar to that behind trial by
ordeal: the God of Justice was the
ultimate umpire, and whoever won,
won rightly; see Dante, *De Monarchia,*
II. x (*Latin Works,* Temple Classics
edn, p. 210), describing the *duellum*:
". . . 'wheresoever human judgment is
at fault . . . we must have recourse to
[Christ] . . . this is what takes place
when by the free assent of either side,
not in hatred but in love of justice, the
divine judgement is sought through

means of mutual clash of strength,
alike of mind and body."

204. *Marshal*] He was the Duke of
Surrey: see note on I. iii. 251–2. The
marshal's duty at a trial by combat
was to maintain public order and
enforce the rules on contestants. For
the reading, see Introduction, p. xviii.

Scene II

MATERIAL. There is nothing corresponding to this scene in Holinshed,
Froissart or the other historians.
Gaunt's attitude of forbearance in the
matter of Gloucester's murder seems
to be Shakespeare's invention, although there are faint analogues to it
in both Hol., 490/1/30 and Froissart,
VI. 338 as well as in *Woodstock* (see also
Introduction, p. xl). The Duchess is
a character in *Woodstock,* and makes
a very brief appearance in v. iii of that
play, weeping, and urging Gaunt and
York to avenge her husband's murder. The two scenes do not correspond, for Gaunt's attitude in *Woodstock* is the reverse of his behaviour
here (see note on ll. 37–41 below).

1. *part . . . blood*] i.e. "my blood-
relationship to Woodstock". Keller

Doth more solicit me than your exclaims
To stir against the butchers of his life;
But since correction lieth in those hands
Which made the fault that we cannot correct,   5
Put we our quarrel to the will of heaven,
Who, when they see the hours ripe on earth,
Will rain hot vengeance on offenders' heads.
Duch. Finds brotherhood in thee no sharper spur?
Hath love in thy old blood no living fire?   10
Edward's seven sons, whereof thyself art one,
Were as seven vials of his sacred blood,
Or seven fair branches springing from one root.

12. Were as] *Q1–3, F;* Were *Q4, 5.*

and Reyher suggest that F reads *Gloustrs* because Gloucester's popular name would no longer be familiar in 1623, the old play about him having been forgotten. If, however, *Woodstock* was revived as late as the actor's names on the MS indicate (see Boas, p. 104; Frijlinck, p. xxviii), this argument does not hold. Greg (*Shakespeare First Folio,* p. 237 n. 1) suggests a better reason: to avoid a solitary use of the *Woodstock* title, which would be confusing to reader or audience.

4. *those hands*] i.e. Richard's: cf. ll. 38–9 below, and see note on i. i. 100.

8. *rain . . . vengeance*] A biblical phrase: cf. Ps., xciv. 1: "O Lord God, to whom vengeance belongeth"; Ps., xi. 7: "Upon the ungodly he shall rain snares, fire and brimstone"; see Noble, p. 151.

9. *brotherhood*] "the fact of your being brothers" or (Herford's suggestion) "the claim made in the name of brotherhood".

11. *Edward's . . . sons*] Edward III's seven sons are catalogued in *2 H 6,* ii. ii. 10–20 and referred to in *Woodstock* by the Ghost of Edward III (v. i. 84) and by Gloucester himself just before his murder (v. i. 161). The recurrence of these dynastic references in close relation to Gloucester's death links the play with both *Woodstock* and *2 H 6*: see note on ii. i. 104.

13–21.] In thinking of the seven sons as branches springing from one root, Shakespeare may have in mind the iconographical device of the family "tree" of which the best-known form is the Tree of Jesse in church windows, depicting Christ's ancestry. Elizabethan versions of family trees differ from the modern diagrammatic kind often by representing actual trees, the founder being at the root and the descendants adorning the various higher branches. This root-and-branch imagery is endemic in Tudor ancestor-pageantry: a tree showing the ancestry of Elizabeth I covers the title-page of Stow's *Chronicles* (1580), and a similar one, with Edward III as Jesse, was used in a pageant for Philip's royal entry in 1554 (see R. Withington, *English Pageantry,* i. 193): cf. the pageant for Charles V and Henry VIII cited in Introduction, p. xl. Scott-Giles (p. 58) points out that one of Edward III's badges, adopted in reference to his manor of Woodstock and used by his son "Thomas of Woodstock", was a gold stock of a tree, uprooted and cut short—a further reinforcement of the chosen image here, if Shakespeare knew of it. For the possible influence of another such family tree, see Paul, *Royal Play of Macbeth,* 1951, p. 174. Tree imagery similar to that found

Some of those seven are dried by nature's course,
Some of those branches by the Destinies cut;   15
But Thomas my dear lord, my life, my Gloucester,
One vial full of Edward's sacred blood,
One flourishing branch of his most royal root,
Is crack'd, and all the precious liquor spilt,
Is hack'd down, and his summer leaves all faded,   20
By envy's hand, and murder's bloody axe.
Ah, Gaunt, his blood was thine! that bed, that womb,
That mettle, that self mould, that fashioned thee
Made him a man; and though thou livest and breathest,
Yet art thou slain in him; thou dost consent   25
In some large measure to thy father's death
In that thou seest thy wretched brother die,
Who was the model of thy father's life.
Call it not patience, Gaunt, it is despair;
In suff'ring thus thy brother to be slaught'red,   30
Thou showest the naked pathway to thy life,
Teaching stern murder how to butcher thee.
That which in mean men we intitle patience
Is pale cold cowardice in noble breasts.
What shall I say? to safeguard thine own life,   35
The best way is to venge my Gloucester's death.
Gaunt. God's is the quarrel—for God's substitute,
His deputy anointed in His sight,

---

23. mettle] *F;* mettall *Qq.*   35. thine] *Q1, 5, F;* thy *Q2–4.*   37. God's ...
God's] *Qq;* Heauens ... heauens *F.*   quarrel—for] *Wilson;* quarrell for *Q1–4;*
quarrell, for *Q5;* quarrell: for *F.*

here occurs in *3 H 6,* II. vi. 47–50.
Reyher cfs. Marlowe, Epilogue to
Faustus: "Cut is the branch that
might have growne ful straight." Behind all may lie the imagery of John,
xv: "The consolation between Christ
and his members, vnder the parable
of the vine".

21. *axe*] See note on I. i. 103.

23. *mettle*] stuff, essence.

self] same. Noble cfs. Job, xxxiii. 6:
"I am even as thou; for I am fashioned
and made even of the same moulde."

28. *model*] "Something representing
on a small scale the qualities of an-

other" (Onions), a copy. Shakespeare
uses *model* with three apparently different connotations in this play: see
notes on III. ii. 153, v. i. 11.

33. *mean men*] i.e. "ordinary" men as
opposed to "nobles".

34. *breasts.*] "The full stop preludes
the final appeal" (Pollard, p. 67).

37–41.] In *Woodstock,* IV. ii. 144,
Gloucester's   sentiments   resemble
Gaunt's here; he says just before his
arrest—"[Richard's] youth is led by
flatterers much astray. / But he's our
King: and God's great deputy; / And
if ye hunt to have me second ye / In

Hath caus'd his death; the which if wrongfully,
Let heaven revenge, for I may never lift   40
An angry arm against His minister.
Duch. Where then, alas, may I complain myself?
Gaunt. To God, the widow's champion and defence.
Duch. Why then, I will. Farewell, old Gaunt.
Thou goest to Coventry, there to behold   45
Our cousin Herford and fell Mowbray fight.

42. alas] *Q1* (*Hunt.*), *2–5, F; not in Q1* (*Cap. and Huth*).   43. God] *Qq;*
heauen *F.*   and] *Qq;* to *F.*

any rash attempt against his state, /
Afore my God, I'll ne'er consent unto
it". For the possible influence of the
Gloucester of *Woodstock* on Shakespeare's Gaunt, see Introduction, pp.
xxxv–xxxix and note to II. i. 128. It is
Woodstock, v. iii, however, which corresponds to the *situation* in this scene—
the widowed Duchess seeking revenge
from her brothers-in-law, the uncles—
and there Gaunt proclaims revenge:
"We will revenge our noble brother's
wrongs; / And force that wanton
tyrant to reveal / The death of his dear
uncle" (*Woodstock*, v. iii. 2–4; and cf.
ibid., v. iii. 19–21). It is likely that
Woodstock and Shakespeare draw independently upon Tudor political
thought, as exemplified by the second
part of the homily "concerning Good
Order and Obedience to Rulers and
Magistrates". This expounds 1 Sam.,
xxvi to show the extreme criminality
of laying hands on an anointed ruler:
see *Homilies*, pp. 100–3 and cf. *ibid.*
("against . . . Rebellion"), pp. 500–4,
and Hart, pp. 46–7: cf. iv. i. 121–9
and note.

38. *deputy*] Richard is twice called
God's deputy in *Woodstock* (iv. ii. 144;
v. iii. 58); Reyher cfs. also *2 H 6*, III.
ii. 286 and *John*, III. i. 136: "Hail, you
anointed deputies of heaven!" The
idea is a commonplace of Tudor political thought, expressed in the
Homilies referred to in the previous
note and having ultimately Biblical
sanction (e.g. Rom., xiii. 1–7; 1 Sam.,
xxiv. 6, xxvi. 9): see Tyndale,

Obedience of a Christian Man (1528):
"Mark, the judges are called gods in
the scriptures, because they are in God's
room, and execute the command-
ments of God", *Doctrinal Treatises*,
Parker Soc. edn, 1848, p. 175. H. F.
Brooks cites the appearance of the
notion in Lyndesay's *Ane Satyre of the
Thrie Estaits* (*Works of D. Lyndesay*,
E.E.T.S., o.s. XXXVII, p. 446) where
the king is "bot ane mortall instrument / To that great God and King
omnipotent", and in Hoby's translation of Castiglione's *Courtier* (Everyman edn, pp. 276–7), and notes
the verbal echo in *Mirror*, p. 178,
"Jack Cade", prose-note: "officers
be Gods deputies". See also note on
the king as "god on earth" at v.
iii. 134.

39. *his*] Gloucester's.

43.] Noble cfs. Ps., lxviii. 5, Ps.,
cxlvi. 9; the widowed Constance of
John, III. i. 108, says: "A widow cries:
be husband to me, heavens" (Reyher).

44. *Farewell . . . Gaunt*] The Duchess
repeats the phrase ten lines later; it is
not quite appropriate here and the
metre of the line is disturbed. It goes
well enough with the next two lines
("Thou goest to Coventry . . ."); but
it and these interrupt the sequence
"why then I will [pray to God]" leading to the actual prayer (ll. 47–53).
Possibly the lack of perfect integra-
tion in the speech means that the
prayer was an afterthought on Shakespeare's part.

O, sit my husband's wrongs on Herford's spear,
That it may enter butcher Mowbray's breast!
Or if misfortune miss the first career,
Be Mowbray's sins so heavy in his bosom   50
That they may break his foaming courser's back
And throw the rider headlong in the lists,
A caitive recreant to my cousin Herford!
Farewell, old Gaunt; thy sometimes brother's wife
With her companion, grief, must end her life.   55
Gaunt. Sister, farewell; I must to Coventry,
As much good stay with thee as go with me!
Duch. Yet one word more—grief boundeth where it falls,
Not with the empty hollowness, but weight.
I take my leave before I have begun,   60
For sorrow ends not when it seemeth done.
Commend me to thy brother Edmund York.
Lo, this is all—nay, yet depart not so,
Though this be all, do not so quickly go;
I shall remember more. Bid him—ah, what?—   65
With all good speed at Plashy visit me.

47. sit] *F;* set *Qq.*   48. butcher] *Q1 (Hunt.),* 2–5, *F;* butchers *Q1 (Cap. and Huth).*   58. it] *Q2–5, F;* is *Q1.*   59. empty] *Q1 (Hunt.),* 2–5, *F;* emptines *Q1 (Cap. and Huth).*   62. thy] *Q1;* my *Q2–5, F.*

47–52.] Q1's reading of *set* in l. 47 may be right (Pollard, p. 61), points out that *set* and *sit* were vulgarly confused in Shakespeare's time); but Reyher hears an echo of *Woodstock,* v. iii. 16–17, the Duchess cursing Gloucester's murderers: "And may their sins sit heavy on their souls / That they in death, this day, may perish all". So also the Ghost of Henry VI curses Richard III, *R 3,* v. iii. 118: "Let me sit heavy on thy soul to-morrow!" For the *set-sit* confusion, cf. v. v. 27.

49. *if . . . career*] "if the first charge of the horses in the combat (=career) is not fatal to Mowbray". To *career* a horse is to run it at full speed for a measured distance and then stop suddenly; see Sieveking in *Shakespeare's England,* ii. 414–15.

53. *caitive recreant*] captive coward. Recreant = "an apostate to his

faith" (cf. 1. i. 144)—"thence used of the apostasy to the faith of chivalry implied in dishonourable surrender" (Herford).

54. *sometimes*] i.e. sometime: "wife of him who was formerly your brother" or "she who was formerly your brother's wife". For *sometimes* cf. v. i. 37; v. v. 75 and note.

55.] Cf. Constance's "Here I and sorrows sit", *John,* iii. i. 73.

58–9.] The Duchess likens the iteration of her grief ("one word more") to the bouncing of a ball; but it is its weight that makes her grief rebound, its emptiness and hollowness the ball.

66. *Plashy*] Gloucester's country-house near Felsted, Essex; several scenes of *Woodstock* are laid there. The place is mentioned in *Mirror,* p. 98, "Thomas, Duke of Gloucester", l. 169.

Alack, and what shall good old York there see
But empty lodgings and unfurnish'd walls,
Unpeopled offices, untrodden stones,
And what hear there for welcome but my groans?   70
Therefore commend me; let him not come there
To seek out sorrow that dwells everywhere.
Desolate, desolate, will I hence and die:
The last leave of thee takes my weeping eye.   [*Exeunt.*

SCENE III.—[*The lists at Coventry.*]

Enter LORD MARSHAL *and the* DUKE AUMERLE.

Mar. My Lord Aumerle, is Harry Herford arm'd?

70. hear] *Q1* (*Hunt.*), *2–5, F;* cheere *Q1* (*Cap. and Huth*), *Malone.*   72. sorrow
that] *Q1–3;* sorrow, that *Q4, 5, F;* sorrow—That *Rann* (*Whalley conj.*).

Scene III
Location.] *Pope; not in Qq, F.*   S.D.] *Qq* (the Lord *Q2–5*); *Enter Marshall, and
Aumerle. F.*

68. *unfurnish'd*] not hung with arras
or tapestry, which was taken down
"on every removal of the family"
(Steevens).

69. *Unpeopled*] Implies "devoid of
servants, or retinue": cf. *LLL.,* II. i.
88.

70. *hear*] " 'There see' [l. 67] is so
excellently complemented by 'heare
there' [in this line] that there can be
little doubt as to the correctness" of
the reading in Q1 Hunt. (Pollard,
p. 36).

Scene III

MATERIAL. The scene derives main-
ly from Hol., 494/2/41–495/2/24;
there are several verbal echoes but
much invented material in the speeches of the two champions; Shakespeare
departs occasionally from the order of
events as prescribed in the chivalric
ordinances (see J. Derocquigny in
Revue Anglo-Américaine, 1 (1923–4),
430–1; and note on S.D. at l. 6).
Richard's embracing of Bolingbroke

and the farewells he exchanges with
both appellants are invented, but Holinshed (494/2/53) mentions that both
combatants took leave of the king on
separate days during the two days
preceding the day fixed for the trial.
Richard's speech giving his reasons
for the sentences of exile (ll. 125–38) is
also, I believe, Shakespeare's invention, but see note on these lines. The
part played by Gaunt, except for
mention of the fact of his consent to
Bolingbroke's exile (see note on l. 234
below), and including the success of
his plea for the shortening of the exile
(see note on l. 211 below), is entirely
invented, as is the parting-scene between him and his son. The latter
part of I. iii is, however, coloured by
borrowings from Lyly's *Euphues: the
Anatomy of Wit* (1578)—see notes on
ll. 145, 206, 236, 275–6, 279–80, 294–
9; Shakespeare must recently have
read or re-read Lyly's letter, adapted
from Plutarch, on bearing exile pati-
ently, and it may have been these few

Aum. Yea, at all points, and longs to enter in.

Mar. The Duke of Norfolk, sprightfully and bold,
    Stays but the summons of the appellant's trumpet.

Mar. Why then, the champions are prepar'd, and stay   5
    For nothing but his Majesty's approach.

The trumpets sound and the KING *enters with his Nobles; when they
    are set, enter* MOWBRAY *in arms, defendant.*

Rich. Marshal, demand of yonder champion
    The cause of his arrival here in arms,
    Ask him his name, and orderly proceed
    To swear him in the justice of his cause.   10

Mar. In God's name and the king's, say who thou art,
    And why thou comest thus knightly clad in arms,
    Against what man thou com'st and what thy quarrel.

6. S.D.] *Qq* (*the Duke of Norfolke*); *Flourish. Enter King, Gaunt, Bushy, Bagot,
Greene, & others: Then Mowbray in Armor, and Harrold. F.*   13. and what] *Q1;*
and what's *Q2–5, F.*

pages in Lyly that gave him the idea
for the scene in which the sage father
offers Plutarchan consolations to the
exiled son.

1–2. *arm'd . . . points*] Cf. the combatants in the *Mirror* account, p. 106,
"Lord Mowbray" l. 135: "At all
poyntes armde to proue our quarels
iust".

2. *enter in*] i.e. into the lists themselves. The stage is imagined as the
actual field of combat; appellant and
defendant are thought of as being
about to leave their tents to wait at
the "barriers of the lists", the appellant at the east entrance, the defendant at the west: the stage-doors in
the public playhouse would serve for
these.

3. *bold*] boldly: dropped adverbial
ending, see Abbott ¶397.

4.] An imaginative touch: the defendant was supposed to be summoned by a herald, not by the
appellant's trumpet.

6. S.D.] The king was umpire, and
would be seated centrally on a stage-
throne. According to Holinshed, it

was Bolingbroke, as appellant, who
entered the lists first (as l. 4 suggests);
this was the correct order according
to the rules for the trial by combat
(G. Neilson, *Trial by Combat*, 1890, p.
161). Shakespeare reverses the order
of entry.

9. *orderly*] according to the rules.

10. *swear . . . cause*] Before being admitted to the lists the combatant was
required solemnly to swear before the
marshal and the constable that his
quarrel was just. Here, the herald is
told to administer the oath ("swear
him"): cf. ll. 29–30 below.

11–13.] The champion had to be
formally identified. Shakespeare's formula here is closer to that given by
Traïson, pp. 18–19/151–2: "the Marshal . . . asked him who he was, what
he wanted, and for what purpose he
was come thither?" than Holinshed's
"[the] marshall . . . demanding of him
what he was". But Bolingbroke's
reply as given by Holinshed could
easily have suggested the form of the
triple question put to him in the
play.

Speak truly on thy knighthood and thy oath,
As so defend thee heaven and thy valour!   15
Mow. My name is Thomas Mowbray, Duke of
        Norfolk,
Who hither come ingaged by my oath
(Which God defend a knight should violate!)
Both to defend my loyalty and truth
To God, my king, and my succeeding issue,   20
Against the Duke of Herford that appeals me,
And by the grace of God, and this mine arm,
To prove him, in defending of myself,
A traitor to my God, my king, and me—
And as I truly fight, defend me heaven!   25

The trumpets sound. Enter BOLINGBROKE, *appellant,*
in armour.

Rich. Marshal, demand of yonder knight in arms,
        Both who he is, and why he cometh hither
        Thus plated in habiliments of war;
        And formally, according to our law,

14. thy oath] *Qq;* thine oath *F.*   15. thee] *Q2–5, F;* the *Q1.*   17. come] *Qq;*
comes *F.*   18. God] *Qq;* heauen *F.*   20. and my] *Qq;* and his *F.*   25.
S.D.] *Qq (Duke of Hereford); Tucket. Enter Hereford, and Harold. F.*   26. demand
of] *Ed. (Ritson conj.);* aske *Qq, F.*   28. plated] *Qq;* placed *F.*   29. formally]
Q1–4; formerly *Q5, F.*

18. *defend*] forbid.

20. *my . . . issue*] Some edd. follow F,
but "Mowbray's issue was, by this
accusation, in danger of an attainder,
and therefore he might come among
other reasons for their sake" (Johnson, who, however, thought the F
reading more just and grammatical).
Herford also defends the F reading.
But the chief argument against Q—
that Mowbray could hardly describe
himself as loyal and true to his own
issue—is not conclusive: a similar
kind of slight awkwardness occurs at
l. 24 below, where Mowbray declares
that Bolingbroke has been a traitor to
"me" as well as to God and the king;
also, as Newbolt says, the *me* of l. 24
balances the *my* of this line.

25.] Some edd. add here a S.D.
for Mowbray to sit down. According
to Holinshed, after each champion
had entered the lists and formally
declared himself, he "sate him down
in his chair", which in Mowbray's
case was of "crimson velvet, courtain-
ed about with white and red damaske". It is not known whether this
would be done on Shakespeare's
stage, nor whether the performance
reflected the fact—which can be inferred from Holinshed, and is plain in
Traïson—that what Holinshed calls a
chair (cf. l. 120) and *Traïson* a *chaïer*
was a small pavilion in which the
knight could be concealed from his
opponent.

26. *demand of*] Ritson's conjecture

Depose him in the justice of his cause.   30

Mar. What is thy name? and wherefore com'st thou hither
    Before King Richard in his royal lists?
    Against whom comest thou? and what's thy quarrel?
    Speak like a true knight, so defend thee heaven!

Bol. Harry of Herford, Lancaster and Derby   35
    Am I, who ready here do stand in arms
    To prove by God's grace, and my body's valour
    In lists, on Thomas Mowbray, Duke of Norfolk,
    That he's a traitor foul and dangerous,
    To God of heaven, King Richard and to me—   40
    And as I truly fight, defend me heaven!

Mar. On pain of death, no person be so bold
    Or daring-hardy as to touch the lists,
    Except the marshal and such officers
    Appointed to direct these fair designs.   45

Bol. Lord Marshal, let me kiss my sovereign's hand,
    And bow my knee before his Majesty;
    For Mowbray and myself are like two men
    That vow a long and weary pilgrimage;
    Then let us take a ceremonious leave   50
    And loving farewell of our several friends.

Mar. The appellant in all duty greets your Highness,
    And craves to kiss your hand and take his leave.

Rich. We will descend and fold him in our arms.

---

33. comest] *Q5;* comes *Q1–4;* com'st *F.*   37. God's] *Qq;* heauens *F.*
39. he's] *F;* he is *Qq.*   43. daring-hardy] *Theobald;* daring, hardy *Qq;*
daring hardie *F.*

---

can now be supported by what seems
the likelihood of memorial corruption
here: see Introduction, p. xix.

  30. *Depose him*] "swear him", or
"examine him on oath": cf. l. 10
above.

  33. *comest*] The Q reading is quite
an admissible form of the 2nd pers.
sing. in Shakespeare, but the metre
requires a disyllable, and the Q compositor could have dropped the *t* by
accident (Wilson).

  43. *daring-hardy*] For compounded
adjectives in Shakespeare, see Abbott

¶2. Cf. *Traïson*, p. 20: ". . . que nulle
personne poure ou riche ne fust si
hardie de mectre la main sur les
lices".

  45. *designs*] enterprises: cf. I. i. 81.

  50 *ceremonious leave*] Mentioned by
Holinshed as occurring prior to the
combat, see note on material. These
leave-takings can hardly have been
a prescribed part of the trial ritual,
and were presumably political gestures; Shakespeare uses them to enhance the general dramatic excite-
ment.

Cousin of Herford, as thy cause is right,   55
So be thy fortune in this royal fight!
Farewell, my blood; which if to-day thou shed,
Lament we may, but not revenge thee dead.

Bol. O, let no noble eye profane a tear
For me, if I be gor'd with Mowbray's spear!   60
As confident as is the falcon's flight   †
Against a bird, do I with Mowbray fight.
My loving lord, I take my leave of you;
Of you, my noble cousin, Lord Aumerle;
Not sick, although I have to do with death,   65
But lusty, young, and cheerly drawing breath.
Lo, as at English feasts, so I regreet
The daintiest last, to make the end most sweet.
O thou, the earthly author of my blood,
Whose youthful spirit in me regenerate   70
Doth with a twofold vigour lift me up
To reach at victory above my head,
Add proof unto mine armour with thy prayers,
And with thy blessings steel my lance's point,
That it may enter Mowbray's waxen coat,   75

---

55. right] *Qq*; iust *F.*   58. thee] *Q 3–5, F*; the *Q 1, 2.*   69. earthly] *Qq*; earthy
F.   71. vigour] *Qq*; rigor *F.*   72. at victory] *Q 1, 2, F*; a victorie *Q 3–5.*

---

55. *as . . . right*] "in so far as thy
cause is right". A perfectly correct
sentiment on the part of the king, who
is acting as umpire or judge.

58. *thee*] Q 1 also made the mistake
of printing *the* for *thee* at I. iii. 15, IV. i.
109, V. i. 41, V. ii. 11.

59–60. *profane . . . me*] Bolingbroke
means that the eye would be misusing
a tear if it wept at the fall of a knight
so unworthy as to be beaten by Mowbray.

67. *English feasts*] The "daintiest"
part of the English feast was the
"banket" of confectionery and fruit
served at the end, the "idle banquet"
which is offered to the ladies in *Tim.*,
I. ii. 149.

regreet] "greet again", though it has
a stronger connotation of "again" at

ll. 142 and 186 below. These are the
only examples of its use as a verb in
Shakespeare; cf. the anonymous
Edward III (entered S.R., 1595,
1 Dec.), III. v. 65: "Lords, I regreet
you all with harty thanks" (*Shakespeare
Apocrypha*, ed. Brooke, p. 89); other
examples are cited by Lucas, *Works of
J. Webster*, III. 235.

68. *sweet.*] The full-stop (in Q 1)
implies a pause while he turns to
address Gaunt.

73. *proof*] " 'Proof armour', or
'armour of proof', was armour the
strength of which had been proved
or tested. So, we still speak of prov-
ing a sword, gun barrel etc." (Deighton).

75. *waxen*] i.e., soft and penetrable
as if it were a coat of wax.

And furbish new the name of John a Gaunt,
Even in the lusty haviour of his son.

Gaunt. God in thy good cause make thee prosperous,
Be swift like lightning in the execution,
And let thy blows, doubly redoubled,   80
Fall like amazing thunder on the casque   †
Of thy adverse pernicious enemy!
Rouse up thy youthful blood, be valiant and live.

Bol. Mine innocence and Saint George to thrive!

Mow. However God or Fortune cast my lot,   85
There lives or dies true to King Richard's throne,
A loyal, just, and upright gentleman.
Never did captive with a freer heart
Cast off his chains of bondage, and embrace
His golden uncontroll'd enfranchisement,   90
More than my dancing soul doth celebrate
This feast of battle with mine adversary.
Most mighty liege, and my companion peers,

---

76. furbish] *Qq;* furnish *F.*   78. God] Heauen *F.*   82. adverse] *Qq;*
amaz'd *F.*   84. innocence] *Qq, F;* innocency *Capell.*   85. God] *Qq;* heauen
F.   86. lives] *Q1, 2, F;* lies *Q3–5.*

---

76. *furbish*] Besides its more general
meaning of "clean up", *furbish* means
"scour the rust from armour"—as in
Mac., I. ii. 32 ("With furbish'd arms");
so Gaunt's "name" (honour, repute)
is also his armour, and the metaphor
continues the references to arms and
armour in the preceding lines.

77. *Even*] = "I mean"; used to
"explain a bold or figurative thought
just expressed" (Herford).

haviour] behaviour.

80. *redoubled*] Cf. *Mac.*, I. ii. 39;
here scanned as four syllables, in *Macbeth*
as three.

81. *amazing*] stupefying. "*Amaze*
was a very strong verb, almost equivalent to 'stun' or 'paralyze'" (Kittredge).

83.] An alexandrine; *valiant* is trisyllabic. *Youthful* may, however, be a
memorial intrusion from ll. 69–70
above: " . . . my *blood*, / Whose *youthful*
spirit"; and to read here "Rouse up

thy blood . . ." (cf. the sentiment with
H 5, III. i. 7) would by reducing the
alexandrine to a pentameter make the
line run better as the opening line of
the rhyming couplet ll. 83–4.

84.] "I rely upon my innocence and
St George for my success." For *innocence* cf. *R 3*, III. v. 20. *Traïson* says that
Bolingbroke's shield had a cross like
St George's (as Wilson points out);
but perhaps Shakespeare hardly needed inspiration from the French
chronicle to make an English knight
swear by St George.

90.] This phrase is, as Herford says,
tautologous. For "golden enfranchisement" cf. Peele's "golden libertie",
Edward I, M.S.R., l. 1077.

92. *feast*] Here simply connotes "re-
joicing", "festivity", without any
sense that battle is an eater of men;
contrast "feast of death" (*1 H 6*, IV. v.
7) and the eating Death of *John*, II. i.
352–5 and *Ham.*, v. ii. 356–7.

Take from my mouth the wish of happy years;
As gentle and as jocund as to jest   95
Go I to fight: truth hath a quiet breast.

Rich. Farewell, my lord, securely I espy
Virtue with valour couched in thine eye.
Order the trial, Marshal, and begin.

Mar. Harry of Herford, Lancaster and Derby,   100
Receive thy lance, and God defend the right!

Bol. Strong as a tower in hope, I cry amen.

Mar. Go bear this lance to Thomas, Duke of Norfolk.

1 Herald. Harry of Herford, Lancaster and Derby,
Stands here, for God, his sovereign, and himself,   105
On pain to be found false and recreant,
To prove the Duke of Norfolk, Thomas Mowbray,
A traitor to his God, his king, and him,
And dares him to set forward to the fight.

2 Herald. Here standeth Thomas Mowbray, Duke of Norfolk,
On pain to be found false and recreant,   111
Both to defend himself, and to approve
Henry of Herford, Lancaster and Derby,
To God, his sovereign, and to him disloyal,
Courageously, and with a free desire,   115
Attending but the signal to begin.

Mar. Sound trumpets, and set forward, combatants.

[*A charge sounded.*

---

94. mouth] *Q1–3, 5, F;* youth *Q4.*   101. God] *Qq;* heauen *F.*   the right]
Q1; thy right *Q2–5, F.*   108. his God] *Q1 (Hunt.), 2–5, F;* God *Q1 (Cap. and
Huth).*   109. forward] *Q1;* forwards *Q2–5, F.*   117. forward] *Q1, F;* forth
Q2–5.   S.D.] *F (after l. 116); not in Qq.*

---

95. *jest*] sport; here probably Mowbray is thinking of a chivalric masque or entertainment. To explain the word, Farmer cited Hieronimo's "pompous iest" in Kyd's *Spanish Tragedy,* I. v. 20 ff; see Wilson's note.

96. *truth . . . breast*] The sentiment is proverbial, although the form of words is Shakespeare's: see Tilley T583.

97. *securely*] confidently; the adv. goes with *couched* in l. 98.

101. *Receive . . . lance*] The com-

batants' lances were measured by the marshal to ensure their being of equal length.

102.] Compare Ps., lxi. 3: "for thou hast ben my hope, and a strong tower for me against the face of the enemie" (Noble).

112. *approve*] prove.

117. *set forward*] As Shakespeare would know from Holinshed, and elsewhere, this trial was conducted on horseback with a certain parade of mounting and dismounting (see I. i. 82 and Appendix, pp. 184–5). It is

Stay, the king hath thrown his warder down.

Rich. Let them lay by their helmets and their spears,
    And both return back to their chairs again.   120
    Withdraw with us, and let the trumpets sound,
    While we return these dukes what we decree.

                                        [*A long flourish.*

    Draw near,
    And list what with our council we have done.
    For that our kingdom's earth should not be soil'd   125
    With that dear blood which it hath fostered;

---

122. S.D.] *F; not in Qq.*   123–4.] *As Theobald; . . . list | . . . done | Qq, F.*
126. hath] *Q1–4, F; hath beene Q5.*

---

usually assumed that horses were
never used on the Elizabethan stage;
an apparent exception occurs, strange-
ly enough, in *Woodstock* itself (III. ii.
129 ff: see Rossiter, p. 223). For the
theory that horses were used in the
arena or pit of the public playhouse,
see W. Hodges, *The Globe Restored*
(London, 1953), p. 49.

118. *thrown*] *throwen* in Q1, a form
which, if reflected in the pronunciation, would regularize the metre of
this line. But we cannot be sure that it
is more than a spelling; see notes on
I. i. 46 and v. ii. 24–5.

warder] truncheon. The casting
down of the umpire's baton was the
recognized procedure for stopping the
fight: see Dillon, 'Barriers and Foot
Combats', *Archaeological Jl*, LXI (1904),
p. 285, and for a fight in 1375 similarly
terminated by the umpire see Coulton,
Life in the Middle Ages, III. 85.

120. *chairs*] See note on l. 20 above.

121. *Withdraw*] This need not mean
that Richard and the council left the
stage.

122. *While we return*] until we inform.

S.D.] The deliberation lasted two
hours in Holinshed.

125–38.] Wilson (pp. liv–v) holds
that the reasons for the banishments
are derived by Shakespeare from
Froissart, VI. 314–16. I think rather
that Shakespeare is engaged in filling
up some gaps in Holinshed with in-

vented matter. Holinshed (495/1/57
ff) says only that Richard stopped the
fight, withdrew to deliberate with his
council, and that Bushy then read out
the sentences. Froissart does give the
details of the deliberations; these
occur not on the field of combat (as in
Holinshed and Shakespeare) but *before*
the combatants meet for the second
time (the meeting represented by this
scene), and are effectively designed to
stop their meeting for actual combat
altogether; Froissart, in fact, has no
knowledge of a second meeting between Bolingbroke and Mowbray. In
Froissart the council uses the following arguments to persuade Richard to
prevent the combat: (i) it is popularly
rumoured that Richard started the
whole controversy; (ii) the Londoners
and others say that it is all part of his
play to destroy his "lygnage and the
realme of Englande"; (iii) the Londoners may therefore rise against
Richard; (iv) they hate him anyway
for his alliance by marriage to
France; (v) if the combatants come to
the field, the Londoners will take the
judgement of the trial out of Richard's
hands, because (vi) Richard should
have kept the peace between the pair,
and (vii) the fact that he did not
shows that Richard is prejudiced in
Mowbray's favour. Therefore, the
council advises Richard to prevent the
trial and banish both contestants;
Bolingbroke must be exiled for ten

And for our eyes do hate the dire aspect
Of civil wounds plough'd up with neighbours' sword,
And for we think the eagle-winged pride
Of sky-aspiring and ambitious thoughts,   130
With rival-hating envy, set on you
To wake our peace, which in our country's cradle
Draws the sweet infant breath of gentle sleep;

128. civil] Q_I (*Hunt.*), *2–5*, *F*; cruell Q_I (*Cap. and Huth*).   sword] *Qq*; swords
F.   129–33.] *not in F*.   131. rival-hating] Q_I (*Hunt.*), *2–5*; *unhyphened in*
Q_I (*Cap. and Huth*).   133. Draws] Q_I (*Hunt.*), *2–5*; Draw Q_I (*Cap. and Huth*).

years, but at the last moment "to please the people withall" Richard must "release four yere of the tenne". Richard agrees to everything, and in Froissart's next chapter (VI. 316), pronounces the sentences, giving the following feeble official reasons: (i) Mowbray—"bycause he hath brought this realme into this trouble, by reason of his wordes, wherin he canne not make profe"; (ii) Bolingbroke—"bycause he hathe displeased us, and that he is the chiefe cause of the banysshment of therle Marshall". I am not convinced that Richard's speech here reflects any of these precisely-described intrigues; it is a generalized homily on civil war and political ambition, which Shakespeare invented, perhaps with help from the *Mirror* (see note on ll. 125–6), to fill the gap left by Holinshed's failure to describe what lay behind Richard's action. Also, the striking discrepancy between the two sentences—life for Mowbray, ten years for Bolingbroke—is, although the political reasons for it are clearly stated by Froissart, left quite unexplained by Shakespeare as also by Holinshed—another indication that Froissart has not affected the passage; see also, on the reduction of Bolingbroke's sentence, note on l. 211 below.

125. *For that*] in order that.

125–6. The only source which mentions this reason for stopping the fight is *Mirror*, p. 106, "Lord Mowbray", ll. 141–5: "And for to auoyde the

sheddynge of our bloode, / with shame and death, which one must nedes haue had / The King through counsaile of the lordes thought good / To banysh both".

127. *for*] because.

129–38. *And for we think . . . kindred's blood*] The passage is confused because the *peace* of l. 132, roused by drums and trumpets, frights the *fair peace* of l. 137. Herford's view that the "picturesque incoherence" of his language shows that Richard is concealing his motives is unconvincing: Kittredge, following Steevens, produces a paraphrase which ignores grammatical difficulties. F solved the problem by omitting ll. 129–33; "This is sense," said Warburton, but Pollard comments that it "leaves the sword which is to plow up civil wounds to be roused by drums in rather an awkward manner . . . the obvious difficulty is surmounted, though in so clumsy a manner as to make it incredible that the omission was either made or approved by Shakespeare himself". The mess may be due to hasty composition: Wilson suggests that ll. 134–8 and ll. 129–33 are alternative drafts left side by side in the MS; that ll. 129–33 was the later attempt, mistakenly cancelled by the prompter, and ll. 134–8 the first attempt which Shakespeare forgot to delete. The omission of five lines would make this important speech, the pivot of the scene, rather short.

131. *set on you*] i.e. "set you on".

Which so rous'd up with boist'rous untun'd drums,
With harsh-resounding trumpets' dreadful bray,   135
And grating shock of wrathful iron arms,
Might from our quiet confines fright fair peace,
And make us wade even in our kindred's blood—
Therefore we banish you our territories.
You, cousin Herford, upon pain of life,   140
Till twice five summers have enrich'd our fields,
Shall not regreet our fair dominions,
But tread the stranger paths of banishment.

Bol. Your will be done; this must my comfort be,
That sun that warms you here, shall shine on me,   145
And those his golden beams to you here lent
Shall point on me and gild my banishment.

Rich. Norfolk, for thee remains a heavier doom,
Which I with some unwillingness pronounce.
The sly slow hours shall not determinate   150
The dateless limit of thy dear exile;
The hopeless word of "never to return"
Breathe I against thee, upon pain of life.

---

134. drums] *Q1, 3–5, F;* drumme *Q2.*   136. wrathful iron] *Q1 (Hunt.), 2–5, F;*
harsh resounding *Q1 (Cap. and Huth).*   140. life] *Qq;* death *F.*   141. fields]
Q1, F; field *Q2–5.*   146. to] *Q1, F;* unto *Q2–5.*

136. *shock*] A technical term for two horses striking together in combat: cf. III. iii. 56 and see Sieveking in *Shakespeare's England,* II. 409.

wrathful iron] Misprinted as *harsh resounding* in Q1 (Cap. and Huth): the compositor had the earlier phrase running in his head, or misheard owing to printing-house dictation.

140. *upon . . . life*] i.e. "upon pain of death"; *life* will be the forfeit paid as a punishment if you disobey: see *O.E.D. s.v.* pain I. b: cf. l. 153 below. Wilson points out that Shakespeare, except here, prefers "upon paine of death" (which F reads at l. 140) and suggests that Shakespeare caught the rarer phrase from Berners' Froissart, where it occurs frequently. But Shakespeare could have found it in *Woodstock* (IV. iii. 171) too: see Rossiter's note, pp. 230–1.

142. *regreet*] See note on l. 67 above.

143. *stranger*] foreign.

145.] Tilley (S985) cfs. with the proverb "the sun shines upon all alike"; cf. the passage from *Euphues* quoted in note to ll. 275–6 below.

146. *lent*] afforded.

147. *point on me*] aim themselves at, or have reference to, me; cf. *Oth.,* v. ii. 49: "These are portents; but yet I hope, I hope, / They do not point on me."

150. *sly*] stealthy.

determinate] put an end to (legal vb.): cf. *Sonn.,* LXXXVII. 4, and *Woodstock,* v. iii. 32: "This day shall here determinate all wrongs."

151. *dateless limit*] *Date* here = limit (cf. *Sonn.,* XIV. 14: "Thy end is . . . beauty's . . . date"), and the phrase means "limitless period".

Mow. A heavy sentence, my most sovereign liege,
 And all unlook'd for from your Highness' mouth; 155
 A dearer merit, not so deep a maim
 As to be cast forth in the common air,
 Have I deserved at your Highness' hands.
 The language I have learnt these forty years,
 My native English, now I must forgo, 160
 And now my tongue's use is to me no more
 Than an unstringed viol or a harp,
 Or like a cunning instrument cas'd up—
 Or being open, put into his hands
 That knows no touch to tune the harmony. 165
 Within my mouth you have engaol'd my tongue,
 Doubly portcullis'd with my teeth and lips,
 And dull unfeeling barren ignorance
 Is made my gaoler to attend on me.
 I am too old to fawn upon a nurse, 170
 Too far in years to be a pupil now:
 What is thy sentence then but speechless death,
 Which robs my tongue from breathing native breath?

159. learnt] *Q1, 2;* learnd *Q3–5, F.* 167. portcullis'd] portculist *Q1 (Cap. and Huth);* portcullist *Q1 (Hunt.), 2, 3;* percullist *Q4, 5, F.* 172. then] *F;* not in *Qq.*

155.] Wilson quotes Hol. 495/2/18: "[Mowbray] was in hope . . . that he should have beene borne out in the matter by the king, which when it fell out otherwise, it greeued him not a little."

156.] "A more valuable reward, not an injury so deep . . ."

161. *my tongue's . . . more*] "My tongue is no more use to me . . ." or "my power of using my tongue [for speaking English] is no more to me . . ." In the similitudes of the next lines, *tongue* is both the physical organ and the "native language" which it speaks: both useless instruments.

162. *viol*] instrument having from three to six strings played with a bow.

165. *knows no touch*] "has no skill in playing"; *touch* = fingering (in music).

166. *engaol'd*] The spelling of Q1

(*engaold* Q1, 2; *ingayld* Q3, 5; *ingaylde* Q4) may indicate hard pronunciation of the *g*; whether the *g* in *gaol/jail* was hard or soft was then as uncertain ås the words' spelling still is: see note on *2 Return from Parnassus* 415, in *Three Parnassus Plays*, ed. Leishman, p. 252.

167.] Tilley (T424) cfs. the line with proverbial references to teeth as guardians of the tongue, e.g. Greene, *Penelope's Web* (1587), *Works,* ed. Grosart, v. 221: "Nature by fortefying the tongue, would teach how precious and necessarie a vertue silence is, for she has placed before it the Bulwarke of the teeth"; the same idea is found in *Euphues,* Bond, I. 279.

170–1.] Mowbray is saying that he is too advanced in years to learn to speak as a baby learns from his nurse.

Rich. It boots thee not to be compassionate;
　　After our sentence plaining comes too late.   175
Mow. Then thus I turn me from my country's light,
　　To dwell in solemn shades of endless night.
Rich. Return again, and take an oath with thee.
　　Lay on our royal sword your banish'd hands,
　　Swear by the duty that you owe to God—   180
　　Our part therein we banish with yourselves—
　　To keep the oath that we administer:
　　You never shall, so help you truth and God,
　　Embrace each other's love in banishment,
　　Nor never look upon each other's face,   185
　　Nor never write, regreet, nor reconcile
　　This louring tempest of your home-bred hate,
　　Nor never by advised purpose meet
　　To plot, contrive, or complot any ill
　　'Gainst us, our state, our subjects, or our land.   190
Bol. I swear.
Mow. And I, to keep all this.
Bol. Norfolk, so far as to mine enemy:
　　By this time, had the king permitted us,

180. you owe] *F;* y'owe *Qq.*   God] *Qq;* heauen *F.*   183. God] *Qq;* heauen
F.   185. never] *Qq;* euer *F.*   186. never] *Qq;* euer *F.*   nor] *Qq;* or *F.*
187. louring] *Q1, 2, F;* louing *Q3–5.*   188. never] *Qq;* euer *F.*   193. far]
F4; fare *Qq, F1;* farre *Q6, F2, 3.*   enemy:] *Q1, 2, 4, 5;* enemie, *Q3, F.*

174. *to be compassionate*] "to be sorry
for yourself" or "to make yourself an
object of pity".
175. *plaining*] complaining.
177.] Cf. v. vi. 43 (of the banished
Exton).
179. *sword*] The oath is taken on the
cross formed by blade, hilt, and
guard.
181.] "In banishing you we absolve
you from your duty to us."
186. *regreet*] Cf. I. iii. 67 and note,
I. iii. 142.
reconcile] "To reconcile a tempest"
is awkward; the metaphor from "to
reconcile a quarrel" is not born until
Shakespeare reaches the second part
of the thought.
189. *plot . . . complot*] This is "legal

tautology", as Craig points out.
193. *Norfolk . . . enemy*] Most edd.
adopt the reading of F2; *fare* (Qq, F)
may be due to Q1's failure to repeat
the "r" in an intended spelling *farre*
(used elsewhere in Q1, e.g., I. iii. 252).
Wilson follows Qq and F, interpreting
the phrase as "Bolingbroke will not
bid Mowbray farewell but only the
'fare' (= condition of life) he would
wish as to an enemy." The grammar
of this seems very queer. The placing
of the phrase at the beginning of the
speech forcibly suggests that it is an
induction to the solemn appeal Bolingbroke is about to make, intimating
(as John says) that "while still holding
Mowbray as his enemy he wishes to
say certain things to him".

One of our souls had wand'red in the air,   195
Banish'd this frail sepulchre of our flesh,
As now our flesh is banish'd from this land—
Confess thy treasons ere thou fly the realm;
Since thou hast far to go, bear not along
The clogging burthen of a guilty soul.   200
Mow. No, Bolingbroke, if ever I were traitor,
My name be blotted from the book of life,
And I from heaven banish'd as from hence!
But what thou art, God, thou, and I do know,
And all too soon, I fear, the king shall rue.   205
Farewell, my liege. Now no way can I stray—
Save back to England all the world's my way.   [*Exit.*
Rich. Uncle, even in the glasses of thine eyes
I see thy grieved heart. Thy sad aspect
Hath from the number of his banish'd years   210
Pluck'd four away. [*To Boling.*] Six frozen winters spent,

198. the] *Qq;* this *F.*   204. God] *Qq;* heauen *F.*   206. stray—] *Wilson;*
stray, *Qq, F;* stray; *Capell.*   207. England] *Q1–3;* England, *Q4, 5, F.*   211.
S.D.] *Steevens; not in Qq, F.*

196. *sepulchre*] Pronounced *sepúlcher*;
cf. the pronunciation of the verb,
Gent., IV. ii. 113; *Lr.*, II. iv. 130.
   200. *clogging*] burdening: cf. V. vi.
20 "With clog of conscience" (Wilson) and note.
   202.] Noble cfs. Rev., iii. 5: "He
that overcommeth, shalbe thus clothed
in white aray, and I wil not blot out
his name out of the booke of life."
The passage is evidence for Shakespeare's use of the Bishops' Bible (first
edn, 1568): see Noble, p. 73, and cf.
IV. i. 236.
   206–7. *Now . . . way*] "I can never
go astray now, except in returning to
England; I am free to wander anywhere in the world" or "I can never
go astray now, I am free to wander
anywhere in the world, save back to
England." The punctuation of Q1
favours the latter, but may be mis-
leading. The sentiment is from Lyly,
Letters of Euphues in *Euphues: the
Anatomy of Wyt*, Bond, I. 315: "When
thou hast not one place assigned

thee wherein to liue, but one forbidden thee which thou must leaue,
then thou beeing denied but one, that
excepted thou maist choose any."
   208–9. *glasses . . . heart*] Gaunt's
weeping eyes are compared to looking-glasses which mirror his internal
disposition: see Tilley E231; cf. *Spanish Tragedie*, ed. Boas, II. v. 50: "close
vp the glasses of his sight".
   210. *banish'd years*] i.e. "the years he
must spend in banishment".
   211.] Shakespeare plainly did not
know, or did not care to follow, the
reasons provided in Froissart for this
reduction in the period of Bolingbroke's exile. Froissart says that the
council advised Richard beforehand
to make this gesture of clemency to
their favourite to "please the people"
(the discontented Londoners). Holinshed gives no explanation, and so
Shakespeare invents his own; the remission of the sentence on the aged
father's plea has obvious dramatic
point.

Return with welcome home from banishment.
Bol. How long a time lies in one little word!
Four lagging winters and four wanton springs
End in a word: such is the breath of kings.   215
Gaunt. I thank my liege that in regard of me
He shortens four years of my son's exile,
But little vantage shall I reap thereby;
For ere the six years that he hath to spend
Can change their moons, and bring their times about,
My oil-dried lamp and time-bewasted light   221
Shall be extinct with age and endless night,
My inch of taper will be burnt and done,
And blindfold Death not let me see my son.
Rich. Why, uncle, thou hast many years to live.   225
Gaunt. But not a minute, king, that thou canst give:
Shorten my days thou canst with sullen sorrow,
And pluck nights from me, but not lend a morrow;
Thou canst help time to furrow me with age,
But stop no wrinkle in his pilgrimage;   230
Thy word is current with him for my death,

---

215. a] *Q1–4, F;* one *Q5.*   222. extinct] *Q2–5, F;* extint *Q1.*   night] *Q4, 5, F;* nights *Q1–3.*   223. inch] *Q3–5, F;* intch *Q1, 2.*   227. sullen] *Qq;* sudden *F.*

---

221. *oil-dried lamp*] Cf. *1 H 6*, II. v. 8, the dying Mortimer: "These eyes, like lamps whose wasting oil is spent, / Wax dim"; *All's W.*, I. ii. 59. The thought may have a proverbial basis: see Tilley O29 and F. P. Wilson, *R.E.S.*, N.S., III (1952), 197.

222. *extinct with*] extinguished by.

223.] One of a series of Shakespearian images in which man's end is compared to the extinction of taper or candle: cf. *3 H 6*, II. vi. 1; *2 H 4*, I. ii. 148; *Mac.*, v. v. 22: see Tilley C41, and cf. Job, xviii. 6, Ps., xviii. 28. For a possible origin of this image in Barnabe Googe's translation of Palingenius, *The Zodiake of Life* (1576 edn) and de la Primaudaye's *The French Academie* (four parts, 1586–1618), see J. E. Hankins, *Shakespeare's Derived Imagery*, 1953, p. 46.

224. *blindfold Death*] The traditional image of Death, which is without eyes because an eyeless skull (cf. *Cym.*, v. iv. 177–8) has perhaps coalesced with that of Atropos, the blindfold thread-cutting Destiny (see Hankins, work cited in preceding note, p. 46). Herford interprets as "the state of death which involves loss of sight"; but *blindfold*, an adj. more easily applied to an emblematic personification than to a state, suggests that Shakespeare is personifying here.

230.] "But stop no wrinkle that comes as time travels onwards."

231–2.] A "buying" metaphor: "Time will accept Richard's order for Gaunt's death as though it were good current coin of the realm, but, once Gaunt has died, the realm itself cannot buy his life again": cf. IV. i. 264.

But dead, thy kingdom cannot buy my breath.
Rich. Thy son is banish'd upon good advice,
Whereto thy tongue a party-verdict gave:
Why at our justice seem'st thou then to lour?   235
Gaunt. Things sweet to taste prove in digestion sour.
You urg'd me as a judge, but I had rather
You would have bid me argue like a father.
O, had it been a stranger, not my child,
To smooth his fault I should have been more mild.   240
A partial slander sought I to avoid,
And in the sentence my own life destroy'd.
Alas, I look'd when some of you should say
I was too strict to make mine own away;
But you gave leave to my unwilling tongue   245
Against my will to do myself this wrong.
Rich. Cousin, farewell—and uncle, bid him so,
Six years we banish him and he shall go.
                 [*Flourish. Exeunt King Richard and train.*]
Aum. Cousin, farewell; what presence must not know,
From where you do remain let paper show.   250

233. upon] *Q1, F;* with *Q2–5.*   234. tongue a party-verdict] *F;* tong a party
verdict *Q1;* tongue, a party, verdict *Q2–5.*   237. urg'd] *Q1, F;* vrge *Q2–5.*
239–42.] *Not in F.*   239. had it] had't *Qq.*   240. should] *Q1;* would *Q2–5.*
241. sought] *Q1 (Hunt. and Huth),* 3–5; ought *Q1 (Cap.),* 2.   248. S.D.]
Wright. Exit. Q1; Exit. Flourish. F; not in Q2–5.

234. *party-verdict*] "one person's
share of a joint verdict" (*O.E.D.*).
That Gaunt agreed to Bolingbroke's
exile is stated in Holinshed's version of
the Bishop of Carlisle's speech at the
deposition (Hol. 512/2/54: see Appendix, p. 195 and IV. i. 114 ff.). It is also
stated in Hall, p. 14, Créton, pp. 106
and 120, and implied in Froissart, VI.
319; it is not necessary to suppose
that Shakespeare required more than
Holinshed's testimony.
236.] A proverb (Tilley M1265,
supplemented by F. P. Wilson,
R.E.S., N.S., III (1952), 197), deriving
from the book in Rev., x. 9–10 that
was "sweet in the mouth and bitter in
the belly". Cf. *Lucr.,* 699, Lucretia's
rape as it appeared to Tarquin: "His

taste delicious, in digestion souring".
Lyly reverses the proverb in his letter
on exile, which Shakespeare uses elsewhere in this scene, Bond, I. 313.
241. *partial slander*] = the reproach
of partiality (Wilson).
243. *look'd when*] expected that.
244. *to make*] in making.
249–50.] It is Aumerle who accompanies Bolingbroke "to the next high
way" (I. iv. 4), so it is strange that he
should take what appears to be a final
leave here. His stilted couplet means:
"As our personal intercourse is sus-
pended, write to me from your new
abode what otherwise I might have
learnt from your own mouth."
Aumerle perhaps leaves the stage
after this.

Mar. My lord, no leave take I, for I will ride
    As far as land will let me by your side.
Gaunt. O, to what purpose dost thou hoard thy words,
    That thou returnest no greeting to thy friends?
Bol. I have too few to take my leave of you,   255
    When the tongue's office should be prodigal
    To breathe the abundant dolour of the heart.
Gaunt. Thy grief is but thy absence for a time.
Bol. Joy absent, grief is present for that time.
Gaunt. What is six winters? they are quickly gone— 260
Bol. To men in joy; but grief makes one hour ten.
Gaunt. Call it a travel that thou tak'st for pleasure.
Bol. My heart will sigh when I miscall it so,
    Which finds it an inforced pilgrimage.
Gaunt. The sullen passage of thy weary steps   265
    Esteem as foil wherein thou art to set
    The precious jewel of thy home return.
Bol. Nay, rather, every tedious stride I make
    Will but remember me what a deal of world
    I wander from the jewels that I love.   270
    Must I not serve a long apprenticehood

266. as foil] *Q1;* a foyle *Q2;* a soyle *Q 3–5, F.*   268–93.] *Not in F.*   269. a deal] *Q1–3;* deale *Q4, 5.*

251–2.] Cf. *Mer. V.,*II.ii.102–3. The marshal (cf. note on I. i. 204) was the Duke of Surrey, a partisan of Richard's (see IV. i. 60 ff); his friendly attitude to Bolingbroke here is surprising. Newbolt suggests that Shakespeare had not realized the marshal's identity (although Holinshed states it); Capell first separated the two persons, placing an additional "Lord Marshal" in his Dramatis Personae.

256. *office*] proper function or duty.
257. *to breathe*] in breathing: cf. l. 244 above.
258–9. *Thy grief . . . grief*] A play on two meanings, "complaint" and "sorrow".
266. *foil*] setting. A thin leaf of metal set behind a *jewel* (l. 267) to enhance its lustre (Deighton): for the image, cf. II. i. 46 and note.
270. *jewels*] Deighton cfs. *Lr.,* I. i.

267, where Cordelia calls her sisters "the jewels of our father".
271–4.] Many differing interpretations of the lines are due to difficulty over the metaphor *apprenticehood— freedom—journeyman* and apparent confusion of tense. Bolingbroke complains that he must serve an apprenticeship in foreign travel and experiences ("passages"), and then, when he has qualified ("having my freedom", a technical term for the apprentice's release from his indentures), will be able to boast that he was only a journeyman (qualified artisan working for day-wages) to grief. A journeyman, however, is exactly what a trained apprentice does become; Shakespeare surely did not confuse the two, and therefore we would expect *am,* not *was,* in l. 274, since Bolingbroke seems to be saying: "When I am no longer a prentice-

To foreign passages, and in the end,
Having my freedom, boast of nothing else
But that I was a journeyman to grief?
Gaunt. All places that the eye of heaven visits　　275
Are to a wise man ports and happy havens.
Teach thy necessity to reason thus—
There is no virtue like necessity.
Think not the king did banish thee,

277. thus—] *Wilson;* thus, *Qq.*

traveller, I shall only be able to say that I am a journeyman to grief, not to a better master." I know no reason for supposing that Bolingbroke is thinking of the apprentice who became merely a journeyman instead of a master as a failure; and the supposition creates fresh problems—for it is *grief* who must be and remain the *master*, if the conceit is to retain any coherence. Theobald thought the allusions "not in the sublime taste".

275–6. *wise man*] A "wiseman" (so Q1) = "philosopher", "sage", with a strong overtone of Stoic meaning (cf. III. ii. 178–9 and note). The sentiment of the lines is proverbial (Tilley M426), but Shakespeare, as Malone first indicated, was reminded of it by a recent reading of Lyly's free version of Plutarch's *De Exilio* in *Euphues: the Anatomy of Wyt* (1578) which had already been drawn upon in ll. 145, 206, and 236: "*Plato* would neuer accompt him banished yt had the Sunne, Fire, Aire, Water & Earth, that he had before, where he felt the Winters blast and the Summers blaze, wher ye same Sunne & the same Moone shined, whereby he noted that euery place was a countrey to a wise man, and all partes a pallaice to a quiet minde" (Bond, I. 314): cf. *ibid.*, p. 316: "the wiseman lyueth as well in a farre country as in his owne home." Baldwin's attempt (*Shakspere's Small Latine . . .* II. 427–8) to prove a direct debt to Ovid, *Fasti*, I. 493: "Omne solum forti patria est", is ingenious but unconvincing.

havens] Kökeritz (p. 84) suggests a homonymic pun on *heavens* and *havens*, and for further discussion of the same pun in *Cym.*, III. ii. 60, see Kökeritz in *R.E.S.*, XXIII (1947), 313–14. Cf. *Eastward Hoe*, IV. i. 22–4: "see one of her passengers labouring for his life, to land at this Hauen here; pray heauen he may recouer it" (Herford and Simpson, *Ben Jonson*, IV. 577).

278.] An old phrase, used by Chaucer (by whose time it was already proverbial: see note on *The Knight's Tale* 3041–2 in *Poetical Works*, ed. F. N. Robinson, p. 785) and twice by Shakespeare—cf. *Gent.*, IV. i. 62.

279.] The line is a foot short. It is possible that Shakespeare wrote "Think not thou the King did banish thee / But thou the King." But this would obscure the antithesis in rather a clumsy way,

279–80. *Think . . . king*] The idea comes from the same passage in Lyly's *Euphues* (see note on l. 275 above): "when it was cast in *Diogenes* teeth that the *Synoponetes* had banished hym *Pontus*, yea, sayde hee, I them of *Diogenes*", Bond, I. 314. Shakespeare uses the idea again in *Cor.*, III. iii. 125. The passage (from l. 278, and cf. l. 262 above) may also owe something to Marlowe, *Edward II*, where Leicester comforts the imprisoned Edward: "Be patient, good my lord, cease to lament, / Imagine Killingworth Castle were your court, / And that you lay for pleasure here a space, / Not of compulsion or necessity."

But thou the king. Woe doth the heavier sit   280
Where it perceives it is but faintly borne.
Go, say I sent thee forth to purchase honour,
And not the king exil'd thee; or suppose
Devouring pestilence hangs in our air,
And thou art flying to a fresher clime.   285
Look what thy soul holds dear, imagine it
To lie that way thou goest, not whence thou com'st.
Suppose the singing birds musicians,
The grass whereon thou tread'st the presence
    strew'd,
The flowers fair ladies, and thy steps no more   290
Than a delightful measure or a dance;
For gnarling sorrow hath less power to bite
The man that mocks at it and sets it light.

Bol. O, who can hold a fire in his hand   †
By thinking on the frosty Caucasus?   295
Or cloy the hungry edge of appetite
By bare imagination of a feast?
Or wallow naked in December snow
By thinking on fantastic summer's heat?
O no, the apprehension of the good   300

---

280. *king. Woe*] *Q1–3;* king, who *Q4, 5.*

281. *faintly*] faint-heartedly.

282. *purchase*] acquire: see note by
F. L. Lucas, *Works of John Webster,* II.
157.

286. *Look what*] whatever; see note
on I. i. 87.

289. *presence strew'd*] the royal presence-chamber strewed with rushes.
See E. K. Chambers in *Shakespeare's
England,* I. 91, quoting from Paul
Hentzer's account of Elizabeth's
procession to chapel at Greenwich,
1598: "We were admitted . . . into
the presence-chamber, hung with
rich tapestry, and the floor after
the English fashion strewed with
hay."

291. *measure*] a slow, stately dance:
see *Ado,* II. i. 67.

292. *gnarling*] snarling: cf. *2 H 6,*

III. i. 192: "wolves are gnarling who
shall gnaw thee first", and see *O.E.D.*
Ll. 292–3 are anthologized in *England's Parnassus,* no. 1560, in the section "Of Sorrow".

294–9. *fire*] Pronounced as a disyllable and spelled *fier* in Q1, 4, 5. As
Malone noted, this passage was suggested by the following in Lyly's
Euphues (see note on l. 275 above):
"hee that is colde doth not couer himselfe wyth care, but wyth clothes, he
that is washed in ye rayne dryeth himselfe by the fire not by his fancie, and
thou which art bannished oughtest
not with teares to bewaile thy hap.
but with wisedome to heale thy hurt"
(Bond, I. 313–14).

299. *fantastic . . . heat*] imagined heat
of summer.

Gives but the greater feeling to the worse.
Fell sorrow's tooth doth never rankle more
Than when he bites, but lanceth not the sore.
Gaunt. Come, come, my son, I'll bring thee on thy way,
Had I thy youth and cause, I would not stay.   305
Bol. Then, England's ground, farewell; sweet soil, adieu,
My mother and my nurse that bears me yet!
Where'er I wander boast of this I can,
Though banish'd, yet a true-born Englishman.   [*Exeunt.*

SCENE IV.—[*The Court*]

[*Enter the* KING *with* BAGOT *and* GREENE *at one door; and
the* LORD AUMERLE *at another.*]

Rich. We did observe. Cousin Aumerle,

301. Gives] *Q 1–4, F*; Giue *Q 5.*   302. never] *Qq*; euer *F.*   303. he] *Q 1*; it
Q 2–5, F.   307. that] *Qq*; which *F.*   309. S.D.] *Qq; not in F.*

Scene IV
Location.] *Theobald; not in Qq, F.*   S.D.] *Wilson; Enter the King with Bushie &c.
at one dore, and the Lord Aumarle at another. Qq; Enter King, Aumerle, Greene, and
Bagot. F.*

301. *the worse*] i.e. the things worse
(than "good") which we endure.
302–3.] i.e. "The biting animal
Sorrow (see l. 292 above) makes the
most festering of his wounds ("doth
never rankle more") when he bites
without making a piercing wound
like that made by a surgeon's lance."
Lanceth carries the idea of curing by
medical treatment. Bolingbroke implies that on occasions Sorrow, in the
act of making its wound ("sore"),
also goes deep enough to probe it like
a surgeon and so starts the cure. He is
complaining that Gaunt is trying to
blunt the probe of surgeon Sorrow (or
the tooth of animal Sorrow) with silly
consolations so that the wound it
makes will fester. These lines are
anthologized in *England's Parnassus*,
no. 1557, in the section "Of Sorrow".
307.] See note on II. i. 51.

Scene IV
MATERIAL. What Richard "observes" in l. 1 of this scene is Bolingbroke's "courtship to the common
people", which he goes on to describe
at ll. 23 ff. This, I believe, derives ultimately from Hol., 495/2/25: see note
on ll. 24–36 below. The cold parting
between Aumerle and Bolingbroke,
described in ll. 3 ff, seems entirely
Shakespeare's invention. The first
mention of the Irish campaign (see
l. 38 below) occurs in Hol., 496/2/70.
Shakespeare tends to represent Richard's fiscal exactions, "farming" and
"blank charters", both of which are
described by Holinshed (496/1/11 ff
and 496/1/64 ff), as if they were contrived especially to pay for the Irish
campaign (see ll. 38–9, 47, 51), but
Holinshed does not connect them, nor
do any of the other sources; Shake-

How far brought you high Herford on his way?

Aum. I brought high Herford, if you call him so,
But to the next highway, and there I left him.

Rich. And say, what store of parting tears were shed?   5

Aum. Faith, none for me, except the north-east wind,
Which then blew bitterly against our faces,
Awak'd the sleeping rheum, and so by chance
Did grace our hollow parting with a tear.

Rich. What said our cousin when you parted with him?   10

Aum. "Farewell"—
And, for my heart disdained that my tongue
Should so profane the word, that taught me craft
To counterfeit oppression of such grief
That words seem'd buried in my sorrow's grave.   15
Marry, would the word "farewell" have length'ned
        hours
And added years to his short banishment,
He should have had a volume of farewells;
But since it would not, he had none of me.

Rich. He is our cousin, cousin, but 'tis doubt,   20

---

7. blew] *Qq;* grew *F.*   faces] *Q1, 2;* face *Q3–5, F.*   8. sleeping] *Q1, 2;*
sleepie *Q3–5, F.*   10. our] *Q1, F;* your *Q2–5.*   11–12. "Farewell" /
. . . tongue /] *As Pope;* Farewel . . . tongue / *Qq, F.*   15. words] *Qq;* word *F.*
20. cousin, cousin] *F;* Coosens Coosin *Qq.*

---

speare may have been adapting from Holinshed's account during the fourth year of Richard's reign (428/2/37) of the "new and strange subsidie or taske granted for the kings use, and towards the charges of this armie that went ouer into France with the earle of Buckingham": see also note on l. 45 below. Gaunt's death is reported by Hol., 496/1/22 on the same page that deals with the beginning of the Irish war; for more on this, see II. i, note on material.

3–4.] Aumerle plays impudently on *high* and *highway.*

6. *for me*] for my part.

8. *rheum*] watery discharge; to be distinguished from "the rheum", a morbid condition (as in *Meas.*, III. i. 31, "the gout, serpigo and the rheum"). The idea of tears as "mere rheum" is several times used by Shakespeare for ironic and diminishing effect, e.g. *Ado*, v. ii. 72, *John*, IV. iii. 108, *Cor.*, v. vi. 46 ("a few drops of women's rheum, which are / As cheap as lies").

12. *for*] because.

13. *that*] defining the previous phrase *for . . . word.*

14. *counterfeit . . . grief*] "pretend I was oppressed with such grief . . ."

15. *my . . . grave*] i.e. a grave made by my sorrow.

20–2. *cousin, cousin*] Aumerle, Richard and Bolingbroke were cousins, being sons of three brothers. "Aumerle is reminded with a touch of formality that Hereford is his own cousin, and there is an ironical suggestion that in spite of this he may not be recalled" (Pollard, pp. 83–4). The

When time shall call him home from banishment,
Whether our kinsman come to see his friends.
Ourself and Bushy
Observ'd his courtship to the common people,

22. come] *Q1, 2, F; comes Q3–5.*   22–3. friends. / Ourself and Bushy /] *Qq; friends, / Our selfe, and Bushy: heere Bagot and Greene / F.*

ironical suggestion in ll. 20–2 may be paraphrased as a threatening sneer: "It's doubtful, when the period of his banishment ends, whether this kinsman of ours will be permitted to come and see his dear cousins." Kittredge's suggestion that Richard means that he suspects that when Bolingbroke comes back he will return as an enemy, not a friend, seems less likely.

23. *Ourself and Bushy*] The half-line here has to be taken together with the S.D. of Q1 at l. 1 and with what occurs at ll. 52–3; see Wilson, p. 150. Q1's version may have happened thus: (i) Shakespeare originally wrote, intending, as the Q1 S.D. shows ["Enter the King with Bushie. &c. . . ."], to have all three favourites on the stage from the beginning of the scene: "Our selfe and Bushie heere, Bagot and Greene". They are all named in order to introduce them to the audience on this their first speaking appearance. (ii) It was decided to economize on actors by having Bushy, rather than a Messenger, bring the news at l. 52 [see note on that line]; ll. 52–3 were altered accordingly. (iii) When the copy for Q1 was prepared Bushy's entrance later on in this scene was noticed (but not his entrance at the beginning of the scene) and *heere*, together with the last three words of the line, was struck out as inconsistent with it. At the same time the alteration of ll. 52–3 was misread, in the way suggested in the note at that point. F's version may have happened thus: (*a*) transcription for the prompt-book from the foul papers was done after stage ii above, and the original line thus preserved in the prompt-book. (*b*) In the prompt-book

the S.D. at l. 1 was eventually brought into line with the S.D. at l. 52 as "Enter King, Aumerle, Greene and Bagot." (*c*) When the copy of Q3 was being prepared for printing for F, the prompt-book was consulted, and the original l. 23 inserted in the copy of Q3. The comma after *friends* and the colon in l. 23 [F] is either an attempt by F to emend with the S.D.s at ll. 1 and 52 in mind, or reflects stage-practice from the prompt-book; either way, the actor is meant to speak the [F] lines as though *Our selfe and Bushie* are in apposition to *friends*. This makes l. 23 a very awkward one. H. F. Brooks suggests that the line may have been altered in the prompt-book: *here* struck out and inserted between *Bagot* and *and Greene* (incidentally, this is the way Q6 emends F: *Our selfe and Bushy, Bagot here and Greene.*). F may have missed these alterations if they were carelessly done. If they were made, it would explain why the prompter did not eventually strike out the last four words of the line as did whoever prepared the foul papers as copy for Q1, since it would seem better to do this than to tolerate the awkwardness of what is represented by the putative emendations of F. The suggested prompt-book change would have preserved Shakespeare's conjectural intention of introducing the three favourites by name, very necessary for the audience's sake.

24–36.] More of Richard's motives for banishing Bolingbroke are revealed. There may be a debt to Daniel, *C.W.*, I, st. 64, who expands a hint in Froissart (VI. 314) to make Richard's fear of Bolingbroke's in-

How he did seem to dive into their hearts   25
With humble and familiar courtesy;
What reverence he did throw away on slaves,
Wooing poor craftsmen with the craft of smiles
And patient underbearing of his fortune,
As 'twere to banish their affects with him.   30
Off goes his bonnet to an oyster-wench;

27. What] *Q1* (*Hunt. and Huth*), *F; With Q1 (Cap.*), *2–5.*   28. smiles] *Qq;* soules *F.*

creasing popularity, should he win the combat, the sole motive for the ban on the trial and the banishment of the appellants. Shakespeare could, however, have read of Bolingbroke's popularity in Holinshed (495/2/25): "A wonder it was to see what number of people ran after him in euerie towne and street where he came, before he tooke the sea, lamenting and bewailing his departure, as who would saie, that when he departed, the onelie shield, defense and comfort of the commonwealth was vaded and gone", and it was not beyond Shakespeare to infer from this Richard's jealousy of Bolingbroke as a motive for exiling him—Shakespeare nowhere makes Richard display this motive for the act of banishment—but for preventing his return (see ll. 20–2 above). The timing of Richard's expression of his jealousy (after Bolingbroke has left) suggests also that Shakespeare thought of Richard becoming aware of Bolingbroke's popularity owing to the national outcry when he set sail: this is consistent with Holinshed's timing, not with Froissart's or Daniel's, who both see Bolingbroke's popularity as a factor in the crisis at an earlier stage of its development than Bolingbroke's final departure from England. It is true, as Wilson says, that Froissart's account of the popular dismay at Bolingbroke's departure is much vivider than Holinshed's, but the point is not, I think, relevant: Froissart (like Holinshed and Daniel) describes how the people behaved to

Bolingbroke; this speech describes how Bolingbroke behaves to the people with a wealth of imaginative detail quite independent of the historical sources. For Wilson's view that the speech is developed from a phrase describing Bolingbroke's behaviour on his *return* to London as king (Froissart, VI. 361), see note on v. ii. 18. G. B. Harrison (*T.L.S.*, 20 Nov. 1930; 15 Oct. 1931) suggested that when the passage was printed in Q1 it would be construed by contemporary readers as a reference to the behaviour of the Earl of Essex; cf. note on l. 31 below and Introduction, p. lviii.

29. *underbearing*] endurance. Wilson points out the use of the verb *underbear* in *John*, III. i. 65; not elsewhere in Shakespeare.

30.] i.e. "as if he were trying to carry away into exile with him the affections which the people ought to have for me as their king."

31.] Brereton (p. 102) points out that this line is echoed in an anonymous poem addressed to Ralegh, apparently written after Ralegh's condemnation in November 1603. The poem contrasts Ralegh's haughty bearing with Essex's humility: "Renowned Essex, as he past the streets, / Would vaile his bonett to an oyster wife, / And with a kind of humble congie greete / The vulgar sorte that did admire his life". The poem is printed in Percy Society (London), *Early English Poetry*, xv, *Poetical Miscellanies*, ed. Halliwell, p. 17. Another possible echo of this line (see G. B. Harrison,

A brace of draymen bid God speed him well,
And had the tribute of his supple knee,
With "Thanks, my countrymen, my loving friends"—
As were our England in reversion his,   35
And he our subjects' next degree in hope.
Greene. Well, he is gone; and with him go these thoughts.
Now for the rebels which stand out in Ireland,
Expedient manage must be made, my liege,
Ere further leisure yield them further means   40
For their advantage and your Highness' loss.
Rich. We will ourself in person to this war;
And for our coffers, with too great a court
And liberal largess, are grown somewhat light,
We are inforc'd to farm our royal realm,   45
The revenue whereof shall furnish us

T.L.S., 15 Oct. 1931) is found in Guilpin's *Skialetheia* (1598), Satire 1 (Shakespeare Assoc. facsimile edn, sig. C3ᵛ) in a passage apparently attacking Essex for wooing the people.

33. *supple knee*] Bolingbroke is *courtesying* with a low bow: perhaps Shakespeare thinks of him here as being on foot—contrast his gestures when on horseback, v. ii. 18–19.

35. *reversion*] A legal term for the reverting of property to the original owner at the expiry of a grant or on the death of the lessee (Deighton).

36. *subjects' . . . hope*] i.e. "the next object of our subjects' hopes after us".

39. *Expedient manage*] speedy arrangements; cf. *expedience*, II. i. 287. *Expedient* is used three times in *John*, once only in each of five other Shakespeare plays. For *manage*, in a different sense, see III. iii. 179 and note.

43. *for*] because.

43–4. *too great . . . largess*] The extravagance of Richard's court is described by Hol., 508/1/55 ff; cf. II. i. 19 ff and note.

45. *to farm . . . realm*] i.e. "to let the realm by lease." *Realm* is metaphorical: Richard intends to grant to

certain persons, in exchange for an immediate sum of money, the profits from the royal taxes. The phrase derives from Hol., 496/1/64: "The common brute ran, that the king had set to farme the realme of England, unto [Scroope, Bushie, Bagot and Greene, the favourites]"; in Holinshed's margin—"the realme let [*sic*] to farme by the king." Edd. have claimed that this reference here (and at II. i. 256) presupposes the audience's knowledge of the fuller treatment of the theme in *Woodstock*, IV. i. 54 ff (Rossiter, p. 225), where the "farming" is anachronistically introduced from a later year of the reign (1398). The emphasis in *Woodstock* may have been in Shakespeare's mind, but the reference in Holinshed is an entirely adequate source; Holinshed and Daniel (*C.W.*, II. st. 19) both refer with equal casualness to the transaction and do not seem to suppose that their remarks would be intelligible only to readers fully informed from elsewhere. For modern readers, though, *Woodstock*, IV. i *is* the best gloss on this line. For similar casual dramatic allusions by Shakespeare, cf. II. i. 202–4 and note.

For our affairs in hand. If that come short,
Our substitutes at home shall have blank charters,
Whereto, when they shall know what men are rich,
They shall subscribe them for large sums of gold,   50
And send them after to supply our wants;
For we will make for Ireland presently.

Enter BUSHY.

Bushy, what news?
Bushy. Old John of Gaunt is grievous sick, my lord,

47. hand. If] *Newbolt;* hand if *Qq;* hand: if *F.*   52. S.D.] *F; Enter Bushie with*
newes. Qq.   53. Bushy . . . news?] *F; not in Qq.*   54. grievous] *Qq;* verie *F.*

48. *blank charters*] documents which
the wealthy were obliged to sign as
promises to pay, the space for the
amount being left blank to be filled up
at the king's pleasure: see Hol.,
496/1/11 ff and 496/2/30 ff. They are
also mentioned in *Mirror,* p. 114,
"King Richard the Second", l. 43.

50. *subscribe them for*] *O.E.D., s.v.*
subscribe 1c, interprets: "put [the
rich men] down for", quoting only
this example. It is not very likely to
mean "write or enter their names
under", since the names are already
on the blank charters as signatures; it
can hardly mean *subscribe* in the
modern connotation of *underwrite,*
since the victims were not giving
assurance but making a gift of the
money. Either of these meanings is
possible if Shakespeare was not thinking carefully of Holinshed's description of the blank charters. These interpretations take the object of *subscribe*
("them") to be the rich men (or their
names), but perhaps "them" = the
charters themselves, as it certainly
does in the next line ("send them
after"): then the phrase describes the
process of writing the amount in
figures on the signed charter and so
making it valid "for" large sums of
gold in the same way that we "make
out [a cheque] for" an amount; this
accords with Holinshed's account of
what was done.

52. *presently*] immediately.
S.D.] Q1 obviously went astray:
see Pollard, p. 87 and Wilson, p.
152. When it was decided, for the
sake of economy, to give Bushy the
Messenger's job (see note on l. 23
above), the foul papers were altered
so that the revision read "Enter
Bushie Ric. Bushie, wt. newes?" Whoever prepared the papers for the
printing of Q1 misread the contraction *wt.* as *with* not *what* and thought
he was dealing with a continuation of
the S.D. "Enter Bushie". H. F.
Brooks points out that the second
Bushie, the opening word of Richard's
line, is likely to have been part of the
correction: this is Bushy's first appearance as a speaker, and he would need
to be identified for the audience. The
second *Bushie* was dropped by Q1;
but the prompt-book represented the
whole alteration correctly from the
foul papers, and from the prompt-
book it supposedly passed intact to F.

54.] Cf. Froissart, VI. 335: "the
physicions and surgyons in Englande
sayd surely, howe that the duke
[Bolingbroke's] father had on hym a
paryllous sicknesse, which shulde be
his dethe." Froissart is the only writer
who implies that Gaunt's death was
preceded by a sickness: but for the
purposes of II. i Shakespeare would in
any case have had to invent the detail.
This was not beyond his powers.

Suddenly taken, and hath sent post-haste   55
To intreat your Majesty to visit him.
Rich. Where lies he?
Bushy. At Ely House.
Rich. Now put it, God, in the physician's mind
To help him to his grave immediately!   60
The lining of his coffers shall make coats
To deck our soldiers for these Irish wars.
Come, gentlemen, let's all go visit him,
Pray God we may make haste and come too late!
All. Amen.   [*Exeunt.*   65

59. God] *Qq;* heauen *F.*   in the] *Q1;* into the *Q2–5;* in his *F.*   65. *All.*]
Staunton: not in Qq, F.

58. *Ely House*] Gaunt died "at the
bishop of Elies place in Holborne"
(Hol., 496/1/23).

59.] Herford cfs. Edward's wish,
Edward II, II. ii. 235–6: "Would Lancaster and he had both carous'd
/ A bowl of poison to each other's
health."

61. *lining*] contents, with quibble on
coat-linings. "The word *lining* was
used colloquially of that which forms
the whole *contents* of anything hollow.
... So especially of money as *lining* a
chest; cf. Jaques' description of the
justice's 'fair round belly with good
capon lin'd' [*AYL.,* II. vii. 154]; and
the mod. colloquial 'to line one's
nest' " (Herford).

ACT II

SCENE I.—[*Ely House.*]

Enter JOHN OF GAUNT *sick, with the* DUKE OF YORK, *&c.*

Gaunt. Will the king come that I may breathe my last

Location.] *Wright; not in Qq, F.*   S.D.] *Qq; Enter Gaunt, sicke with Yorke. F.*

MATERIAL. The first half of the scene (to l. 155), comprising the death of Gaunt, is discussed in the Introduction, pp. xxxiv–xxxv ff, and see notes below. Richard's seizure of Gaunt's property immediately after his death and York's reaction derive from Hol., 496/1/26 ff: see Appendix. In Holinshed, York does not protest personally to the king, but the material in his protest-speech is from Holinshed (see notes on ll. 165–8, 202–4); Holinshed reports that York withdrew to his house at Langley and dissociated himself from affairs (see l. 211). For sources of York's character in general, see note on l. 221. Richard's decision to go to Ireland, already introduced in I. iv, and his appointment of York as "lieutenant generall" ("lord governor", l. 220) derive from Hol., 496/2/70 ff, but these events did not happen in such rapid succession as Shakespeare depicts. The last part of the scene (from l. 224), depicting the treasonable conversation between Northumberland, Ross, and Willoughby, is based on Hol., 497/2/54 ff, with some details from other places in Holinshed. Holinshed does not name the persons who first engaged in plotting against Richard on behalf of the

exiled Bolingbroke, but Shakespeare takes the names from Holinshed's list of those who first flocked to Bolingbroke's standard (see note on II. ii. 53–5). Shakespeare also runs together the first plotting and the reception of the news of Bolingbroke's imminent arrival (to which, without warrant from Holinshed, he makes Northumberland privy before the other conspirators), whereas, in Holinshed, Bolingbroke sets forth only as a result of the pleas of Thomas Arundell, Archbishop of Canterbury, who is sent to France as emissary of the malcontent nobles. The part played by Northumberland is thus greater in Shakespeare than Holinshed allows. It is therefore possible that Shakespeare owed something to the mention of the Percies' treasonable mutterings in Froissart, chap. ccxxxiii (vi. 347): "There were many knightes and squyers in the kynges company that shulde go with hym into Irelande that were nat content with him. . . Such wordes [of discontent] were so multiplyed, that the lorde Henry Percy and sir Henry his sonne spake certayne wordes, whiche came to the kynges knowlege and to his counsayle." On the other hand, it is equally possible that Shakespeare's

In wholesome counsel to his unstaid youth?

York. Vex not yourself, nor strive not with your breath;
For all in vain comes counsel to his ear.

Gaunt. O, but they say the tongues of dying men   5
Inforce attention like deep harmony.
Where words are scarce they are seldom spent in vain,
For they breathe truth that breathe their words in pain.
He that no more must say is listened more
Than they whom youth and ease have taught to glose; 10
More are men's ends mark'd than their lives before.
The setting sun, and music at the close,

10. have] *Q1, 2, F;* hath *Q 3–5.*   12. at the close] *Q1;* at the glose *Q2–5;* is the close *F.*

awareness of the fact, as reported by Holinshed, that Northumberland had been "declared traitor" (see note on II. ii. 56–61) sufficiently accounts for Shakespeare's emphasis on Northumberland's share in the discontent and plotting in this scene. (The later conduct of the Percies—their refusal to appear before the king when summoned, their prudent retreat northwards out of his reach and subsequent banishment—is not reflected in Shakespeare.) The facts given in Northumberland's speech at ll. 277 ff are reproduced almost verbatim from Hol., 498/1/9 ff, and represent one of two conflicting reports about the strength of Bolingbroke's forces both recorded by Holinshed; but the reasons given for Bolingbroke's delay in landing are not in Holinshed (see note on ll. 289-90).

S.D. Enter . . . sick] As Wilson suggests, Gaunt may have been carried in in a chair: cf. *Lr.,* IV. vii. 20 (F): "Enter Lear in a chaire carried by Seruants".

3. *nor strive . . . breath*] "do not strive by words ["your breath"] to admonish the king."

5.] The passage up to l. 14 is anthologized in *England's Parnassus,* no. 311, in the section entitled "Death".

5–6.] Tilley M514 cites many parallels to the thought in these lines, and cf. *Mer. V.,* I. ii. 25: "holy men at their death have good inspirations".

8.] H. Craig sees the passage as influenced by a contemporary belief that weakened physical powers increase the sight of the soul (see Craig, *The Enchanted Glass,* 1936, pp. 45–6) and cfs. *Ham.,* III. iv. 114: "Conceit in weakest bodies strongest works." J. B. Leishman points out to me a similar statement in Lucretius, *De Rerum Natura,* trans. Bailey, III. 55: "it is more fitting to watch a man in doubt and danger, and to learn of what manner he is in adversity; for then at last a real cry is wrung from the bottom of the heart: the mask is torn off, and the truth remains behind."

8–12.] The rhymed quatrain as here (and cf. III. ii. 76–82) is frequent in *Err., LLL.,* and *MND.* and is parodied in *John,* II. i. 504–9.

9. *listened*] Cf. *Cæs.,* IV. i. 41: "Listen great things" (Wilson).

10. *glose*] talk smoothly and speciously.

12. *close*] cadence, the conclusion of a musical phrase, theme or movement *O.E.D.*); cf. *H 5,* I. ii. 180–3: "government . . . doth keep in one consent, / Congreeing in a full and natural close, / Like music."

As the last taste of sweets, is sweetest last,
Writ in remembrance more than things long past:
Though Richard my life's counsel would not hear,   15
My death's sad tale may yet undeaf his ear.
York. No, it is stopp'd with other flattering sounds,
As praises, of whose taste the wise are fond,
Lascivious metres, to whose venom sound
The open ear of youth doth always listen,   20
Report of fashions in proud Italy,

18. of . . . fond] *Collier;* of whose taste the wise are found *Q1;* of whose state the wise are found *Q2;* of his state: then there are found *Q3–5,* F (sound *F*); of whose taste th' unwise are fond *Lettsom conj.*

13. *As . . . sweets*] "like the last taste of sweet things".

sweetest last] *Last* might mean "at the last", "in its ending"; or, "latest", i.e. retaining its sweetness for the longest time. The latter relates the meaning better to that of the next line.

16 *My . . . tale*] i.e. "My solemn dying words" (Herford).

undeaf] Herford suggests that the word is "a free coinage" of Shakespeare's; it is not found elsewhere; *undeafen* would be more regular, see Abbott ¶290. M. Joseph (*Shakespeare's Use of the Arts of Language*, p. 140) notes the large number of negative or privative terms in this play, and cites *unhappied,* III. i. 10, *uncurse,* III. ii. 137, *unking'd,* IV. i. 220, v. v. 37, *unkiss,* v. i. 74.

17. *other . . . sounds*] i.e. other sounds, viz. flattering ones (Herford).

18. *As . . . fond*] Collier's emendation of Q1's *found* has been accepted by most edd. (see Pollard, pp. 15–17, who shows that Q3's version was an attempt to emend a line which had been further damaged by the compositor of Q2), and the phrase is then taken to mean "of whose taste even the wise (much more the unwise Richard) are fond [or, with a quibble, "made foolish by"]". This is rather forced. and perhaps the original sense and wording are now irrecoverable.

19. *metres*] verses: the part is named

for the whole. The emphasis on Richard's luxury here derives essentially from Holinshed (501/2/39, 508/1/4) and has its counterpart in *Woodstock,* as Reyher noted. Marlowe's *Edward II* refers (1. i. 51–3) to the "wanton poets, pleasant wits, / Musicians, that with touching of a string / May draw the pleasant king which way I [Gaveston] please"; cf. note on ll. 21–3 below.

venom] venomous.

21–3. *proud Italy . . . imitation*] Gaunt's combination of an attack on foreign fashions with a patriotic appeal is matched in A. Marten's *Exhortation* (1588) in *Harleian Miscellany,* 1809 edn, II. 99. Cf. *Woodstock,* II. iii. 88–95: "[Richard and his minions] sit in council to devise strange fashions, / And suit themselves in wild and antic habits / Such as this kingdom never yet beheld: / French hose, Italian cloaks, and Spanish hats . . ." and *Edward II,* I. iv. 412–14. Complaints about imported finery are endemic in English satire from the earliest times; the specific references to Italian fashions are characteristic of the 16th century rather than the 14th —Richard's court was more under French influence—and Shakespeare is here one of the many writing in the tradition of R. Ascham's famous attack on the "Italianated Englishman" in Book I of *The Scholemaster*

Whose manners still our tardy-apish nation
Limps after in base imitation.
Where doth the world thrust forth a vanity—
So it be new, there's no respect how vile—   25
That is not quickly buzz'd into his ears?
Then all too late comes counsel to be heard,
Where will doth mutiny with wit's regard.
Direct not him whose way himself will choose:
'Tis breath thou lack'st and that breath wilt thou lose.

Gaunt. Methinks I am a prophet new inspir'd,   31
And thus expiring do foretell of him:
His rash fierce blaze of riot cannot last.
For violent fires soon burn out themselves;
Small showers last long, but sudden storms are short;   35
He tires betimes that spurs too fast betimes;
With eager feeding food doth choke the feeder;
Light vanity, insatiate cormorant,
Consuming means, soon preys upon itself.

---

22. tardy-apish] *Dyce (S. Walker conj.)* ; *unhyphened Qq,F.*   27. Then] *Qq*; That
F.   30. wilt thou] *Q1–4, F*; thou wilt *Q5.*

(*English Works of Ascham*, ed. Wright, pp. 222–37).

22. *tardy-apish*] imitative, though lagging far behind the model (Kittredge).

25. *there's . . . vile*] "there's no regard for its vileness."

28. *with . . . regard*] "against the thoughtful consideration of the understanding". *Lucr.*, 277, "Sad pause and deep regard beseems the sage", shows the meaning of *regard* here. For the antithesis between wit and will cf. *Lucr.*, 1299: "What wit sets down is blotted straight with will". The rebellion of Will against Understanding or Reason is cardinal to the Elizabethan psychologists' theory about the readiness with which the "faculties of the soul" come into conflict with one another: cf. *Ant.*, III. xiii. 4–5, and see R. L. Anderson, *Elizabethan Psychology and Shakespeare's Plays*, 1927, chap. VIII.

30. *breath*] An uncomic quibble:

"As a sick man you're short of breath, so don't waste words on him."

31. *prophet*] Cf. note on l. 8 above, and note on II. iv. 11.

31–2. *inspir'd . . . expiring*] Another tragic conceit, which continues the one in l. 30: "I have obtained through 'inspiration' (breathing in) a fresh supply of 'breath', and, 'breathing it out' (dying), . . ."

34–9.] Gaunt uses the rhetorical device of auxesis, arranging his sentences in a sequence of increasing force, to illustrate the idea that a thing whose property is to operate violently "fordoes itself", in Polonius's words (see *Ham.*, II. i. 103, and cf. *Ham.*, III. ii. 191–2, *Rom.*, II. vi. 9). For proverbial images, see Tilley N321 ("Nothing violent can be permanent"), illustrating l. 34. Similar auxesis characterizes the rest of this speech.

36.] "He soon tires who rides too fast early in the day" (Kittredge)— a play on *betimes.*

This royal throne of kings, this scept'red isle,   40 †
This earth of majesty, this seat of Mars,
This other Eden, demi-paradise,

40–68.] Part of this passage (up to l. 55) is anthologized in *England's Parnassus*, no. 1927, in the section "Of Albion", where it is wrongly attributed to Drayton. Elements in this speech have antecedents or parallels (see the notes that follow for discussion) in various places, viz. (*a*) Shakespeare's own work, *3 Henry VI*, *John*, and *Cymbeline*. (*b*) Classical authors, Virgil, Caesar, Dio Cassius, Plutarch. (*c*) contemporary patriotic propaganda. (*d*) Froissart, VI. 311: a report of Gaunt's meditations on the future of England (quoted by Wilson, p. lvii). (*e*) Holinshed's account of early British history. (*f*) *The Mirror for Magistrates*. (*g*) John Eliot's *Ortho-epia Gallica or Eliot's Fruits from the French* (1593), a French-English conversation book, which contains a translation of part of a passage in praise of France from Du Bartas's *Creation du Monde* (Bk II, *La Seconde Sepmaine: Les Colonies*): see J. W. Lever, *Shakespeare Survey*, VI (1953), 89, and see Appendix, p. 206. (*h*) Joshua Sylvester's translation of the same passage from Du Bartas (which Sylvester adapted into a praise of England) in his *Deuine Weekes and Workes*: the date of the first appearance of Sylvester's verses is uncertain—see A. S. T. Fisher in *Times Literary Supplement*, 28 Nov. 1952, and P. Ure, 'Sylvester's Du Bartas and ... *Richard II*' in *N. & Q.*, CXCVIII (1953), 374–7, and see Appendix, p. 207. (*j*) G. Peele's *Edward I* and *Arraignment of Paris*. (*k*) Daniel's *Delia*, sonnet XLIV (first printed 1592). (*l*) Daniel's *Ciuile Warres* (1595). The speech is shaped by its dramatic context, and none of these passages is a complete analogue. In one of its aspects, the relation of England to the sea (see especially note on ll. 47–9), the speech is part of a growing tradi-

tion which pictured England as Queen of the seas: Hakluyt's dedicatory epistle to Walsingham in the 1589 edn of his *Voyages* boldly proclaims the idea (on this see S. B. Liljegren in his edn of J. Harrington's *Oceana* [Heidelberg, 1924]), and it swells to a chorus in the work of Daniel, Drayton, and Selden: cf. the Proclamation of Union (1603): the Isle is guarded by the "Ocean Sea, making the whole a little world [cf. l. 45] within itself".

40. *This ... kings*] Peele twice (in *The Arraignment of Paris*, M.S.R., l. 1249, and in *Edward I*, M.S.R., l. 15) uses the phrase "ancient seat of kings" in panegyrics on England: see the passage from *Edward I* cited in note to ll. 53–6 below.

41. *earth of majesty*] i.e. "this land, which is the proper domain of 'majesty' " (Herford).

42. *This other Eden*] Cf. "our sea-walled garden, the whole land", III. iv. 43, and cf. France as a "garden" in *H 5*, v. ii. 36. The panegyrical comparison of England to a garden may take its origin from the habit of comparing a country to a garden in other respects, which may be called the "political" use of the metaphor, and which is discussed in the Introduction and notes to III. iv; or it may derive from some untraced source and may itself have contributed to the garden/state analogy. Sylvester used the phrase in his translation of the panegyric on France-England in Du Bartas ("The Worlds rich Garden") without warrant from his original; he may be imitating Shakespeare or Shakespeare may be imitating him. 17th century occurrences of the phrase "garden of the world" applied as praise to a particular land are discussed by J. B. Leishman, *T.L.S.*, 7 Nov. 1952. Cf. also Greene, *Spanish Masquerado*

This fortress built by Nature for herself
Against infection and the hand of war,
This happy breed of men, this little world,   45 †

(1589), sig. E3ᵛ: "Seeing then we are euery way blest and fauoured from aboue: that the Lord our mercifull God maketh ENGLAND like EDEN, a second Paradice: let us fear to offend him..."; and cf. W. Lightfoote on "a land much resembling the happinesse of *Paradise*" in his *Complaint of England* (1587), sig. C1ʳ.

demi-paradise] Implying perhaps not simply "half-Paradise" (on the analogy of *demi-god*) but "one of two Paradises" or "sharing the function of Paradise"; cf. *Ant.*, I. v. 23: "demi-Atlas of this earth", where Antony is, with Caesar, one of two "Atlases" who share the support of the globe traditionally attributed to Atlas the Titan. But *demi* may merely have the sense of *quasi* in both places, and cf. *Tp.*, v. i. 36 and F. Kermode's note, Arden edn of *Tp.*, p. 113. The phrase is found in both Eliot ("O earthly paradise!") and Sylvester ("Earths rare Paradice") rendering Du Bartas's "ô paradis du monde!"

44. *infection*] Cf. *John*, v. ii. 20, where Salisbury speaks of the "infection of the time". Gaunt seems to mean specifically *infection* coming from without, perhaps the kind of imported foreign corruptions glanced at in ll. 21 ff above. Daniel twice refers to the *contagion* of foreign iniquities: "With what contagion *France* didst thou infect / The land by thee made proud, to disagree?" (*C. W.*, IV, st. 43): "*Neptune* keepe out from thy imbraced Ile / This foule contagion of iniquitie" (*ibid.*, IV, st. 90). Holinshed also says that the private vices of the king and his followers "infected" the land. Because of these echoes it is hard to agree with Kittredge that *infection* simply = "pestilence".

45. *this ... world*] Cf. *Cym.*, "Britain is / A world by itself" (III. i. 13–14)

and "I' th' world's volume / Our Britain seems as of it, but not in't" (III. iv. 136–7). This notion, which suffuses the whole speech, is used also by Daniel (see passages cited in note to ll. 47–9 below). Virgil's famous line, *Eclogues*, I. 5, "Et penitus toto divisos orbe Britannos", may be the origin of Daniel's repeated phrase "divided from the world"; cf. its use by Chapman, *Masque of the Middle Temple, Comedies*, ed. Parrott, p. 449: "But poets (our chief men of wit) ... ingeniously affirming that the isle is (for the excellency of it) divided from the world (divisus ab orbe Britannus [*sic*])". There are other classical parallels to the idea besides Virgil: (i) Caesar, *De Bello Gallico* (Loeb edn, 1922, p. 204), emphasizes the remoteness of Britain, visited only by traders. (ii) Dio Cassius, in his account of Aulus Plautius's campaign in Britain (A.D. 43; see *Dio's Roman History*, Loeb edn, 1924, VII. 414), says that Plautius's soldiers "were indignant at the thought of carrying on a campaign outside the limits of the known world". Shakespeare could have read about this in Holinshed's first 1587 volume, Bk IV of *The Historie of England*, 34/1/11: "the soldiers were loth to go with [Plautius], as men not willing to make warre in another world". (iii) Plutarch says that Caesar was "the first that enlarged the Roman empire, beyond the earth inhabitable" (*Lives*, trans. Sir T. North [1579], Temple Classics edn, VII. 150–1). Cf. also *Parts Added to the Mirror for Magistrates*, ed. Campbell, 1946, p. 197, "Nennius" [1574], ll. 140–1, and A. Marten's *Exhortation*, edn cit., p. 90: "we be here removed in a corner from the rest of the world ... measured with a span, in comparison of all Christendom".

This precious stone set in the silver sea,
Which serves it in the office of a wall,

46.] Cf. the metaphor from jewellery at I. iii. 266 and *R 3*, v. iii. 250-1, where Richmond describes Crookback as "A base foul stone made precious by the foil / Of England's chair, where he is falsely set" (and see Thompson's note on this passage, Arden edn of *R 3*, p. 201). Both Eliot ("O pearle of rich *European* bounds!") and Sylvester ("*Europes* Pearle of price") provide parallels (from Du Bartas: "O perle de l'Europe!").

47-9.] Cf. ll. 61-3 below. Both passages emphasize England's insularity and the sea which both guards it and cuts it off from the rest of the world. Cf. the emphasis on these ideas in *3 H 6*, IV. i. 42-4: " 'Tis better using France than trusting France. / Let us be back'd with God, and with the seas / Which He hath giv'n for fence impregnable"; *ibid.*, IV. viii. 20; *John*, II. i. 23-8: "[England] that pale, that white-fac'd shore, / Whose foot spurns back the ocean's roaring tides / And coops from other lands her islanders— / Even till that England, hedg'd in with the main, / That water-walled bulwark, still secure / And confident from foreign purposes". Daniel uses the idea in *Delia*, sonnet XLIV (1592 and subsequent editions): "Florish faire *Albion*, glory of the North, / *Neptunes* darling helde betweene his armes: / Deuided from the world as better worth, / Kept for himselfe, defended from all harmes"; he repeats it in *C.W.*, IV, st. 90 (passage quoted in note to l. 44 above), and in *ibid.*, I, st. 68: "Why *Neptune* hast thou made us stand alone / Deuided from the world . . .?" (Here, however, the phrase is part of a complaint against being cut off by the waves from escape and so made an easy prey to internal tyranny.) For the repeated phrase *deuided from the world*, see note on l. 45 above. There is also a passage in *C.W.*, II, st. 49 (first pointed out by Reyher), describing the place near Flint where Richard was ambushed, a rock whose "proud feet" "spurnes the waues", which Shakespeare may have had in mind when he wrote the passage in *John*, II. i, quoted above, and which would therefore entitle it to be ranked as an antecedent, through *John*, of these lines in *R 2* (see Wilson, p. 158. This is not certain, because *John*, usually dated 1595-7, may have been written earlier, before the publication of *C.W.*). In his praise of England, adapted from Du Bartas's praise of France, Sylvester has a passage, corresponding to nothing in his original, which provides further parallels, but the date of which is also uncertain (*Deuine Weekes and Workes*, 1605 edn, sig. Hh6^r: see Appendix, p. 207, ll. 17-21). It is impossible to arrange these parallels in any satisfactory "family-tree", because of the uncertainty attaching to the chronology of most of the works mentioned. Daniel's *Delia* sonnet may well have the priority, since it is stated in the 1594 edn of *Delia* that he composed his sonnet in Italy, which he visited probably soon after 1585. H. F. Brooks points out the traditional element in the idea of the sea as England's defensive wall: it is found in *The Libelle of Englyshe Polycye* (written ca. 1436-9; printed by Hakluyt in the 1598 edn of his *Voyages*): "Kepe than the see abought in speciall, / Whiche of England is the rounde wall, / As thoughe England were lykened to a cite / And the wall environ were the see. / Kepe then the see, that is the wall of Englond / And than is Englond kepte by Goddes sonde" (ed. Sir G. Warner, 1926, ll. 1092-7). It also featured in contemporary patriotic propaganda, e.g., Greene's *Spanish Masquerado*, sig. B4^r: "seeing how secure we slept . . . for that we were hedged in with the sea . . . [God] brought in these Spaniards to waken us out of our dreams".

Or as a moat defensive to a house,
Against the envy of less happier lands;
This blessed plot, this earth, this realm, this
    England,   50
This nurse, this teeming womb of royal kings,
Fear'd by their breed, and famous by their birth,
Renowned for their deeds as far from home,
For Christian service and true chivalry,
As is the sepulchre in stubborn Jewry   55 †
Of the world's ransom, blessed Mary's son;
This land of such dear souls, this dear dear land,
Dear for her reputation through the world,
Is now leas'd out—I die pronouncing it—
Like to a tenement or pelting farm.   60

48. as a] *Q4, 5, F;* as *Q1–3.*   52. by . . . by] *Qq;* by . . . for *F.*   53. for] *Q1, 2, F;* in *Q3–5.*   60. or] *Q1–4, F;* and *Q5.*

49. *less happier*] A grammatical anomaly, formed on the analogy of "more happier": see Abbott ¶11, and Herford's note.

51. *This . . . womb*] Cf. Eliot, *Ortho-epia-Gallica*: "this nurse of many learned wits", "mother of many artist-hands"; Sylvester: "thrice-happy mother", translating Du Bartas's "Mere de tant d'ouvriers", "Mere de tant d'esprits"; see Appendix, p. 207 and cf. I. iii. 307.

53–6.] These references to the chivalric renown of English crusaders are the most striking of the parallels to the words of Du Bartas and his translators: see Appendix, pp. 206–7. They are also one of the few patches of deliberately introduced historical colour in the play: cf. IV. i. 92–100 and note. A similar claim for the world-wide reputation of English chivalry is advanced in Peele's *Edward I* (printed 1593), M.S.R., ll. 15–26, and in A. Marten's *Exhortation*, edn cit., p. 90: "yet have we been ever as ready . . . to travel over sea and land, to spend our lives, lands, and goods, to resist the fury and invasion of the Turks, and other heathen nations; whereas we ourselves, being

an island, and defended by the ocean sea, had less cause than any other to fear the infidels, being so far remote from us".

55. *Jewry*] the lands of the Jews; but *stubborn* applies to the Jews themselves, either in the general sense of "barbarous" (cf. the adj. as used in the passage from Peele cited in the preceding note) or because they "stubbornly" rejected Christianity.

56. *ransom*] For the idea of Christ as ransom Noble cites 1 Tim., ii. 6 and Matt., xx. 28.

60. *tenement*] real estate held by a tenant.

pelting farm] paltry farm: cf. *Woodstock*, ed. Frijlinck, M.S.R., l. 1888 (IV. i. 147 in Rossiter), "rent out [o]ur kingdome like a pelting ffarme". Frijlinck (p. xxxiii) points out that the word she prints as *pelting* is obscurely written and has been altered in the MS, and Rossiter (p. 198) thinks that the editorial reading of *pelting* in *Woodstock* is influenced by the supposed echo in Shakespeare: "Why should we assume that Shakespeare did not know the word *pelting* till he read it in *Woodstock*?" He certainly

England, bound in with the triumphant sea,
Whose rocky shore beats back the envious siege
Of wat'ry Neptune, is now bound in with shame,
With inky blots and rotten parchment bonds;
That England, that was wont to conquer others,   65
Hath made a shameful conquest of itself.
Ah, would the scandal vanish with my life,
How happy then were my ensuing death!

Enter KING, QUEEN, AUMERLE, BUSHY. GREENE, BAGOT,
ROSS, *and* WILLOUGHBY.

York. The king is come, deal mildly with his youth,

68. S.D.] *F; Enter King and Queene &c. Qq (after l. 70).*

used it later (*Lr.*, II. iii. 18, *Meas.*, II. ii.
112), but here it is not just the word
but the whole idea of the line that
echoes, and it seems certain that
Shakespeare is remembering *Woodstock* or *Woodstock* Shakespeare: see
Introduction, pp. xxxv–xxxix.

61–3.] See note on ll. 47–9 above.

64. *rotten . . . bonds*] i.e. the leases by
which Richard has "let the realme to
farme", in Holinshed's phrase. There
need not be a specific reference to
Tresillian's documents in *Woodstock*,
IV. i: see note on l. 114 below.

65–6.] These lines clinch the rhetorical development. The sentiment
and implication, that England can
never be conquered except from within and must rest true to herself, are
certainly not original to Shakespeare
and are found in the passage from
Froissart (VI. 311) which Wilson prof-
fers as the germ of the whole speech
(see Introduction, p. xxxiv). When
they were used by the anonymous
author of *The Troublesome Raigne of
King John*, Part II (edn in the Furness
Variorum *John*, sc. ix, ll. 25–9, 45–6,
53–4), he was probably imitating the
Bastard's patriotic speech in *John*, v.
vii. 112–18, which, as Wilson notes,
reads like a first draft of the lines in *R 2*
(on this, see E. A. J. Honigmann,

Arden edn of *John*, 1954). An emphasis
similar to Shakespeare's is found in
T. Churchyard's *Discourse of Rebellion*
(1570) and A. Borde's *Fyrst Boke of the
Introduction to Knowledge* (ca. 1542?)—
see the passages quoted in the Furness
Variorum *John*, p. 427; in *Edmond
Ironside*, M.S.R., ll. 375–9, and in contemporary patriotic propaganda, e.g.
G. D.'s *Briefe Discoverie* (1588), sig.
R3v: "when our realme was not so
strong, yet hath it conquered other
Nations and was neuer conquered by
any so long as it was true within it
selfe"; in Sylvester's Du Bartas (see
passage cited in note to ll. 47–9 above);
and, as Reyher noted, in Daniel, *C. W.*,
I, st. I: "[England] a mighty land: /
Whose people hauty, proud with
forain spoyles / Vpon themselues,
turne back their conquering hand".

67–8.] Rossiter cfs. *Woodstock*, III. ii.
108: "I would my death might end
the misery / My fear presageth to my
wretched country". But Shakespeare
himself had already used the sentiment in *2 H 6*, III. i. 148–50: and cf.
True Tragedy of Richard III, M.S.R.,
ll. 658–60.

69. *mildly . . . youth*] Cf. *Woodstock*,
I. i. 186, where Gloucester hopes that
Richard's marriage "will mildly calm
his headstrong youth".

For young hot colts being rein'd do rage the more.   70
Queen. How fares our noble uncle, Lancaster?
Rich. What comfort, man? how is't with aged Gaunt?
Gaunt. O, how that name befits my composition!
    Old Gaunt indeed, and gaunt in being old.
    Within me grief hath kept a tedious fast,   75
    And who abstains from meat that is not gaunt?
    For sleeping England long time have I watch'd,
    Watching breeds leanness, leanness is all gaunt.
    The pleasure that some fathers feed upon
    Is my strict fast—I mean my children's looks,   80
    And therein fasting hast thou made me gaunt.
    Gaunt am I for the grave, gaunt as a grave,
    Whose hollow womb inherits nought but bones.
Rich. Can sick men play so nicely with their names?
Gaunt. No, misery makes sport to mock itself: 85
    Since thou dost seek to kill my name in me,
    I mock my name, great king, to flatter thee.
Rich. Should dying men flatter with those that live?

70. rein'd] *Singer, ed. 2;* ragde *Qq, F;* inrag'd *Pope;* ragged *Wilson.*   87. I] *Q1, F;* O *Q2–5.*   88. with] *Q1; not in Q2–5, F.*

70. *being rein'd*] O.E.D. gives no other examples of *raged* (Qq, F) used transitively, and, as Sisson says (*New Readings,* II. 19), "it is pointless to say that a horse if deliberately tormented will rage the more for being *raged*". Wilson takes Q1's *ragde* as Shakespeare's spelling of *ragged* (cf. "great rag'd hornes", *Wiv.,* [F] IV. iv. 30), and makes the lines refer to the use of *ragged colt* in the proverb "Of a ragged [= shaggy, untamed] colt comes a good horse" (Tilley, C522), as actually used by Hall (p. 12) in his version of Richard's abdication-speech. The objection to this view is that it makes nonsense of the comparative meaning plainly intended by Q: "Don't [anger or restrain] the king; young and hot as he is, it will only make him worse." Singer's reading (= "restrain") is preferable.

73. *composition*] constitution.

77.] Rossiter cfs. *Woodstock,* v. i.

124–5: "bear record, righteous heaven, / How I have nightly waked for England's good"; but this itself probably derives from *2 H 6,* III. i. 110–11.

watch'd] kept awake, keeping guard or vigil.

78. *Watching*] sleeplessness.

79–80. *The pleasure . . . looks*] "From the pleasure that some fathers nourish themselves with, their children's looks, I strictly abstain." The reference is to Bolingbroke's exile.

83. *inherits*] possesses.

84. *nicely*] subtly + foolishly and fancifully.

85. *misery . . . itself*] "it is misery that takes pleasure in mocking itself."

86. *kill my name*] i.e. by banishing Bolingbroke, his heir. Gaunt is playing on *name* and *name* = family reputation, or the "name" that symbolizes it.

88–93.] Stichomythia: cf. I. iii. 258–62. This device, caught from Seneca and his French imitators such as

Gaunt. No, no, men living flatter those that die.
Rich. Thou now a-dying sayest thou flatterest me.   90
Gaunt. Oh no, thou diest, though I the sicker be.
Rich. I am in health, I breathe, and see thee ill.
Gaunt. Now He that made me knows I see thee ill,
    Ill in myself to see, and in thee, seeing ill.
    Thy death-bed is no lesser than thy land,   95
    Wherein thou liest in reputation sick,
    And thou, too careless patient as thou art,
    Commit'st thy anointed body to the cure
    Of those physicians that first wounded thee:
    A thousand flatterers sit within thy crown,   100
    Whose compass is no bigger than thy head,
    And yet, incaged in so small a verge,
    The waste is no whit lesser than thy land.
    O, had thy grandsire with a prophet's eye
    Seen how his son's son should destroy his sons,   105
    From forth thy reach he would have laid thy shame,
    Deposing thee before thou wert possess'd,

92. and] *Q1; not in Q2–5, F.*   95. thy land] *Q1;* the land *Q2–5, F.*   102. incaged] *F;* inraged *Qq.*   106. thy reach] *Q1, 2, 4, 5, F;* they reach *Q3.*

Jodelle and Garnier, was used by the dramatists of the "Countess of Pembroke's Circle", such as Daniel and Fulke Greville, and also by Kyd and some other popular dramatists.

88. *flatter with*] "Flatter *with*" is not usual in Shakespeare, but cf. *Gent.*, iv. iv. 184, *Tw. N.*, i. v. 287.

93–9. *see thee ill . . . wounded thee*] Gaunt develops three ideas out of his simple retort in l. 93 to Richard's ". . . see thee ill": (*a*) "I see that *you* are (politically) ill"; this notion is developed in ll. 95–9, where Richard's political sickness is compared by metaphor to bodily sickness ("death-bed" . . . "patient" . . . "physicians"). (*b*) l. 94: "Ill in myself to see" = "I see you ill because my own sight is impaired by sickness". (*c*) l. 94: "and in thee, seeing ill" = "in you, I see evil". The last two ideas thus lead to a postponement of the development inherent in the first quibble.

101. *compass*] Here used in its obsolete sense, "circle".

102. *verge*] A quibble on 'limit', with special reference to the metal rim of a diadem (cf. *R 3*, iv. i. 59), and *verge* as the term for the area extending to a distance of twelve miles round the king's court, wherever he happened to be, which was under the jurisdiction of the Lord High Steward of the Household (from L. *virga*, the Steward's wand of office).

103. *waste*] Another quibble: *waste* can mean injury done to a property by a tenant.

104. *thy grandsire*] Edward III; for other references to him cf. i. ii. 11, ii. i. 124. In *Woodstock*, v. i. 78 ff, the Ghost of this monarch indulges in reproaches similar to those imagined for him here by Gaunt.

107–8. *possess'd . . . possess'd*] "possessed of the crown" and "possessed of the devil".

Which art possess'd now to depose thyself.
Why, cousin wert thou regent of the world,
It were a shame to let this land by lease;   110
But for thy world enjoying but this land,
Is it not more than shame to shame it so?
Landlord of England art thou now, not king,
Thy state of law is bondslave to the law,
And thou—

Rich.   A lunatic lean-witted fool,   115
Presuming on an ague's privilege,
Darest with thy frozen admonition
Make pale our cheek, chasing the royal blood
With fury from his native residence.

---

109. wert] *Qq;* were *F.*   110. this] *Qq;* his *F.*   113. now, not] *Theobald;*
now not, not *Q1–4;* now not, nor *Q5;* and not *F.*   115. And . . . lunatic] *Q1,*
2 (thou/); And thou./ *King.* Ah lunatick *Q3–5;* And— / *Rich.* And thou, a
lunaticke *F.*   118. chasing] *Qq;* chafing *F.*

---

109. *regent*] ruler.
111. *for thy world*] for thy domain.
113. *Landlord*] "a person who lets
land to a tenant" (*O.E.D.*). For the
way in which this word connects *R 2*
with *Woodstock*, see Introduction, p.
xxxviii. Sir John Hayward (*Life and
Raigne of Henrie IIII*, p. 55), when he
uses the word of Richard, may be
borrowing from either play.
114.] Gaunt means that Richard's
legal status as king is now "amenable
to the common law like that of any
other mortgagee" (Newbolt). It is
unnecessary to suppose with Rossiter
(p. 48) that the line is "hopelessly
obscure" unless the audience is expected to have in mind the scene in
Woodstock (IV. i) where Richard is
shown signing and sealing indentures
on land and commodities prepared for
the favourites by the corrupt lawyer
Tresillian. Gaunt has just made clear
what he means in ll. 110, 113 above;
and the dramatic sense is plain
enough—cf. note on ll. 202–4 below.
115.] Richard breaks into Gaunt's
speech and uses his *thou* as if it referred
to Gaunt himself: "And thou a lunatic . . . darest". H. F. Brooks cfs.

Richard III's attempt to make Mar-
garet's curse apply to herself by inter-
rupting it with her own name, *R 3*,
I. iii. 233.
118–19. *Make pale . . . With fury*]
Richard turns pale again at III. ii. 75–
9, and he is twice referred to as a
"rose" (*R 2*, v. i. 8; *1 H 4*, I. iii. 175);
he is red with fury at III. iii. 62 (see
note). All this may imply that "high
colour, easily yielding to deadly
pallor, was part of Shakespeare's conception of Richard" (Herford). But
pallor is also a conventional sign of
shock in Shakespeare: cf. *R 3*, II. i.
83 ff—the whole court turns pale
when they hear of Clarence's death;
and *R 3*, III. vii. 26 where the Londoners collectively "look'd deadly
pale". Wilson argues that Shakespeare depended upon hints in the historical sources for Richard's complexion. Holinshed says that Richard
was "seemelie of shape and fauour",
which might account for the "rose"
comparison; Froissart says that
Richard "chaunged colours" once (VI.
367) and "chaunged countynaunce"
(VI. 314); but the phrases are conventional, and could have told Shake-

Now by my seat's right royal majesty,   120
Wert thou not brother to great Edward's son,
This tongue that runs so roundly in thy head
Should run thy head from thy unreverent shoulders.
Gaunt. O, spare me not, my brother Edward's son,
For that I was his father Edward's son;   125
That blood already, like the pelican,
Haꜱt thou tapp'd out and drunkenly carous'd:
My brother Gloucester, plain well-meaning soul,

---

124. brother] *Q2–5;* brothers *Q1, F.*
out] *Q1, F; not in Q2–5.*

127. Hast thou] *Qq;* Thou hast *F.*

---

speare little, for "chaunged colour" is
also applied to Bolingbroke (vi. 344)
when he is angry and abashed.

122. *roundly*] glibly, bluntly.

123. *unreverent*] disrespectful; see
note on v. vi. 25–6.

124–5.] The references to Edward
III here, though allied to previous
dynastic allusions (see note on l. 104
above) are perhaps related to Gloucester's cry when he is arrested,
Woodstock, IV. ii. 180: "Villains,
touch me not! / I am descended of the
royal blood, / King Richard's uncle /
... his princely father's brother".

124. *brother*] Q1's *brothers*, repeated
by F, is probably a misprint like *butchers* in I. ii. 48, which latter, however,
was corrected in the Huntington copy:
see Pollard, p. 36, n. 1.

126. *pelican*] Richard is compared to
the young pelican that, according to
fable, is revived by the mother-bird
with her own blood: see Onions in
Shakespeare's England, I. 495 and illustration. When applied to the parent
the story commemorates self-sacri-
fice (see *Edward III*, III. v. 110–14;
Ham., IV. v. 143–4) and became a
popular emblem for Christ's sacrifice
(see R. Freeman, *English Emblem Books*,
1948, pp. 145–6); when to the children, ingratitude (as here, and cf. *Lr.*,
III. iv. 74 and *Mirror*, p. 448).

128.] The plain well-meaning
Gloucester is unhistorical, and the
line epitomizes rather the hero of

Woodstock, who is represented as well-
meaning and often referred to as
"plain" (rough, out-spoken, "frank")
both in clothes and manner. Commentators have held with Keller that
the line connects *R 2* unmistakably
with *Woodstock*, and it is of course
more likely in that case that Shakespeare is epitomizing *Woodstock* than
that the author of that play developed
his hero out of this hint. The case is
not watertight, however: *Woodstock*
itself provides overwhelming evidence
that the "plain Thomas" therein emphasized had an existence independent of the anonymous author, perhaps through a family or local tradition which did not get much admis-
sion to the history-books. Thus the
title "plain Thomas" is twice stated to
be a popular nickname (*Woodstock*,
I. i. 99–100, I. i. 198–9; and cf. v. i.
55), Richard uses it ironically as
though it were a nickname (II. ii. 143,
II. ii. 27) and Gloucester constantly
refers to it as though it were an
appellation given to him by others of
which he is rather proud (e.g., I. i.
216, I. iii. 34, II. ii. 34, III. ii. 235, IV. ii.
75, IV. ii. 151). It is hard to believe
that all this sprang simply from the
dramatist's head without support in a
tradition of some kind; to that tradition Shakespeare may have had access
without going through *Woodstock*.
Even if we admit that "plain" here
connects with the nickname in *Wood-*

Whom fair befall in heaven 'mongst happy souls,   †
May be a president and witness good   130
That thou respect'st not spilling Edward's blood.
Join with the present sickness that I have,
And thy unkindness be like crooked age,
To crop at once a too long withered flower.
Live in thy shame, but die not shame with thee!   135
These words hereafter thy tormentors be!
Convey me to my bed, then to my grave—
Love they to live that love and honour have.   [*Exit.*

Rich. And let them die that age and sullens have,
    For both hast thou, and both become the grave.   140

York. I do beseech your Majesty, impute his words
    To wayward sickliness and age in him;
    He loves you, on my life, and holds you dear,
    As Harry Duke of Herford, were he here.

Rich. Right, you say true; as Herford's love, so his;   145
    As theirs, so mine; and all be as it is.

Enter NORTHUMBERLAND.

North. My liege, old Gaunt commends him to your Majesty.
Rich. What says he?
North.   Nay nothing, all is said:

140. the] *Q1, 3–5, F;* thee *Q2.*   146. all] *Q1, F; not in Q2–5.*   S.D.] *F; not in Qq.*   148. Nay] *Q1–3, F; not in Q4, 5.*

stock, we must remember that a "well-meaning" and outspoken Gloucester is one aspect of the figure in the chroniclers and the *Mirror,* as H. F. Brooks has pointed out to me, and is not confined to *Woodstock.* Holinshed is generally hostile to him ("a noble man* [*marg.,* for he was son to a King and uncle to a King], fierce o. nature, hastie, wilfull and giuen more to war than to peace", 489/2/5) but he reports his brothers' defence of him to the king: "a man sometimes rash in woords . . . and the same proceeded of a faithfull heart" (488/1/43); Grafton (*Chronicles,* 1809 edn, I. 468) speaks of him as "this honourable and good man miserable put to death". Such

sentiments are repeated in *Mirror,* p. 91—"a man muche mynding the common weale"; p. 104—"the warder of the common weale . . . gyltles"; and in "Thomas, Earl of Salisbury", ll. 22–35, he is held up as a historical example of how reputations change: his execution was regarded as just for two years afterwards, but ever since as "sore tiranny and wrong"—a fact which reflects a change of opinion about Richard as well.

130. *president*] precedent.
133. *crooked*] Steevens suggested that Time's traditional crooked sickle prompted the image in the next line.
139. *sullens*] sulks.
140. *become*] are fit for.

His tongue is now a stringless instrument;
Words, life, and all, old Lancaster hath spent.   150
York. Be York the next that must be bankrout so!
Though death be poor, it ends a mortal woe.
Rich. The ripest fruit first falls, and so doth he;
His time is spent, our pilgrimage must be.
So much for that. Now for our Irish wars: 155
We must supplant those rough rug-headed kerns,
Which live like venom where no venom else,
But only they, have privilege to live.
And for these great affairs do ask some charge,
Towards our assistance we do seize to us   160
The plate, coin, revenues, and moveables,
Whereof our uncle Gaunt did stand possess'd.
York. How long shall I be patient? ah, how long
Shall tender duty make me suffer wrong?   †
Not Gloucester's death, nor Herford's banishment,   165

156. rug-headed] *Q4, 5, F;* rugheaded *Q1–3.*   kerns] *Q1 (Huth), 3–5, F;*
kerne *Q1 (Cap. and Hunt.), 2.*   161. coin] *Q1 (Huth, Cap. and Hunt.), 2–5, F;*
coines *Q1 (Petworth).*

149.] For the image, cf. I. iii. 161–2.
151. *bankrout*] bankrupt. This form
(It., *banca rotta,* Fr., *banqueroute*) is
twice used in Q1: cf. l. 257 below. The
alternative form (caused by assimila-
tion to L. *ruptus*) occurs at IV. i. 267 in
the part of the play not printed in Q1.
Here, the adj. continues the thought
in Northumberland's *spent*: cf. *poor* in
the next line.
152. *death*] the state of being dead.
mortal] deadly + fleshly.
153. *The ripest . . . falls*] Proverbial:
see Tilley R133.
154. *our . . . be*] i.e. "we have still to
run our pilgrimage on earth."
156. *rug-headed*] shaggy-headed; cf.
2 H 6, III. i. 367: "shag-haired crafty
kern", and cf. Dekker, *2 Honest Whore,*
III. i. 152. Spenser in *The Present State of
Ireland* describes the long hair worn by
the Irish fighters of his time.
kerns]   light-armed Irish foot-
soldiers; Shakespeare uses the word
several times and it is found in Holinshed: see Arden edn of *Mac.,* ed. K.

Muir, note on I. ii. 13, and cf. *Edward
II,* II. ii. 162. Their method of making
war is described in *Mirror,* p. 88, "The
Two Mortimers", ll. 120–40.
157–8.] Refers to the legend that St
Patrick banished snakes from Ireland.
Steevens cfs. Dekker, *2 Honest Whore,*
III. i. 201, where Bryan, an Irish foot-
man, is described as "that Irish Iudas,/
Bred in a Country where no venom
prospers / But in the Nations blood".
159. *for*] because.
ask . . . charge] require some expen-
diture.
161. *moveables*] Includes furniture,
clothing and jewellery: cf. *R 3,* III. i.
195.
165–8.] The first two "wrongs" are
mentioned in the source-passage in
Hol., 496/1/45–7. Of the three others,
"Gaunt's rebukes" (i.e. the rebukes
administered to Gaunt), "England's
private wrongs" and the "prevention
. . . / . . . marriage", only the last
needs explanation. Bolingbroke, during his exile in France, projected mar-

Nor Gaunt's rebukes, nor England's private wrongs,
Nor the prevention of poor Bolingbroke
About his marriage, nor my own disgrace, †
Have ever made me sour my patient cheek,
Or bend one wrinkle on my sovereign's face. 170
I am the last of noble Edward's sons,
Of whom thy father, Prince of Wales, was first.
In war was never lion rag'd more fierce,
In peace was never gentle lamb more mild,
Than was that young and princely gentleman. 175
His face thou hast, for even so look'd he,
Accomplish'd with the number of thy hours;
But when he frown'd it was against the French,
And not against his friends; his noble hand
Did win what he did spend, and spent not that 180
Which his triumphant father's hand had won;
His hands were guilty of no kindred blood,

168. my own] Q1 (Huth, Cap. and Hunt.), 2–5, F; his owne Q1 (Petworth). 171.
noble] Q1, F; the noble Q2–5. 173. rag'd] Q1–4, F; rage Q5. 177. the] F;
a Qq.

riage with the French king's cousin, but Richard intervened to stop the match, alleging "heinous offences" against Bolingbroke. Froissart's account is very detailed (chap. CCXXXII), enlarging especially on Bolingbroke's anger at being called a traitor at the French court. Holinshed also moralizes on the wrong done to him: "This was a pestilent kind of proceeding . . . so sharpe, so seuere, & so heinous an accusation, brought to a strange king from a naturall prince, against his subiect . . ." There is no further reference to the incident in the play, but Holinshed's emphasis accounts for the events having stayed in Shakespeare's mind and earning a reference here. There is no need to suppose with Wilson (p. lxvi) that we have a "loose thread" from the hypothetical "old play".

168. nor . . . disgrace] York voluntarily retired to Langley from the court after Gaunt's death in 1398, just as the previous year he and Gaunt,

displeased with Richard, withdrew "into their own countries". This phrase might refer to York's loss of favour as indicated by either or both of these retirements, but, since the retirements were voluntary, whereas the phrase implies Richard's active displeasure, Rossiter suggests there is an echo of Gloucester's historically unjustified complaint, Woodstock, III. ii. 3–4: "Richard with a . . . mind corrupt / Disgraced our names and thrust us from his court."

170. wrinkle] i.e. a frown, which causes wrinkles. York is saying: "I have never looked on you frowningly": cf. John, IV. ii. 90.

172–83.] A speech in Woodstock (I. i. 29–45) similarly compares the king to his father, the Black Prince, to Richard's disadvantage, as did the Londoners mentioned by Froissart (VI. 352).

177.] i.e. "When he was the same age as you"; Accomplish'd with = "furnished with".

But bloody with the enemies of his kin.
O Richard! York is too far gone with grief,
Or else he never would compare between——   185
Rich. Why, uncle, what's the matter?
York.   O my liege,
Pardon me, if you please; if not, I pleas'd
Not to be pardoned, am content withal.
Seek you to seize and gripe into your hands
The royalties and rights of banish'd Herford?   190
Is not Gaunt dead? and doth not Herford live?
Was not Gaunt just? and is not Harry true?
Did not the one deserve to have an heir?
Is not his heir a well-deserving son?
Take Herford's rights away, and take from time   195
His charters, and his customary rights;
Let not to-morrow then ensue to-day:
Be not thyself. For how art thou a king
But by fair sequence and succession?
Now afore God—God forbid I say true!—   200
If you do wrongfully seize Herford's rights,
Call in the letters patents that he hath

---

185. between—] *Hanmer;* between. *Qq, F.*   186-7. *Rich. . . . O*] *Om. Q1* (*Pet-worth*).   186-8.] *As Theobald; . . . matter? / . . . please, / . . . with all, / Qq; . . .* Vncle, / . . . matter? / . . . if not / . . . with all: / *F.*   195. rights] *Q1-4, F;* right *Q5.*   200. say] *Q1* (*Cap. and Huth*), *2-5, F;* lay *Q1* (*Hunt.*).   201. rights] *Q1;* right *Q2-5, F.*   202. the] *Qq;* his *F.*

185-6. *compare between*] Some edd. take this to be used absolutely for "to make comparisons". If so, the usage is very unusual, and this is the only example cited by *O.E.D.* Pollard (p. 66) maintains more convincingly that York leaves his sentence unfinished, the full-stop in Q1 here indicating a pause. Richard has not been listening properly to York (Pollard suggests that he is "walking round the room appraising the value of its contents"), and when York breaks down asks him casually why he is so upset.

189. *gripe*] clutch, grasp.

190. *royalties*] rights granted to a subject by the king (*O.E.D.*, s.v.

"royalty" 6): cf. II. iii. 119; III. iii. 113.

197. *ensue*] follow upon.

202-4.] From Holinshed: Richard had granted Bolingbroke letters-patent allowing him to employ attorneys to "sue his livery", i.e. to institute suits for the obtaining his father Gaunt's lands, which under feudal law would revert to the sovereign until it had been proved that the heir was of age. When the lands were legally restored to the heir, he was required to make an act of homage to the sovereign. Here, Richard is said to revoke the letters-patent (l. 202) and refuse (l. 204) the homage, which, under the letters-patent now revoked,

By his attorneys-general to sue
His livery, and deny his off'red homage,
You pluck a thousand dangers on your head,   205
You lose a thousand well-disposed hearts,
And prick my tender patience to those thoughts
Which honour and allegiance cannot think.
Rich. Think what you will, we seize into our hands
His plate, his goods, his money and his lands.   210
York. I'll not be by the while. My liege, farewell.
What will ensue hereof there's none can tell;
But by bad courses may be understood
That their events can never fall out good.   [*Exit.*
Rich. Go, Bushy, to the Earl of Wiltshire straight,   215
Bid him repair to us to Ely House
To see this business. To-morrow next
We will for Ireland, and 'tis time, I trow.
And we create, in absence of ourself,
Our uncle York Lord Governor of England;   220
For he is just, and always loved us well.
Come on, our queen, to-morrow must we part;

210. lands] *Q1, 2, F;* land *Q3-5.*

was to be "respited with making a reasonable fine" (presumably because the banished Bolingbroke could hardly appear in person to pay homage). By revoking the letters-patent, Richard may be said to be rejecting the homage altogether, and Gaunt's land automatically reverts to the crown. These lines would not be immediately intelligible to an audience, but Shakespeare, copying Holinshed, did not worry about this (cf. note on l. 114 above): a little legal jargon sounds well on the stage.

203. *By*] i.e. by means of, through.

209-10.] The phraseology is close to Holinshed: "he seized into his *hands* all the goods that belonged to [Gaunt], and also receiued all the rents and reuenues of his *lands* which ought to have descended unto the duke of Hereford". Shakespeare may owe Richard's jingle to this; but note that the same rhyme and form is used

by *Mirror,* p. 107, recounting Mowbray's loss of his goods upon his being exiled, "Lord Mowbray", ll. 151-2: "I went my way: the kyng seasde in his hande, / My offyces, my honours, goods and lande". (I owe these suggestions to H. F. Brooks.)

213. *by*] i.e. concerning.

214. *events*] outcomes.

217. *see*] see to.

221. *he is just*] Richard in *Woodstock* makes a similar remark about York, II. i. 126, "... York is gentle: mild and generous"; but there is ample testimony in Holinshed to supply Shakespeare with a mild-tempered York: "a man of a gentle nature, wished that the state of the common-wealth might have been redressed without losse of any man's life" (464/2/46; cf. 485/2/25 and 486/2/20, and note on II. ii. 100). York's "mild sprite" is also referred to by Daniel, *C.W.,* I, st. 30.

Be merry, for our time of stay is short.

    [Exeunt King, Queen, Aumerle, Bushy, Greene and Bagot.]

North. Well, lords, the Duke of Lancaster is dead.

Ross. And living too, for now his son is Duke.   225

Will. Barely in title, not in revenues.

North. Richly in both, if justice had her right.

Ross. My heart is great, but it must break with silence,
    Ere't be disburdened with a liberal tongue.

North. Nay, speak thy mind, and let him ne'er speak more
    That speaks thy words again to do thee harm.   231

Will. Tends that that thou wouldst speak to the Duke of
    Herford?
    If it be so, out with it boldly, man;
    Quick is mine ear to hear of good towards him.

Ross. No good at all that I can do for him,   235
    Unless you call it good to pity him,
    Bereft, and gelded of his patrimony.

North. Now afore God 'tis shame such wrongs are borne
    In him, a royal prince, and many mo
    Of noble blood in this declining land;   240
    The king is not himself, but basely led
    By flatterers; and what they will inform,
    Merely in hate, 'gainst any of us all,
    That will the king severely prosecute
    'Gainst us, our lives, our children, and our heirs.   245

Ross. The commons hath he pill'd with grievous taxes,

---

223. S.D.] *Capell; Exeunt King and Queene: Manet North. Qq; Flourish. Manet North. Willoughby, and Ross. F.* 232. that that... wouldst] *Keightley;* that thou wouldst *Qq;* that thou'dst *F.* 238. God] *Qq;* heauen *F.* 243. 'gainst] *Q1,F;* against *Q2-5.* 245. 'Gainst] *Q1,F;* Against *Q2-5.*

---

228. *great*] pregnant, "big" with eelings; Wilson cfs. *Ham.,* i. ii. 159.

229. *liberal*] unrestrained.

232.] F attempts to mend the metre on the (wrong) assumption that *Herford* (*Hereford* in F) is trisyllabic. Without the second *that* there is an unnatural stress on *wouldst* in Q1's version, which Keightley's emendation smooths away.

239. *mo*] more.

241–2. *The king . . . flatterers*] Cf. *Woodstock,* IV. ii. 143: "His youth is

led by flatterers much astray", and *Mirror,* p. 113, "King Richard the Second", l. 33 "[I] . . . alway put false Flatterers most in trust".

246. *pill d*] despoiled. Keller cfs. *Woodstock,* I. iii. 112: "They would not tax and pill the Commons so!" The verb is fairly common—see its punning use in *1 Return from Parnassus,* l. 751 and Leishman's note in his edn of *The Three Parnassus Plays;* Shakespeare used it in *R 3,* I. iii. 159 (see A. H. Thompson's note in the Arden

And quite lost their hearts. The nobles hath he fin'd
For ancient quarrels and quite lost their hearts.
Will. And daily new exactions are devis'd.
As blanks, benevolences, and I wot not what—   250†
But what a God's name doth become of this?
North. Wars hath not wasted it, for warr'd he hath not,
But basely yielded upon compromise
That which his ancestors achiev'd with blows;

251. But] *Q1–3, F; North.* But *Q4, 5.*   a] *Qq;* o' *F.*   252. *North.* Wars] *Q1,*
F; Willo. Wars *Q2–5.*   254. ancestors] *F;* noble auncestors *Qq.*

edn) and Hayward (p. 63) used it in a similar context: "great summes of money are pulled and pilled from good subiectes to be throwne away amongst vnprofitable vnthrifts".

246–7.] Richard's unpopularity with the common subject is recorded by *Mirror*, p. 114, "King Richard . . .", ll. 43–4: "Blanke charters, othes, & shiftes not knowen of olde, / For whych my Subiectes did me sore detest."

247–8. *quite lost their hearts*] The repetition may be a printer's blunder; but the second use refers to the nobles (as the first to the commons) and there may be an intentional emphasis, as Kittredge thinks. Rossiter cfs. *Woodstock*, v. iii. 94, York to Richard: "thou well may'st doubt their loves that lost their hearts."

250. *blanks, benevolences*] For *blanks* see I. iv. 48 and note. *Benevolences* were forced loans. Holinshed first mentions them in connection with the exactions of Edward IV (1474), Hol., 694/1/50 ff; there is a further paragraph in Hol., 771/2/65 ff on benevolences under Henry VII (1489), where it is again stated that Edward IV introduced this kind of levy. Shakespeare was therefore guilty of anachronism, and he does not use the word in this sense elsewhere, but the *Mirror* mentions the novel methods employed by Richard in extortion (see note on ll. 246–7 above). Hayward committed the same anachronism in his *Life and Raigne of Henrie IIII*, p. 55; at

Hayward's trial for treason on 11 July 1600, according to notes left by the Attorney-General, the famous Sir E. Coke, he confessed that "he has red of a Benevolence in the time of Richard III and not before and yet that he inserted the same in the raigne of Richard II" (quoted by M. Dowling, 'Sir John Hayward's Troubles . . .' in *Library*, 4th ser., XI (1930–1, 214). Hayward may have picked up the word from Shakespeare: see Introduction, p. lxii.

252. *Wars hath*] *Hath* (so Qq, F) is quite commonly used as a plural in the 16th century: see Abbott ¶334.

253.] The reference is to the cession of Brest by Richard to the Duke of Brittany in 1596: see Hol., 487/2/28. From it arose the beginnings of the quarrel with his uncle Gloucester. Northumberland's criticism of Richard here is derived, as Wilson points out, from Gloucester's words of reproach about Brest as given by Hol., 487/2/65: "Sir, your grace ought to put your bodie in paine to win a strong hold or towne by feats of war, yet you take upon you to sell or deliuer anie towne or strong hold gotten with great aduenture by the manhood and policie of your noble progenitours." The cession of Brest was one of the facts about Richard which would be popularly known from the emphasis placed upon it by *Mirror*, p. 114, "King Richard the Second", ll. 45–50.

254. *ancestors*] The extra-metrical

More hath he spent in peace than they in wars.   255
Ross. The Earl of Wiltshire hath the realm in farm.
Will. The king's grown bankrout like a broken man.
North. Reproach and dissolution hangeth over him.
Ross. He hath not money for these Irish wars,
  His burthenous taxations notwithstanding,   260
  But by the robbing of the banish'd Duke.
North. His noble kinsman—most degenerate king!
  But, lords, we hear this fearful tempest sing,
  Yet seek no shelter to avoid the storm;

257. king's] *Q3–5, F;* King *Q1, 2.*

noble of Qq, omitted by F, seems to have been intruded from *noble kinsman* eight lines later. This is probably too far for an ordinary catching by the compositor, and is likely to be a memorial anticipation by a transcriber. "Noble" occurs at l. 240 above, where it is clearly correct; if it is correct here also, then Shakespeare, rather clumsily, used the epithet three times in twenty-three lines. The idea of "kinsman" is close enough to "ancestors" to have prompted the scribe's shift: cf. v. ii. 28 and Introduction, pp. xvi–xix. It is not likely that F had any special authority for its emendation: it frequently regularizes metre, or attempts to, by omission of single words.

256. *The Earl . . . farm*] See note on I. iv. 45.

257. *bankrout*] See note on l. 151 above.

broken] financially ruined.

258. *hangeth*] The singular verb is used after two nouns where these stand for a single conception or for two things not meant to be thought of apart; it is also sometimes attracted to the number of the neatest substantive (Herford): see Abbott ¶336. For the sentiment, Reyher cfs. *Woodstock,* II. ii. 47, Gloucester to Richard: "Confusion hangeth o'er thy wretched head", but the phrase and thought are commonplace. Wilson's parallel with Hall (p. 6) of how York implored God's aid

in diverting "the darke clowde which he saw dependyng ouer his hed" is likewise inconclusive; cf. note on ll. 263–9 below.

262. *degenerate*] Probably implies "degenerate from his noble father" (the Black Prince), as *Woodstock* has it, I. i. 29: cf. ll. 172–83 above and note.

263–9.] The image of persons threatened by political dangers likened to those threatened with a storm is not recondite—Shakespeare had already used it in *3 H 6,* v. iii. 1–5 (and cf. *R 2,* I. iii. 187)—and it is not surprising that there are analogies in Hall and Daniel, which prove very little. In Hall (p. 6) Archbishop Arundel, in his plea to Bolingbroke to invade England, speaks of this "tempestuous world and ceason (in the which no manne of our nacion is sure of his life . . .)" [Reyher]. In Daniel, *C.W.,* I, st. 113, we have: "Calme these tempestuous spirits O mighty Lord / This threatning storme that ouer hangs the land" (cf. l. 258 above), and cf. *ibid.,* I, st. 80: "There where they little thinke the storme doth rise, / And ouercasts their clear security"—a passage, which, since it has the *security-storm* contrast and describes the situation at about the time of the king's departure for Ireland, may be the closer to Shakespeare: in Daniel, however it is Richard himself who is foolishly "secure" and ignorant of the coming danger from Bolingbroke.

We see the wind sit sore upon our sails,   265
And yet we strike not, but securely perish.

Ross. We see the very wrack that we must suffer,
And unavoided is the danger now,
For suffering so the causes of our wrack.

North. Not so, even through the hollow eyes of death   270
I spy life peering; but I dare not say
How near the tidings of our comfort is.

Will. Nay, let us share thy thoughts as thou dost ours.

Ross. Be confident to speak, Northumberland:
We three are but thyself, and, speaking so,   275
Thy words are but as thoughts; therefore be bold.

North. Then thus: I have from le Port Blanc,
A bay in Brittaine, receiv'd intelligence
That Harry Duke of Herford, Rainold Lord Cobham,
[The son of Richard Earl of Arundel,]   280
That late broke from the Duke of Exeter,
His brother, Archbishop late of Canterbury,

271. spy] *Q1,F;* espie *Q2–5.*   277. le Port Blanc] *Wright;* le Port Blan *Qq;* Port
le Blan *F.*   278. Brittaine] *Q1;* Brittanie *Q2–4;* Britaine *Q5,F.*   280.] *Malone;
not in Qq, F.*

266. *strike*] "strike or furl sails" with
quibble on "strike a blow".
   securely] over-confidently, unsuspici-
ously: cf. III. ii. 34, v. iii. 42.
   268. *unavoided*] unavoidable: cf. *R 3,*
IV. iv. 217, "unavoided is the doom";
"the Passive Participle is often used to
signify, not that which *was* and *is,* but
that which *was* and therefore *can be
hereafter*" (Abbott ¶375).
   270–1.] An image which suggests
the well-known emblem-book figure of
the soul trapped inside an anatomy
and looking outwards: see Quarles,
Emblems Divine and Moral. Bk v, no. 8
(London edn of 1778) and accom-
panying cut. *Eyes* = eye-sockets: see
note on I. iii. 224.
   272. *tidings . . . is*] Tidings is sometimes singular and sometimes plural
in Shakespeare.
   277. *le Port Blanc*] From Holinshed,
like all the other place and personal
names in this passage, this is the

modern Port le Blanc, near Tréguier,
Côtes du Nord.
   278. *Brittaine*] Brittany, or Bretagne:
cf. l. 285 below. It seems best to follow Q1's spelling here, since we would
have to modernize to *Bretagne* rather
than to *Britain*: cf. *John,* II. i. 156.
   280.] A line appears to have been
dropped out in Qq and F. Something
like Malone's conjecture is necessary,
because according to Hol., 496/1/70 it
was not Lord Cobham who "broke
from the Duke of Exeter" but the
Earl of Arundel's son who fled the
realm to join his uncle the Archbishop
of Canterbury. The list of proper
names has also caused metrical disturbances at l. 277, which is a foot
short, and at l. 279 and ll. 283–4. It
may be, as Herford suggests, that
Shakespeare did not attempt to fit
them into better verse.
   282. *His brother*] i.e. the Earl of
Arundel's brother.

Sir Thomas Erpingham, Sir John Ramston,
Sir John Norbery, Sir Robert Waterton, and Francis
　　Quoint—
All these well furnished by the Duke of Brittaine   285
With eight tall ships, three thousand men of war,
Are making hither with all due expedience,
And shortly mean to touch our northern shore.
Perhaps they had ere this, but that they stay
The first departing of the king for Ireland.   290
If then we shall shake off our slavish yoke,
Imp out our drooping country's broken wing,
Redeem from broking pawn the blemish'd crown,
Wipe off the dust that hides our sceptre's gilt,
And make high majesty look like itself,   295
Away with me in post to Ravenspurgh;
But if you faint, as fearing to do so,
Stay, and be secret, and myself will go.
Ross. To horse, to horse! urge doubts to them that fear.
Will. Hold out my horse, and I will first be there.   300
　　　　　　　　　　　　　　　　　　　　　　　[*Exeunt.*

283. Ramston] *Qq;* Rainston *F.*   284. Quoint] *F;* Coines *Qq.*   291. slavish]
Q1, F; Countries slauish *Q2–5.*   293. broking] *Q1, 2, F;* broken *Q3–5.*

284. *Quoint*] So F; the Qq reading
Coines seems to be a mistake for the
name that appears in Holinshed as
Coint. This misprint could hardly have
arisen if Q1 had in its copy the F
spelling with *Qu-.* F's spelling may be
a prompt-book spelling and does not
seem to derive from Holinshed or Q1;
for the significance of this, see Introduction, p. xxi.

287. *expedience*] speed: cf. i. iv. 39.

289–90. *stay . . . Ireland*] i.e. "they
wait till the king has first departed
. . ." (Herford). The reason given in
Holinshed (498/1/31) for Bolingbroke's delay in landing is his wish to
find out "what countenance was made
by the people, whether they meant
enuiouslie to resist him, or freendlie to
receiue him." Shakespeare has so tele-
scoped the various events in this scene
in the interests of dramatic timing that

the situation has now become quite
unhistorical in its chronology, for
Richard was safely in Ireland long
before Bolingbroke approached the
coast of Yorkshire.

292. *Imp*] A falconers' term, meaning to engraft new feathers in the wing
and so restore and improve the powers
of flight (Onions).

293. *broking pawn*] A reminder of
the "king as landlord" theme, ll. 113–
14 above.

296. *in post*] with speed, literally
"travelling by relays of horses".

Ravenspurgh] Between Hull and
Bridlington; in Edward I's time the
most considerable port on the Hum-
ber (Clarendon edd.).

297. *if you faint*] if you are faint-
hearted.

300. *Hold out*] last out.

SCENE II.—[*Windsor Castle.*]

Enter the QUEEN, BUSHY, *and* BAGOT.

Bushy. Madam, your Majesty is too much sad.
  You promis'd, when you parted with the king,
  To lay aside life-harming heaviness,
  And entertain a cheerful disposition.
Queen. To please the king I did—to please myself   5
  I cannot do it; yet I know no cause
  Why I should welcome such a guest as grief,
  Save bidding farewell to so sweet a guest
  As my sweet Richard. Yet again methinks

Scene II

Location.] *Clarendon edd.; not in Qq, F.*   3. life-harming] *Q1, 2;* halfe-harming
Q3–5; selfe-harming *F.*

MATERIAL. Queen Isabel has appeared in the previous scene. Her
marriage with Richard is described at
length by Holinshed, pp. 486–7: for
her unhistorical maturity in years, see
Introduction, p. xliii. The passage between Bushy and Isabel up to
l. 40 is all Shakespearian invention,
although there may be a couple of
analogues in *Woodstock* and Créton
(see note on ll. 10–11). The disasters
to Richard's cause reported by
Greene—the landing of Bolingbroke
(l. 49), the accessions to his standard
(ll. 53 ff), the proclamation of Northumberland and "all the rest" as traitors (ll. 56–7) and the death of the
Duchess of Gloucester (l. 97)—are
derived from scattered places in Holinshed: see notes on these lines. The
discussion of them by the favourites in
Isabel's presence is Shakespeare's invention. York's behaviour derives
from Holinshed's statement (498/1/36
ff) that York sent for certain privy
councillors, including Bushy, Bagot,
and Greene, "to know what they
thought good to be done in this matter, concerning the duke of Lancaster,
being on the seas", and l. 108 derives

from their decision to "gather an
armie to resist the duke in his landing".
But York's confusion and feebleness of
mind is part of Shakespeare's general
conception of the character: see notes
on II. i. 221 and l. 100 below. York's
plan to ask the Duchess of Gloucester
for help seems to have been invented
by Shakespeare so that he could bring
in the news of her death and thus increase the feeling that the disasters, as
Reyher says, "fondent en effet coup
sur coup". The final colloquy between
Bushy, Bagot, and Greene (ll. 125 ff)
is based on Hol., 498/1/56 ff.

Location] Holinshed says that
Isabel remained at Windsor when
Richard left for Ireland.

3. *life-harming heaviness*] Noble cites
Ecclus., xxx. 23: "as for sorowe and
heauinesse, driue it farre from thee:
for beauinesse hath slayne many a
man, and bringeth no profit." As
Wilson notes, grief was thought to
impoverish the blood: cf. *Rom.*, III. v.
59.

7. *guest . . . grief*] The image of
grief as a guest lodging in a sorrowful
man is repeated by Isabel at v. i. 13-
15.

Some unborn sorrow ripe in Fortune's womb   10
Is coming towards me, and my inward soul
With nothing trembles; at some thing it grieves,
More than with parting from my lord the king.
Bushy. Each substance of a grief hath twenty shadows,
Which shows like grief itself, but is not so.   15
For sorrow's eye, glazed with blinding tears,
Divides one thing entire to many objects,
Like perspectives, which, rightly gaz'd upon,

---

12. With] *Q1 (Huth, Cap. and Hunt.)*, *2–5, F;* At *Q1 (Petworth).*   trembles; at
some thing it] *Ed.;* trembles at some thing it *Qq, F (something Q1, 2, F);*
trembles, yet at something *Pope.*   16. eye] *F;* eyes *Qq.*

10.] For the later development of
the image, see ll. 62–6 below. Isabel's
foreboding recalls the foreboding
dreams of the Duchess of Gloucester
in *Woodstock*, IV. ii. 5 ff. Créton, p.
31/100, describes how he suffered
from an obscure heaviness of heart
during Richard's Irish campaign.

12. *some thing*] The accent falls
on *thing* (Herford). Pope's smooth-
ing of the line is defended by Wilson.

14. *substance . . . shadows*] i.e. "for
every real grief, there are twenty il-
lusory ones": cf. IV. i. 292–9 and
notes. Shakespeare was very interested in this contrast: cf. *3 H 6*, IV. iii.
50, *Tit.*, III. ii. 79–80, *Mer. V.*, III. ii.
127, *Ham.*, II. ii. 261, *All's W.*, v. iii.
301–2, *Rom.*, v. i. 10–11.

15. *shows*] "a sing. verb often follows the *relative* in spite of a pl. antecedent" (Herford).

17.] "Breaks up one thing, entire in
itself, into many separate objects"
(Deighton).

18–20.] Cf. Henry Porter's *Two
Angrie Women of Abington* (1599),
M.S.R., ll. 12-18: "Kinde sir, neere
dwelling amitie indeed, / Offers the
hearts enquirie better view, / Then
loue thats seated in a farther soile, /
As prospectiues [t]he nearer that they
be, / Yeeld better iudgement to the
iudging eye, / Things seene farre off,
are lessened in the eye, / When their

true shape is seene being hard by".
(I owe this reference to J. M. Nos-
worthy.)

18. *perspectives*] perspective pictures:
scan, pérspectíves. The perspective
picture, a Renaissance toy, is described by Tollet quoting from *Humane
Industry* (1661) in his note to *Tw. N.*,
v. i. 244 in the Johnson-Steevens 1821
Variorum: "it is a pretty art that in a
pleated paper and table furrowed or
indented, men make one picture to
represent several faces—that being
from one place or standing, did shew
the head of a Spaniard, and from another the head of an ass." This
variety is referred to in *Ant.*, II. v. 116–
17. A simpler example is the portrait
of Edward VI in the National Portrait
Gallery (reproduced in *Shakespeare's
England*, II. 12), where the subject's
face appears grotesquely distorted unless viewed through a spyhole in the
frame. This is the variety referred to
by Bushy. But in ll. 16–17 he also
seems to be thinking of another kind
of "perspective", the "multiplying
glass cut into a number of facets each
giving a separate image . . . [an] illu-
sion produced naturally by some
specimens of Iceland spar" (see F. L.
Lucas, *Works of John Webster*, I. 208):
to these multiplying glasses he compares the tear-filled eye of Isabel,
whose facets multiply grief. Neither
the perspective pictures nor the per-

Show nothing but confusion; ey'd awry,
Distinguish form. So your sweet Majesty,　　20
Looking awry upon your lord's departure,
Find shapes of grief more than himself to wail,　　†
Which, look'd on as it is, is nought but shadows
Of what it is not; then, thrice-gracious queen,
More than your lord's departure weep not—more's not
　　seen,　　25
Or if it be, 'tis with false sorrow's eye,

19. Show] *Q1* (*Huth, Cap. and Hunt.*), *2–5, F; Shows Q1* (*Petworth*).　　24. thrice-gracious queen] *F;* thrice (gracious Queene) *Qq.*　　25. more's] *F;* more is *Qq.*
26. eye] *Q1, F;* eyes *Q2–5.*

spective multiplying glasses (so called because they were cut by "art perspective") must be confused with the *perspective* (or "prospective") *glass*, a kind of magic crystal which could be used to look into the distance or the future. This is not referred to here, but is important in *Mac.*, IV. i. 111 ff (and cf. Jonson, *Alchemist*, III. iv. 87 ff, Greene, *Friar Bacon*, scenes vi and xiii). Chapman is fond of using the perspective picture to illustrate moods or morals, e.g. *Eugenia*, ll. 173–8 (*Poems*, ed. Bartlett, and note on p. 456); and cf. Drayton, *Mortimeriados*, ll. 2332–8 (*Works*, ed. Hebel, I, and K. Tillotson's note, V. 43).

rightly] "directly" with quibble on "properly".

20. *Distinguish form*] show distinct forms (Herford).

21–2.] In these lines the two comparisons, from perspective pictures and multiplying glasses, get mixed up. Isabel, "looking awry" (that is to say, not from the prescribed angle) at the perspective picture, is said to see multiplied shapes of grief, which is what one would expect to see if looking at a multiplying glass. The passage is made harder by the quibble on "looking awry": Isabel is "looking awry" (wrongly) on the perspective picture of her lord's departure because she is *not* "looking awry" at it (i.e. from the prescribed angle at the side of the pic-

ture, as explained in note to l. 18 above).

22. *Find*] 2nd pers. sing., the subject being "you", understood from "your sweet Majesty" in l. 20 (Wilson).

more than himself] in addition to the original grief itself.

wail] bewail.

23–4. *Which . . . not*] i.e. "Which [= shapes of grief], if looked on 'rightly', are nothing but shadows of something which they are not." The "something" which the shapes of grief illusorily counterfeit is "grief" itself, but, because they are illusions, they are not, therefore, the grief and cause for grief which they pretend to be. "Which" in this interpretation is attracted into the sing. and has a sing. verb because it is relative to the whole situation as well as to the "shapes" themselves. Alternatively, the passage might be a further stage in the argument: "which [= grief itself at your lord's departure], if looked on 'rightly', is itself nothing but shadows of something that doesn't exist." But this interpretation conflicts with l. 25 below, where Bushy allows the queen to grieve for Richard's going, and with the whole tenour of the argument, which is directed not against Isabel's admittedly genuine cause for grief at losing Richard but against the "more than" this of which she complains in ll. 12–13 above.

Which, for things true, weeps things imaginary.
Queen. It may be so; but yet my inward soul
    Persuades me it is otherwise. Howe'er it be,
    I cannot but be sad; so heavy sad,   30
    As, though on thinking on no thought I think,
    Makes me with heavy nothing faint and shrink.
Bushy. 'Tis nothing but conceit, my gracious lady.
Queen. 'Tis nothing less: conceit is still deriv'd
    From some forefather grief; mine is not so,   35
    For nothing hath begot my something grief,
    Or something hath the nothing that I grieve—
    'Tis in reversion that I do possess—
    But what it is that is not yet known what,
    I cannot name: 'tis nameless woe, I wot.   40

Enter GREENE.

Greene. God save your Majesty! and well met, gentlemen.
    I hope the king is not yet shipp'd for Ireland.
Queen. Why hopest thou so? 'tis better hope he is,

27. weeps] *Qq;* weepe *F.*   31. though] *Q2–5,F;* thought *Q1.*   33–4. *Bushy...*
Queen.] *om. Q1 (Petworth).*   39–40. But ... name:] *Q1* (name,)*;* But what it is,
that is not yet knowne, what / I cannot name, *Q2–5, F.*   40. S.D.] *F; not in Qq.*
41. God] *Qq;* Heauen *F.*

27.] "Which, instead of weeping for true things, weeps for imaginary things". For *weep* in the sense of "weep for", cf. l. 25 above, *R 3,* ii. iv. 59.

31. *though . . . think*] "Though I think on thinking no thought", i.e. "Though I set myself to think about nothing" (Newbolt). Johnson's view that "thought" here means "melancholy" does not accord with the "heavy nothing" of the next line, which implies that Isabel's mind is vacant (though mysteriously burdened by this vacancy), not merely free from melancholy.

33. *conceit*] fancy

34–40.] *nothing less* = "anything but mere fancy!" She continues: "for a fanciful condition of grief is always engendered by some real preceding grief; but my grief is not; no-

thing has begot the grief that I suffer from. Or, something else actually possesses the reality of the apparent nothingness which now grieves me [l. 36]; what I've got, I've got 'in reversion'. But what is not yet known, I cannot give a name to; therefore, I suppose, it's 'Nameless Woe'." The image from engendering ("forefather", "begot", and cf. ll. 62–6 below) switches to legal imagery at l. 36 with the change in the direction of her thought. For "in reversion", see note on i. iv. 35—the woe is due to pass to Isabel when whoever now has it yields it up.

43–6. *hope*] The placings of the word bring out the different shades of meaning: *hope* in "good hope" = "good expectation"; in "our hope" = "our means of succour, the person from whom we hope for aid".

For his designs crave haste, his haste good hope.
Then wherefore dost thou hope he is not shipp'd?   45
Greene. That he, our hope, might have retir'd his power,
And driven into despair an enemy's hope,
Who strongly hath set footing in this land:
The banish'd Bolingbroke repeals himself,
And with uplifted arms is safe arriv'd   50
At Ravenspurgh.
Queen.   Now God in heaven forbid!
Greene. Ah, madam, 'tis too true; and that is worse,
The lord Northumberland, his son young Henry Percy,
The lords of Ross, Beaumond, and Willoughby,
With all their powerful friends, are fled to him.   55
Bushy. Why have you not proclaim'd Northumberland

53. son young] *Q1;* yong sonne *Q2-5, F.*   54. lords] *Q1 (Huth, Cap. and Hunt.),*
2-5, F; lord *Q1 (Petworth).*

46. *retir'd . . . power*] pulled back [from Ireland] his forces.

49. *repeals*] recalls from exile. Regularly used in this sense by Marlowe and Shakespeare: cf. iv. i. 85.

51. *Ravenspurgh*] See note on ii. i. 296.

52. *and . . . worse*] also, that which is worse.

53. *his son young Henry Percy*] The line may be an alexandrine, but the phrase duplicates ii. iii. 21, which was perhaps anticipated in the memory of a transcriber; or *his son* may have been an afterthought—did Shakespeare originally write: "The lord Northumberland, yong Harry Percie [H. Percie in Q1]"?

53-5.] A selection from the supporters of Bolingbroke named by Holinshed at 498/1/73 ff: "The first that came to him, were the lords of Lincolnshire, and other countries adioining, as the lords Willoughbie, Ros, Darcie, and Beaumont. At his comming into Doncaster, the earle of Northumberland, and his sonne sir Henrie Persie, wardens of the marches against Scotland, with the earl of Westmoreland, came unto him . . ." There is no debt to Hall, as Zeeveld

(p. 322) mistakenly claims. For Northumberland, cf. note on material for ii. i, and note on ll. 56-61 below.

56-61.] The proclamation of Northumberland as a traitor and the Earl of Worcester's subsequent displeasure are further referred to at ii. iii. 26-30 and are recorded by Hol., 499/2/74: "Sir Thomas Persie earle of Worcester, lord steward of the king's house, either being so commanded by the king, or else upon displeasure (as some write) for that the king had proclaimed his brother the earle of Northumberland traitor, brake his white staffe, and without delaie went to duke Henrie." The *Mirror* enlarges upon the fact of Northumberland's being proclaimed traitor (p. 133, "Henry, Earl of Northumberland", ll. 31-5) and also mentions Worcester's breaking of his staff of office (p. 115, "Richard the Second", ll. 75-6). Froissart, who gives a very different and much more elaborate account of the Percies' behaviour during the crisis (see note on material, ii. i) says only: "they were openly banysshed the realme of Englande, tyll the kynge dyd repeale them agayne" (vi. 348).

And all the rest revolted faction traitors?

Greene. We have; whereupon the Earl of Worcester
  Hath broken his staff, resign'd his stewardship,
  And all the household servants fled with him   60
  To Bolingbroke.

Queen. So, Greene, thou art the midwife to my woe,   †
  And Bolingbroke my sorrow's dismal heir;
  Now hath my soul brought forth her prodigy,
  And I, a gasping new-deliver'd mother,   65
  Have woe to woe, sorrow to sorrow join'd.

Bushy. Despair not, madam,

Queen.   Who shall hinder me?
  I will despair, and be at enmity
  With cozening Hope—he is a flatterer,
  A parasite, a keeper-back of Death,   70
  Who gently would dissolve the bands of life,
  Which false Hope lingers in extremity.

---

57. all the rest] *Q1;* the rest of the *Q2–5, F.* revolted] *Q1–3, F;* revolting
Q4, 5. 59. broken] *Q1;* broke *Q2–5, F.* 60–1.] *As Pope;* And ... Bulling-
brook / *Qq, F.* 62. to] *Q1;* of *Q2–5, F.* 69. cozening] *Q1–3, F;* couetous
Q4, 5. 72. Hope lingers] *Qq;* hopes linger *F.*

57. *all ... faction*] "all the rest of the
revolted faction". But see Abbott
¶246, who proposes ellipsis of a relative and interprets: "And all the rest
[that are] revolted, faction-traitors".
The line seems to have been puzzling
to Q2.

59. *broken his staff*] The reading of F
and Q2–5 may be correct, since
broken disturbs the metre. The phrase
is not only tautologous (since breaking
the wand of office was equivalent to
"resigning the stewardship") but a
near-repetition of II. iii. 27: "*Broken
his staff* of office".

62–6.] The imagery continues the
"generating" imagery of the lines on
Isabel's sorrow, l. 10 and ll. 34–40
above. Cf. *The First Part of Ieronimo*
(?1600), ed. Boas (*Works of Kyd*), I.
iii. 6–8: "I haue mischiefe / Within
my breast, more then my bulke can
hold: / I want a midwiue to deliuer
it" Day, *Ile of Gulls* (1606), C4ᵛ: "My
thoughts come like a saile afore the

wind, swolne big with newes, and
thine eares the midwife must deliuer
me of this burthen", and the imagery
in Daniel, *C.W.*, II, st. 97 (part of
a passage that probably influenced
Shakespeare) which is quoted in the
Appendix, p. 205.

63. *heir*] offspring: Wilson cfs. "the
first heir of my invention", dedication
to *Ven.*

64. *prodigy*] Usually in Shakespeare
means "portent", here "monstrous
birth" as well: cf. *3 H 6,* I. iv. 75,
where the word is abusively applied
to Crookback. Bolingbroke himself is
the "child" who has been born:
"[Isabel] is like a woman whose new-
born infant is so monstrous a creature
that his birth does not relieve her sufferings but adds to them" (Kittredge).

69. *cozening*] cheating.

71. *bands*] bonds.

72. *lingers in extremity*] prolongs to
the utmost degree. For transitive use
of *linger* cf. *Oth.*, IV. ii. 224.

Enter YORK.

Greene. Here comes the Duke of York.

Queen. With signs of war about his aged neck;
  O, full of careful business are his looks!   75
  Uncle, for God's sake, speak comfortable words.

York. Should I do so, I should belie my thoughts;
  Comfort's in heaven, and we are on the earth,
  Where nothing lives but crosses, cares, and grief.
  Your husband, he is gone to save far off,   80
  Whilst others come to make him lose at home.
  Here am I left to underprop his land,
  Who weak with age cannot support myself;
  Now comes the sick hour that his surfeit made,
  Now shall he try his friends that flatter'd him.   85

Enter a Servant.

Serv. My lord, your son was gone before I came.

York. He was? why, so go all which way it will!
  The nobles they are fled, the commons cold,

72. S.D.] *F; not in Qq.*   76. God's] *Qq; heauens F.*   77.] *Not in F.*   78. on] *Q1
(Huth, Cap. and Hunt.), 2–5, F; in Q1 (Petworth).*   79. cares] *Q1; care Q2–5, F.*
85. S.D.] *F; not in Qq.*   88. cold] *Pope; they are colde Qq, F.*

74.] York must be wearing a gorget, the piece of armour that protected the throat. In Shakespeare's time it was a prerogative of military men to wear the gorget, and no other armour, with civilian dress. See the portrait of Sir P. Sidney by an unknown artist in the National Portrait Gallery, and G. Reynolds, *Costume of the Western World: Elizabethan* . . . (1951), p. 16.

75. *careful business*] anxious preoccupation (Herford).

76. *Uncle, . . . sake*] The line is a long one, and may have been corrupted by anticipation of III. i. 36–7: "*Uncle*, you say the *queen* is at your house; / *For God's sake* . . ." But Isabel's use of the word "Uncle", as she bursts out in a plea to York and an acknowledgement of his entry, seems very natural here.

speak . . . words] Noble cites the Communion Service in the Book of

Common Prayer ("Hear what comfortable words our Saviour Christ saith . . ."), and Zech., i. 13 (Genevan version), but argues (pp. 62–3) that in view of the use of *discomfortable* elsewhere in *R 2* (see III. ii. 36 and note) Isabel's phrase is probably caught from its variant in the Bishops' or Genevan Bible's version of Ecclus., xviii. 4: "speake no discomfortable words".

84.] For the language and sentiments cf. *Lr.*, I. ii. 121: "when we are sick in fortune, often the surfeits of our own behaviour".

85. *try*] put to the test, i.e. find out if they have any real worth in the crisis.

S.D. Servant] The speech-prefixes for this speaker in Q1–3 are "Serving-man".

86. *your . . . gone*] Aumerle, who had gone to the king in Ireland.

88.] Wilson thinks that the repeti-

And will, I fear, revolt on Herford's side.
Sirrah, get thee to Plashy, to my sister Gloucester,   90
Bid her send me presently a thousand pound.
Hold, take my ring.
Serv. My lord, I had forgot to tell your lordship:
To-day as I came by I called there—
But I shall grieve you to report the rest.   95
York. What is't, knave?
Serv. An hour before I came the Duchess died.
York. God for his mercy, what a tide of woes

92–4.] *As in Qq;* . . . forgot / . . . there / *F.*   94. as I came by I] *Q1;* I came by and *Q2–5, F.*   98. God] *Qq;* Heau'n *F.*

tion of *they are* in Qq and F may be a compositor's blunder—cf. I. iii. 136; it is certainly harder to justify than the similar repetition at II. i. 247–8.

91. *presently*] immediately.

97.] Hol., 514/2/3 reports that the Duchess died in 1399 through "sorrow (as was thought) . . . for the losse of her sonne and heire the lord Humfrie". Her death at this precise point in the play is an imaginative stroke by Shakespeare. It also releases the actor playing her part to play that of the Duchess of York in Act V.

98–121.] The metrically dislocated character of several lines in this speech has led editors to attempt rearrangements; Pope's at ll. 120–1 is generally accepted as preserving an intended rhyme. The speech contains a number of phrases that seem to echo each other (e.g., ll. 111–14: "Both are my kinsmen . . . both my oath . . . th' other again / Is my kinsman . . ."; ll. 105 and 116: "Come, sister—cousin . . ." and "Come, cousin . . ."; ll. 108 and 117) and these are found in conjunction with metrical disturbances. If the theory that a transcriber who was liable to memorial errors had something to do with the copy for Q1 is correct (see Introduction, pp. xvi–xix) it looks as though the confusion may be his work; the kind of phrase (exclamations and forms of address) on which damage

seems to centre belongs in the categories which D. L. Patrick in his study of *Richard III* showed to be particularly susceptible of memorial corruption. (i) l. 98: *God for his mercy*: cf. the same exclamation at V. ii. 75. This may be York's consistency in swearing or it may be a memorial error at either place. (ii) l. 109: the metre is disturbed. A similar phrase is found in the first Quarto of *R 3*, IV. ii. 171: "But how or in what place I do not know." In *R 3* this is a memorial corruption, corrected in the F text of *R 3* (IV. iii. 30) to "But where (to say the truth) I do not know" (see D. L. Patrick, p. 102). We note the similar phrase-pattern of l. 109 here and the corrupt line in *R 3*, and the associative link "I do not know / If I know". This suggests that the phrases in Q1 *R 3* and Q1 *R 2* are related through a single mind, and that the putative scribe of *R 2* allowed his memory of *R 3* to operate during work on our play. This is reinforced by (iii) l. 116, again metrically irregular: cf. first Quarto of *R 3*, III. i. 216–17: "Chop off his head, man, somewhat we will doe"; this is a memorial corruption of *R 3*, F, III. i. 193: "Chop off his head—something we will determine" (see Patrick, p. 74). It hardly seems possible to restore here what Shakespeare wrote, since there is no check on the corruptions such as is provided

Comes rushing on this woeful land at once!
I know not what to do, I would to God,   100
So my untruth had not provok'd him to it,
The king had cut my head off with my brother's.
What, are there no posts dispatch'd for Ireland?
How shall we do for money for these wars?   104
Come, sister—cousin, I would say, pray pardon me.   †
Go, fellow, get thee home, provide some carts
And bring away the armour that is there. [*Exit Servant.*]
Gentlemen, will you go muster men?
If I know how or which way to order these affairs,
Thus thrust disorderly into my hands,   110
Never believe me. Both are my kinsmen:
Th'one is my sovereign, whom both my oath
And duty bids defend; th' other again
Is my kinsman, whom the king hath wrong'd,
Whom conscience and my kindred bids to right.   115
Well, somewhat we must do. Come, cousin,
I'll dispose of you. Gentlemen, go muster up your
    men,
And meet me presently at Berkeley.
I should to Plashy too,

99. Comes] *Qq;* Come *F.*   100. God] *Qq;* heauen *F.*   103. no] *Q1;* two
Q2-5; not in F.   107. S.D.] *Capell; not in Qq, F.*   110. thrust disorderly]
Steevens (1793); disorderly thrust *Qq, F.*   118. Berkeley] *Qq;* Barkley Castle *F.*
119-21.] *As Pope; . . . permit: | . . . seauen. | Qq, F.*

by the F text in the case of *R 3.*
  99.] Reyher cfs. *Woodstock,* IV. ii. 62:
"this woeful land will all to ruin run."
  100. *I know . . . do*] Shakespeare
conceives York as not only mild (cf.
note on II. i. 221) but flustered by
affairs: see Hol., 485/2/25: "the duke
of Yorke was a man rather coueting to
live in pleasure, than to deale with
much businesse, and the weightie
affairs of the realme." Reyher cfs.
York's situation with Gloucester's in
Woodstock, and cites as parallels to this
line and ll. 110-13 below Gloucester's
repeated: "Afore my God / I know
not which way to bestow myself" (I. i.
126-7, I. iii. 240) and "Afore my God,
I know not what to do" (I. iii. 246).

  101. *untruth*] disloyalty. York is not
implying that he *has* been disloyal
(Newbolt).
  105. *sister*] "The recent death of his
sister is uppermost in his mind"
(Steevens).
  106. *carts*] When describing how
Richard's Constable made off with
the king's valuables, Créton, p. 99/
326, says: "La auoit il moult mer-
veilleux desroy / Nes escrangier &
chargier le charroy". Both passages
thus mention "carts"—a fairly insig-
nificant coincidence.
  108. *men*] i.e. tenantry and re-
tainers for the fighting: cf. *R 3,* IV. iii.
56, *3 H 6,* IV. viii. 9 ff.
  112. *oath*] See note on IV. i. 235.

But time will not permit. All is uneven,   120
And everything is left at six and seven.
                    [*Exeunt York and Queen.*]
Bushy. The wind sits fair for news to go for Ireland,
        But none returns. For us to levy power
        Proportionable to the enemy
        Is all unpossible.   125
Greene. Besides, our nearness to the king in love
        Is near the hate of those love not the king.
Bagot. And that's the wavering commons, for their love
        Lies in their purses, and whoso empties them,
        By so much fills their hearts with deadly hate.   130
Bushy. Wherein the king stands generally condemn'd.
Bagot. If judgment lie in them, then so do we,
        Because we ever have been near the king.
Greene. Well, I will for refuge straight to Bristow castle,
        The Earl of Wiltshire is already there.   135
Bushy. Thither will I with you; for little office
        The hateful commons will perform for us,
        Except like curs to tear us all to pieces.
        Will you go along with us?
Bagot. No, I will to Ireland to his Majesty.   140

121. S.D.] *Wright; Exeunt Duke, Qu. man Bush. Green. Qq (manent. Q3–5);
Exit F.*   122. for] *Qq;* to *F.*   124–5.] *As Pope;* Proportionable . . . un-
possible. / *Qq, F.*   125. unpossible] *Qq;* impossible *F.*   128. that's] *F;*
that is *Qq.*   133. ever have been] *Qq;* haue been euer *F.*   134. Bristow]
Brist. *Qq;* Bristoll *F.*   137. The . . . commons will]*Pope;* Will the . . . commons *Qq, F.*   138. to pieces] *Q1;* in pieces *Q2–5, F.*

121. *at . . . seven*] Shakespeare's only
use of the phrase, originally derived
from dicing: see Tilley A208.
    128. *that's*] An F contraction adopt-
ed here; see Introduction, p. xxix.
    132.] "If the commons' hearts are
to be judges, then we are condemned
too."
    134. *I will*] See Introduction, p.xxix.
    136. *office*] i.e. "good office" or
"service".
    137. *hateful*] full of hate.
    140.] Hol., 498/1/61 says that Bagot
"got him to Chester and so escaped into Ireland, the other [i.e. Bushy
and Greene] fled to the castell of

Bristow". But this line here contradicts II. iii. 164, where we find Bushy
and Bagot at Bristol. Rossiter (p. 239)
ascribes the contradiction to Shakespeare's following *Woodstock*, v. vi.
6–7, where Bagot is said to be at Bristol: Shakespeare might have concluded therefrom that Bagot never got as
far as Ireland in spite of his declared
intention and the statement in Holinshed. I do not think Shakespeare used
Woodstock in this way, and suggest
that the contradiction between here
and II. iii. 164 is due to sheer careless-
ness. For a further tangle about
Bagot, see note on III. ii. 122–3.

Farewell. If heart's presages be not vain,
We three here part that ne'er shall meet again.
Bushy. That's as York thrives to beat back Bolingbroke.
Greene. Alas, poor Duke! the task he undertakes
Is numb'ring sands and drinking oceans dry;   145
Where one on his side fights, thousands will fly.
Farewell at once—for once, for all, and ever.
Bushy. Well, we may meet again.
Bagot.   I fear me, never.   [*Exeunt.*

SCENE III.—[*In Gloucestershire.*]

Enter BOLINGBROKE *and* NORTHUMBERLAND.

Bol. How far is it, my lord, to Berkeley now?
North. Believe me, noble lord,

147. Farewell] *Qq; Bush.* Farewell *F.*   148. Bushy.] *Qq; not in F.*

Scene III

Location] *Pope; not in Qq, F.*   S.D.] *Ed.; Enter Hereford, Northumberland. Qq;
Enter the Duke of Hereford, and Northumberland. F.*

141–2.] Keller cfs. *Woodstock,* III. ii.
102 ff, the parting of Richard's three
uncles: "Adieu . . . farewell for ever. /
I have a sad presage comes suddenly / That I shall never see these
brothers more: / On earth, I fear, we
never more shall meet. / Of Edward
the Third's seven sons we three are
left . . ."

145.] Both proverbial expressions
for attempting the impossible (Tilley
S91 and O9), not used elsewhere by
Shakespeare.

Scene III

MATERIAL. The basic facts derive
from Hol., 498/2/23 ff. The way that
Shakespeare handles them is original,
although, as Wilson says, the entries
of Percy, Ross, and Willoughby on the
scene give effect to Holinshed's words:
"And thus what for loue, and what for
feare of losse, [supporters] came flock-
ing unto [Bolingbroke] from euerie
part." The manner of the entry of

Henry Percy ("Hotspur") and his
formal presentation to Bolingbroke,
and the brush between Berkeley and
Bolingbroke at ll. 69 ff are Shakespeare's inventions. Except for Northumberland's declaration that Bolingbroke comes "but for his own" (l. 148)
and Bolingbroke's precisely worded
complaints at ll. 128 ff (see notes), the
substance of the colloquy between
York and Bolingbroke is invented, but
Holinshed records the fact of their
meeting. Holinshed has nothing
about York's "remaining neuter";
Froissart (VI. 371) speaks of York's
complete inaction and does not mention his meeting with Bolingbroke on
the latter's landing: but this is hardly
the same as "remaining neuter".

Location] Derived from Holinshed,
who speaks of Bolingbroke's proceeding from Doncaster (where he had
met with Northumberland) "by Eue-
sham unto Berkelie [Castle, in Glou-
cestershire]".

I am a stranger here in Gloucestershire.
These high wild hills and rough uneven ways
Draws out our miles and makes them wearisome,   5
And yet your fair discourse hath been as sugar,
Making the hard way sweet and delectable.
But I bethink me what a weary way
From Ravenspurgh to Cotshall will be found
In Ross and Willoughby, wanting your company,   10
Which I protest hath very much beguil'd
The tediousness and process of my travel.
But theirs is sweet'ned with the hope to have
The present benefit which I possess,
And hope to joy is little less in joy   15
Than hope enjoy'd. By this the weary lords
Shall make their way seem short, as mine hath done
By sight of what I have, your noble company.
Bol. Of much less value is my company
        Than your good words. But who comes here?   20

Enter HARRY PERCY.

North. It is my son, young Harry Percy,
        Sent from my brother Worcester, whencesoever.
        Harry, how fares your uncle?

---

3. here] *Q1, F; not in Q2–5.*   6. your] *Qq;* our *F.*   14. which] *Q1;* that *Q2–5, F.*

4. *high . . . ways*] The Gloucester-shire Cotswolds are high, although they no longer appear to be par-ticularly wild. Since the characters are here thought of as travelling towards Richard, the line may owe something to Daniel, who describes Richard as immured at Conway and comforted by Salisbury thus: "And hither to approach [Bolingbroke] will neuer dare, / Where deserts, rockes and hils, no succours giue, / Where desolation and no comforts are"(*C.W.*, II, st. 33).

5. *draws*] Either a compositor's error, or because " 'wild hills' etc. are thought of, not as separate and dis-tinct features of the country, but as together expressing its general charac-ter" (Herford).

7. *delectable*] pronounced déléctáble.

9. *Cotshall*] Cotswold. The spelling preserves what may have been Shakespeare's pronunciation: cf. *2 H 4,* III. ii. 23: "a Cotsole man" (Wilson). See Kökeritz, p. 320.

10. *In*] by.

12. *tediousness and process*] = tedious process.

15. *little . . . joy*] i.e. "little less enjoyable".

16. *By this*] i.e. by anticipating the pleasure of Bolingbroke's conversa-tion.

22. *whencesoever*] from somewhere or other.

Percy. I had thought, my lord, to have learn'd his health of
    you.
North. Why, is he not with the queen? 25
Percy. No, my good lord, he hath forsook the court,
    Broken his staff of office and dispers'd
    The household of the king.
North.   What was his reason?
    He was not so resolv'd when last we spake together.
Percy. Because your lordship was proclaimed traitor. 30
    But he, my lord, is gone to Ravenspurgh
    To offer service to the Duke of Herford,
    And sent me over by Berkeley to discover
    What power the Duke of York had levied there,
    Then with directions to repair to Ravenspurgh. 35
North. Have you forgot the Duke of Herford, boy?
Percy. No, my good lord, for that is not forgot
    Which ne'er I did remember: to my knowledge,
    I never in my life did look on him.
North. Then learn to know him now. This is the Duke. 40
Percy. My gracious lord, I tender you my service,
    Such as it is, being tender, raw, and young,
    Which elder days shall ripen and confirm
    To more approved service and desert.
Bol. I thank thee, gentle Percy, and be sure 45

28–9 What . . . reason? / . . . together. /] *As F;* What . . . resolude /
. . . togither? / *Qq.*   29. last we] *Qq;* we last *F.*   33. over] *Qq, F;* o'er
Pope.   35. directions] *Qq;* direction *F.*   36. Herford, boy] *Q3–5, F;*
Herefords boy *Q1, 2.*

30.] On this and what immediately precedes, see note on ii. ii. 56–61.

33–5.] There seems to be no historical foundation for this errand of Percy's. Shakespeare also departed from Holinshed in making Percy join up with Bolingbroke at Berkeley and not along with his father Northumberland at Doncaster.

33. *over*] As is not the case with *over* at iii. iii. 17, it seems impossible to scan this line comfortably if *over* is pronounced as a disyllable; perhaps a contracted form was expanded in Q1 —see Introduction, p. xxviii.

36. *boy*] Cf. ll. 42–3 below. Newbolt (p. xli) notes that the historical Hotspur Percy was actually two years older than Bolingbroke himself.

41, 42. *tender*] For the pun, John cfs. *Ham.*, i. iii. 99–109, *Cym.*, iii. iv. 11–12: "Why tender'st thou that paper to me with / A look untender?"

45–50.] Bolingbroke's replies and promises here and at ll. 65–7 below are the "candy deal of courtesy" which disgust in retrospect when Hotspur recalls this conversation in *1 H 4*, i. iii. 251–5.

I count myself in nothing else so happy
As in a soul rememb'ring my good friends,
And as my fortune ripens with thy love,
It shall be still thy true love's recompense.
My heart this covenant makes, my hand thus seals it.   50
North. How far is it to Berkeley? and what stir
Keeps good old York there with his men of war?
Percy. There stands the castle by yon tuft of trees,
Mann'd with three hundred men, as I have heard,
And in it are the Lords of York, Berkeley, and
Seymour—   55
None else of name and noble estimate.

Enter Ross *and* WILLOUGHBY.

North. Here come the Lords of Ross and Willoughby,
Bloody with spurring, fiery-red with haste.
Bol. Welcome, my lords; I wot your love pursues   †
A banish'd traitor. All my treasury   60
Is yet but unfelt thanks, which, more inrich'd,
Shall be your love and labour's recompense.
Ross. Your presence makes us rich, most noble lord.
Will. And far surmounts our labour to attain it.
Bol. Evermore thank's the exchequer of the poor,   65 †
Which, till my infant fortune comes to years,
Stands for my bounty. But who comes here?

---

53. yon] *Qq;* yond *F.*   56. estimate] *Q1–3, F;* estimation *Q4, 5.*   S.D.] *F;*
not in *Qq.*   65. thank's] *Q1–4;* thankes *Q5, F.*

57.] Ross and Willoughby actually
joined Bolingbroke on his landing at
Ravenspurgh, not at Berkeley: cf.
note on material and on ll. 33–5 above.
  61. *unfelt*] intangible.
  64.] "Your presence is much greater
in value than the labour we have
spent attaining it."
  65. *Evermore . . . poor*] "Thank is always the exchequer of the poor," i.e.,
all that they have to repay favours
with. Editors, except Wilson, follow F,
as against the *thanke's* of Q1–4, and
take the phrase "exchequer of the
poor" to be in apposition to "evermore thanks". *Evermore* must mean

"always in the future" or "always,
continually" (*O.E.D.,* sense 2) and
those who follow F presumably interpret the line: "thanks continually,
which continual thanks are the exchequer of the poor". But the phrase
is better understood as a gnomic saying rather than a *direct* expression of
thanks. *Thank* = "expression of
gratitude" or "gratitude" (*O.E.D.,*
s.v. thank, 3, 4); not a common usage,
but there are examples as late as 1642
and 1677 respectively, and cf. Jonson,
Sad Shepherd, I. vii. 7: "spend a thanke
for't". Cf. the sentiment to that of
Sebastion in *Tw. N.,* III. iii. 14–15.

Enter BERKELEY.

North. It is my Lord of Berkeley, as I guess.
Berk. My Lord of Herford, my message is to you.
Bol. My lord, my answer is—to Lancaster,   70
     And I am come to seek that name in England,
     And I must find that title in your tongue,
     Before I make reply to aught you say.
Berk. Mistake me not, my lord, 'tis not my meaning
     To race one title of your honour out.   75
     To you, my lord, I come, what lord you will,
     From the most gracious regent of this land,
     The Duke of York, to know what pricks you on
     To take advantage of the absent time,
     And fright our native peace with self-borne arms.   80

Enter YORK.

Bol. I shall not need transport my words by you;
     Here comes his grace in person. My noble uncle!
                                                    [*Kneels.*]
York. Show me thy humble heart, and not thy knee,
     Whose duty is deceivable and false.
Bol. My gracious uncle—   85
York. Tut, tut! grace me no grace, nor uncle me no uncle,

67. S.D.] *F; not in Qq.*   70. is—to] *Malone;* is to *Qq, F.*   77. gracious regent of] *Q1;* ghorious of *Q2;* glorious of *Q3–5, F.*   80. S.D.] *F; not in Qq.* 82. S.D.] *Rowe; not in Qq, F.*   86. no uncle] *Qq; not in F.*

70. *my answer . . . Lancaster*] i.e., "I answer only to the title 'Lancaster'."

75. *race out*] Here means "erase", "scrape away" (*O.E.D.*, s.v., rase 3), the title being imagined as something inscribed, like the *imprese* which are razed out in III. i. 25: cf. *Meas.*, I. ii. 7.

title] Quibble on *title* and *tittle*: cf. *LLL.*, IV. i. 73 and note in Arden edn, and see Kökeritz, p. 84.

79. *absent time*] time of absence.

80. *self-borne*] i.e. borne for one's own sake and not one's country's. But in this period *borne* and *born* are not distinguished in spelling, and *self-borne* might therefore mean "arising

amongst ourselves", an antonym to "foreign", as Kittredge suggests.

84. *deceivable*] deceptive. Used only once elsewhere in Shakespeare (*Tw. N.*, IV. iii. 21) and perhaps caught from the opposite page in Hol., 499/2/60: "such is the deceiuable [here means "apt to be deceived"] iudgement of man".

86. *Tut, tut!*] An extra-metrical expression of annoyance, possibly an actor's exclamation intruded by the transcriber through his memory of the sound heard on the stage (see Introduction, p. xvii, Wilson, *Manuscript of Shakespeare's Hamlet*, pp. 78–9, Patrick, *Textual History of Richard III*, pp. 91–2,

I am no traitor's uncle, and that word "grace"
In an ungracious mouth is but profane.
Why have those banish'd and forbidden legs
Dar'd once to touch a dust of England's ground?   90
But then more "why?"—why have they dar'd to march
So many miles upon her peaceful bosom,
Frighting her pale-fac'd villages with war
And ostentation of despised arms?
Com'st thou because the anointed king is hence?   95
Why, foolish boy, the king is left behind,
And in my loyal bosom lies his power.
Were I but now the lord of such hot youth,
As when brave Gaunt, thy father, and myself,
Rescued the Black Prince, that young Mars of men,   100
From forth the ranks of many thousand French,
O then how quickly should this arm of mine,
Now prisoner to the palsy, chastise thee,
And minister correction to thy fault!
Bol. My gracious uncle, let me know my fault: 105
On what condition stands it and wherein?

89. those] *Qq;* these *F.*   98. the] *F; not in Qq.*   99. myself] *Q1–3, F;* thy
selfe *Q4, 5.*   101. thousand] *Q1, F;* thousands *Q2–5.*

and cf. note on v. ii. 101). It seems un-
desirable that the words, although
extra-metrical, should stand in what
Wilson in a similar case (op. cit., p.
222) calls "solitary grandeur" in a
line by themselves.

90. *dust*] a grain of dust; cf. *John,*
iv. i. 93.

94. *despised*] despicable; cf. ii. i. 268
and note.

98–104.] Reyher suggests that the
incident referred to is the famous one
at the Battle of Crécy (1346) when the
Black Prince won his spurs and his
father Edward III refused to aid him
when he was surrounded—"for I will
that this iournie be his, with the honor
thereof" (Holinshed's account, 372/2/
19 ff). This seems unlikely, for the
point of the story in our text is the
valiancy of the rescuers, and that of
the Black Prince's story that he rescued himself. No incident in which his

two brothers rescued the Prince has
been traced. The Clarendon editors
suggest that York's claim is due to his
memory of a similar claim to youthful
prowess made by Nestor in *Iliad,* vii.
157 ff, which was later to be used by
Shakespeare in *Troil.,* i. iii. 291–301.
It seems likely that the passage may
be connected with 16th century traditions about Gaunt's exploits, for
traces of which see Introduction,
p. xl, n. 2.

103. *chastise*] With accent on the
first syllable: cf. *Mac.,* i. v. 24.

106–8.] *Condition* means both "quality" and "circumstances": *Bol.* "On
what personal quality does [my fault]
depend, and in what act has it shown
itself?" (Herford, Deighton). York
replies, with a quibble on *condition*:
"[It has shown itself] in the very
worst of 'conditions', rebellion and
treason."

York. Even in condition of the worst degree—
    In gross rebellion and detested treason;
    Thou art a banish'd man, and here art come,
    Before the expiration of thy time,   110
    In braving arms against thy sovereign.
Bol. As I was banish'd, I was banish'd Herford;
    But as I come, I come for Lancaster.
    And, noble uncle, I beseech your grace
    Look on my wrongs with an indifferent eye.   115
    You are my father, for methinks in you
    I see old Gaunt alive. O then my father,
    Will you permit that I shall stand condemn'd
    A wandering vagabond, my rights and royalties
    Pluck'd from my arms perforce, and given away   120
    To upstart unthrifts? Wherefore was I born?
    If that my cousin king be King in England,
    It must be granted I am Duke of Lancaster.
    You have a son, Aumerle, my noble cousin;
    Had you first died, and he been thus trod down,   125
    He should have found his uncle Gaunt a father
    To rouse his wrongs and chase them to the bay.
    I am denied to sue my livery here,
    And yet my letters patents give me leave.
    My father's goods are all distrain'd and sold,   130
    And these, and all, are all amiss employ'd.
    What would you have me do? I am a subject,
    And I challenge law; attorneys are denied me,   †

111. thy] *Q1, F;* my *Q2–5.*   116. for] *Q1, 2, F;* or *Q3–5.*   122. in] *Q1;* of
Q2–5, F.   124. cousin] *Qq;* kinsman *F.*   133. I] *Qq; not in F.*

111. *braving*] daring; cf. l. 142 below.

115. *indifferent*] impartial.

119–21. *my rights . . . unthrifts*] Zee-veld claims a parallel with Hall (p. 5) where Hall says that Richard "distributed the duke's landes to his parasites and flattering foloers". I think rather that "rights and royalties" corresponds to Holinshed's "rents and revenues", which the king is said to have received. Holinshed does not say that he distributed them, but the idea is fundamental to *Woodstock* and to the *Mirror.* Hayward's "great summes of

money are pulled and pilled from good subiects, to be throwne away amongst vnprofitable vnthrifts" (p. 63) seems to echo Shakespeare. For *royalties,* cf. II. i. 190 and note.

127.] A metaphor from hunting, in which the "wrongs" are the quarry: *rouse,* to startle from the lair; *bay,* the quarry's last stand.

128–9.] Cf. l. 133 below, and see note on II. i. 202–4. Bolingbroke's complaints in this speech up to l. 135 echo Hol., 496/1/29 ff.

133.] The abnormal metre suggests

And therefore personally I lay my claim
To my inheritance of free descent.   135
North. The noble Duke hath been too much abused.
Ross. It stands your grace upon to do him right.
Will. Base men by his endowments are made great.
York. My lords of England, let me tell you this:
I have had feeling of my cousin's wrongs,   140
And labour'd all I could to do him right.
But in this kind to come, in braving arms,
Be his own carver, and cut out his way,
To find out right with wrong—it may not be.
And you that do abet him in this kind   145
Cherish rebellion, and are rebels all.
North. The noble Duke hath sworn his coming is
But for his own; and for the right of that
We all have strongly sworn to give him aid.
And let him ne'er see joy that breaks that oath!   150
York. Well, well, I see the issue of these arms.   †
I cannot mend it, I must needs confess,

142. kind to come,] *Q1*; kind, to come *Q2–5, F*.   144. wrong] *Qq*; wrongs *F*.
150. ne'er] *F4*; neuer *Q1, 2*; ne're *Q3–5*; neu'r *F*.

the possibility of textual disturbance:
And in this line may be intrusive,
caught by the compositor from the
And which opens the line immediately
following.

137. *It . . . upon*] "It is incumbent
upon your grace." For the phrase,
with preposition following object, cf.
Ant., II. i. 50–1.

138. *endowments*] property which
has been endowed upon, not by,
Bolingbroke.

143. *Be . . . carver*] i.e. "take or
choose for himself". The expression is
used before Shakespeare by Lyly,
Greene, and Nashe, and may be proverbial (Tilley C110): cf. *Ham.*, I. iii.
20, and Gascoigne, *Supposes*, III. iii. 25
(in *Early Plays from the Italian*, ed.
Bond): "to such detestable offences no
punishment can seeme sufficient, but
onely death, and in such cases it is not
lawful for a man to be his own
carver." In *R 2* the metaphor sug-

gests not only greed at table (Wilson) but also the wielding of a sword
in battle, as in "carv'd out his passage" (*Mac.*, I. ii. 19); cf. *Oth.*, II. iii.
165.

147–50.] This is what Bolingbroke
later declares to Richard at III. iii.
196. It derives from Hol. 498/2/6: "he
sware unto these lords, that he would
demand no more, but the lands that
were to him descended by inheritance
from his father". The phrase "his
own" (also at III. iii. 196) perhaps
echoes Daniel's subtle account of
Bolingbroke's policy on landing—
"Sought but his owne, and did no
more expect" (*C.W.*, I, st. 94). Daniel
continues to explore Bolingbroke's
attitude for a further six stanzas: for
quotation and discussion, see Introduction, p. lxxiv.

150. *ne'er*] For the contracted form,
see Introduction, p. xxix, and cf. III.
iii. 17.

Because my power is weak and all ill left.
But if I could, by Him that gave me life,
I would attach you all, and make you stoop 155
Unto the sovereign mercy of the king;
But since I cannot, be it known unto you,
I do remain as neuter. So, fare you well,
Unless you please to enter in the castle,
And there repose you for this night. 160
Bol. An offer, uncle, that we will accept.
But we must win your grace to go with us
To Bristow castle, which they say is held
By Bushy, Bagot, and their complices,
The caterpillars of the commonwealth, 165
Which I have sworn to weed and pluck away.
York. It may be I will go with you; but yet I'll pause
For I am loath to break our country's laws.
Nor friends, nor foes, to me welcome you are.
Things past redress are now with me past care. 170
                                              [*Exeunt.*

157. unto] *Q1;* to *Q2–5, F.*   169. foes,] *Q2–5, F;* foes *Q1.*   170. S.D.] *Q1, 2 F; not in Q3–5.*

153. *all ill left*] left utterly inadequate. The reasons York gives for his inaction here are strikingly different from those in Hol., 498/2/27: "[York] assembled a puissant power of men of armes and archers . . . but all was in vaine, for there was not a man that willinglie would thrust out one arrow against the duke of Lancaster, or his partakers, or in anie wise offend him or his friends."

155. *attach*] arrest.

158. *remain . . . neuter*] remain neutral; cf. *Edmond Ironside*, M.S.R., l. 1584: "I here remaine a newter free from feare".

165. *caterpillars*] "parasites on society". The word *caterpiller*, as it was often spelt, was associated with the better-known *piller*, "pillager" (for the verb, see II. i. 246 and note), and was used synonymously with it (*O.E.D.*): cf. III. iv. 47.

166. *weed*] For "weeding the commonwealth", see note on III. iv. 37–9 and Introduction, p. lii and p. xlvii, n. I.

169.] "I cannot welcome you as either friends or foes" (Wilson).

170.] The thought is related to the proverb (Tilley C921) "Past cure, past care".

SCENE IV.—[*A Camp in Wales.*]

Enter EARL OF SALISBURY *and a* Welsh Captain.

Capt. My Lord of Salisbury, we have stay'd ten days,
And hardly kept our countrymen together,
And yet we hear no tidings from the king;
Therefore we will disperse ourselves. Farewell.
Sal. Stay yet another day, thou trusty Welshman: 5
The king reposeth all his confidence in thee.
Capt. 'Tis thought the king is dead; we will not stay.
The bay-trees in our country are all wither'd,
And meteors fright the fixed stars of heaven,
The pale-fac'd moon looks bloody on the earth,   10
And lean-look'd prophets whisper fearful change,

Scene IV

Location] Capell; *not in* Qq, F.   S.D.] *Qq; Enter Salisbury and a Captaine. F.*
1, 7. *Capt.*] *F; Welch.* Qq.   8. are all] *Q1, F;* all are *Q2–5.*

MATERIAL. The scene follows Hol., 499/1/32 ff, and Salisbury's part in it is derived therefrom. One detail comes from another place in Holinshed (see note on l. 8). For the identity of the Welsh Captain, see note on III. i. 43.

1. *ten days*] Holinshed says that the Welshmen waited fourteen days.

5–6. *thou . . . thee*] From Hol., 499/2/41: "[Richard] had also no small affiance [= confidence] in the Welshmen, and Cheshire men." Zeeveld's claim (p. 333 and n. 29) that Hall (p. 8) is the only authority for Richard's trust in the Welsh, and that Shakespeare is following him, cannot therefore be admitted. For Richard, Bolingbroke and the Welsh, cf. note on III. i. 43.

8.] From Hol., 496/2/65, where the withering of the bay-trees occurs in England, not Wales: "In this yeere in a manner throughout all the realme of England, old baie trees withered, and afterwards, contrarie to all mens thinking, grew greene againe, a strange sight, and supposed to import some unknowne euent." This passage

occurs first in the second (1586–7) edn of Holinshed, which must therefore have been the edition used in this play. The bay-tree was a prophylactic (Steevens) and, like other evergreens, emblematic of the soul's immortality (Macquoid in *Shakespeare's England*, II. 149).

9.] Knight cfs. Daniel, *C.W.*, I, st. 114–15, describing portentous stars and meteors occurring at this time. The history-plays are so full of such things that the mere mention of men's feelings about the bay-trees in Holinshed was probably enough to set Shakespeare's pen describing other and commoner portents also.

11. *prophets*] In Shakespeare *prophet* usually means "prognosticator" rather than "inspired divine spokesman" in the fullest Biblical sense. The prophets in Daniel, *C.W.*, I, st. 110 are decidedly of the Biblical kind, not Shakespearian prognosticators "whispering fearful change", as here, but divines and divine spokesmen: "graue religious fathers . . . / As Prophets warne, exclaime, disswade these crimes / By the examples fresh of other times." There

Rich men look sad, and ruffians dance and leap—
The one in fear to lose what they enjoy,
The other to enjoy by rage and war.
These signs forerun the death or fall of kings.   15
Farewell: our countrymen are gone and fled,
As well assured Richard their king is dead.   [*Exit.*
Sal. Ah, Richard! with the eyes of heavy mind
I see thy glory like a shooting star
Fall to the base earth from the firmament.   20
Thy sun sets weeping in the lowly west,
Witnessing storms to come, woe, and unrest.
Thy friends are fled to wait upon thy foes,
And crossly to thy good all fortune goes.   [*Exit.*

15. or fall] *Q1; not in Q2–5, F.*   17. S.D.] *F; not in Qq.*   18. the] *Q1; not in Q2–5, F.*   24. S.D.] *F; not in Qq.*

is not necessarily therefore any connection between Shakespeare's lean-looked soothsayers and Daniel's religious fathers. But that even the prognosticator can have a kind of inspiration that links him to the Jewish prophet is shown in the solemnity with which Gaunt (II. i. 31), Carlisle (IV. i. 136), and Antony (*Cæs.*, III. i. 260) assume the role. Prophet-prognosticators occur elsewhere in Shakespearian histories; for a Welsh "pro-phet" in especial, see Peele's *Edward I*, M.S.R., ll. 500 ff and 2651 ff. There are several references to prophecies about Richard's fall amongst the suggested sources: see Froissart, VI. 341; *Traïson*, p. 62/213; Créton, p. 169/374; this last elaborates, with remarks upon English credulity. I do not think Shakespeare was indebted to any of these.

14. *to enjoy*] in hope of enjoying.
24. *crossly*] adversely.

ACT III

SCENE I.—[*Bristol. Before the castle.*]

[*Enter* BOLINGBROKE, YORK, NORTHUMBERLAND, *with* BUSHY *and* GREENE, *prisoners.*]

Bol. Bring forth these men.
 Bushy and Greene, I will not vex your souls,
 Since presently your souls must part your bodies,
 With too much urging your pernicious lives,
 For 'twere no charity; yet, to wash your blood   5
 From off my hands, here in the view of men
 I will unfold some causes of your deaths:
 You have misled a prince, a royal king,
 A happy gentleman in blood and lineaments,
 By you unhappied and disfigured clean;   10

ACT III

Scene 1

Location.] Capell; not in Qq, F.   S.D.] *Wilson; Enter Duke of Hereford, Yorke, Northumberland, Bushie and Greene prisoners. Qq; Enter Bullingbrooke, Yorke, Northumberland, Rosse, Percie, Willoughby, with Bushie and Greene Prisoners. F.*   7. deaths] *Q1, F;* death *Q2–5.*

MATERIAL. The facts are from Hol., 498/2/60 ff and 518/2/53 ff (see note on l. 43). The substance of Bolingbroke's long speech and the defiance of the favourites are invented. The Earl of Wiltshire, who is mentioned by Holinshed as being at Bristol Castle (and cf. II. ii. 135) and at III. ii. 141–2 and III. iv. 53 is said to have been beheaded at Bristol along with Bushy and Greene, surprisingly does not appear in this scene, or anywhere else in the play: Shakespeare may have been economizing on characters, satisfied that the appearance of three favourites was enough to convey the impression that he wanted, but for the possibility that he wrongly identified him with "Bagot", see note on III. ii. 122. Bolingbroke's kind words about Isabel, his account of his wrongs, and his ruthless act of state, all appearing in this scene, form a notable example of Shakespeare's workmanship and invention in creating a character: but for possible influences from *Woodstock* and Marlowe see notes on ll. 12–15.

3. *presently*] immediately.
part] part from.

4.] "With insisting too much upon the perniciousness of your lives".

10. *unhappied*] Not used elsewhere by Shakespeare, see note on II. i. 16.

You have in manner, with your sinful hours,
Made a divorce betwixt his queen and him,
Broke the possession of a royal bed,

13. possession] *Q₁–4, F;* profession *Q5.*

11. *in manner*] i.e. "in a manner of speaking": see *O.E.D.,* s.v. manner 10.

12–15.] An accusation unsupported by history and inconsistent with the portrayal of Isabel's relations with Richard in the rest of the play. Explanations offered have included: (i) that the lines are a vestige of the hypothetical "old play" (Wilson); but it is hard to conceive any "old play" containing any expansion of this element which yet retained sketches for the "Isabel" and "Richard" of Shakespeare, and harder still to see why "Shakespeare's unknown predecessor, soaked in the history of England" (Wilson, p. lxxv) should so wilfully depart from history. (ii) That it is Shakespeare's echo of the charges brought against Gaveston by the Queen in *Edward II,* I. iv. 150 ff: "thou corrupts my lord, / And art a bawd to his affections . . . / Villain! 'tis thou that robb'st me of my lord." (iii) That it is an echo of the hostility between Richard's first Queen, Anne of Bohemia, and his favourites, as hinted at in *Woodstock,* II. iii. 10–37 (Wilson, followed in more detail by Rossiter): the passage is vague and obscure compared with those in *Edward II* but it is certainly true that Anne was no friend of the minions. (iv) That the passage is Shakespeare's imagination at work on Hol., 508/1/32 [a summary of Richard's behaviour]: ". . . there reigned abundantlie the filthie sinne of leacherie and fornication, with abhominable adulterie, speciallie in the king, but most cheefelie in the prelacie". His invention here may have been aided by the emphasis on the same point in *Mirror,* p. 113, a passage quoted in the Introduction, p. xli. (v) That it is inserted so that Bolingbroke may acquire in the audi-

ence's eyes "an air of chivalrous magnanimity" as Queen's champion (Herford), (vi) or so that the audience may recognize that Bolingbroke is master of the situation by the confidence with which he tells an obvious lie (Reyher). The first of these explanations must, I think, be rejected; the last seems unlikely; but the rest do not contradict one another and may be accepted *en bloc.* Nothing that Bolingbroke says here need imply that the relation between Richard and the favourites was imagined by Shakespeare to be like the passionate Gaveston-Edward affair as depicted by Marlowe: the favourites are merely "flatterers", those who, according to 16th century *moralia,* weaken a monarch's power to rule by encouraging his vices. Handbooks for princes, such as those by Machiavelli, Erasmus, or Castiglione, castigate flattery, which keeps the prince ignorant of the world and himself.

13. *Broke . . . bed*] Meaning clear, but form difficult: it is not officialese for "violated Richard's possession of Isabel's bed", for that would imply that it was Richard who was wronged by Isabel's adultery with the favourites—which is nearly the opposite of what Bolingbroke means. *Bed,* so often used as a metaphor for "person", in marriage" and "possessed" by one or other partner (cf. "I got possession of Julietta's bed", *Meas.,* I. ii. 139) has here come to mean, by extension of the metaphor, "the royal marriage relation". This could not be "legally owned" (possessed) by either of the pair; if thought of as owned at all, it is the joint "possession" of both. Thus in the phrase *break the possession,* "break" has the sense of "violate contract, bond, or covenant" (cf. Coverdale's Bible, Matt., xix. 18, "thou

And stain'd the beauty of a fair queen's cheeks
With tears, drawn from her eyes by your foul wrongs;
Myself—a prince by fortune of my birth,   16
Near to the king in blood, and near in love,
Till you did make him misinterpret me—
Have stoop'd my neck under your injuries,
And sigh'd my English breath in foreign clouds,   20
Eating the bitter bread of banishment,
Whilst you have fed upon my signories,
Dispark'd my parks and fell'd my forest woods,
From my own windows torn my household coat,
Rac'd out my imprese, leaving me no sign,   25
Save men's opinions and my living blood,
To show the world I am a gentleman.
This and much more, much more than twice all this,
Condemns you to the death. See them delivered over
To execution and the hand of death.   30
Bushy. More welcome is the stroke of death to me
       Than Bolingbroke to England. Lords, farewell.
Greene. My comfort is, that heaven will take our souls,
       And plague injustice with the pains of hell.

---

15. by] *Q1;* with *Q2–5, F.*   18. you] *Q1, F;* they *Q2–5.*   22. Whilst] *Q1;*
While *Q2–5, F.*   24. my own] *Q1, 2;* mine owne *Q3–5, F.*   32. Lords, fare-
well] *Qq; not in F.*

shalt not break wedlocke", and see
O.E.D., s.v. break, III. 15d). The
favourites *broke* the "bond of joint
ownership of the marriage by and
between" the pair, by making one
of the partners unfaithful to the
covenant.

20. *sigh'd . . . clouds*] Bolingbroke's
breath augments the foreign clouds,
as well as being sighed forth amidst
them: cf. *Rom.*, I. i. 131: "Adding to
clouds more clouds with his deep
sighs".

21. *Eating . . . bread*] Biblical phraseology: Noble c s. 1 Kings, xxii., 27.

22. *signories*] estates; cf. IV. i. 89.

23. *Dispark'd*] Dispark = "throw
open parkland or convert it to other
uses than that of preserving game".
Not found elsewhere in Shakespeare;

but cf. Chapman, *Tragedy of Bussy
d'Ambois* (revised version, ?ca. 1610),
I. i. 122.

24.] i.e. "broken from my windows
my coat-of-arms blazoned in the
painted glass" (Herford). Defacing a
knight's arms was considered very
abominable: see *2 H 6*, IV. i. 42.

25. *Rac'd*] razed; see note on II. iii.
75.

imprese] Plural form of It. *impresa*;
this is Q6's spelling, spelled *impreese*
in Q1–4, *impresse* in Q5 and F. The
impresa was a miniature allegorical
picture, with a motto, used as a
heraldic device on arms and equip-
ment; Shakespeare helped to devise
one for the Earl of Rutland at a
Whitehall tournament, 1613: see
Barron in *Shakespeare's England*, II. 88.

Bol. My lord Northumberland, see them dispatch'd.   35
          [*Exeunt Northumberland and prisoners.*]
     Uncle, you say the queen is at your house;
     For God's sake fairly let her be intreated,
     Tell her I send to her my kind commends;
     Take special care my greetings be delivered.
York. A gentleman of mine I have dispatch'd   40
     With letters of your love to her at large.
Bol. Thanks, gentle uncle. Come, lords, away,
     To fight with Glendor and his complices:
     A while to work, and after holiday.   [*Exeunt.*

35. S.D.] *Ed.; not in Qq, F.*   37. God's] *Qq;* Heauens *F.*

36.] The references to Isabel are perhaps partly in preparation for III. iv., partly to soften the rigour of the scene and Bolingbroke's behaviour (cf. Herford's suggestion, note on ll. 12–15 above). Shakespeare has no authority for Isabel's being at Langley, York's house. Froissart, VI. 346, says that she and her household were left at Windsor when Richard went to Ireland, and later, after Richard's capture, that she was "at Ledes in Kent" (VI. 370). The juxtaposed sentences in Hol., 497/1/9 may have suggested the point: ". . . the king departed . . . leauing the queene with her traine still at Windesor: he appointed for his lieutenant generall in his absence his uncle the duke of Yorke."
     37. *intreated*] treated.
     41. *at large*] in full.
     43. *Glendor*] Owen Glendower (Glyndwr) of Conway. A bit of historical colour—we hear no more of him in this play, but he is prominent in *1 H 4*. The suggestion that Bolingbroke fought Glendower in 1399 is unhistorical, though the presence of Glendower in Richard's neighbourhood is not. It was in 1400 that Bolingbroke, then Henry IV, led an army against Glendower "and his unrulie complices" (Hol., 519/1/8), and it must be this later passage that Shakespeare had in mind, although the recurrence of *complices* may be sheer

coincidence: Bolingbroke has already used the word in II. iii. 164. Perhaps Shakespeare mentioned Glendower here because in the same place (518/2/67) Holinshed says that Glendower "serued king Richard at Flint castell, when [Richard] was taken by Henrie duke of Lancaster", and Shakespeare may already have been thinking of Glendower's part in *1 H 4*. Craig supposes that Shakespeare may have identified the Welsh Captain of II. iv with Glendower, whom Holinshed describes as "capteine" of the Welshman (518/2/56). For the hostility of the Welsh to Bolingbroke and their friendliness to Richard there is evidence in Holinshed (cf. note on II. iv. 5–6). Créton, pp. 104 ff/327 also refers to the Welsh hostility to the Lancastrians and describes how they waylaid Sir T. Percy, who was absconding with Richard's valuables. Wilson's view that the reference to Glendower is a vestige of the hypothetical "old play" was answered in anticipation by Ritson: "It is evident from the preceding scene, that there was a force in Wales, which Bolingbroke might think it necessary to suppress; and why might not Shakespeare call it Glendower's?" In view of what Holinshed says in the passages cited above, it was the obvious name to choose. For a similar isolated name, cf. v. iii. 135 and note.

SCENE II.—[*The coast of Wales.*]

Drums: flourish and colours. Enter KING RICHARD, AUMERLE,
the BISHOP OF CARLISLE, *and* Soldiers.

Rich. Barkloughly castle call they this at hand?
Aum. Yea, my lord. How brooks your grace the air,
　　After your late tossing on the breaking seas?
Rich. Needs must I like it well: I weep for joy
　　To stand upon my kingdom once again.   5
　　Dear earth, I do salute thee with my hand,
　　Though rebels wound thee with their horses' hoofs.
　　As a long-parted mother with her child
　　Plays fondly with her tears and smiles in meeting,
　　So weeping, smiling, greet I thee, my earth,   10
　　And do thee favours with my royal hands;
　　Feed not thy sovereign's foe, my gentle earth,
　　Nor with thy sweets comfort his ravenous sense,
　　But let thy spiders that suck up thy venom
　　And heavy-gaited toads lie in their way,   15

Scene II

Location.] Capell, adding "*A castle in view*"; not in Qq, F.   S.D.] Wright. *Enter the
King, Aumerle, Carleil &c.* Qq; Drums: Flourish, and Colours. Enter Richard, Aumerle,
Carlile and Soldiers. F.   1. they] *Q1;* you *Q2–5,* F.   9. tears] *Q1, 4;* teares,
Q2, 3, 5, F.   11. favours] *Q1;* fauour *Q2–5,* F.

MATERIAL. Richard's landing at
"Barclowlie" in Wales, after a stormy
passage (suggested by Hol., 499/1/17),
and hearing news of various disasters
to his cause, viz., the loss of the
Welsh, the "great forces which the
duke of Lancaster had got togither"
(Hol., 499/1/74; ll. 106 ff), the execution of the favourites, and various
defections north and south, all appear
on the same page (499) of Holinshed.
According to Holinshed, Richard had
already heard in Ireland of Bolingbroke's *coup*; in Shakespeare, he enters conscious of what has happened
but knowing no details. His melancholy and despair are immensely expanded and vivified from Holinshed's
account. There is no need to suppose
with Wilson that any of the French

chroniclers influenced this scene; but
see notes on ll. 64, 119.

1. *Barkloughly*] Holinshed's "Barclowlie" Castle, an error for Hert-
lowli, the form used by the Monk of
Evesham, Holinshed's authority at
this point, for the modern Harlech.

2. *brooks*] endures, with some of the
O.E. sense, "enjoys" (Herford).

6. *salute*] to greet with word or gesture; now restricted to the military
sense.

8–10.] The imagery recalls Joan's
plea to the Duke of Burgundy, *1 H 6,*
III. iii. 47–51.

9. *tears and smiles*] Cf. v. ii. 32 and
note.

15–22. *heavy-gaited*] Not used elsewhere by Shakespeare, but cf. *2 Return from Parnassus*, ed. Leishman,

Doing annoyance to the treacherous feet,
Which with usurping steps do trample thee;
Yield stinging nettles to mine enemies;
And when they from thy bosom pluck a flower,
Guard it, I pray thee, with a lurking adder,   20
Whose double tongue may with a mortal touch
Throw death upon thy sovereign's enemies.
Mock not my senseless conjuration, lords:
This earth shall have a feeling, and these stones
Prove armed soldiers ere her native king   25
Shall falter under foul rebellion's arms.

Car. Fear not, my lord. That Power that made you king
Hath power to keep you king in spite of all.
The means that heaven yields must be imbrac'd
And not neglected; else, heaven would,   30
And we will not; heavens offer, we refuse
The proffered means of succour and redress.

Aum. He means, my lord, that we are too remiss;
Whilst Bolingbroke, through our security,
Grows strong and great in substance and in power.   35

Rich. Discomfortable cousin! know'st thou not

19. thy] *Q1–4, F;* my *Q5.*   20. pray thee] *Qq;* prethee *F.*   26. rebellion's]
Q1, 2; rebellious *Q3–5, F.*   27. Power] *F;* power *Qq.*   29–32.] *Not in F.*
29. heaven yields] *Pope;* heauens yeeld *Qq.*   30. heaven] *Qq;* if heaven *Pope.*
31. will] *Q1, 2;* would *Q3–5.*   32. succour] *Pope;* succours *Qq.*   35. power]
Qq; friends *F.*

l. 1213: "old heauy-gated iades". In
this passage Richard invokes, like
Lear, the powers of the "dear goddess", Nature; not, as Herford opines,
"a fairyland full of wise and faithful
beasts".

19–20.] For the snake hidden in the
flower, cf. *2 H 6*, III. i. 228, *Mac.*, I. v.
62–3; related to the proverb about the
snake in the grass (Tilley S585).

23. *senseless*] i.e. he is speaking to
things generally supposed to be without sense, he admits; but goes on to
claim that the earth *shall* have "a
feeling".

24. *these stones*] Craig cfs. Luke,
xix. 40 and iii. 8. For the turn of
thought, cf. III. iii. 85 ff.

29–32.] F omitted (suggests H. F.
Brooks) because the compositor, after
setting l. 28, eye-skipped from *The
means* to the very similar *He means* (l.
33). Most editors accept Pope's *if*, but
T. W. Baldwin (*M.L.N.*, LXXII [1957],
377–8) defends Q: "If we do not obey,
then 'heaven would, and we will not';
heavens offer [verb], we refuse the
proffered means. . ." Q1 punctuates:
*. . . would, . . , not, . . . offer, . . . refuse, . . .
redress.*

34. *security*] over-confidence; cf. II. i.
266, v. iii. 42.

36. *Discomfortable*] disheart-
ening. Not elsewhere in Shakespeare, but
found in Coverdale's Bible (Ecclus.,
xviii. 14) and retained by the

That when the searching eye of heaven is hid
Behind the globe and lights the lower world,
Then thieves and robbers range abroad unseen
In murthers and in outrage boldly here;   40
But when from under this terrestrial ball
He fires the proud tops of the eastern pines,
And darts his light through every guilty hole,
Then murthers, treasons, and detested sins,
The cloak of night being pluck'd from off their backs, 45
Stand bare and naked, trembling at themselves?
So when this thief, this traitor, Bolingbroke,
Who all this while hath revell'd in the night,
Whilst we were wand'ring with the Antipodes,
Shall see us rising in our throne the east,   50
His treasons will sit blushing in his face,
Not able to endure the sight of day,
But self-affrighted tremble at his sin.
Not all the water in the rough rude sea
Can wash the balm off from an anointed king;   55

---

38. and] *Hanmer;* that *Qq, F.*   40. boldly] *Dyce (Collier conj.);* bouldy *Q1;* bloudy, *Q2–5, F.*   41. this] *Q1, F;* his *Q2–5.*   43. light] *Qq;* lightning *F.* 49.] *Not in F.*   53. tremble] *Q1, F;* trembled *Q2–5.*   55. off] *Qq; not in F.*

Bishops' and Genevan; see Noble, pp. 63 and 154, and note on II. ii. 76.

38.] Hanmer's emendation clears up the line; editors have taken Q1's "that lights the lower world" to be in apposition to "eye of heaven" in l. 37, and a very tangled sentence results. The "globe" is the earth as it conceals the sun at night (see "*under* this terrestrial ball" at l. 41); the "lower world" is, as Malone suggested, "a world lower than this of ours", viz., the "Antipodes" of l. 49 below. Richard is implying a comparison between the sun's voyage to the Antipodes, when his light is hidden from England, and his own absence in Ireland. Q1's *that* perhaps occurred through the compositor's catching the *That* from the preceding line.

39–46.] For the passage on Night, Noble cfs. Job, xxiv. 13–17 on

the secret judgement of the wicked and their detestation of light. Shakespeare might also have been remembering Prince Arthur's apostrophe to Night, *Faerie Queene,* III. iv, st. 58–9. For the imagery and thought of the whole speech, cf. *1 H 4,* I. ii. 190–6.

40. *boldly*] Many editors follow F's *bloody,* which weakens the line and seems less likely than *boldly* to be what Q1's *bouldy* was intended for: cf. *Faerie Queene,* II. ii, st. 23, l. 2: *bloudy* (1596), *boldy* (1609), *boldly* (modern editions).

49. *with . . . Antipodes*] i.e. "with the people [not the region] who dwell on the opposite side of the earth".

54–8.] Anthologized in *England's Parnassus,* no. 862, in the section "Kings".

55. *balm*] the oil of consecration: cf. IV. i. 207, *3 H 6,* III. i. 17.

off] The omission of *off* by F regu-

The breath of worldly men cannot depose
The deputy elected by the Lord;
For every man that Bolingbroke hath press'd
To lift shrewd steel against our golden crown,
God for his Richard hath in heavenly pay   60 †
A glorious angel: then, if angels fight,
Weak men must fall, for heaven still guards the right.

Enter SALISBURY.

Welcome, my lord: how far off lies your power?
Sal. Nor near nor farther off, my gracious lord,
Than this weak arm; discomfort guides my tongue,   65
And bids me speak of nothing but despair.
One day too late, I fear me, noble lord,
Hath clouded all thy happy days on earth.
O, call back yesterday, bid time return,

60. God] *Qq;* Heauen *F.*   67. me,] *Q1, 2* (me) *; my Q3–5, F.*

larizes the metre; the same omission
was made by *England's Parnassus,*
copying from one of the first three
Quartos.

57. *deputy*] Cf. I. ii. 38–41 and note,
IV. i. 126, and III. iii. 77–8.

58. *press'd*] conscripted.

59. *shrewd*] harmful and accursed.

60–3. *heavenly pay*] i.e., the angels
are on heaven's pay-roll: the image
continues from the *press'd* of l. 58
above. For the sentiments, cf. III. iii.
85–7. The idea can hardly be attributed to any precise source: *Faerie
Queene,* II. viii. st. 1–10 might be cited
along with Matt., xxvi. 53. It is unlikely that Shakespeare was thinking
of the several passages where Richard
supposes God to be on his side in
Créton (pp. 114/337, 115/339, 140/
359). Scott-Giles (p. 64) suggests that
Shakespeare had seen "the double
rank of angels in Westminster Hall [a
building restored by Richard], each
bearing a shield of Richard's arms,
and the angels grouped about his
shield at the entrance to the Hall",
and that the impression they made
came out in these lines. Ll. 61–2 (*if*

angels . . . right) were anthologized in
England's Parnassus, no. 5.

64. Salisbury] "It is *Traïson* (p. 190)
and Créton (p. 97), not Holinshed,
which make Salisbury bring tidings of
the desertion of the army" (Wilson).
This need not mean that Shakespeare
was dependent on either: Salisbury
was the messenger whom Richard
sent from Ireland to gather an army
for him (Hol., 499/1/32 ff) and has
already appeared in II. iv with the
Welshmen he had collected; he is
therefore the obvious person to bring
the bad news of the Welsh defection.
Shakespeare had to find some such
bearer, since none is mentioned by
name in Holinshed, and solved a
similar problem similarly when he
chose Scroope at l. 91 below (see note).

near] nearer.

67. *One . . . late*] i.e. "your being one
day too late".

69. *call . . . yesterday*] Has a quite
literal applicability to Richard's
dilemma, but is also a proverbial expression for trying to undo things
done, like "to cry over spilt milk":
see Tilley Y31.

And thou shalt have twelve thousand fighting men!   70
To-day, to-day, unhappy day too late,
O'erthrows thy joys, friends, fortune and thy state;
For all the Welshmen, hearing thou wert dead,
Are gone to Bolingbroke, dispers'd and fled.
Aum. Comfort, my liege, why looks your grace so pale?   75
Rich. But now the blood of twenty thousand men
Did triumph in my face, and they are fled;
And till so much blood thither come again,
Have I not reason to look pale and dead?
All souls that will be safe, fly from my side,   80
For time hath set a blot upon my pride.
Aum. Comfort, my liege, remember who you are.
Rich. I had forgot myself, am I not king?
Awake, thou coward majesty! thou sleepest.
Is not the king's name twenty thousand names?   85
Arm, arm, my name! a puny subject strikes
At thy great glory. Look not to the ground,
Ye favourites of a king, are we not high?
High be our thoughts. I know my uncle York
Hath power enough to serve our turn. But who comes
          here?   90

Enter SCROOPE.

Scroope. More health and happiness betide my liege
Than can my care-tun'd tongue deliver him.
Rich. Mine ear is open and my heart prepar'd.
The worst is worldly loss thou canst unfold.
Say, is my kingdom lost? why, 'twas my care,   95
And what loss is it to be rid of care?

---

72. O'erthrows] *F;* Ouerthrowes *Qq.*   84. coward] *Q1;* coward, *Q2–5;*
sluggard *F.*   85. twenty] *Qq;* fortie *F.*   90. Hath . . . here?/] *As Qq;*
. . . turne. / . . . here? / *F.*

76–81.] Richard's highly emotional
speech is in the form of a sestet
(Craig).

79. *pale and dead*] Dead = "death-
like". Rossiter cfs. *Woodstock,* IV. ii.
110 and *1 H 6,* IV. ii. 38 On Richard's
pallor, see note on II. i. 119–20.

91. Scroope] This must be Sir
Stephan (*sic,* in Hol.) Scroope, men-

tioned as being attendant on Richard
at the crisis in Hol., 499/2/32, not "Sir
William Scroope earle of Wiltshire",
on whom see note on l. 122 below and
III. i, note on material. Stephan
appears again in III. iii.

92 *care-tun'd*] "tuned to the key of
sorrow" (Onions).

deliver] communicate to.

Strives Bolingbroke to be as great as we?
Greater he shall not be. If he serve God,
We'll serve Him too, and be his fellow so.
Revolt our subjects? that we cannot mend;   100
They break their faith to God as well as us.
Cry woe, destruction, ruin, and decay—
The worst is death, and death will have his day.

Scroope. Glad am I that your Highness is so arm'd
To bear the tidings of calamity.   105
Like an unseasonable stormy day,
Which makes the silver rivers drown their shores,
As if the world were all dissolv'd to tears,
So high above his limits swells the rage
Of Bolingbroke, covering your fearful land   110
With hard bright steel, and hearts harder than steel.
White-beards have arm'd their thin and hairless scalps
Against thy majesty; boys, with women's voices,
Strive to speak big, and clap their female joints
In stiff unwieldy arms against thy crown;   115
Thy very beadsmen learn to bend their bows
Of double-fatal yew against thy state;
Yea, distaff-women manage rusty bills
Against thy seat: both young and old rebel,

---

102. and] *Qq;* Losse F.   107. makes] *Q1, 2, F;* make *Q3–5.*   shores] *Q1–4,*
F; showers *Q5.*   112. White-beards] *Reed (1803);* White beards *Qq;* White
beares *F.*   113. boys] *Q1;* and boyes *Q2–5, F.*   116. bows] *Q1, 2, F;*
browes *Q3–5.*   117. double-fatal] *Warburton; unhyphened in Qq, F.*   yew]
Hanmer; ewe *Q1, 2;* woe *Q3–5;* Eugh F.

100–1.] For the later development
of this theme of the subjects' faith to
the God-appointed ruler, see note to
IV. i. 235.

109. *his*] = "its" (Bolingbroke's
rage).

114–15. *clap . . . arms*] thrust their
womanish joints into stiff unwieldy
armour.

117. *double-fatal yew*] "Called so,
because the leaves of the yew are
poison, and the wood is employed for
instruments of death" (Warburton).

118. *manage*] wield.

rusty bills] Bills had a long wooden
shaft with a spiked blade or axe-

head; *rusty,* because long out of use.

119. *both . . . rebel*] Perhaps derived
from Holinshed's account of Bolingbroke's triumphant progress, 501/2/
55: "For in euerie towne and village
where he passed, children reioised,
women clapped their hands, and men
cried out for ioy." Froissart, VI. 360,
has a similar passage. A closer parallel
is found in Créton, p. 53/311, but
the events occur after the Archbishop's speech: "Then might you
have beheld young and old, the feeble
and the strong, make a clamour,
and regarding neither right nor
wrong, stir themselves up with one

And all goes worse than I have power to tell.   120
Rich. Too well, too well thou tell'st a tale so ill.
      Where is the Earl of Wiltshire? where is Bagot?
      What is become of Bushy? where is Greene?
      That they have let the dangerous enemy
      Measure our confines with such peaceful steps?   125
      If we prevail, their heads shall pay for it:
      I warrant they have made peace with Bolingbroke.
Scroope. Peace have they made with him indeed, my lord.
Rich. O villains, vipers, damn'd without redemption!
      Dogs, easily won to fawn on any man!   130
      Snakes, in my heart-blood warm'd, that sting my heart!

accord", and cf. Créton, p. 55/312.

122–3. *Bagot*] Four favourites are mentioned by name in *R 2* and Holinshed—Bushy, Bagot, Greene, and the Earl of Wiltshire. Bushy and Greene died in III. i; Wiltshire never appears in the play; Bagot re-appears alive in IV. i. Although these four are all named here, Richard refers to *three* Judases at l. 132 below, and in ll. 141–2 we learn that of the quartet only three (Bushy, Greene, and Wiltshire) have been executed, the audience having had plain evidence of the execution of two of these in III. i. It is natural to assume that the fourth, Bagot, whom we meet again in IV. i, somehow escaped from the trap at Bristol (see II. iii. 164): Shakespeare perhaps thought of him as turning informer and being kept alive as prisoner to supply the needed evidence about the death of Gloucester in IV. i: he has "made peace" (l. 127) with Bolingbroke, though hardly in the grim sense uppermost in l. 137 below. Why, then, after *four* are mentioned here, should Richard, before he has heard that only *three* died (at ll. 141–2) cry out upon *three* Judases at l. 132? Wilson suggests that only three favourites are really involved throughout, because Shakespeare thought of "Wiltshire" and "Bagot" as one and the same person, then forgot that "he" had been killed, and resurrected him

in IV. i. This would entail Shakespeare's making two mistakes: ignoring what Holinshed says (and there seems no particular reason why any reader of Holinshed should confuse "Bagot" with "sir William Scroope earl of Wiltshire"), and forgetting what he had written. I suggest that Shakespeare, when he wrote l. 132, was already thinking ahead to ll. 141–2 and IV. i; he was planning to have one of the four men alive for IV. i, but forgot that Richard could not yet know, when he breaks out at l. 132, what Shakespeare was arranging to have him told at ll. 141–2: Shakespeare carelessly anticipated but did not grossly resurrect.

125. *confines*] territories.

127–8.] For the quibble on "peace" cf. *Mac.*, IV. iii. 178–9.

129.] Cf. Matt., xxiii. 33: "Ye serpentes, ye generation of vipers, how wyl ye escape the dampnation of hell?" (Noble).

131.] For the image applied to traitors, cf. v. iii. 56, *2 H 6*, III. i. 343. It is very common; a far from complete list is given by Tilley V68. For an origin in Aesopic fable, see A. Yoder, *Animal Analogy in Shakespeare's Character Portrayal* (New York, 1947), pp. 18, 117–18: a peasant was bitten by a snake which he found almost dead from cold and warmed in his breast.

Three Judases, each one thrice worse than Judas!
Would they make peace? Terrible hell,
Make war upon their spotted souls for this!
Scroope. Sweet love, I see, changing his property,   135
Turns to the sourest and most deadly hate.
Again uncurse their souls; their peace is made
With heads and not with hands; those whom you curse
Have felt the worst of death's destroying wound,
And lie full low, grav'd in the hollow ground.   140
Aum. Is Bushy, Greene, and the Earl of Wiltshire dead?
Scroope. Ay, all of them at Bristow lost their heads.
Aum. Where is the Duke my father with his power?
Rich. No matter where—of comfort no man speak.
Let's talk of graves, of worms, and epitaphs,   145
Make dust our paper, and with rainy eyes
Write sorrow on the bosom of the earth.
Let's choose executors and talk of wills.
And yet not so—for what can we bequeath
Save our deposed bodies to the ground?   150
Our lands, our lives, and all, are Bolingbroke's,
And nothing can we call our own but death;
And that small model of the barren earth

133–4.] *As Qq; . . . warre / . . . Offence./ F.*   134. this] *Qq;* this Offence *F.*
135. love] *Q1, 2, F;* loue's *Q3, 4;* Ioue's *Q5.*   138. heads] *Q1, F;* head *Q2–5.*
139. wound] *Qq;* hand *F.*   142. Ay] *Q1* (I); Ye *Q2;* Yea *Q3–5, F.*

132. *Judases*] Political betrayers are often referred to thus, and we need not suppose that Richard is at this point comparing himself to Christ: cf. *True Tragedy of Richard III*, M.S.R., l. 600; Peele's *Edward I*, M.S.R., l. 965; *Edmond Ironside*, M.S.R., ll. 1625, 1641 ff (and see note on IV. i. 169 below); *3 H 6*, v. vii. 33–4.

133. *Would*] "Were they willing to . . ."

133.] "In [line 133] the words 'make peace?' are a cry of rage which can only be adequately rendered by giving to each the time of a whole foot" (Pollard, p. 85).

135. *property*] quality.

137. *uncurse*] See note on II. i. 16.

140. *grav'd*] laid in the grave. Not

elsewhere in this sense in Shakespeare; cf. J. Hall, *Virgidemiarum* (1598), III. ii. 23 (*Poems*, ed. Davenport, p. 36); *2 Return from Parnassus*, ll. 405, 1401 (*Three Parnassus Plays*, ed. Leishman, pp. 252, 308). For possible analogues to the thought in this passage, see note to IV. i. 219.

153. *model*] Q1 has *modle*, a possibly Shakespearian spelling of *model*, and also at III. iv. 42, v. i. 11. The sentence expects a word like "portion", but *model* usually implies "something that accurately resembles something else"; hence Clarendon editors' suggestion that Richard is thinking of the characteristic grave-mound as the "model" (in length and breadth) of the body beneath. Other suggestions

Which serves as paste and cover to our bones.
For God's sake let us sit upon the ground   155
And tell sad stories of the death of kings:
How some have been depos'd, some slain in war,
Some haunted by the ghosts they have deposed,
Some poisoned by their wives, some sleeping kill'd,
All murthered—for within the hollow crown   160

155. God's] *Qq;* Heauens *F.*

have been that "model" is equivalent
to "mould: something that envelops
closely" (*O.E.D.*); that Richard is
thinking of a "model", or effigy, on a
tomb (but it is difficult to see how this
could serve as "paste" to the bones);
that the grave which he anticipates is
the "whole world" of the dead, and
hence a "small model of the barren
earth"; or that "model" refers to the
flesh, the feature which represents in
man the "earth" (which must in this
interpretation be equivalent to "soil")
of the macrocosm, and which in the
next line is compared to "paste"
(i.e. pastry: cf. Webster, *Duchess of
Malfi,* IV. ii. 124: "what's this flesh? a
little cruded milke, phantasticall puff-
paste"). This interpretation links
"model" most pleasingly with the
image in the next line, one "not of the
most sublime kind, taken from a pie"
(Johnson). But this last image suggests another possibility, that Richard
may be thinking of the "small model
[made out] of the . . . earth", i.e. the
grave and its contents, as the "model"
of a pie: other dramatists besides
Shakespeare (*Tit.,* v. ii. 189) had
quibbled on "coffin" in the double
sense of *cercueil* and "pie-crust" (see
O.E.D., s.v. coffin 4), which might
have helped: on this see *Ben Jonson,* ed.
Herford and Simpson, x. 269 (note to
The Staple of News, II. iii. 74).

156.] Richard is thinking of *The
Mirror for Magistrates* and similar
metrical "tragedies" about the falls of
illustrious men; see W. Farnham,
*Medieval   Heritage   of   Elizabethan
Tragedy,* 1936, pp. 416-17.

158. *ghosts . . . deposed*] i.e. ghosts of
persons whom they have deprived [of
life]; *deposed* is here used with a different connotation from *depos'd* in l.
157 above, for which cf. IV. i. 192.

160-2. *within . . . court*] Cf. II. i. 100
(for flatterers sitting within the
crown) and *John,* v. ii. 176: "and in
his forehead sits / A bare-ribb'd
death". Douce (*Illustrations to Shakespeare,* 1807, I. 140) suggested the influence of a woodcut in the Dance of
Death series attributed to Hans Holbein the Younger (first pub. 1538: see
*Les Simulachres & Historiees Faces de la
Mort,* an edition of the 1538 vol., ed.
H. Green, 1869; the woodcut is also
reproduced as no. 7 ["The Emperor"]
in *Holbein's Dance of Death,* ed. Douce,
1878). Douce's description of the
woodcut is very inaccurate. Chamberlain (*Hans Holbein the Younger,*
1913, I. 217), who also reproduces it,
says correctly: "The Emperor sits on
his throne . . . surrounded by his
counsellors and on the right a poor
man kneels demanding justice. The
Emperor . . . turns from him with
frowning face towards the rich op-
pressor, who attempts, with little
success, to excuse himself. Death has
sprung upon the throne behind the
monarch, and is about to tear the
imperial crown from his head." This
does not approach very closely to
Shakespeare's lines (except for "kill
with looks" at l. 165); the general
influence on them of the *imagines
mortis* may be admitted, but no closer
iconographic parallel has yet been
traced.

That rounds the mortal temples of a king
Keeps Death his court, and there the antic sits,
Scoffing his state and grinning at his pomp,
Allowing him a breath, a little scene,
To monarchize, be fear'd, and kill with looks;   165
Infusing him with self and vain conceit,
As if this flesh which walls about our life
Were brass impregnable; and, humour'd thus,
Comes at the last, and with a little pin
Bores thorough his castle wall, and farewell king!   170
Cover your heads, and mock not flesh and blood
With solemn reverence; throw away respect,
Tradition, form, and ceremonious duty;
For you have but mistook me all this while.
I live with bread like you, feel want,   175
Taste grief, need friends—subjected thus,
How can you say to me, I am a king?

Car. My lord, wise men ne'er sit and wail their woes,
But presently prevent the ways to wail.   †
To fear the foe, since fear oppresseth strength,   180
Gives in your weakness strength unto your foe,

170. thorough] *Q1;* through *Q2–5, F.*   wall] *Q1;* walls *Q2–5, F.*   178. sit
. . . woes] *Qq;* waile their present woes *F.*

161. *rounds*] encircles.
162. *antic*] buffoon, jester: because
death in the *imagines mortis* is a skele-
ton with a "grinning" skull, and because, like the jester, he makes fools of
men.
163. *Scoffing his state*] scoffing at his
regality.
164. *scene*] The theatrical term continues the suggestion in "antic".
167–8. *flesh . . . brass*] Cf. Job, vi.12:
"Is my strength the strength of
stones? or is my flesh of brasse?"
(Noble). For brass as a symbol of im-
perishability cf. *Sonn.*, LXIV. 4.
168–9. *humour'd thus . . . Comes*]
Humour'd might refer either to the
king or to death, who is the subject of
the verb *comes* in the next line. Thus
the meaning might be: "When the
king has been indulged in this way,
death comes . . ." or "When death has

amused himself in this way, he comes
. . ." *Humour'd* might also mean "being in this humour" (= mood,
bodily and mental condition) and
could still apply to either death or the
king: "When the king is in this mood,
death comes . . ." or "Because death
feels like doing so, he comes . . ."
170. *thorough*] Here and at v. v. 20
Q1's *thorough* is retained; if any metrical irregularity was entailed, it
might well be Shakespeare's intention.
176. *subjected*] "With a play on the
sense of 'liable to' and 'made a subject'" (Newbolt).
178–9.] Cf. *3 H 6*, v. iv. 1: "wise
men ne'er sit and wail their loss, / But
cheerly seek how to redress their
harms." For *wise men* (*wisemen* Q1–3),
see note on I. iii. 275–6.
179. *presently*] immediately.

And so your follies fight against yourself.
Fear and be slain—no worse can come to fight;
And fight and die is death destroying death,
Where fearing dying pays death servile breath.   185
Aum. My father hath a power; inquire of him,
And learn to make a body of a limb.
Rich. Thou chid'st me well. Proud Bolingbroke, I come
To change blows with thee for our day of doom.
This ague fit of fear is overblown;   190
An easy task it is to win our own.
Say, Scroope, where lies our uncle with his power?
Speak sweetly, man, although thy looks be sour.
Scroope. Men judge by the complexion of the sky
The state and inclination of the day;   195
So may you by my dull and heavy eye:
My tongue hath but a heavier tale to say.
I play the torturer by small and small
To lengthen out the worst that must be spoken:
Your uncle York is join'd with Bolingbroke,   200
And all your northern castles yielded up,
And all your southern gentlemen in arms
Upon his party.
Rich.   Thou hast said enough.

182.] *Not in F.*   203. party] *Qq;* Faction *F.*

183. *no . . . fight*] "Nothing worse [than being slain] can happen to you in fighting."

184-5.] "To die fighting is to destroy death by means of death, whereas to die in the fear of death is to pay death a slavish tribute of your breath of life."

186. *power*] army: ct. l. 211 below.

189. *change*] exchange.

194. *complexion*] Refers to the general visible aspect, not specifically the colour, of the sky.

196-7.] The colon after *eye* (in Q1) seems to indicate that the sense is: "So may you [judge] by my dull and heavy eye [that] my tongue . . ." This interpretation is strengthened by what seems to be the natural balance between the sense of these lines and the

comparison in ll. 194-5, the four lines together forming a quatrain.

198. *by small and small*] little by little.

203. *Upon his party*] on his side. F reads *Faction* here and, as H. F. Brooks, following A. S. Cairncross, notes, at *R 3*, v. iii. 13: "the King's name is a tower of strength, / Which they upon the adverse faction want." In *R 3*, F is correcting Q1's *partie.* Had Shakespeare's *Faction* been memorially changed to the perhaps more usual *partie* first in *R 3* (by memorial recollection from *R 3*, IV. iv. 190) and then more readily in *R 2* by a transcriber who had something to do with the copy for both Q1 *R 3* and Q1 *R 2*? If so, F's reading here must come from the prompt-book.

Beshrew thee, cousin, which didst lead me forth   †
                                        [*To Aumerle.*]
Of that sweet way I was in to despair!   205
What say you now? What comfort have we now?
By heaven, I'll hate him everlastingly
That bids me be of comfort any more.
Go to Flint Castle, there I'll pine away—
A king, woe's slave, shall kingly woe obey.   210
That power I have, discharge, and let them go
To ear the land that hath some hope to grow,   †
For I have none. Let no man speak again
To alter this, for counsel is but vain.
Aum. My liege, one word.
Rich.   He does me double wrong   215
That wounds me with the flatteries of his tongue.
Discharge my followers; let them hence away,
From Richard's night, to Bolingbroke's fair day. [*Exeunt.*

SCENE III.—[*Wales. Before Flint Castle.*]

Enter, with drum and colours, BOLINGBROKE, YORK,
      NORTHUMBERLAND, Attendants.

Bol. So that by this intelligence we learn

204. S.D.] *Theobald; not in Qq, F.*   211. them] *Qq;* 'em *F.*   218. S.D.] *F;
not in Qq.*

Scene III

Location] *Capell; not in Qq, F.*   S.D.] *F; Enter Bull. Yorke, North. Qq.*

205. *way*] Richard compares learning to despair to the acquisition of a
skill or habit which he was "getting
into the way of".

209. *Flint Castle*] From a marginal
note in Hol., 499/2: "K. Richard
stealeth awaie from his armie, and
taketh the castell of Flint"—Holinshed's mistake for the "Conwaie" of
the body of his text.

212. *ear*] plough.

213. *none*] i.e. "no hope to grow":
Richard compares himself to barren
land.

218. *Richard's . . . day*] Smith cfs.
Daniel's images, also applied to
Richard and Bolingbroke: "All turn'd
their faces to the rising sunne / And
leaues his setting-fortune night begun," *C. W.,* II, st. 1 and cf. II. iv. 21–2.

Scene III

MATERIAL. All the authorities, except Froissart, describe how Richard
went to Conway after landing in
Wales; that he was there persuaded
by Northumberland, Bolingbroke's
emissary, who promised him safe con-

The Welshmen are dispers'd; and Salisbury
Is gone to meet the king, who lately landed
With some few private friends upon this coast.
North. The news is very fair and good, my lord;   5
Richard not far from hence hath hid his head.
York. It would beseem the Lord Northumberland
To say "King Richard". Alack the heavy day,
When such a sacred king should hide his head!
North. Your grace mistakes; only to be brief,   10
Left I his title out.
York.   The time hath been,   †

11–12. The time . . . been / . . . he would /] *As F;* The time . . . with him / He
would . . . *Qq.*

duct on oath, to repair to a rendez-vous with Bolingbroke; that on his way between Conway and Flint Richard rode into an ambush previously laid by Northumberland and was thence conveyed under duress to Flint Castle. During this manœuvre Bolingbroke remained at Chester. When Richard was safely lodged at Flint, Bolingbroke mustered his army before the Castle, and, after various negotiations in which Northumberland played a leading part, eventually presented himself before the king in the outer ward of the Castle. Shakespeare, like Froissart and Daniel, omits everything up to the final arrival of Bolingbroke and his army before Flint. It is possible that if Shakespeare had any kind of historical conscience about his omissions it was salved by his finding similar omissions in Froissart. Since Shakespeare had been following Holinshed throughout the play for his primary historical data, it is illogical to suppose that he departed from Holinshed here *because* Froissart differed from him. His motive must have been his judgement of what would be dramatically effective, not Froissart's example. In the scene itself there is a strong contrast between Froissart (VI. 367 ff), vivid and powerful though his account is, and Shakespeare, except

in the one detail noted in l. 53. In Froissart there is no mention of Northumberland's role, and Bolingbroke's conduct is that of a victorious bully, quite different from the "reuerend dutie" shown by Holinshed's and Shakespeare's victor. If Shakespeare was following Froissart at any stage, why does he cease to follow him at the very point where his episode runs parallel with Froissart's and revert to Holinshed? In the character of Bolingbroke's demands on Richard, first through Northumberland (ll. 113 ff) and then in his own person (l. 196), Holinshed is followed with some significant omissions (see notes on these lines). For a further important debt to Holinshed, see note on l. 176. The part played by Aumerle, and, of course, the substance of Richard's speeches on kingship and his own fate, are invented.

11–13. *The time . . . shorten you*] Q1 has: "The time hath bin, would you haue been so briefe *with him / He would haue bin so briefe to shorten you / [*these two words are in a turn-down in the next line]". Its omission of *with you* may be due to lack of space, since the line in which it occurs would not, if it had been given uncut, have fitted into the space left after the last two words of the previous line had been turned down

Would you have been so brief with him, he would
Have been so brief with you to shorten you,
For taking so the head, your whole head's length
Bol. Mistake not, uncle, further than you should.   15
York. Take not, good cousin, further than you should,
Lest you mistake: the heavens are o'er our heads.
Bol. I know it, uncle; and oppose not myself
Against their will. But who comes here?

Enter PERCY.

Welcome, Harry. What, will not this castle yield?   20
Percy. The castle royally is mann'd, my lord,
Against thy entrance.
Bol. Royally!
Why, it contains no king?
Percy.   Yes, my good lord,
It doth contain a king; King Richard lies   25
Within the limits of yon lime and stone;
And with him are the Lord Aumerle, Lord Salisbury,

12. Would you] *Q1–3, F;* should you *Q4, 5.*   13. with you] *F; not in Qq.*
17. mistake:] *Wilson* (mis-take); mistake *Qq, F;* mistake; *Rowe.*   o'er] *F;*
over *Qq.*   our heads] *Qq* (your *Q3–5*); your head *F.*   19. will] *Q1–3, F;*
willes *Q4, 5.*   21. royally is] *Q1, F;* is royally *Q2–5.*   23–4. Royally! /
... king?] *As Steevens (1793);* Royally, ... King. / *Qq, F.*   26. yon] *Qq;* yond
F.   27. are] *Q1; not in Q2–5, F.*

(Wilson). The compositor could, however, have found room for a turn-up
in the space above the first line, and it
is possible therefore that the trouble
originated in the MS copy for Q1, as
H. F. Brooks suggests. Q1's first line
may be due to his copy's having had
one and a half lines written as one, or
even two and a half as two, thus—
"The time hath bin would you haue
been so briefe with him / He would
haue bin so briefe with you to
shorten you"; *with you* may then have
been struck out because it disturbed
the metre of the second "line" and
was believed to be Shakespeare's first
and cancelled draft for "to shorten
you". F's version may come from the
prompt-book: see Introduction, p.
xxii.

14. *taking . . . head*] A quibble on "to
act without restraint, to take undue
liberties" (Johnson), and "to curtail
Richard of his 'head' or title of king".
17. *mistake:*] Rowe's punctuation
gives "better rhythm and greatly
superior sense" (Wilson). Coleridge
followed this sense, too (II. 190). *Mistake* is here used intransitively to mean
"go astray", "transgress", and is a
quibble on the *mistake* of l. 15 above;
the latter means "misapprehend".
The quibble is on the difference between an intellectual (*mistake*) error
and a moral (*mis-take*) error.
23.] Bolingbroke's surprise at finding Richard at Flint is quite unhistorical, since the whole manœuvre had
been planned by him: see note on
material.

Sir Stephen Scroope, besides a clergyman
Of holy reverence; who, I cannot learn.
North. O belike it is the Bishop of Carlisle.   30 †
Bol. Noble lord,
    Go to the rude ribs of that ancient castle,
    Through brazen trumpet send the breath of parle
    Into his ruin'd ears, and thus deliver:
    Henry Bolingbroke   35
    On both his knees doth kiss King Richard's hand,
    And sends allegiance and true faith of heart
    To his most royal person; hither come
    Even at his feet to lay my arms and power,
    Provided that my banishment repeal'd   40
    And lands restor'd again be freely granted;
    If not, I'll use the advantage of my power
    And lay the summer's dust with showers of blood
    Rain'd from the wounds of slaughtered Englishmen—
    The which, how far off from the mind of Bolingbroke 45
    It is such crimson tempest should bedrench
    The fresh green lap of fair King Richard's land,
    My stooping duty tenderly shall show.
    Go, signify as much, while here we march
    Upon the grassy carpet of this plain.   50
    Let's march without the noise of threat'ning drum,
    That from this castle's tottered battlements   †
    Our fair appointments may be well perus'd.

---

31. lord] *F;* lords *Qq.*   33. parle] *F;* parlee *Qq.*   35–8.] *As Steevens* (*1793*);
... hand, / ... heart / ... come / *Qq;* ... kisse / ... allegeance / ... come / *F.*
36. On both] *Qq;* vpon *F.*   38. most] *Q1, 2; not in Q3–5, F.*

32. *rude ribs*] Cf. v. v. 20, and *John,*
II. i. 384: "The flinty ribs of this con-
temptuous city." The ribs are the
castle's protective walls. The ana-
tomizing of the castle is continued in
l. 34 below.

34. *his . . . ears*] i.e. the castle's ruinous casements or loopholes.

40–1.] "Provided that the repeal of
my banishment and the restoration of
my lands be unconditionally granted"
(Deighton).

45. *The which*] as to which; see
Abbott ¶272.

52. *tottered*] A variant spelling for
tattered (so in Q3–5, F), also in *Sonn.,*
II. 4 and cf. *John,* v. v. 7; cf. W. Cart-
wright, *Royal Slave* (1636), IV. iii. 1142:
"those totter'd cloaths" (*Poems and
Plays,* ed. Evans, p. 236); and for the
adjective applied to buildings cf. J.
Austen, *Sense and Sensibility,* vol. 1,
ch. xviii: "I do not like ruined, tattered cottages". See Kökeritz, p. 165.

53.] Holinshed says that Bolingbroke "mustered his armie before the
kings presence, which undoubtedlie
made a passing faire shew . . . The

Methinks King Richard and myself should meet
With no less terror than the elements   55
Of fire and water, when their thund'ring shock
At meeting tears the cloudy cheeks of heaven.
Be he the fire, I'll be the yielding water;
The rage be his, whilst on the earth I rain
My waters—on the earth, and not on him.   60
March on, and mark King Richard how he looks.

Parle without, and answer within: then a Flourish. Enter on the walls,
RICHARD, CARLISLE, AUMERLE, SCROOPE, SALISBURY.

See, see, King Richard doth himself appear,
As doth the blushing discontented sun
From out the fiery portal of the East,
When he perceives the envious clouds are bent   65
To dim his glory and to stain the track
Of his bright passage to the occident.
York. Yet looks he like a king. Behold, his eye,
As bright as is the eagle's, lightens forth
Controlling majesty; alack, alack for woe   70
That any harm should stain so fair a show!
Rich. [*To North.*] We are amaz'd, and thus long have we stood
To watch the fearful bending of thy knee,
Because we thought ourself thy lawful king;
And if we be, how dare thy joints forget   75

56. shock] *Q1;* smoke *Q2-5, F.*   59. whilst] *Qq;* while *F.*   60. waters—on]
Wilson; water's on *Qq, F.*   61. S.D.] *F; The trumpets [Trumpet Q4, 5] sound,
Richard appeareth on the walls. Qq.*   66. track] *Qq;* tract *F.*   72. S.D.] *Rowe;
not in Qq, F.*   74. thy] *Q1-4, F;* the *Q5.*

king that was walking aloft on the
braies of the wals, to behold the comming of the duke afarre off, might see,
that the archbishop . . . were come . . .
to talke with him" (501/1/3); cf. Froissart, VI. 368: "all the countrey about
the castell was full of men of warre:
they within the castell myght se them
out at the wyndowes, and the kynge
. . . myght se them hymselfe."

56. *shock*] See note on I. iii. 136.

62-7.] The red morning sky is used
as a sign of discontent, because it fore-
tells a stormy day, to describe Adonis's

angry mouth, *Ven.,* 453 ff. Richard is
angry here and red-faced, "pale with
fury" at II. i. 118-19 (see note): the
changes in his complexion seem to be
literary and conventional rather than
linked to any special idea of his physical appearance as a whole.

69-70. *lightens . . . majesty*] i.e.
"causes controlling majesty to flash
forth". Shakespeare's only use of
transitive *lighten forth;* cf. Greene,
Friar Bacon, M.S.R., ll. 55-6, Daniel,
Complaynt of Rosamond, ll. 232-3 (*Poems
. . .* ed. Sprague, p. 46).

To pay their awful duty to our presence?
If we be not, show us the hand of God
That hath dismiss'd us from our stewardship;
For well we know no hand of blood and bone
Can gripe the sacred handle of our sceptre,   80
Unless he do profane, steal, or usurp.
And though you think that all, as you have done,
Have torn their souls by turning them from us,
And we are barren and bereft of friends,
Yet know, my master, God omnipotent,   85
Is mustering in his clouds, on our behalf,
Armies of pestilence, and they shall strike
Your children yet unborn, and unbegot,
That lift your vassal hands against my head,
And threat the glory of my precious crown.   90
Tell Bolingbroke, for yon methinks he stands,
That every stride he makes upon my land
Is dangerous treason. He is come to open
The purple testament of bleeding war.

91. yon] *Qq;* yond *F.*   stands] *Qq;* is *F.*   93. open] *Qq;* ope *F.*

76. *awful*] reverential.

77–80.] Note the quibble on *hand, hand, handle,* the first hand being equivalent to "written hand", "signature" or "sign manual". For *hand/handle,* cf. *2 H 6,* v. i. 7, *Tit.,* III. ii. 29.

78. *stewardship*] Cf. II. ii. 59, the only other occurrence in Shakespeare.

80. *gripe*] seize.

81. *Unless . . . profane*] without committing sacrilege.

83. *Have . . . souls*] i.e. "Have wounded their souls [by the sin of treason]", with quibble on *torn/turning.*

85–7.] Like sentiments are expressed by Créton's Richard but are frequent in Elizabethan political pamphlets: see W. Lightfoote, *Complaint of England,* 1587, sig. B3ʳ. Noble cfs. *2 Kings,* xix. 35. Cf. note on III. ii. 60.

88.] Reyher cfs. Daniel, *C.W.,* I, st. 90: "The babes vnborne, shall ô be borne to bleed / In this thy quarrell".

92. *stride . . . land*] Wilson suggests a link with another line in the same stanza of Daniel's cited in preceding note: "Stay here thy foote, thy yet vnguilty foote". In Daniel, Bolingbroke is being addressed in a vision by the Genius of England.

94.] In the 16th century *testament* means "will", or else has a specific reference to the biblical "testament" (= covenant) or to the Old and New Testaments as books. Neither of the two latter meanings seems appropriate here—a covenant is not "opened", and Richard is certainly not thinking of the Bible. Steevens must be right when he takes *testament* in the legal sense: "Bolingbroke is come to open the testament of war, that he may peruse what is decreed there in his favour." But the associations of the word *testament* in its theological sense of a covenant entailing the shedding of blood underlie the legal conceit: *purple* and *bleeding* refer us to, e.g., 1 Cor. ix. 25, "this cup is the newe testament in my blood"; Delius cfs.

But ere the crown he looks for live in peace,   95
Ten thousand bloody crowns of mothers' sons
Shall ill become the flower of England's face,
Change the complexion of her maid-pale peace
To scarlet indignation and bedew
Her pastures' grass with faithful English blood.   100
North. The King of Heaven forbid our lord the king
Should so with civil and uncivil arms
Be rush'd upon! Thy thrice noble cousin,
Harry Bolingbroke, doth humbly kiss thy hand,
And by the honourable tomb he swears,   105
That stands upon your royal grandsire's bones,
And by the royalties of both your bloods,
Currents that spring from one most gracious head,
And by the buried hand of warlike Gaunt,
And by the worth and honour of himself,   110
Comprising all that may be sworn or said,
His coming hither hath no further scope
Than for his lineal royalties, and to beg

---

98. her] *Qq; not in F.*   100. pastures'] *Capell;* pastors *Qq, F;* pastor's *Pope*

First Part of Ieronimo (?1600), ed. Boas (*Works of Kyd*), II. ii. 87: "Then I vnclaspe the purple leaues of war".

97–100. *flower . . . face*] "the blossomy surface of the land, stained by the bleeding slain, but with a secondary suggestion, made prominent in the next lines, of a flower-like human countenance" (Herford). *Flower* also carries a third suggestion, explained by Warburton: "By *the flower of England's face* is meant the choicest youth in England, who shall be slaughtered . . . or have bloody crowns." Knight noted the parallel in thought with Daniel, *C.W.*, I, st. 121: "Th' vngodly bloudshed that did so defile / The beauty of thy fields. And euen did marre / The flowre of thy chiefe pride".

98. *maid-pale*] Cf. *1 H 6*, II. iv. 47: "pale and maiden blossom".

105–6.] The "royal grandsire" is Edward III, whose tomb is in Westminster Abbey. So, at *Woodstock*, II. i.

142–3, York swears by, amongst other things, his father's tomb.

107. *royalties*] Does not carry the precise meaning attached to it in l. 113 below of "royal prerogative" and rights-hereditary (and cf. II. i. 190 and note, II. iii. 119, *O.E.D.*, s.v. royalty 6), but implies "royal status or qualities belonging to both houses [of York and Lancaster]": see *O.E.D.* art. cit., 3.

107–8.] The *bloods* are compared to rivers rising from their fountain-*head*, Edward III: see note on I. ii. 12–21.

112. *scope*] aim.

113–14.] Derived, like l. 196 below, from Hol., 501/2/14 ff, the actual words said by Bolingbroke in his personal meeting with Richard at Flint, not what Northumberland had said were Bolingbroke's demands when Northumberland negotiated with Richard at Conway before the ambush—an incident cut by Shakespeare

Infranchisement immediate on his knees,
Which on thy royal party granted once,   115
His glittering arms he will commend to rust,
His barbed steeds to stables, and his heart
To faithful service of your Majesty.
This, swears he as he is a prince and just;   †
And, as I am a gentleman, I credit him.   120

Rich. Northumberland, say thus the king returns:
His noble cousin is right welcome hither,
And all the number of his fair demands
Shall be accomplish'd without contradiction;
With all the gracious utterance that thou hast   125
Speak to his gentle hearing kind commends.
[*To Aum.*] We do debase ourselves, cousin, do we not,
To look so poorly, and to speak so fair?

---

119. a . . . just] *Sisson* [*see additional notes*]; princesse iust *Q 1, 2*; a Prince iust *Q 3–5*;
a prince, is just *F.*   127. S.D.] *Rowe; not in Qq, F.*   ourselves] *Qq;* our selfe *F.*

(see note on material). Northumberland had demanded on Bolingbroke's
behalf a Parliament which would do
justice on Bolingbroke's enemies,
especially the murderers of his uncle
Gloucester. (In the corresponding
passages in Créton, p. 134/356 and
Traïson, p. 48/198 Northumberland
makes similar demands: for the
appointment of *juges* to bring about a
general conciliation [*Traïson*]; for a
trial of Bolingbroke's enemies with
Bolingbroke as judge [Créton].) Here,
and at l. 196, all that Bolingbroke asks
for are "his own", his "lineal royalties" and "infranchisement immediate". This corresponds to Holinshed's
"My soueraigne lord and king, the
cause of my coming . . . is . . . to have
againe restitution of my person, my
lands and heritage, through your
fauourable licence." The last item,
"infranchisement immediate" (Holinshed's "restitution of my person")
receives special emphasis in Richard's
angry lament at ll. 133 ff below; Holinshed is the only authority who mentions this particular demand.

113. *lineal royalties*] See note on l. 107
above. One of them was the right to
the hereditary office of "grant iuge"
(Lord High Steward) of England, according to Créton, whom Stow follows.
115. *on . . . party*] i.e. "by you, the
king, as party to the agreement"
(Deighton).
116. *commend*] "commit", not "re-
commend"; cf. *Wint.*, II. iii. 181. Quite
devoid of the kindly feeling in *commends* at II. i. 147 or l. 126 below.
117. *barbed*] armed or caparisoned
with *barbs* or *bards*, protective cover-
ings of metal, leather or cloth on
the horse's chest and flanks. *Barbed*
and *barded* are alternative forms both
in use at this time. Hol., 494/2/70, in
what is probably the source for this
detail speaks of Bolingbroke's horse as
"barded with . . . velvet", whereas
Hall (p. 4) uses *barbed*. Zeeveld (p.
320) sees in this a proof of Shakespeare's use of Hall, but, since the
forms were interchangeable, *barbed*
could easily have occurred without
Hall's intervention.
121. *returns*] replies.

Shall we call back Northumberland and send
Defiance to the traitor, and so die?   130
Aum. No, good my lord, let's fight with gentle words,
Till time lend friends, and friends their helpful swords.
Rich. O God! O God! that e'er this tongue of mine,
That laid the sentence of dread banishment
On yon proud man, should take it off again   135
With words of sooth! O that I were as great
As is my grief, or lesser than my name!
Or that I could forget what I have been!
Or not remember what I must be now!
Swell'st thou, proud heart? I'll give thee scope to beat,
Since foes have scope to beat both thee and me.   141
Aum. Northumberland comes back from Bolingbroke.
Rich. What must the king do now? Must he submit?
The king shall do it. Must he be depos'd?
The king shall be contented. Must he lose   145
The name of king? a God's name, let it go.
I'll give my jewels for a set of beads;
My gorgeous palace for a hermitage;
My gay apparel for an almsman's gown;
My figur'd goblets for a dish of wood;   150
My sceptre for a palmer's walking staff;
My subjects for a pair of carved saints,
And my large kingdom for a little grave,
A little little grave, an obscure grave,
Or I'll be buried in the king's highway,   155

135. yon] *Qq;* yond *F.*   146. king] *Q1, F;* a King *Q2–5.*   a] *Qq;* o' *F.*

131–2.] For the sentiments, J. E. Hankins (*Shakespeare's Derived Imagery*, 1953, p. 273) cfs. B. Googe's translation of Palingenius, *The Zodiake of Life* (edn 1576, p. 59): "The wyseman will refraine, / And spie hys time, and eke geue place his foe with wordes to traine / That pleasant seme".

136. *sooth*] appeasement.

138–9.] W. D. Briggs (edn of *Edward II*, p. 185) cfs. *Edward II*, v. i. 110–11: "Come, death and with thy fingers close my eyes; / Or if I live, let me forget myself."

141. *scope*] Here used in the modern sense of "permission" or "opportunity", but perhaps an ironical echo of *scope* in l. 112 above.

149. *gay apparel*] Holinshed speaks of Richard's fine clothes; cf. I. iv. 43–4 and note, II. i. 19, 21–3 and notes.

150. *figur'd*] ornamented with patterns.

151. *palmer's*] pilgrim's; so called because the palmer carried a palm-branch to signify that he had visited Jerusalem.

Some way of common trade, where subjects' feet
May hourly trample on their sovereign's head;
For on my heart they tread now whilst I live:
And buried once, why not upon my head?
Aumerle, thou weep'st (my tender-hearted cousin!),   160
We'll make foul weather with despised tears;
Our sighs and they shall lodge the summer corn,
And make a dearth in this revolting land.
Or shall we play the wantons with our woes,
And make some pretty match with shedding tears?   165
As thus to drop them still upon one place,
Till they have fretted us a pair of graves
Within the earth, and therein laid—there lies
Two kinsmen digg'd their graves with weeping eyes!
Would not this ill do well? Well, well, I see   170
I talk but idly, and you laugh at me.
Most mighty prince, my Lord Northumberland,
What says King Bolingbroke? Will his Majesty
Give Richard leave to live till Richard die?   †
You make a leg, and Bolingbroke says "ay".   175
North. My lord, in the base court he doth attend

166. As] *Q1, F;* And *Q2–5.*   171. laugh] *Qq;* mock *F.*

156. *trade*] M.E. *trede* (="tread")
came to mean "path" and then "passing to and fro over the path",
"traffic", which seems to be the primary meaning here. Note the quibble
with *tread* in l. 158 below.

162. *lodge*] beat down: cf. *2 H 6,* III.
ii. 176, where the strangled Duke
Humphrey's beard is compared to the
"summer's corn by tempest lodged";
Mac., IV. i. 55.

165. *make . . . match*] "devise some
pretty competition or game".

166. *still*] always.

175. *make a leg*] make an obeisance
or "courtesy". Richard describes in
his ironical fantasy the anticipated
answer to the sinister trick-question of
the preceding line—a question that
demands the answer "ay", whatever
Bolingbroke's intentions really are in
regard to Richard's life. Richard sees

Bolingbroke and Northumberland as
carrying out the set lines of a policy
which has been determined elsewhere.

176. *base court*] the outer and lower
castle-courtyard (Fr. *basse cour*). Here
and in ll. 180 and 182, as Brereton
(pp. 107 ff) has shown, Shakespeare
is echoing an earlier passage in Holinshed, the account of Richard's arrest
of Gloucester in 1397. Hol. 489/1/10
tells how Richard came "riding into
the base court, his trumpets sounding
before him. The duke herewith came
downe into the base court", and greet-
ed the king who told him to make
ready for a ride: "And within a while
they came foorth againe all togither
into the base court . . . shortlie after
that the king and all his companie
were gone foorth of the gate of the base
court, he commanded the earle marshall to apprehend the duke . . ." Bre-

　　To speak with you; may it please you to come down?
Rich. Down, down I come, like glist'ring Phaeton,
　　Wanting the manage of unruly jades.
　　In the base court? Base court, where kings grow base,
　　To come at traitors' calls, and do them grace!　　181
　　In the base court? Come down? Down, court! down,
　　　　king!
　　For night-owls shriek where mounting larks should sing.
　　　　　　　　　　　　　　　　　　　[*Exeunt from above.*]
Bol. What says his Majesty?
North.　　　　　　　　　　Sorrow and grief of heart
　　Makes him speak fondly like a frantic man;　　185
　　Yet he is come.

　　　[*Enter* KING RICHARD *and his* Attendants *below.*]

180. base court?] *F;* base court, *Qq.*　　182. court? . . . down?] *Capell;*
court . . . downe: *Qq, F.*　　183. S.D.] *Capell; not in Qq, F.*　　186. S.D.]
Capell; not in Qq, F.

reton comments: "Here is a memorable passage, in which we are told how
the duke, who is subsequently slain in
prison, is brought down unto the base
court—and the words 'base court' are
several times repeated—to meet the
perfidious enemy—his kinsman, who
desires to have him in his power to
effect his overthrow. Shakespeare
shows that enemy in a precisely similar
situation, and by an echoing repetition of the 'base court' . . . reminds us
that the wheel has come full circle."
Wilson's suggestion (p. lix) that
Shakespeare's "base court" echoes "la
basse court" of *Traïson*, p. 59, is much
less convincing.
　178. *glist'ring*] glittering.
　Phaeton] Pronounced Pháëtón.
Phaeton, too weak to control the
horses of his father Apollo's sun-
chariot, drove it so near the earth that
Zeus struck him with a thunderbolt to
save the world from combustion. A
very common image for rash failure
(cf. *3 H 6*, I. iv. 33, II. vi. 11–13) and
an appropriate symbol for a fallen
Yorkist monarch, since the sun was a
Yorkist badge, besides being Richard's

own badge; the story of how Edward
IV assumed the badge at the Battle of
Mortimer's Cross, 1461, is recounted
by Hol., 660/1/22.
　179.] "Lacking horsemanship over
unruly steeds". *Manage* is a term used
for the training of a horse in a riding-
school, especially after the Italian
techniques were introduced into England: see Sieveking in *Shakespeare's
England*, II. 412. Cf. Sidney's use of
terms of manage in *Astrophel and Stella*,
XLIX, XLI, *Faerie Queene*, II. iv, st. 1–2,
and, for a description of the elaborate
manœuvres involved see Florio's
Montaigne, I. xlviii (Everyman edn,
I. 331, 335).
　185. *fondly*] foolishly.
　186. S.D.] "After the fluid fashion
of the Elizabethan theatre the locality
changes from without the walls to
within, in the base court" (Wilson).
Richard descends from the upper
stage by the stairs concealed in the
tiring-house and emerges through one
of the stage-doors on to the platform
stage. This change seems to take place
during Bolingbroke's words at l. 184
above.

Bol. Stand all apart,
And show fair duty to his Majesty.   [*He kneels down.*
My gracious lord.

Rich. Fair cousin, you debase your princely knee   190
To make the base earth proud with kissing it.
Me rather had my heart might feel your love,
Than my unpleased eye see your courtesy.
Up, cousin, up; your heart is up, I know,
Thus high at least, although your knee be low.   195

Bol. My gracious lord, I come but for mine own.

Rich. Your own is yours, and I am yours, and all.

Bol. So far be mine, my most redoubted lord,
As my true service shall deserve your love.

Rich. Well you deserve. They well deserve to have   200
That know the strong'st and surest way to get.
Uncle, give me your hands; nay, dry your eyes—
Tears show their love, but want their remedies.   †
Cousin, I am too young to be your father,
Though you are old enough to be my heir;   205
What you will have, I'll give, and willing too,
For do we must what force will have us do.
Set on towards London, cousin, is it so?

Bol. Yea, my good lord.

Rich.   Then I must not say no.
                              [*Flourish. Exeunt.*

188. S.D.] *Qq; not in F.*   190.] *As Qq; . . . Cousin, / . . . Knee, F.*   200. you deserve] *Qq;* you deseru'd *F.*   200.] *As Qq; . . . deseru'd: / . . . haue, F.*   202. hands;] *Qq* (handes,); Hand: *F.*   205. my] *Q1, F; not in Q2–5.*   208.] *As Qq; . . . London: / . . . so? / F.*   209. S.D.] *F; Exeunt. Q4, 5; not in Q1–3.*

192. *Me . . . had*] I had rather.

194–5.] Cf. *Mirror*, p. 497, "Wolsey", ll. 46–7, where Wolsey is describing the kind of conduct that led to his advancement: "Then downe I lookt, with sober countnaunce sad, / But heart was vp, as high as hope could go."

195. *Thus high*] Richard means "as high as my crown", which he perhaps touches.

196. *mine own*] See note on ll. 113–

14 above and on II. iii. 147–50.

198. *redoubted*] dreaded.

202–3.] Addressed to York, who has been silent and overcome since l. 71. Richard's aphorism in l. 203 seems to mean: "Tears show that they have the quality of being (an expression of) love, but they lack the quality of being remedies (for themselves, or the situation)."

204–5.] In history, Richard and Bolingbroke were both thirty-three.

SCENE IV.—[*The Duke of York's garden.*]

Enter the QUEEN, *and two* Ladies.

Queen. What sport shall we devise here in this garden,
  To drive away the heavy thought of care?
Lady. Madam, we'll play at bowls.
Queen. 'Twill make me think the world is full of rubs
  And that my fortune runs against the bias.   5
Lady. Madam, we'll dance.
Queen. My legs can keep no measure in delight,
  When my poor heart no measure keeps in grief:
  Therefore no dancing, girl—some other sport.
Lady. Madam, we'll tell tales.   10
Queen. Of sorrow or of joy?
Lady.   Of either, madam.
Queen. Of neither, girl.
  For if of joy, being altogether wanting,
  It doth remember me the more of sorrow;

Scene IV

Location] Capell, *adding "Langley"; not in Qq, F.*   S.D.] *F; Enter the Queene with her attendants Qq.*   11. joy] *Rowe (ed. 2); griefe Qq, F.*

MATERIAL. The scene is unhistorical; see Introduction, pp. li–lvii.
  Location] Inferred from II. ii. 116–17 and ll. 69–71 below.
  3. *bowls*] The game is frequently referred to in Shakespeare: see Sieveking in *Shakespeare's England*, II. 463–5. Bowling greens or alleys were common in Elizabethan gardens. For an elaborate bowling scene which makes similar play with bowling terminology, see Day, *Ile of Gulls* (1606), Shakespeare Assoc. Facsimile, E1ʳ–E2ʳ.
  4. *rubs*] A technical term for any impediment to the course of a "wood" in the game of bowls; used often as a metaphor for "difficulty": cf. *LLL.*, IV. i. 140, *H 5*, II. ii. 187–8, *Ham.*, III. i. 65. There was later current a proverb: "He who plays at bowls must look out for rubs" (Apperson, p. 62).
  5. *runs . . . bias*] i.e., "runs with un-

natural crookedness". The *bias* is the leaden weight in the "wood", whose function is explained in Pope's versicle "Of the Byass of a Bowl": "Which, as more pond'rous, makes its Aim more true, / And guides it surer to the Mark in view; / The more it seems to go about, to come / The nearer to its End, or Purpose, home." (*Minor Poems*, ed. Ault and Butt, p. 55); cf. *Shr.*, IV. v. 24–5: "Well, forward, forward! thus the bowl should run, / And not unluckily against the bias." In *John*, II. i. 574 ff Shakespeare uses the *bias*, not, as here, to indicate the natural and proper course, but as a symbol of the artificial and crooked, because it unbalances the "wood".
  6–7.] i.e., "I cannot dance a 'delightful measure' (cf. I. iii. 291) when my grief is immeasurable."

Or if of grief, being altogether had,   15
It adds more sorrow to my want of joy;
For what I have I need not to repeat,
And what I want it boots not to complain.
Lady. Madam, I'll sing.
Queen.   'Tis well that thou hast cause,
But thou shouldst please me better wouldst thou weep.
Lady. I could weep, madam, would it do you good.   21
Queen. And I could sing, would weeping do me good,
And never borrow any tear of thee.

Enter a Gardener *and two* Servants.

But stay, here come the gardeners.
Let's step into the shadow of these trees.   25
My wretchedness unto a row of pins,
They'll talk of state, for everyone doth so
Against a change: woe is forerun with woe.
Gard. Go, bind thou up young dangling apricocks,

15. had] *Q1–4, F;* sadd *Q5.*   23. S.D.] *F; Enter Gardeners. Qq.*   24. come]
Q1; commeth *Q2–5;* comes *F.*   26. pins] *F* (Pinnes); pines *Qq.*   27. They'll]
F; They will *Qq.*   29. young] yong *Q1;* yon *Q2–5;* yond *F.*   apricocks]
Q2–5, F; Aphricokes *Q1.*

15. *being ... had*] being possessed in its entirety.

18. *complain*] bewail.

22–3.] i.e., "And I could sing for joy if my troubles were only such as weeping could alleviate, and then I would not ask you to weep for me" (Wright).

26.] "I will wager my wretchedness against a row of pins", i.e. something very great against something very trivial by comparison (Deighton). Deighton cfs. the 18th and 19th century proverb "All Lombard Street to a China orange" (see Apperson, p. 377). The phrase "not worth a row of pins" was used by a speaker in the House of Lords on 27 October 1954.

28. *Against a change*] i.e., "When a change is about to occur": cf. *Ham.,* II. ii. 477: "against some storm".

forerun with] heralded by. The fore-running woe that Isabel laments is, by

implication, the disturbance of mind that has led "everyone", aroused by the expected change, to talk about affairs of state.

29. *young*] Q1's *yong,* a reading superior to F's *yond,* which is simply F's usual variant for Q3's *yon* that itself derives from Q2's *yon,* a reading without authority and probably a simple misprint by Q2. "Surely the picture of the new shoots ... borne down by the weight of the young green fruit, is vivid enough to stand, and it is the word 'yong' that suggested the comparison of the fruit to 'vnruly children' in the next line" (Pollard, p. 56). Also, the whole phrase "young dangling apricocks" (cf. "too fast growing sprays" in l. 34 below) strikes exactly the note of generalized wisdom which is characteristic of the gardeners' talk.

dangling] Suggests that Shakespeare

Which like unruly children make their sire   30
Stoop with oppression of their prodigal weight,
Give some supportance to the bending twigs.
Go thou, and like an executioner
Cut off the heads of too fast growing sprays,
That look too lofty in our commonwealth: 35
All must be even in our government.
You thus employed, I will go root away

34. too] *F;* two *Qq.*

thought of the trees as standards; training fruit-trees against walls was as yet a novelty: see Prothero in *Shakespeare's England,* I. 371.

apricocks] apricots. The *-cot* ending is <Fr.; the *-cock* ending < Portuguese or Spanish.

33–6. *like an executioner*] This first introduces the explicit comparison between garden and kingdom, on which see Introduction, p. lii. H. J. Leon (*P.Q.,* XXIX [1950], 65–70) cites passages in classical literature where the lopping of tall plants (lilies, poppies, corn) symbolizes the suppression of ambitious men. There is Tarquin's message to his son Sextus to destroy the leading men among the Gabii (reported by Livy, I. 54; Ovid, *Fasti,* II. 701–10, and many others) and what may be its source, Herodotus's story (v. 92) of how Thrasybulus, tyrant of Miletus, sent a similar message to Periander, tyrant of Corinth, by walking before the messenger in a wheatfield and cutting off such stalks as projected above the rest. Aristotle in *Politics* twice alludes to the story, and it continues into the Middle Ages. Shakespeare certainly knew *Fasti* and *Politics,* and had probably read Livy for *Lucr.,* but it is impossible to tell where he met the story first, though it may be significant that when it is related of Tarquin the episode occurs in a garden, when of Thrasybulus in a field. One of its main points in the originals, the manner of sending a message cryptic enough to prevent the mes-

senger himself understanding it, is not found in Shakespeare. Jonson later used the same idea in *Catiline,* III. i. 644–7, with a specific reference to Tarquin.

37–9.] Political allegory continues here and at ll. 44–5 and 50–3 below, the main idea being the comparison of the elements of disorder in the kingdom to weeds which must be rooted up from the garden. For the bearing of this set of images on the scene as a whole, see Introduction, p. lii. The comparison of the bad to weeds is proverbial (see *O.E.D.,* s.v. weeds 1d, proverb: "the weed overgroweth the corn"; Tilley W242; Apperson, pp. 672–3: his earliest citation is from BM/MS Harl. 5396, a political poem on Henry VI's reign, ca. 1450, but this is antedated by an example in *Piers Plowman,* Skeat's edn, I. 478) and may derive ultimately from the seed and tares parable in Matt., xiii. Examples of the extended comparison of bad political elements to "weeds" in the commonwealth are discussed in the Introduction. The image is used in non-Shakespearian history plays: e.g., *Troublesome Raigne of King John* (?1590), Part I, sc. xiii, 90–1; Peele's *Edward I* (1593), M.S.R., l. 2581; *A Knacke to Knowe a Knave* (1592) in Hazlitt's Dodsley, VI. 543. A good example is in *The True Tragedy of Richard III,* a play which there are reasons for supposing Shakespeare to have known (see note on v. vi. 45), M.S.R., ll. 1687–95: "I will so deale in gouerning the state, /

The noisome weeds which without profit suck
The soil's fertility from wholesome flowers.
Man. Why should we, in the compass of a pale,   40
Keep law and form and due proportion,
Showing, as in a model, our firm estate,
When our sea-walled garden, the whole land,
Is full of weeds, her fairest flowers chok'd up,
Her fruit-trees all unprun'd, her hedges ruin'd,   45
Her knots disordered, and her wholesome herbs
Swarming with caterpillars?
Gard.   Hold thy peace—
He that hath suffered this disordered spring
Hath now himself met with the fall of leaf.
The weeds which his broad-spreading leaves did shelter,
That seem'd in eating him to hold him up,   51

38. which] *Q1*; that *Q2–5, F*.   40. *Man.*] *Qq; Ser. F.*   42. as] *Q1, F*;
not in Q2–5.

Which now lies like a sauage shultred
groue, / Where brambles, briars, and
thornes, ouer-grow those sprigs, /
Which if they might but spring to
their effect, / And not be crost so by
their contraries, / Making them subiect to these outrages, / Would proue
such members of the Common-weale,/
That England should in them be
honoured". Shakespeare's own uses,
prior to *R 2*, of the "weed" image (see
especially *2 H 6*, III. i. 31–3; *3 H 6*, II.
vi. 21) are exhaustively discussed in
relation to similar figures by Spurgeon, *Shakespeare's Imagery*, 1935, pp.
216 ff; Spurgeon does not enter into
the question of their provenance. It is
impossible to agree with those who
seek a single "germ" for the idea in a
particular source, whether *Traïson*
(Bolingbroke's remark on cleaning his
garden, p. 93/247, quoted in Introduction, p. xlvii, n. 1), as Wilson suggests; *Woodstock*, v. vi. 3–5, as Rossiter
suggests; Puttenham's *Arte of English
Poesie*, III. xxv, as M. C. Bradbrook
suggests (in *Shakespeare and Elizabethan Poetry*, 1951, p. 37); or Googe's
translation of Palingenius, *The Zodiake
of Life*, as J. E. Hankins suggests (in

Shakespeare's Derived Imagery, 1953, pp
192–3).

40. *pale*] paling.

42. *model*] Here used in one of its
ordinary modern senses (contrast III.
ii. 153) implying "our garden is a
model, or small copy, of what gardens, and kingdoms, ought to be."

43. *sea-walled*] Cf. II. i. 47–9 and
note.

45. *Her . . . unprun'd*] Cf. *Troublesome Raigne of K. John*, Part I, sc. xiii.
28–9, referring to anti-papal measures: "Sith we have prun'd the more
than needful branch / That did
oppress the true well-growing stock".

46. *knots*] flowerbeds arranged in a
precise and intricate pattern: see
illustration (from *The Gardeners Laby-
rinth*, 1577) in *Shakespeare's England*, I.
379; for full discussion, see E. Singleton, *The Shakespeare Garden* (London,
n.d. [1932]), pp. 31–89, 298–301.

47. *caterpillars*] Cf. II. iii. 165 and
note.

48. *suffered*] permitted.

spring] The word is balanced against
fall of leaf in the next line.

51. *in eating him*] "while they were
really devouring him" (Kittredge).

Are pluck'd up root and all by Bolingbroke—
I mean the Earl of Wiltshire, Bushy, Greene.
Man. What, are they dead?
Gard.   They are; and Bolingbroke
Hath seiz'd the wasteful king. O, what pity is it   55
That he had not so trimm'd and dress'd his land
As we this garden! We at time of year
Do wound the bark, the skin of our fruit-trees,
Lest, being over-proud in sap and blood,
With too much riches it confound itself;   60
Had he done so to great and growing men,
They might have liv'd to bear, and he to taste
Their fruits of duty. Superfluous branches
We lop away, that bearing boughs may live;
Had he done so, himself had borne the crown,   65
Which waste of idle hours hath quite thrown down.
Man. What, think you the king shall be deposed?
Gard. Depress'd he is already, and depos'd
'Tis doubt he will be. Letters came last night

52. pluck'd] *Q1, 2;* puld *Q3–5,* F.   53. *Man.] Qq; Ser.* F.   54–7. They are . . . year /] *As Capell;* . . . They are. / . . . king, / . . . trimde, / . . . yeare / *Qq,* F.   55. is it] *Q1,* F; it is *Q2–5.*   57. garden! We at time] *Capell;* garden at time *Qq,* F (garden, *Q3–5,* F).   58. Do] *Qq;* And F.   59. over-proud] *Q2–5,* F; *unhyphened Q1.*   in] *Q1;* with *Q2–5,* F.   66. of] *Qq;* and F.   67. *Man.] Qq; Ser.* F.   you] *Qq,* F; you then *Pope.*   69. doubt] *Qq;* doubted F.

57. *garden! We*] The *We* in Capell's emendation is balanced by the *he* of l. 61 below, and the same antithesis recurs in ll. 64 and 65. The corruption in Q1 may have come about in two stages: (i) One and a half lines of verse written as one in MS: "They are. And Bullingbrooke hath ceasde the wastefull king. O what pitie is it / that he had not so trimde, and drest his land". Q1's misdividing of these lines led to an extra-metrical line: "And drest his land as we this garden We at time of yeare". (ii) The second "We" of this line was then rejected by Q1, which mistook it for an erroneous repetition; see Introduction, p. xv.
    at time of year] in season; cf. Chapman, *Masque of the Middle Temple*: "Jests and merriments are but wild

weeds in rank soil, which, being well manured, yield the wholesome crop of wisdom and discretion at time o' th' year."
    59. *over-proud*] too luxuriant. The allegory here (to l. 63) is related to the view (of Plutarch and others) that great natures grow rankly unless they are early pruned: cf. Intro., p. lvi.
    65. *crown*] Quibble on "royal diadem" and "crown" of a tree. For the crown thrown down, cf. v. i. 24–5.
    67.] Possibly an irregular line. Pope's emendation might be justified if Shakespeare wrote "thē" (*then* abbreviated) and if the compositor missed the abbreviation sign and thought *the* had been erroneously repeated.
    68. *Depress'd*] brought low.
    69. *'Tis doubt*] it is feared.

To a dear friend of the good Duke of York's   70
That tell black tidings.

Queen. O, I am press'd to death through want of speaking!
Thou, old Adam's likeness set to dress this garden,
How dares thy harsh rude tongue sound this unpleasing
    news?
What Eve, what serpent, hath suggested thee   75
To make a second fall of cursed man?
Why dost thou say King Richard is depos'd?
Dar'st thou, thou little better thing than earth,
Divine his downfall? Say, where, when, and how
Cam'st thou by this ill tidings? Speak, thou wretch.   80

Gard. Pardon me, madam, little joy have I
To breathe this news, yet what I say is true.
King Richard he is in the mighty hold
Of Bolingbroke. Their fortunes both are weigh'd;
In your lord's scale is nothing but himself,   85
And some few vanities that make him light.
But in the balance of great Bolingbroke,
Besides himself, are all the English peers,
And with that odds he weighs King Richard down.
Post you to London and you'll find it so;   90
I speak no more than everyone doth know.

Queen. Nimble mischance, that art so light of foot,
Doth not thy embassage belong to me,
And am I last that knows it? O, thou thinkest
To serve me last that I may longest keep   95
Thy sorrow in my breast. Come, ladies, go
To meet at London London's king in woe.

---

70. good] *Q1, 2; not in Q3–5, F.*   80. Cam'st] *Q2–5, F; Canst Q1.*   82. this]
Q1; these Q2–5, F.   90. you'll] *F; you will Qq.*

---

72. *press'd . . . speaking*] Prevented
from speaking hitherto, Isabel compares her situation to that of the
accused person who, on refusing to
plead, was "pressed" to death with
weights. For discussion of other
places where Shakespeare used this
metaphor, see K. B. Danks, 'Shakespeare and "Peine Forte et Dure"',
N. & Q., N.S., 1 (1954), 377–9.
  73. *dress this garden*] Echoes Gen., ii.

15: "God tooke the man, and put him
into the garden of Eden, to dresse it".
  75. *suggested*] incited; cf. i. i. 101.
  83. *hold*] custody.
  84–9. *both . . . down*] Shakespeare is
probably echoing Ps., lxii. 9, but cf.
also Daniel, v. 26–9, Job, xxxi. 6.
  90. *Post*] hasten; see note on i. i.
56.
  93.] "Is not your errand (or mission)
directed to me?"

What, was I born to this, that my sad look
Should grace the triumph of great Bolingbroke?
Gard'ner, for telling me these news of woe,   100
Pray God the plants thou graft'st may never grow.

[Exeunt Queen and Ladies.]

Gara. Poor queen, so that thy state might be no worse,
I would my skill were subject to thy curse.
Here did she fall a tear; here in this place
I'll set a bank of rue, sour herb of grace.   105
Rue, even for ruth, here shortly shall be seen,
In the remembrance of a weeping queen.   *[Exeunt.*

100. these] *Qq;* this *F.*   101. Pray God] *Qq;* I would *F.*   S.D.] *Pope; Exit*
Qq, F.   104. fall] *Q1;* drop *Q2-5, F.*   105. herb of grace] *Q1-3, F;*
hyphened in Q4, 5.   107. the] *Q1, F;* not in *Q2-5.*

99. *triumph*] Isabel, like Cleopatra
(*Ant.*, v. ii. 207 ff), thinks of the Roman
triumphal procession (Herford). The
idea is expanded in the scenes (v. i, ii,
v) which deal with Bolingbroke's processional rides, but the word is used
in a different sense at v. ii. 52 (see
note).

102. *so that . . . worse*] i.e. "if in that
way you could be benefited".

105. *rue . . . grace*] Garden rue, also
called Herb Grace or herb-of-grace (as
in Q4, 5, and cf. *Ham.*, IV. v. 177-8:
"There's rue . . . we may call it herb

of grace a Sundays") acquired its
second name because *rue* also means
"repentance", supposed to come by
God's grace. It was believed to be
"good for the head, eyes, breast,
liver, heart, spleen", according to the
great 17th century gardener John
Parkinson; Gerarde in his *Herball*
(1597) says it is a prophylactic against
bites and stings (E. Singleton, *The
Shakespeare Garden*, p. 229). Its special
association here, as explained in the
next line, is not with *rue* (repentance)
but with *ruth* (pity).

ACT IV

SCENE I.—[*Westminster Hall.*]

[*Enter as to the Parliament* BOLINGBROKE, AUMERLE, NORTHUM-
BERLAND, PERCY, FITZWATER, SURREY, *the* BISHOP of CAR-
LISLE, *the* ABBOT of WESTMINSTER, *and another* Lord, Herald,
Officers, *and* BAGOT.]

Bol. Call forth Bagot.

ACT IV

Scene 1

Location] Malone; *not in* Qq, F.   S.D.] *Wright. Enter Bullingbrooke with the Lords
to parliament.* Q1, 2; *Enter Bullingbrooke, Aumerle, and others.* Q4, 5; *Enter as to the
Parliament, Bullingbrooke, Aumerle, Northumberland, Percie, Fitz-Water, Surrey,
Carlile, Abbot of Westminster. Herauld, Officers, and Bagot. F; not in* Q3.   1. *Qq
have S.D. in margin: Enter Bagot.*

MATERIAL. The chief incidents are:
(i) the challenges, followed by news of
Mowbray's death; (ii) Carlisle's
speech, followed by York's entry;
(iii) the abdication, including a formal act of discrowning and the un-
rehearsed looking-glass incident; (iv)
the opening move of the Abbot of
Westminster's plot. This table shows
which parts Shakespeare found in
Holinshed and the modifications he
made: (i) [1399] Monday, 29 Sept.,
the Tower; Hol., 503/1/73. Richard
abdicated in the presence of certain
commissioners and subscribed an
instrument of resignation, the sentiments of which are echoed in part
in the speech beginning at l. 204.
(ii) Tuesday, 30 Sept., Westminster;
504/2/60–506/1/3. The commissioners
reported to Parliament; Bolingbroke
claimed the throne and ascended it
with the assent of lords and commons. Shakespeare compresses this
incident into ll. 107–13, and York

stands for all the commissioners. (iii)
Thursday, 16 Oct., Westminster;
511/2/44. Bagot accused Aumerle in
Parliament. (iv) Saturday, 18 Oct.,
Westminster; 512/1/58. Fitzwater
accused Aumerle. (v) Wednesday, 22
Oct., Westminster; 512/2/36. Carlisle's speech: in Holinshed made not
against the deposition, but against the
proposal that Richard "might haue
iudgement decreed against him, so as
the realme were not troubled by him".
(vi) Monday, 27 Oct. ["morrow after
all Soules day"], Westminster; 513/2/
70. Bolingbroke, now Henry IV, promised that Mowbray should be sent
for from exile and the challenges proceeded with. (vii) In 1400, soon after
the Parliament, Abbot of Westminster's house; 514/2/10. First news
of the Abbot's conspiracy.

Shakespeare runs these events together in time and place for obvious
dramatic reasons and alters their
order to make the abdication their

Now, Bagot, freely speak thy mind—
What thou dost know of noble Gloucester's death,
Who wrought it with the king, and who perform'd
The bloody office of his timeless end.   5
Bagot. Then set before my face the Lord Aumerle.
Bol. Cousin, stand forth, and look upon that man.
Bagot. My Lord Aumerle, I know your daring tongue
Scorns to unsay what once it hath delivered.
In that dead time when Gloucester's death was plotted,
I heard you say "Is not my arm of length,   11
That reacheth from the restful English court
As far as Callice, to mine uncle's head?"
Amongst much other talk that very time

9. once it hath] *Qq;* it hath once *F.*   13. mine] *Qq;* my *F.*

climax and the Abbot's plot a preparation for Act v. I do not think
that because *Traïson* places Carlisle's
speech soon after Bolingbroke's assumption of the throne Shakespeare
is following *Traïson*, as Wilson (pp.
198–9) maintains: where Shakespeare has altered a whole sequence
of events for dramatic reasons, the
fact that a part of the altered sequence
corresponds with a part of the
Traïson sequence proves no connexion.
Other problems of provenance, entailing discussion of many other
sources besides Holinshed, are given
in notes and Introduction; my conclusion is that it cannot be shown with
certainty that Shakespeare used any
of them in this scene. The parts played
by York and Northumberland are
invented (but see note on l. 106); so
also are the formal discrowning (but
see note to l. 180), the business with
the articles (see note to l. 222) and the
scene with the mirror.

1. *Bagot*] See note on III. ii. 122–3.
4. *wrought . . . king*] Wrought is the
now largely obsolete past tense and
past participle of *work* (see Fowler,
Modern English Usage, s.v. work); i.
the phrase is rendered, "who worked
it with the king", this slang paraphrase (see Partridge, *Dictionary of*

Slang, s.v. work) conveys the ambiguity which has troubled commentators,
some holding that the phrase means
"worked upon the king so that the
murder was effected", others, "joined
with the king in effecting the murder". The passage from Holinshed
quoted in note to l. 6 might have
allowed Shakespeare to mean either
or both of these.

5. *office*] duty.
timeless] untimely.
6. *Aumerle*] Newbolt quotes Hol.,
512/1/6: "there was no man in the
realme to whom king Richard was so
much beholden, as to the duke
Aumerle: for he was the man that to
fulfill his mind, had set him on hand
with all that was done against
[Gloucester]".

10. *dead*] "fatal" and hence "dark
and dreary", a combination of the
connotations of *dead* in *MND.*, III. ii.
57: "So should a murderer look—so
dead, so grim", and *Ham.*, I. i. 65:
"this dead hour" (midnight).

14–17.] Shakespeare has mistaken
his chronology here, as Craig notes:
Gloucester's murder was contrived
and executed long before Bolingbroke
went into exile, so that the two con-
versations could not have occurred at
the same time, as Bagot asserts.

I heard you say that you had rather refuse   15
The offer of an hundred thousand crowns
Than Bolingbroke's return to England—
Adding withal, how bless'd this land would be,
In this your cousin's death.

Aum.   Princes and noble lords,
What answer shall I make to this base man?   20
Shall I so much dishonour my fair stars
On equal terms to give him chastisement?
Either I must, or have mine honour soil'd
With the attainder of his slanderous lips.
There is my gage, the manual seal of death,   25
That marks thee out for hell. I say thou liest,
And will maintain what thou hast said is false
In thy heart-blood, though being all too base
To stain the temper of my knightly sword.

Bol. Bagot, forbear, thou shalt not take it up.   30

Aum. Excepting one, I would he were the best
In all this presence that hath mov'd me so.

Fitz. If that thy valour stand on sympathy,
There is my gage, Aumerle, in gage to thine;

17–19.] *As Capell;* ... withall / ... death / ... Lords / *Qq,F.*   22. him] *Q 3–5,*
F; them *Q 1;* my *Q 2.*   26. I say] *Q 1; not in Q 2–5, F.*   33. sympathy] *Qq;*
sympathize *F.*

16. *hundred . . . crowns*] "twentie
thousand pounds" in Hol., 512/1/
18.

21. *fair stars*] i.e., "honourable
birth ":"the *birth* is supposed to be influenced by the *stars,* therefore our
author, with his usual licence, takes
stars for *birth*" (Johnson).

24. *attainder*] accusation.

25. *manual seal*] Aumerle compares
his gage to a seal affixed to a document with his own hand, thus giving
it authority. The commoner term is
sign manual, but cf. the *seal manual* of
Ven., l. 516. For *manual seal* cf. *Ed-*
mond Ironside, M.S.R., l. 439: "Then
for a manuell seale receaue this kisse".
(This may be an echo of the *Ven.* line),
and Drayton, *Endimion and Phoebe,* l.
206. *Manual* = "autograph", "by my
own hand", suggests that Shake-

speare thought of the gage as a glove
(not a hood, as in Holinshed: see note
on l. i. 69), and that Aumerle is being
grimly witty here. Cf. note on ll. 83–4
below.

29. *stain . . . temper*] Aumerle is
thinking of the bright surface of a well-
tempered sword stained with blood.

31–2.] Aumerle is complex with
rage: "I wish the man who has made
me so angry had been the best knight
here—I mean, the knight who is best
after Bolingbroke—for he of course is
the best of all."

33.] "If your valour depends on
correspondence in rank". At once a
sneer and an assertion that Fitzwater
is as well-born as Aumerle. Onions
observes that Shakespeare nowhere
uses *sympathy* in its usual modern
connotation.

By that fair sun which shows me where thou stand'st, 35
I heard thee say, and vauntingly thou spak'st it,
That thou wert cause of noble Gloucester's death.
If thou deniest it twenty times, thou liest;
And I will turn thy falsehood to thy heart,
Where it was forged, with my rapier's point.   40

Aum. Thou dar'st not, coward, live to see that day.

Fitz. Now by my soul, I would it were this hour.

Aum. Fitzwater, thou art damn'd to hell for this.

Percy. Aumerle, thou liest, his honour is as true
In this appeal as thou art all unjust;   45
And that thou art so, there I throw my gage,
To prove it on thee to the extremest point
Of mortal breathing. Seize it, if thou dar'st.

Aum. And if I do not, may my hands rot off,
And never brandish more revengeful steel   50
Over the glittering helmet of my foe!

Another Lord. I task the earth to the like, forsworn Aumerle,
And spur thee on with full as many lies
As may be hollowed in thy treacherous ear
From sun to sun. There is my honour's pawn;   55

35. which] *Q1;* that *Q2–5, F.*   38. it] *Qq;* it, *F.*   41. live] *Q1, F;* liue I
Q2–5.   that] *Qq;* the *F.*   43. Fitzwater] *F;* Fitzwaters *Qq.*   52–9.] *Not
in F.*   52. task] *Q1;* take *Q2–5.*   54. As] *Capell;* As it *Qq.*   55. sun to sun]
Capell; sinne to sinne *Qq.*

39. *turn*] fling back; cf. *1 H 6,* II. iv.
79.

40. *rapier*] Rapiers came into use only
in Shakespeare's own time; Johnson
censured this anachronism severely.

49. "*And if*] "suppose that", "if
indeed": see *O.E.D.,* s.v. and C1;
Abbott, p. 75. *O.E.D.* (s.v. An) remarks: "modern editors substitute
[*an*] for the full form *and* usual in
Shakespeare and his contemporaries."
In *R 2, And if* is consistently printed in
both Qq and F: see l. 264 below (*And
if,* Q4, 5, F) and v. iii. 111 (*And if,*
Qq, F). There is no point in a modern
editor replacing one archaism by
another.

52. *I . . . like*] "I lay on the earth the
task of bearing the like gage" (Clarendon editors).

54. *hollowed*] shouted loudly. The
usual Shakespearian spelling; the more
exact modern equivalent would be
hollered rather than *hallooed* or *holloaed,*
which last is now obsolescent.

55. *From . . . sun*] i.e. from sunrise to
sunset, the prescribed period for a
combat, which ceased at nightfall: cf.
Cymb., III. ii. 67. The same phrase is
used in Harl. MS 941 (15th century?)
printed by Wright, *Reliquae Antiquae,*
I. 319: "And so the xix day is xiiij
owres long and a half, fro son to son"
and by S. Butler, "Repartee between
Cat and Puss" (*Satires and Miscel-
laneous Works,* Cambridge, 1928, p.
138): ". . . Thieves, that rob themselves 'twixt Sun and Sun, / Make
others pay for what themselves have
done", i.e. thieves, who squander

Ingage it to the trial if thou darest.

Aum. Who sets me else? By heaven, I'll throw at all!
I have a thousand spirits in one breast
To answer twenty thousand such as you.

Surrey. My Lord Fitzwater, I do remember well   60
The very time Aumerle and you did talk.

Fitz. 'Tis very true; you were in presence then,
And you can witness with me this is true.

Surrey. As false, by heaven, as heaven itself is true.

Fitz. Surrey, thou liest.

Surrey.   Dishonourable boy,   65
That lie shall lie so heavy on my sword
That it shall render vengeance and revenge
Till thou, the lie-giver, and that lie do lie
In earth as quiet as thy father's skull.
In proof whereof there is my honour's pawn;   70
Ingage it to the trial if thou darest.

Fitz. How fondly dost thou spur a forward horse!
If I dare eat, or drink, or breathe, or live,
I dare meet Surrey in a wilderness,
And spit upon him whilst I say he lies,   75
And lies, and lies. There is my bond of faith

60–1.] *As Qq;* ... Fitz-water / ... time / ... talke / *F.*   62. 'Tis] *Qq;* My
Lord, / 'Tis *F.*   64.] *As Qq;* ... by heauen / ... true *F.*   65–6.] *As F;*
... liest / ... sword / *Qq.*   70. my] *Q1, 4, 5;* mine *Q2, 3, F.*   76. my] *Q3–5,
F;* the *Q2; not in Q1.*

their money between sunrise and sunset, recoup their losses by robbing
others at night. (I owe this reference
to J. C. Maxwell.) Wilson believes
that the phrase is Shakespeare's version of "entre deux soleilz" (which
also means "from sunrise to sunset")
in *Traïson*, p. 15, but he disregards the
evidence that Shakespeare was merely
using an English idiom already current. In the fragmentary translation
of *Traïson* in Harl. MS 6219 the
phrase is (wrongly) rendered "w^tin ij
listes".

56. *Ingage ... trial*] "Make a gage
of it, with a view to a trial by combat." Such a meaning of *engage* is not
recorded elsewhere, but seems the

only one that will fit here; cf. l. 71
below.

57. *Who ... else?*] "Who else puts
up a stake?"

throw] cast. Both these are dicing
metaphors.

62. *in presence*] present.

65. *boy*] An insult; cf. *Cor.*, v. vi.
113.

72. *fondly*] foolishly.

74.] Cf. i. i. 65 and note.

76. *my*] Q3's emendation for a missing word is somewhat less than self-
evidently right, says Pollard (p. 60).
The "bond of faith" is a gage which
Fitzwater throws down and everyone
else in the scene so far has referred to
"my" gage. H. F. Brooks conjectures

To tie thee to my strong correction.
As I intend to thrive in this new world,
Aumerle is guilty of my true appeal.
Besides, I heard the banished Norfolk say   80
That thou, Aumerle, did'st send two of thy men
To execute the noble Duke at Callice.

Aum. Some honest Christian trust me with a gage,
That Norfolk lies—here do I throw down this,
If he may be repeal'd to try his honour.   85

Bol. These differences shall all rest under gage
Till Norfolk be repeal'd—repeal'd he shall be,
And, though mine enemy, restor'd again
To all his lands and signories. When he's return'd,
Against Aumerle we will inforce his trial.   90

Car. That honourable day shall ne'er be seen.
Many a time hath banish'd Norfolk fought

---

82. at] *Q1, F;* of *Q2–5.*   85. repeal'd] *Qq;* repeal'd, *F.*   89. he's] *F;* he is *Qq.*   91. ne'er] *F* (ne're); neuer *Qq.*

this, the compositor's eye having skipped it because of the preceding *is.* Fitzwater has already thrown down one gage (l. 34) and he might well emphasize now: "here's this—yet another gage!"

78. *this . . . world*] i.e. created by Bolingbroke's rebellion (Wilson), cf. the sentiments at v. ii. 50 and v. v. 59.

79. *appeal*] Cf. I. i. 4 and note.

83–4. *gage, . . . lies—*] Qq and F have a comma after *gage* and *lies.* It is not clear from the punctuation whether Aumerle means: ". . . trust me with a gage [pledge wherewith I may prove] that Norfolk is lying! Here do I . . ." or ". . . trust me with a gage! [Pause, while he borrows one.] To prove that Norfolk is lying, here do I . . ." Since Aumerle has so far thrown down only one gage, his need to borrow one here suggests that Shakespeare is no longer thinking of the gages as gloves (see note on l. 25 above) but as hoods.

85. *repeal'd*] recalled from exile; cf. II. ii. 49.

89. *signories*] estates. The line in Q1

may be an alexandrine suffering from expansion of a Shakespearian contraction *he's;* see Introduction, p. xxviii.

92–100.] Holinshed states only that Mowbray died at Venice (495/2/14, 514/1–2); Stow, *Chronicles* (1580), p. 544, adds "in his returne from Jerusalem". Wilson holds that Mowbray's association with the crusades derives from the passage in *Traïson,* p. 22/158, describing Mowbray's sentence after the trial: "That [Mowbray] shall quit the realm for the rest of his life, and shall choose whether he would dwell in Prussia, in Bohemia, or in Hungary, or would go right beyond sea to the land of the Saracens and unbelievers; and that he shall never return to set foot again on Christian land". This is not very close to Shakespeare, and implies in its last sentence a contradiction of Shakespeare and Holinshed, whom Shakespeare follows in respect of the death at Venice. Froissart, vi. 317, associates Bolingbroke with the crusades after *his* exile, where people speculate on his fate abroad: "thoughe he may have

For Jesu Christ in glorious Christian field,
Streaming the ensign of the Christian cross
Against black Pagans, Turks, and Saracens;   95
And, toil'd with works of war, retir'd himself
To Italy; and there at Venice gave
His body to that pleasant country's earth,
And his pure soul unto his captain Christ,
Under whose colours he had fought so long.   100
Bol. Why, Bishop, is Norfolk dead?
Car. As surely as I live, my lord.
Bol. Sweet peace conduct his sweet soul to the bosom
    Of good old Abraham! Lords appellants,
    Your differences shall all rest under gage   105

93. Christ . . . field,] *Q1, 3*; Christ . . . field. *Q2*; Christ, . . . field, *Q4, 5, F*
(field).   98. that] *Q1, F*; a *Q2–5*.   102. surely] *Q1*; sure *Q2–5, F*.   103–
5.] *As Qq*; . . . Soule / . . . Abraham / . . . gage / *F*.

been sore traveyled in his dayes in
farre countreis, as into Pruce, and to
the Holy Sepulchre, to Cayre, and to
saynt Katheryn's mount . . . When
he commeth into Spaygne he maye
move theym to make warre upon
the Sarazyns". Shakespeare may
have transferred Froissart's hint about
Bolingbroke to Mowbray, enlarged
upon Stow's information or upon
Traison's, and combined any one of
these with the death at Venice. It
seems more likely that he invented the
whole reference to the crusades as a
piece of dramatic and historical
colour: for a very similar invention,
which may be the origin of this passage, cf. ii. i. 53–6 and note.

96. *toil'd*] For this usage, cf. *MND.*,
v. i. 74.

98. *pleasant country's*] Wilson suggests an echo of the phrase in Hall's
proem: "who can reherce what mis-
chefes and what plages the pleasant
countree of Italy hath tasted . . .?"
This is possible, but Shakespeare had
earlier used a similar phrase in *Shr.*, I. i.
4. In *Mirror*, p. 108, "Lord Mowbray",
l. 185, it is mentioned that Mowbray
found "more ease and frendlynes" at
Venice than during his sojourn in

"Almayne", to the unpleasantness of
which the three previous stanzas (ll.
164–82) are devoted.

101.] Bolingbroke's apparent surprise at the news of Mowbray's death
is sometimes read as being assumed,
on the theory that Shakespeare wished
to represent Bolingbroke's promise to
repeal Mowbray, which he knew he
could not fulfil, as an act of statesman-
like hypocrisy. There is no warrant in
Holinshed for inferring such a move
on Bolingbroke's part: the mention of
Mowbray's death is quite separate
from Bolingbroke's promise about his
repeal. By running the two together,
Shakespeare may have wished to convey an impression that Bolingbroke
knew that Mowbray had been finally
exiled by death; but he may as easily
have had no wish but to fit in information about the fate of a character
prominent in earlier scenes.

102. *As . . . live*] This is swearing
"like a comfit-maker's wife", according to Hotspur, *1 H 4*, III. i. 248–51.

103–4. *bosom . . . Abraham*] See the
parable of Dives, Luke, xvi. 22, and
for other Shakespearian references to
Abraham's bosom, *R 3*, IV. iii. 38, *H 5*
II. iii. 10 ff.

Till we assign you to your days of trial.

Enter YORK.

York. Great Duke of Lancaster, I come to thee
From plume-pluck'd Richard, who with willing
　　soul
Adopts thee heir, and his high sceptre yields
To the possession of thy royal hand.　　　　　　110
Ascend his throne, descending now from him,
And long live Henry, fourth of that name!
Bol. In God's name, I'll ascend the regal throne.
Car. Marry, God forbid!
Worst in this royal presence may I speak,　　　115
Yet best beseeming me to speak the truth.
Would God that any in this noble presence
Were enough noble to be upright judge
Of noble Richard! then true noblesse would

109. thee] *Q2-5, F; the Q1.*　　112. fourth . . . name!] *Qq* (name.)*; of that
Name the Fourth. F.*　　114. Marry] *F3; Mary Qq, F1, 2.*　　God] *Qq;
Heauen F.*　　115. may I] *Q1, F; I may Q2-5.*　　117. that] *Q1, F; not in Q2-5.*
119. noblesse] *Q1; noblenesse Q2-5, F.*

106. S.D. York] Wilson ascribes the
presence of York to Shakespeare's
following Froissart (VI. 378) and Hall
(p. 12) both of whom say that York
was in London and well received by
Bolingbroke. York provides continuity
with the earlier part of the play, and
his actions here are invented, not
warranted by Froissart or Hall. As
Shakespeare planned the play, some
dramatis persona had to do what York
does here. Similar arguments apply to
the presence and acts of Northumberland (Froissart, but no one else, mentions that Northumberland was in
London). The theory that Shakespeare relied for such things on historical authority and that this proves
he was following a particular source
implies the strange corollary that, in
the absence of such authority, he
would either have been left without
any characters to perform essential
tasks or would have had to keep inventing fresh ones instead of making

use of the old. For a similar point, cf.
note on III. ii. 64.

108. *plume-pluck'd*] i.e. humbled: a
reference to the Aesopian fable of the
crow that dressed itself in stolen
feathers and was shamed when the
other birds plucked them away: see
Yoder, *Animal Analogy in Shakespeare's
Character Portrayal*, pp. 11, 79, and cf.
the analogous fable of the jay in *1 H 6,*
III. iii. 5–7.

112. *Henry*] Probably pronounced
"Henery": cf. *2 H 6*, II. ii. 23 The
formula, both this version and the
transposed form in F, perhaps echoes
Mirror, e.g., "Sonne to kyng Edward
third of that name" (p. 92, and cf. pp.
86, 140, 446)

115–16.] "Though I who speak be
the least worthy person present, yet I
speak as one whom (being an ecclesi-
astic) it best beseems to tell the
truth" (Herford).

119. *noblesse*] nobility; not elsewhere in Shakespeare.

Learn him forbearance from so foul a wrong.   120
What subject can give sentence on his king?
And who sits here that is not Richard's subject?
Thieves are not judg'd but they are by to hear,
Although apparent guilt be seen in them,
And shall the figure of God's majesty,   125
His captain, steward, deputy elect,
Anointed, crowned, planted many years,
Be judg'd by subject and inferior breath,
And he himself not present? O forfend it, God,   †
That in a Christian climate souls refin'd   130
Should show so heinous, black, obscene a deed!   †
I speak to subjects, and a subject speaks,
Stirr'd up by God thus boldly for his king.

---

122. here] *Q1, 5, F*; not here *Q2–4*.   126. deputy] *F*; deputy, *Qq*.   129.
forfend] *Qq*; forbid *F*.   133. God] *Qq*; Heauen *F*.

120. *Learn . . . forbearance*] Teach
him to refrain.

121–9.] In Holinshed, Carlisle's
speech occurs after the abdication and
is directed against the plan that
Richard should be tried for his crimes;
this fact is reflected in these lines,
although the actual wording is closer
to Daniel, *C.W.*, III, st. 22 than to
Holinshed: "Neuer shall this poore
breath of mine consent / That he that
two and twentie yeeres hath raignd /
As lawfull Lord, and king by iust
discent, / Should here be iudg'd vn-
heard, and vnaraigned / By subiects
two [*sic*]: Iudges incompetent / To
iudge their king . . ." The general idea
of the wickedness of subjects attempting to "judge" their king in any way
is reflected in many history plays, and
is found in the Holinshed source
(Appendix, p. 195), and in such pamphlets as Lightfoote's *Complaint of England* (1587), sig. B3ʳ, and G. D.'s *Briefe
Discouerie* (1588), p. 120, against
Roman Catholic attacks on Elizabeth.
It was an essential part of Tudor
political doctrine, expressed at length
in the two official sermons on "Obedience" and against "Rebellion" which
were read in church in Elizabeth's

reign: e.g. *Homilies*, p. 494: "what
perilous thing were it to commit unto
the subjects the judgement, which
prince is wise and godly, and his
government good, and which is otherwise; as though the foot should judge
the head . . .", and cf. *ibid.*, p. 497.
Daniel and Shakespeare may well be
drawing independently on the ideas
and language of the *Homilies*: cf. I. ii.
38-41 and note, on *Woodstock*, Shakespeare and *Homilies*, and cf. below
notes on ll. 137–49. The rhetorical
point about thieves and kings on trial
(ll. 123 ff) is copied from Hol., 512/2/
43.

124. *apparent*] manifest; cf. I. i. 13.

125. *figure*] image.

126. *steward, deputy*] See I. ii. 38 and
note.

130.] Hayward, p. 115, may be
remembering this passage when he
makes the people of Bordeaux exclaim after Richard's deposition:
"Who would euer haue thought that
Christian, that ciuill people, that any
men, would thus have violated all
religion, all lawes, and all honest and
orderly demeanure?" But his main
source for the reaction at Bordeaux
was Froissart, VI. 385.

My Lord of Herford here, whom you call king,
Is a foul traitor to proud Herford's king,   135
And if you crown him, let me prophesy—
The blood of English shall manure the ground,
And future ages groan for this foul act,
Peace shall go sleep with Turks and infidels,
And, in this seat of peace, tumultuous wars   140
Shall kin with kin, and kind with kind, confound.
Disorder, horror, fear, and mutiny,
Shall here inhabit, and this land be call'd
The field of Golgotha and dead men's skulls—
O, if you raise this house against this house,   145
It will the woefullest division prove
That ever fell upon this cursed earth.
Prevent it, resist it, let it not be so,
Lest child, child's children, cry against you woe.
North. Well have you argued, sir, and, for your pains,   150
Of capital treason we arrest you here.
My Lord of Westminster, be it your charge

---

138. this] *Q1;* his *Q2–5, F.*   145. raise] *Qq;* reare *F.*   against this] *Q1, 2,*
F; against his *Q3–5.*   148. Prevent it] *Qq, F;* Prevent *Pope.*   let] *Q1;* and
let *Q2–5, F.*

136. *prophesy*] See note on II. iv. 11.
137–49.] The passage reflects the various warnings against rebellion found in the Tudor homily on the subject; cf. especially: "countrymen to disturb the public peace and quietness of their country ... the brother to seek, and often to work the death of his brother; the son of the father, the father to seek or procure the death of his sons ... and by their faults to disinherit their innocent children and kinsmen their heirs for ever" (*Homilies,* p. 511, and Hart, pp. 52–3, who cfs. *Cæs.,*III.i. 260–76). The theme is already classical in the history plays: see *3 H 6,* II. v. 55 ff and *R 3,* v. v. 23 ff.

141. *with*] by means of.
kind] race, breed.
confound] ruin and destroy. Cf. the line with Daniel, *C.W.,* I, st. 1: "Whil'st Kin their Kin, brother the brother foyles".

144.] Golgotha is described as "place of a skull" in the King James Bible, but as "a place of dead mens skulles" in Bishops', Mark, xv. 22 etc. (Noble).

145. *raise*] F, puzzled by *his house* in the line in Q3, may have consulted the prompt-book about it, and *reare* may be a genuine correction from that source.

145–6. *house ... division*] The houses are those of Lancaster and York *and* of Mark, iii. 25: "And yf a house be diuided agaynst it selfe, that house can not continue" (Noble).

148. *Prevent it*] The irregular metre makes for dramatic effect, but Pope's conjecture may be right, especially if it can be reinforced by possible signs of memorial corruption deriving from this line at v. ii. 55 (see note).

151. *Of*] on a charge of.
152–3.] All sources say that Car-

To keep him safely till his day of trial.
May it please you, lords, to grant the commons' suit?
Bol. Fetch hither Richard, that in common view   155
He may surrender; so we shall proceed
Without suspicion.
York.   I will be his conduct.   [*Exit.*
Bol. Lords, you that here are under our arrest,
Procure your sureties for your days of answer.
Little are we beholding to your love,   160
And little look'd for at your helping hands.

[*Re-enter* YORK, *with* RICHARD, *and* Officers *bearing the regalia.*]

Rich. Alack, why am I sent for to a king
Before I have shook off the regal thoughts
Wherewith I reign'd? I hardly yet have learn'd
To insinuate, flatter, bow, and bend my knee.   165
Give sorrow leave awhile to tutor me
To this submission. Yet I well remember
The favours of these men. Were they not mine?

154–318.] *Not in Q1–3.*   154. commons'] *F*; common *Q4, 5.*   155. *Bol.*
Fetch] *F*; Fetch *Q4, 5.*   155–7.] *As F*; . . . view / . . . suspition / . . . conduct /
Q4, 5.   157. S.D.] *F*; *not in Q4, 5.*   158. here are] *F*; are here, are *Q4, 5.*
161. look'd] *F*; looke *Q4, 5.*   S.D.] *Capell; Enter king Richard. Q4, 5; Enter
Richard and Yorke. F.*   165. knee] *F*; limbes *Q4, 5.*   166–70.] *As F*; . . . sub-
mission / . . . men / . . . hayle / . . . twelue / *Q4, 5.*   166. tutor] *Q4, 5;* tuture *F.*

lisle was consigned to the Abbot of St
Albans, not of Westminster (e.g. Hol.,
512/2/64). Wilson ascribes this to a
misreading by Shakespeare of *Traïson.*
But all the arguments which Wilson
advances would apply equally well to
a misreading from the corresponding
passage in Hol., 514/2/10 ff: "The
abbat of Westminster [mistrusting
Bolingbroke's intentions towards the
church] . . . became an instrument to
search out the minds of the nobilitie.
. . . The abbat after he had felt the
minds of sundrie of them, called to his
house on a day in the terme all such
lords and other persons . . . [here
follows a list of eight names, the sixth
being "John the bishop of Carleill"]."
To anyone who remembered Holin-

shed's statement at 512/2/64 that Carlisle was in St Albans' charge, the
inference that he had been transferred to Westminster's is plausible.
There were also obvious reasons of
dramatic convenience for the naming
of Westminster here, since Westminster and Carlisle are to remain on
the stage to represent, in ll. 321–34,
the passage just quoted from Holinshed.

154. *the . . . suit*] i.e. the proposal of
22 October 1399 that Richard should
have "iudgement decreed against
him"—against which the historical
Carlisle's speech was directed nearly a
month after the abdication.

168. *favours*] A quibble on "faces"
and "benefits"; cf. *Volpone,* II. ii. 16.

Did they not sometime cry "All hail!" to me?
So Judas did to Christ. But he, in twelve,   170
Found truth in all but one; I, in twelve thousand, none.
God save the king! Will no man say amen?
Am I both priest and clerk? well then, amen.
God save the king! although I be not he;
And yet, amen, if heaven do think him me.   175
To do what service am I sent for hither?
York. To do that office of thine own good will
Which tired majesty did make thee offer:
The resignation of thy state and crown
To Henry Bolingbroke.   180
Rich. Give me the crown. Here, cousin, seize the crown.

169. sometime] *F;* sometimes *Q4, 5.*   180. Henry] *F;* Harry *Q4, 5.*   181.]
F; Sease the Crowne. *Q4, 5;* Seize the Crown. Here, cousin, *Malone.*

169–71.] On the view that connects this passage with *Traïson* and
Créton, see Introduction, p. xlviii.
   173. *clerk*] The clerk uttered the
responses to the priest's prayers.
   181.] In Holinshed, Richard's abdication takes the form of the signing
of an instrument in which he releases
his liegemen from their oaths (cf.
l. 210, 214–15), renounces his titles
and possessions and the "name, worship, and regaltie and kinglie highnesse" (504/2/8 ff). Froissart, Hall,
and Daniel all represent a formal act
of abdication (in the Tower) during
which Richard personally hands the
crown to Bolingbroke, and in Hall
and Froissart the sceptre as well. There
are three possible verbal echoes of
Daniel in Shakespeare, two that may
be coincidental (see notes on l. 208,
216–17) and one which is also found
in Holinshed (see note on l. 210) and
no conclusive reminiscences of Hall or
Froissart. It is hard to imagine how an
abdication could be staged without
the formal acts that Richard here performs and difficult to believe that
Shakespeare depended for the idea
and treatment on these sources:
plainly, the mere signing of a docu-

ment is undramatic and uncharac-
teristic of Shakespeare's Richard, and
the dramatist would have had to
amplify, whether or not aware of
other sources, the historian's "bare
Was", just as the poet Daniel, and
Marlowe, did. Because of the echoes,
Daniel has the best claim to a connection with the passage, and the
deposition-scene in *Edward II* has also
left traces.
   181–3.] Q4, 5 read: "Sease the
Crowne. / Heere Coosin, on this side
my hand, and on that side yours".
Malone thought this was correct,
except for "Heere Coosin" having
slipped into the wrong line. In reported texts, however, like Q4, 5, the
repetition and near-repetition of
"Giue me the crowne" and "Heere
Coosin" could easily have dropped
out, while F hints at dramatic business much better. Its second "Here
Cousin" (in l. 183 in F) perhaps reflects the putative manuscript copy as
a mistaken printing of a metrically
detached phrase with the line that
succeeds it (see Introduction, p. xv);
it resulted in an over-long line which
F regularized by omitting the *and,*
which we can restore from Q4, 5.

Here, cousin,
On this side my hand, and on that side thine.
Now is this golden crown like a deep well
That owes two buckets, filling one another,   185 †
The emptier ever dancing in the air,
The other down, unseen, and full of water.
That bucket down and full of tears am I,
Drinking my griefs, whilst you mount up on high.

Bol. I thought you had been willing to resign.   190

Rich. My crown I am, but still my griefs are mine.
You may my glories and my state depose,
But not my griefs; still am I king of those.

Bol. Part of your cares you give me with your crown.

Rich. Your cares set up do not pluck my cares down.   195
My care is loss of care, by old care done;
Your care is gain of care, by new care won.
The cares I give, I have, though given away,
They 'tend the crown, yet still with me they stay.

Bol. Are you contented to resign the crown?   200

Rich. Ay, no; no, ay; for I must nothing be.

182–3.] *As Wright;* Here . . . thine / *Q4, 5, F.*   183. and] *Q4, 5;* not in *F*
thine] *F;* yours *Q4, 5.*   189. griefs] *F;* griefe *Q4, 5.*

184–9.] The figure of buckets and well is adapted from the medieval and Elizabethan figure of Fortune's buckets, as noticed by Patch, *The Goddess Fortuna in Medieval Literature,* 1927, pp. 53–4, and rated as a proverb by Tilley B695. The raising and lowering of well-buckets as a symbol of the "commyng and goyng" of Fortune (or, in Chaucer, Venus—see Patch, p. 90) is used in *Knightes Tale,* ll. 1531–3; and by G. de Machaut, *Remède de Fortune* (ca. 1342), ll. 969–84, *Œuvres,* ed. Hoepffner, II. 35–6, quoted by Wilson, p. 209, and in the story of the Fox and the wolf's wife in Caxton's *History of Reynard the Fox* (1481) and his *Fables of Aesop etc.,* ed. Jacobs, II. 278. (I owe this last reference to J. C. Maxwell.) Tudor examples of the figure are found in J. Heywood, *Three Hundred Epigrams* (1562), no. 110, R. Sempill, *Ane Complaint upon Fortoun*

(1581) and Sir J. Davies, *Epigrammes* (?ca. 1599), no. 29. As Tilley's examples show, the figure remained alive long after Shakespeare, whose use of it here influenced G. Herbert in his "Justice" (II), on which see Herbert's *Works,* ed. Hutchinson, p. 141 and note.

195.] From here to l. 199 Richard manipulates several shades of meaning in *care,* personal grief or worry and the "cares" of high office, responsibility.

196. *by . . . done*] "through having finished with old care".

199. *'tend*] attend upon, accompany; the apostrophe is F's.

200.] Cf. *Edward II,* v. i. 49–50: "My lord, why waste you thus the time away? / They stay your answer; will you yield your crown?"

201.] The sense is clear if it is remembered that *Ay* and *I* are pro-

Therefore no "no", for I resign to thee.
Now, mark me how I will undo myself.
I give this heavy weight from off my head,
And this unwieldy sceptre from my hand,   205
The pride of kingly sway from out my heart;
With mine own tears I wash away my balm,
With mine own hands I give away my crown,
With mine own tongue deny my sacred state,
With mine own breath release all duteous oaths;   210
All pomp and majesty I do forswear;
My manors, rents, revenues, I forgo;
My acts, decrees, and statutes I deny.
God pardon all oaths that are broke to me,
God keep all vows unbroke are made to thee!   215
Make me, that nothing have, with nothing griev'd,
And thou with all pleas'd, that hast all achiev'd.
Long may'st thou live in Richard's seat to sit,
And soon lie Richard in an earthy pit.
God save King Henry, unking'd Richard says,   220
And send him many years of sunshine days!
What more remains?

202. no "no"] *Wilson;* no no *Q4, 5;* no, no *F.*   210. duteous oaths] *F;* duties
rites *Q4, 5.*   215. are made] *F;* that sweare *Q4, 5.*   219. earthy] *Q4, F;* earthly
Q5.   220. Henry] *F;* Harry *Q4, 5.*   221. sunshine] *Q4, F;* sun-shines *Q5*

nounced alike (and were often both
written *I*), thus bringing out the
elaborate quibble; cf. *Rom.,* III. ii. 45–
50.
  208. *With . . . hands*] R. M. Smith
cfs. Daniel, *C.W.,* II, st. 119: "Tis said
with his owne hands he gaue the
crowne / To *Lancaster*". Daniel himself may have owed the phrase to
Froissart, VI. 378: "Than kynge
Rycharde toke the crowne fro his
heed with bothe his handes".
  210, 214–15.] In the "instrument"
signed by Richard and reproduced by
Holinshed, Richard formally annuls
the oaths of fealty and homage made
to him; cf. Daniel, *C.W.,* II, st. 118:
". . . he his subiectes all in generall /
Assoyles and quites of oth and fealty".
  216–17.] Cf. Daniel, *C.W.,* II, st.
119: ". . . he gaue the crowne / To

Lancaster, and wisht to God he might/
Haue better ioy thereof then he had
knowne".
  219. *earthy pit*] The thought was
perhaps suggested both here and
more elaborately at III. iii. 153 ff by
the passage in Hol., 507/2/44 ff
describing Richard's misery, which
quotes lines from T. Watson's *Amintas*
(1585, a Latin paraphrase of Tasso's
Aminta): "O qui me fluctus, quis me
telluris hiatus / Pertæsum tetricæ
vitæ deglutiat ore / Chasmatico?"
  220. *unking'd*] Cf. v. v. 37, the only
other Shakespearian occurrence, and
see note on II. i. 16.
  221. *sunshine*] For the adjectival use
Herford cfs. *3 H 6,* II. i. 187, *Edward
II,* v. i. 26–7; cf. also *Edmond Ironside,*
M.S.R., l. 1355: "A sunne shine Day
is quicly ouercaste".

North.   No more; but that you read
 These accusations, and these grievous crimes
 Committed by your person and your followers
 Against the state and profit of this land;   225
 That, by confessing them, the souls of men
 May deem that you are worthily depos'd.
Rich. Must I do so? and must I ravel out
 My weav'd-up follies? Gentle Northumberland,
 If thy offences were upon record,   230
 Would it not shame thee, in so fair a troop,
 To read a lecture of them? If thou wouldst,
 There shouldst thou find one heinous article,
 Containing the deposing of a king,
 And cracking the strong warrant of an oath, 235
 Mark'd with a blot, damn'd in the book of heaven.

229. follies] *F;* folly *Q4, 5.*

222.] The idea that Richard was to be required to read over in public the articles drawn up against him—which are given in Holinshed (p. 502)—seems to be a Shakespearian invention. Shakespeare may have wanted to give Northumberland some prominent action and to make clear that the articles did exist, but to avoid the dramatically unmanageable business of presenting them with Holinshed's fullness by making Richard evade the task.

226. *by confessing*] by your confessing.

232. *read a lecture*] i.e. "give a public 'reading'".

233. *heinous article*] Caught from Holinshed, who refers to the articles as "33 solemne articles, heinous to the eares of all men" (Reyher). Also in Hall. Richard ironically emphasizes the word *article.*

235. *oath*] The line may be Shakespeare's only reference to an episode which was certainly known to him, but which he otherwise withheld from his audience, viz. Northumberland's perjury at Conway (see III. iii, material). But it also associates with the previous references to subjects' oaths to their prince by Richard himself in this scene (which derive from Holinshed, see notes on ll. 181, 210) and in II. ii. 112, III. ii. 100–1. The notion that a rebel breaks his oath to God and the king is emphasized in the homily against rebellion: "rebels, by breach of their faith given, and oath made, to their prince, be guilty of most damnable perjury" (*Homilies,* p. 508; see Hart, pp. 49–50). It is probably this general idea to which Richard refers here rather than the specific perjury at Conway. There is no need to suppose that Shakespeare was influenced by *Traïson* or Créton: see Introduction, p. xlvii.

236.] A lawful oath is "a part of God's glory", says the Tudor homily "against swearing and perjury" (*Homilies,* p. 64). Noble cites numerous passages on the sanctity of oaths, especially Ezek., xvii. 16. For "blot" and "book of heaven", cf. I. iii. 202 and note. For the political sentiments, cf. *Homilies,* p. 512: "heaven is the place of good obedient subjects, and hell the prison and dungeon of rebels against God and their prince."

Nay, all of you, that stand and look upon me
Whilst that my wretchedness doth bait myself,
Though some of you, with Pilate, wash your hands,
Showing an outward pity—yet you Pilates   240
Have here deliver'd me to my sour cross,
And water cannot wash away your sin.

North. My lord, dispatch, read o'er these articles.

Rich. Mine eyes are full of tears, I cannot see.
And yet salt water blinds them not so much   245
But they can see a sort of traitors here.
Nay, if I turn mine eyes upon myself,
I find myself a traitor with the rest.
For I have given here my soul's consent
T'undeck the pompous body of a king;   250
Made glory base, and sovereignty a slave;
Proud majesty a subject, state a peasant.

North. My lord—

Rich. No lord of thine, thou haught insulting man;
Nor no man's lord. I have no name, no title;   255
No, not that name was given me at the font,

---

237. all] *F; not in Q4, 5.*   me] *F; not in Q4, 5.*   250. T'] *F;* To *Q4, 5.*
251. and] *Q4, 5;* a *F.*   254. haught insulting] *Q4, 5;* hyphened in *F.*   255.
Nor] *Q4, 5;* No, nor *F.*

239–42.] For discussion of the provenance of this, see Introduction, p. xlviii.

246. *sort*] pack, "crew"; cf. *R 3*, v. iii. 316: "a sort of vagabonds".

253–4.] Verity cfs. *Edward II*, v. i. 112–13: "*B. of Win.* My lord— *K. Edw.* Call me not lord; away—out of my sight".

254. *haught*] haughty; cf. *R 3*, II. iii. 28, *Edward II*, III. ii. 28 (Verity).

256–7.] Rossiter (note on *Woodstock*, II. i. 100) thinks that Richard may be saying: "If I am not KING Richard I am Nobody", and the same point is persuasively put by Kittredge: "Richard reasons with the logic of despair and completely 'undoes [i.e. unmakes] himself' (l. 203). The usurper has stripped him of his royalty, which was his by right of birth, and so has destroyed his identity. If not a *king* how

can he be *Richard*? He is a nameless outcast"; cf. also how Richard in Holinshed renounces the "name" of king (see note on l. 181 above), and Edgar in *Lr.*, v. iii. 121–2, who, when asked his name, replies: "Know, my name is lost, / By treason's tooth baregnawn and canker-bit". Others interpret more narrowly as meaning "My baptismal name has been taken away from me." It was W. A. Harrison's explanation of the line, interpreted in this latter way, that started the hunt for French chronicle sources of the play (*New Shakespeare Society Transactions*, 12 Jan. 1883), the line being understood as an allusion to the Lancastrian story that Richard was not the son of the Black Prince, but the bastard of a Bordeaux priest, whence he is given the name "Jehan". The story is mentioned three times in

But 'tis usurp'd. Alack the heavy day,
That I have worn so many winters out,
And know not now what name to call myself!
O that I were a mockery king of snow,   260
Standing before the sun of Bolingbroke,
To melt myself away in water-drops!
Good king, great king, and yet not greatly good,
And if my word be sterling yet in England,
Let it command a mirror hither straight,   265
That it may show me what a face I have
Since it is bankrupt of his majesty.

Bol. Go some of you, and fetch a looking-glass.

          [Exit an Attendant.]

North. Read o'er this paper while the glass doth come.
Rich. Fiend, thou torments me ere I come to hell.   270
Bol. Urge it no more, my Lord Northumberland.
North. The commons will not then be satisfi'd.
Rich. They shall be satisfi'd. I'll read enough
  When I do see the very book indeed
  Where all my sins are writ, and that's myself.   275

Enter one with a glass.

Give me that glass, and therein will I read.

260. mockery] *Q4, 5*; Mockerie, *F.* 264. word] *F*; name *Q4, 5.* 268. S.D.]
Capell; not in Q4, 5, F. 275. S.D.] *F; not in Q4, 5.* 276. that] *F*; the *Q4, 5.*
and . . . read] *F; not in Q4, 5.*

Traïson (64/215, 72/223, 94/248) but
the passages would be very cryptic to
one not already acquainted with the
tale: (i) [The people say] Now we are
well revenged of this wicked bastard
who has governed us so ill. (ii) it is
ordered . . . that John of Bordeaux,
who has been called Richard King of
England be sentenced . . . (iii) He
commanded a knight . . . to go down
and deliver straightway from the
world, John of London, called
Richard. . . Froissart, on the other
hand, has a full account as from
Bolingbroke's own mouth, of the bas-
tardy legend: see Intro., p. xxxvi.

260-3.] Verity cfs. Marlowe, *Faustus*, ed. Greg, B text, ll. 2086-8.

264. *And if*] Cf. l. 49 above and note.
sterling] Metaphor from coinage:
cf. *current* in I. iii. 231 (Herford).
265.] On the significance of the
mirror, see Introduction, p. lxxxii.
267. *his*] its.
268. *some of you*] i.e. "some one of
you"; J. C. Maxwell cfs. *Per.*, v. i. 9-
10: "there is some of worth would
come aboard; / I pray greet him
fairly."
270.] Perhaps another (general)
reminiscence of Faustus's last speech
in *Faustus*; cf. note on l. 260 above.
torments] A usual Shakespearian
form of the second pers. sing. pres.
(Wilson): cf. v. iii. 120, and Abbott
§340.

No deeper wrinkles yet? hath sorrow struck
So many blows upon this face of mine
And made no deeper wounds? O flatt'ring glass,
Like to my followers in prosperity,   280
Thou dost beguile me. Was this face the face
That every day under his household roof
Did keep ten thousand men? Was this the face
That like the sun did make beholders wink?
Is this the face which fac'd so many follies,   285
That was at last out-fac'd by Bolingbroke?
A brittle glory shineth in this face;
As brittle as the glory is the face,
                    [*Dashes the glass against the ground.*]
For there it is, crack'd in an hundred shivers.
Mark, silent king, the moral of this sport—   290
How soon my sorrow hath destroy'd my face.
Bol. The shadow of your sorrow hath destroy'd
    The shadow of your face.

276–80.] As *F*; . . . yet / . . . this / . . . woundes / . . . prosperitie / *Q4, 5.*
277. struck] *F*; stroke *Q4, 5.*   281–5.] As *F*; . . . his / . . . men / . . . follies /
Q4, 5.   281. Thou . . . me] *F*; *not in Q4, 5.*   this . . . face] *F*; this the face
Q4, 5.   283–4. Was . . . wink] *F*; *not in Q4, 5.*   285. Is] *F*; Was *Q4, 5.*
which] *F*; that *Q4, 5.*   286. That] *F*; And *Q4, 5.*   288. S.D.] *Theobald; not
in Q4, 5, F.*   289. an] *F*; a *Q4, 5.*   293–8.] As *F*; . . . face / . . . sorrow /
. . . griefe / . . . manners / . . . vnseene / . . . soule / *Q4, 5.*

283.] Whether or not the passage
from l. 281 echoes the Helen speech in
Faustus (ed. Greg, B text, l. 1874), as
many think, this detail derives from
Holinshed's account of Richard's
"noble housekeeping", 508/1/8: "For
there resorted dailie to his court aboue
ten thousand persons that had meate
and drinke there allowed them."

285. *fac'd*] To *face* is literally to trim
or cover a garment with new cloth: cf.
1 H 4, v. i. 74: "To face the garment
of rebellion / With some fine colour".
Richard covered over many follies by
adorning them with the splendour of
his own state—he "countenanced"
them. For other puns on *face*, cf. *Shr.*
IV. iii. 122 ff.

286. *out-fac'd*] stared down; cf.
LLL., v. ii. 615.

287–9.] For the brittleness of glass
as a symbolic quality in Shakespeare,
cf. *R 3*, IV. ii. 63, and for man as a
"glassy essence", cf. *Meas.*, II. ii. 120
and M. Lascelles in *R.E.S.*, N.S., II
(1951), 140–2.

289. *shivers*] splinters.

292–3.] i.e. "The shadow [= darkness of grief] cast by your sorrow hath
destroyed the shadow [= unreal
image] of your face." Bolingbroke
quibbles on *shadow*, noting that
Richard has destroyed only something unreal, his reflected face in the
glass; a use of *shadow* to mean something unreal is common in Shakespeare: cf. *3 H 6*, IV. iii. 50, "be true
King indeed; thou but the shadow";
Tit., III. ii. 79, *2 H 4*, I. i. 192, *All's W.*,
v. iii. 301–2, *Mac.*, v. vi. 24.

Rich.   Say that again.
The shadow of my sorrow? ha! let's see—
'Tis very true, my grief lies all within,   295
And these external manners of lament
Are merely shadows to the unseen grief
That swells with silence in the tortur'd soul.
There lies the substance. And I thank thee, king,
For thy great bounty, that not only giv'st   300
Me cause to wail, but teachest me the way
How to lament the cause. I'll beg one boon,
And then be gone, and trouble you no more.
Shall I obtain it?

Bol.   Name it, fair cousin.

Rich. Fair cousin! I am greater than a king;   305
For when I was a king, my flatterers
Were then but subjects; being now a subject,
I have a king here to my flatterer.
Being so great, I have no need to beg.

Bol. Yet ask.   310

Rich. And shall I have?

Bol. You shall.

Rich. Then give me leave to go.

Bol. Whither?

Rich. Whither you will, so I were from your sights.   315

296. manners] *Q4, 5;* manner *F.*   lament] *Capell;* laments *Q4, 5, F.*   299. There . . . substance] *F; not in Q4, 5.*   299–300. And . . . king / . . . giv'st /] *As F;* And . . . giuest / *Q4, 5.*   300. For . . . bounty] *F; not in Q4, 5.*   304. Shall . . . it] *F; not in Q4, 5.*   305. cousin!] *F* (Cousin?); Coose, why: *Q4, 5.* 306–9.] *As F;* . . . subiects / . . . heere / . . . beg / *Q4, 5.*   311. have] *F;* haue it *Q4, 5.*   313. Then] *F;* Why then *Q4, 5.*

294–9.] Richard develops the well-loved Shakespearian contrast between *shadow* and *substance* (cf. II. ii. 14 and note), implicit in Bolingbroke's remark, and in l. 297 deliberately alters the meaning which Bolingbroke had given to his first *shadow*: "The shadow [= darkness] cast by my sorrow? Let's see—'tis very true; my sorrow—these external ways of lamenting—are simply shadows [= unreal images] of the grief within . . ." Richard thus uses Bolingbroke's own quibble to prove, not, as Bolingbroke had wished to, that the image in the glass is unreal, but that Richard's lamentation reflects a real substance, just as the image in the glass though itself unreal, as Bolingbroke claims, none the less reflects a real face. A shadow is unreal compared with the substance that it is a shadow of; this fact can be used either, as by Bolingbroke, to insist on the unreality of the shadow, or, as by Richard, to insist on the reality of the substance. For the general sentiment, Malone cfs. *Ham.,* I. ii. 83–6.

315. *sights*] Shakespeare thinks of

Bol. Go some of you, convey him to the Tower.
Rich. O, good! Convey! Conveyers are you all,
   That rise thus nimbly by a true king's fall.
                           [*Exeunt Richard and Guard.*]
Bol. On Wednesday next we solemnly set down
   Our coronation. Lords, prepare yourselves.   250
                 [*Exeunt all except the Bishop of Carlisle,
                    the Abbot of Westminster, and Aumerle.*]
Abbot. A woeful pageant have we here beheld.
Car. The woe's to come; the children yet unborn
   Shall feel this day as sharp to them as thorn.
Aum. You holy clergymen, is there no plot
   To rid the realm of this pernicious blot?   325
Abbot. My lord,
   Before I freely speak my mind herein,

317. good!] *Wright;* good *Q4, 5;* good: *F.*   Convey!] *Alexander;* conuey, *Q4,
5;* conuey: *F.*   318. S.D.] *Ed.; not in Q4, 5, F.*   319–20.] *Q4, 5, F;* Let it be
so, and loe on wednesday next, / We solemnly proclaime our Coronation, /
Lords be ready all. / *Q1–3.*   320. S.D.] *Wright; Exeunt. Manent [Manet Q2–5]
West. Carleil, Aumerle. Qq; Exeunt. F.*   322. woe's] *Qq;* woes *F.*   326.] *Q1, 2*
(*beginning l. 327*); *not in Q3–5, F.*

the individual beholders as possessing one "sight" apiece; cf. *Lr.*, IV. vi. 35.

317. *Convey! Conveyers*] Euphemisms for "steal" and "thieves", still current in the 19th century. Cf. *Edward II*, I. i. 200–1: "Convey this priest to the Tower. *Bp. of Coventry.* True, true,"; cf. *Wiv.*, I. iii. 27, and note to v. i. 51–2.

319–20.] The two lines proclaiming the usurper's final triumph of coronation are the natural conclusion of the deposition scene, and would be found in any MS of it. When the scene was cut out of the copy for Q1, someone added the words *Let it be so and loe* to form the link with l. 154 above, and made two other minor alterations. The fact that Q4, 5, and F restore the original lines need not mean that F is dependent on these Quartos; Quartos and F may have derived the lines independently from whatever were their respective sources for the scene (see Hasker, *Studies in Bibliography*, v (1952–3), 61). For the

information, cf. Hol., 507/2/2 ff: "A proclamation was made, that the states should assemble againe in parlement on mondaie then next insuing [6 Oct.] . . . and that the monday then next following [13 Oct.] . . . the feast day of saint Edward the king and confessor, the coronation should be solemnized". Créton, p. 205/395, gives "St Edward's day, the eighth of October" and on the next page refers to this as *mercredi*, a curious coincidence with Shakespeare's "Wednesday". Créton was mistaken, for Bolingbroke was crowned on 13 October, a Monday, and Edward the Confessor's Day. I do not think that Shakespeare's "Wednesday" has anything to do with Créton's error; he may have looked hastily for a day, and picked up "Wednesday" by accident from Hol., 512/2/29, where the phrase "on Wednesdaie following" (actually 22 Oct.) opens the paragraph describing Carlisle's speech and arrest.

You shall not only take the sacrament
To bury mine intents, but also to effect
Whatever I shall happen to devise.   330
I see your brows are full of discontent,
Your hearts of sorrow, and your eyes of tears.
Come home with me to supper; I will lay
A plot shall show us all a merry day.   [*Exeunt.*

329. intents] *Q1–4, F;* intent *Q5.*   332. hearts] *Q1;* heart *Q2–5, F.*   333–
4. I will lay / A plot] *Malone;* Ile lay a plot, / *Qq, F.*

328. *take . . . sacrament*] R. M. Smith
cfs. Daniel, *C.W.*, III, st. 34: "The Sacrament the pledge of faith they take".
Hol., 514/3/65 says "they sware on the
holie euangelists". The phrase here =
"swear on the sacrament to . . ."

Cf. Webster, *White Devil*, IV. iii. 75–6:
"You have tane the sacrament to pro-
secute / Th' intended murder?"; Heywood, *If You Know not Me*, II (Sh. Soc.
edn, p. 143): "I have ta'en the Sacrament to do it . . ."

ACT V

SCENE I.—[*London. A street leading to the Tower.*]

Enter the QUEEN *with her* Attendants.

Queen. This way the king will come; this is the way
To Julius Caesar's ill-erected tower,

ACT V
Scene I

Location.] Capell; *not in Qq, F.*   S.D.] *Qq; Enter Queene, and Ladies. F.*

MATERIAL. Only Daniel, *C.W.*, II, st. 66–98, supplies a last meeting between Richard and Isabel after Richard's fall. Daniel's treatment is different: his scene begins, like Shakespeare's, in a London street, but the greater part of the thirty-two stanzas is taken up by an extended soliloquy from Isabel. She first mistakes the applauded Bolingbroke for Richard as she looks from a window, faints when she recognizes the "pensiue" Richard in his "base araie", recovers, avows her continuing love for him ("I loue thee for thy selfe not for thy state"). She next proceeds by a concealed way to the "chamber where he was alone"; Richard puts on a cheerful air, and after his brief welcome of her they both become speechless with sorrow. A final stanza declares that Richard attempts to comfort her, but his actual words are not given. Shakespeare's treatment is dramatic, not, like Daniel's, modelled on Lucan and the *Heroides.* This accounts for some divergences, while his conception of Richard's character may explain why it is Isabel rather than Richard who acts as comforter. There are good verbal parallels (see especially notes on ll. 7 and 40–50) and there seems a

strong possibility that Daniel influenced the scene—see Introduction, p. xliii. The entry of Northumberland and all that follows from it are invented by Shakespeare, except for ll. 51–2, which derive from Holinshed.

2. *Julius . . . tower*] Among the writers who mention the legend that the Tower was built by Julius Caesar are Lydgate, Polydore Vergil, William Lambarde (1576), Stow, Grafton, and G. Peele in *Edward I.* There is no need to believe that Shakespeare relied on a particular written source for the belief, despite his making Buckingham in *R 3*, III. i. 74, refer to it as being a fact "upon record". It is on the assumption that Shakespeare had a written source that G. L. Frost (*M.L.N.*, LI [1936], 431–3) and H. Nearing (*ibid.*, LXIII [1948], 228–33) document pre-Shakespearian mentions of the belief, without, however, claiming any specific one as Shakespeare's source; Shakespeare lived in London, and in any city there are oral traditions about the famous buildings.

2. *ill-erected*] built for ill ends or with evil results. Black's suggestion that Isabel is thinking specifically about the defeat of Cassivellaunus by Julius

145

To whose flint bosom my condemned lord
Is doom'd a prisoner by proud Bolingbroke.
Here let us rest, if this rebellious earth   5
Have any resting for her true king's queen.

Enter RICHARD *and* Guard.

But soft, but see, or rather do not see,
My fair rose wither—yet look up, behold,
That you in pity may dissolve to dew,
And wash him fresh again with true-love tears.   10
Ah, thou, the model where old Troy did stand!   †
Thou map of honour, thou King Richard's tomb,
And not King Richard! Thou most beauteous inn,
Why should hard-favour'd grief be lodg'd in thee,
When triumph is become an alehouse guest?   15

6. S.D.] *F; Enter Richard. Qq.*   10. true-love] *F; unhyphened Qq.*

Caesar (*English Institute Essays, 1947*, pp. 129–30) is unconvincing; to her, the Tower is ill-erected because it was destined to become Richard's prison.

3. *flint*] flinty; cf. v. v. 20.

7. *but . . . see*] Cf. Daniel, *C.W.*, II, st. 83, where Isabel is described as "Wishing to see, what seene she grieud to see" (Reyher).

8. *rose*] Cf. *1 H 4*, I. iii. 175, where Hotspur refers to Richard as "that sweet lovely rose".

9. *you*] i.e. Isabel herself.

10.] Isabel now turns to address Richard.

11. *model*] For the spelling, see note on III. ii. 153; usually taken to mean here "ground plan": "Troy symbolizes ruined greatness, which only the outline of its walls is left to tell of. The choice of this particular symbol is due to the recent mention of the Tower; tradition said that London was first built by Trojan refugees, who called it Troynovant" (Newbolt). For the reader, *model* gains force through its previous associations with earth and death (cf. III. ii. 153) and with *module* ="model") as used in *John*, v. vii.

58: "all this thou see'st is but a clod / And module of confounded royalty." But it is doubtful whether Shakespeare had these in mind. For the comparison of man to a ruined city, Hankin (*Shakespeare's Derived Imagery*, p. 217) cites Prov., XXV. 27: "He that can not rule him selfe, is lyke a citie which is broken downe and hath no walles."

12. *map*] = "image". *Map* is used figuratively for "image", "embodiment" with emphasis on the *resemblances* between a map and that which it represents, in *Tit.*, III. ii. 12 ("map of woe"), *2 H 6*, III. i. 203 ("map of honour"), the anonymous *Locrine*, M.S.R., l. 2141 ("map of magnanimitie"), the anonymous *Selimus*, M.S.R., l. 178 ("map of many valures"). Here the stress seems to be on the way a map *differs* from the thing it represents.

13. *And . . . Richard*] Cf. Daniel, *C.W.*, II, st. 82: "Let me not see him, but himselfe, a king; / . . . This is not he" (Reyher).

13–15.] Richard is the "beauteous inn" where grief is lodged, Bolingbroke is the common "alehouse" where triumph is entertained.

Rich. Join not with grief, fair woman, do not so,
  To make my end too sudden. Learn, good soul,
  To think our former state a happy dream;
  From which awak'd, the truth of what we are
  Shows us but this. I am sworn brother, sweet,   20
  To grim Necessity, and he and I
  Will keep a league till death. Hie thee to France
  And cloister thee in some religious house.
  Our holy lives must win a new world's crown
  Which our profane hours here have thrown down.   25
Queen. What, is my Richard both in shape and mind
  Transform'd and weak'ned? hath Bolingbroke depos'd
  Thine intellect? hath he been in thy heart?
  The lion dying thrusteth forth his paw
  And wounds the earth, if nothing else, with rage   30 †

20. this.] *F;* this: *Qq.*   25. thrown] *Qq;* stricken *F;* throwen *Wilson.*
27–8.] *As Wright;* . . . Bullingbrooke / Deposde . . . *Qq, F.*

20. *this.*] The colon after *this* in Q1 might indicate either an emphatic pause or an introduction to reported speech. In the latter case, *this* must refer to Richard's next remark, as most editors apparently assume; in the former, *this* is Richard's and Isabel's wretched condition in general, indicated perhaps by a gesture at his "base araie". I think an emphatic pause altogether more likely and punctuate accordingly, as F.

  sworn brother] An allusion to the chivalric custom whereby knights swore to share one another's trials and rewards (John, following Whalley); cf. *H 5*, II. i. 10.

23. *religious house*] convent.

24–5. *a new* . . . *down*] "Our holy lives must win us a 'crown of righteousness' [see 2 Tim., iv. 8 and Noble]. since our profane hours here have thrown down the earthly crown." The thought and language is a near-repetition of III. iv. 65–6, but the metre here is disturbed, since *throwne* (Q1–4) must be scanned as a disyllable. Wilson reads *throwen*; but does this common Shakespearian spelling indicate any real difference in pronunciation from the *throwne* of Q1–4? To scan Q1's *throwen* at v. ii. 30 as a disyllable would disturb the metre there (see also notes on *throwen* and *right-drawen* at I. iii. 118, and I. i. 46). It is possible, as H. F. Brooks suggests, that there is memorial corruption, owing to a scribe's memory being confused from the near-repetition at III. iv. 65–6, and even that F's *stricken* is not an attempt to restore the metre by guess but a genuine correction from the prompt-book, the consultation of which was motivated by the disturbed metre.

29. *lion*] The comparison of a monarch to a lion is very common, but this one may have been suggested by *Edward II*, v. i. 11–14: "But, when the imperial lion's flesh is gor'd / He rends and tears it with his wrathful paw, / And highly scorning that the lowly earth / Should drink his blood, mounts up into the air." Cf. *ibid.*, II. ii. 202. Richard is compared to an escaped lion by reason of his unbridled passions in one of Daniel's epic similes. *C. W.*, I, st. 58.

To be o'erpow'r'd, and wilt thou, pupil-like,
Take the correction mildly, kiss the rod,
And fawn on rage with base humility,
Which art a lion and the king of beasts?

Rich. A king of beasts, indeed—if aught but beasts,   35
I had been still a happy king of men.
Good sometimes queen, prepare thee hence for France.
Think I am dead, and that even here thou takest,
As from my death-bed, thy last living leave.
In winter's tedious nights sit by the fire   40
With good old folks, and let them tell thee tales
Of woeful ages long ago betid;
And ere thou bid good night, to quite their griefs
Tell thou the lamentable tale of me,
And send the hearers weeping to their beds;   45

32. the correction] *Q1;* thy correction *Q2–5, F.*   correction mildly,] *F;* correction, mildly *Qq.*   34. the king] *Q1;* a king *Q2–5, F.*   35. but beasts] *Q1, 2, F;* but beast *Q3–5.*   37. sometimes] *Q1, 2;* sometime *Q3–5, F.* 39. thy] *Q1;* my *Q2–5, F.*   41. thee] *Q2–5, F;* the *Q1.*   42. betid] *Q1* (betidde)*; betide *Q2–5, F.*   43. quite] *Qq;* quit *F.*   griefs] *Q1;* griefe *Q2–5, F.*   44. tale] *Qq;* fall *F.*

31. *To be*] = at being.
32. *correction mildly,*] Most editors follow F's punctuation, but Pollard points out that "the transference of the comma from before to after *mildly* . . . needlessly augments the idea fully conveyed in *pupill-like*"; but the phrase *kiss the rod*, proverbially conveying the idea of submission to punishment, hardly needs the augmentation *mildly* either. It is true that the phrase may not have been so well-known in Shakespeare's time, but the first use of it recorded by *O.E.D.* and by Tilley (R156), from Sidney's *Arcadia* (1593 etc.), is long antedated by this from Tyndale's *Obedience of a Christian Man* (1528): "If [the child] knowledge his fault, and take the correction meekly, and even kiss the rod . . . then is the rod . . . burnt" (*Doctrinal Treatises*, Parker Soc. edn, 1848, p. 196). Noting the position of Tyndale's *meekly*, I follow F's punctuation.

37. *sometimes*] Cf. i. ii. 54, v. v. 75 and notes.
40–50.] Cf. iii. ii. 156 ff. But the parallel in Daniel, *C.W.*, iii, st. 65, from Richard's soliloquy in Pomfret prison on the difference between himself and the peasant is much closer: "Thou sit'st at home safe by thy quiet fire, / And hear'st of others harmes, but feelest none; / And there thou telst of kinges and who aspire, / Who fall, who rise, who triumphs, who doe mone: / Perhappes thou talkst of mee, and dost inquire / Of my restraint, why here I liue alone, / O know tis others sin not my desart, / And I could wish I were but as thou art."
42. *betid*] happened.
43. *to . . . griefs*] i.e. "to requite (or cap) their tragic tales" (Herford).
44. *tale*] Conceivably a memorial or printing slip induced by the mention of *tales* in l. 41 above. F's reading may be right, if it is derived from the prompt-book.

For why, the senseless brands will sympathize
The heavy accent of thy moving tongue,
And in compassion weep the fire out,
And some will mourn in ashes, some coal-black,
For the deposing of a rightful king.   50

Enter NORTHUMBERLAND.

North. My lord, the mind of Bolingbroke is chang'd;
You must to Pomfret, not unto the Tower.
And, madam, there is order ta'en for you:
With all swift speed you must away to France.
Rich. Northumberland, thou ladder wherewithal   55
The mounting Bolingbroke ascends my throne,
The time shall not be many hours of age
More than it is, ere foul sin gathering head
Shall break into corruption: thou shalt think,

46. why,] *Qq*; why? *F.*   sympathize] *Q1* (simpathize), *F*; simpathie *Q2*;
simpathy *Q3–5.*

46. *For why*] because ("of the tale's
sadness", understood).
   sympathize] agree in emotion with.
   48. *fire*] A disyllable. Wilson cfs. the
lines to Arthur's remark that the
"fire is dead with grief", *John*, IV. i.
106; cf. also Ferdinand's logs "weeping" with resinous drops, *Tp.*, III. i.
19. The notion may have a classical
origin in the ominous failure of the
sacrificial fires. Hankins (*Shakespeare's
Derived Imagery*) cfs. Seneca, *Thyestes*,
trans. J. Heywood, 1560, where the
fire refuses to heat the Thyestean
banquet (v. iii. 41 in *Thyestes*, ed.
McIlwraith, *Five Elizabethan Tragedies*,
1938, p. 57).
   51–2.] Hol., 507/2/64: "For shortlie
after his resignation, he was conveied
to the castell of Leeds in Kent, & frō
thence to Pomfret [= Pontefract,
Yorks.]".
   53. *there . . . ta'en*] arrangements
have been made.
   54.] Isabel was not sent back to
France immediately after the deposition, as this passage suggests, but was
kept by the English as long as they

could because they did not want to
carry out the agreement for the refund
of her dowry. The forced and hasty
parting here has obvious dramatic
point; Froissart, VI. 370, says that one
of the first things Bolingbroke did was
to send home Isabel's French attendants, and this may have suggested
the idea to Shakespeare.
   55–6. *thou . . . throne*] Edricus
describes himself as the ladder upon
which Canute climbed to the throne
in *Edmond Ironside*, M.S.R., ll. 76–7,
and cf. Daniel, *C.W.*, I, st. 74: "Who
will throw downe himselfe for other
men / That make a ladder by his fall
to clime?" Wilson cfs. *Cæs.*, II. i. 21–7
(see note at ll. 59–68).
   55–9.] At *2 H 4*, III. i. 70–7, Henry,
meditating on the changes in the
relations with Northumberland,
quotes these lines in somewhat compressed form.
   59–68.] Reyher cfs. Daniel, *C.W.*,
II, st. 2–3, where the poet reproaches
Northumberland for his treachery
and predicts a similar relation between usurper and king-maker whose

Though he divide the realm and give thee half,   60
It is too little, helping him to all;
He shall think that thou, which knowest the way
To plant unrightful kings, wilt know again,
Being ne'er so little urg'd, another way
To pluck him headlong from the usurped throne.   65
The love of wicked men converts to fear,
That fear to hate, and hate turns one or both
To worthy danger and deserved death.

North. My guilt be on my head, and there an end.
    Take leave and part, for you must part forthwith.   70 †

Rich. Doubly divorc'd! Bad men, you violate
A two-fold marriage—'twixt my crown and me,
And then betwixt me and my married wife.
Let me unkiss the oath 'twixt thee and me;
And yet not so, for with a kiss 'twas made.   75
Part us, Northumberland: I towards the north,
Where shivering cold and sickness pines the clime;
My wife to France, from whence set forth in pomp,
She came adorned hither like sweet May,
Sent back like Hollowmas or short'st of day.   80

---

62. He] *Qq, F;* And he *Rowe.*   knowest] *Q1;* knowst *Q2–5, F.*   63. wilt]
Q1–3, F; will *Q4, 5.*   66. men] *Qq;* friends *F.*   71. divorc'd! Bad] *F*
[diuorc'd? (bad); diuorst (bad *Qq* [diuorst, *Q2–5*]).   you] *Qq;* ye *F.*
72, 74. 'twixt] *Q1, F;* betwixt *Q2–5.*   78. wife] *Qq;* Queene *F.*

great services embarrass his master;
cf. *Cæs.,* II. i. 21–7.

61. *helping him*] = "since you helped
him".

62.] The line must be treated as a
whole. There does not seem much
point in accepting, for the sake of
improving the flow and rhythm,
Rowe's *And* (which Pollard, however,
considered "necessary"), and yet rejecting Q2–5 and F's *knowst,* because
that rejection still leaves the line
irregular, though in a different way.
I have rejected Rowe and Q2–5, F
altogether: *He shall think* is balanced
against *thou shalt think* at l. 59.

66. *converts*] changes; cf. v. iii. 62.

67. *one or both*] i.e. the king or the
king-maker or both.

68. *worthy*] well-deserved.

74. *unkiss the oath*] i.e. "unmake the
oath with a kiss"; for *unkiss,* see note
on II. i. 16.

75. *a kiss*] i.e. the kiss which was
part of the marriage-ceremony. *And
yet not so* might mean "Don't let us
kiss, since, after all, it's by a kiss that a
marriage is made, not unmade" or
"Even if we kiss, we can't unmake the
marriage—as I have suggested we
might—because it was by just such a
kiss that the marriage was made in the
first place."

77. *pines the clime*] afflicts the land.

78. *pomp*] The pomp attending upon
Isabel's wedding is described by Hol.,
487/1/5 ff.

80. *Hollowmas*] Hallowmas, 1 Nov-

Queen. And must we be divided? must we part?
Rich. Ay, hand from hand, my love, and heart from heart.
Queen. Banish us both, and send the king with me.
North. That were some love, but little policy.
Queen. Then whither he goes, thither let me go.   85
Rich. So two, together weeping, make one woe.
        Weep thou for me in France, I for thee here;
        Better far off than, near, be ne'er the near.
        Go count thy way with sighs; I mine with groans.
Queen. So longest way shall have the longest moans.   90
Rich. Twice for one step I'll groan, the way being short,
        And piece the way out with a heavy heart.
        Come, come, in wooing sorrow let's be brief,
        Since, wedding it, there is such length in grief:
        One kiss shall stop our mouths, and dumbly part;   95
        Thus give I mine, and thus take I thy heart.
Queen. Give me mine own again; 'twere no good part
        To take on me to keep and kill thy heart.
        So, now I have mine own again, be gone,
        That I may strive to kill it with a groan.   100

84. *North.*] *F; King Qq.*   87. thou] *Q1, F; not in Q2–5.*   88. off than, near,]
Ed.; off, then neare, F; unpunctuated Qq.   95. dumbly] *Q1, F; doubly Q2–5.*
97. mine] *Q1–4, F; my Q5.*

ember, corresponding in Shakespeare's time to our 12 November and
so nearer the "short'st of day"
(22 December) then than now. Isabel
comes adorned "like sweet May"; she
is sent back *unadorned* (understood)
like dreary November.

84. *little policy*] bad politics.

85.] Cf. Ruth, i. 16: "Entreate me
not to leaue thee, and to returne from
thee: for whyther thou goest, I will go
also".

88.] "It is better that we should be
far from each other than, being near
in place, be no nearer meeting or
happiness." Johnson: "To be *never the
nigher*, or, as it is commonly spoken in
the midland counties, *ne'er the ne'er*,
[*sic*] is, to make no advance towards
the good desired": cf. the proverb
"Early up and never the nearer",

included in Tilley E27.

92. *piece . . . out*] "lengthen", with
perhaps a quibble on "pace".

95. *dumbly part*] Cf. *Edward II*, i. iv.
134: "Therefore, with dumb em-
bracement, let us part".

96–100.] A conceit such as is often
found in Elizabethan sonnets is here
developed. Richard introduces the
well-worn idea of the lovers exchang-
ing hearts in a kiss; after the kiss (at
l. 96), Isabel insists on having her own
heart back, because she does not want
to keep her lord's heart and kill it
with the grief that she will suffer for
his absence; so they kiss again (at
l. 98), and Isabel bids Richard be
gone so that the pain of his departure
may quickly kill the heart, her own,
of which she has re-possessed herself
in the second kiss.

Rich. We make woe wanton with this fond delay.
   Once more, adieu; the rest let sorrow say.   [*Exeunt.*

SCENE II.—[*The Duke of York's house.*]

Enter DUKE *of* YORK *and the* DUCHESS.

Duch. My lord, you told me you would tell the rest,
   When weeping made you break the story off,
   Of our two cousins' coming into London.
York. Where did I leave?

Scene 11

Location] Ed.; not in Qq, F.   S.D.] Qq; Enter Yorke, and his Duchesse. F.
2. off] F; of Q1; not in Q2–5.

101. *wanton*] unrestrained.
fond] tender-foolish.

Scene 11

MATERIAL. Ll. 1–40 show a general
indebtedness to Daniel, *C.W.*, 11, st.
66–70, as R. M. Smith noted. Daniel
describes a processional entry with
Isabel looking from the window, and
pictures the king as treated with contempt by the crowd rather than with
the murderous hatred described by
the chroniclers. Shakespeare's invention, though, could have also worked
upon Hol., 501/2/43–502/1/3: Holinshed describes the great crowds that
welcomed Bolingbroke, and their
cries of joy, and follows this with an
account of the "manie euill disposed
persons" who on the next day designed to seize and kill Richard until prevented by the graver citizens. The
juxtaposition of these two very different receptions might have suggested the sharp contrasts of this passage,
whereas in Froissart, which Wilson
strongly urges as a source for this
scene, there is no such juxtaposition.
(Indeed, *Traïson* and Créton are
nearer to Shakespeare and Holinshed
than Froissart in that they describe
two contrasting entries occurring on
two consecutive days, Créton reversing

the order of the entries.) Further,
Froissart specifically states that Richard was *not* forced to ride publicly
through London. Suggested parallels
between Froissart and Shakespeare
(see ll. 16, 18–20 and notes) and
Créton and *Traïson* and Shakespeare
(see ll. 32, 34–6 and notes) seem very
strained.

The rest of the scene derives from
Hol., 515/1/18. Reyher's view that the
scene is based on Hall, pp. 17–18,
rather than on Holinshed's less vivid
account, has been adopted by Zeeveld
and Wilson independently. The parallels are not wholly convincing (see ll.
44, 61–2, 112 and notes) and the logic
of the argument unclear, since the
particular features in which Hall
really is more vivid than Holinshed
(e.g. York's remark to Aumerle: "by
the holy rode I had leauer see the
strangeled on the gibbet") are not reflected in Shakespeare's text. Wilson's
elaborate proof (p. 220) that Shakespeare must be using Hall rather than
Traïson because it is only Hall who
mentions that the sealed bond was
sticking out of Aumerle's bosom (cf.
l. 56) ignores the fact that this detail is
found in Hol., 515/1/21. The part
played by the Duchess of York is
entirely Shakespearian invention.

Duch.   At that sad stop, my lord,
   Where rude misgoverned hands from windows' tops   5
   Threw dust and rubbish on King Richard's head.
York. Then, as I said, the Duke, great Bolingbroke,
   Mounted upon a hot and fiery steed
   Which his aspiring rider seem'd to know,
   With slow but stately pace kept on his course,   10
   Whilst all tongues cried "God save thee, Bolingbroke!"
   You would have thought the very windows spake,
   So many greedy looks of young and old
   Through casements darted their desiring eyes
   Upon his visage; and that all the walls   15
   With painted imagery had said at once
   "Jesu preserve thee! Welcome, Bolingbroke!"
   Whilst he, from one side to the other turning,

11. Whilst] *Q1;* While *Q2–5, F.*   thee] *F;* the *Qq.*

6.] A detail referred to by the Archbishop when he recalls this episode in *2 H 4*, I. iii. 101–5.

8.] The steed is "roan Barbary", Richard's own horse (cf. v. v. 76–92). Wilson holds that York's failure to make specific mention here of this fact suggests that Shakespeare had not yet come to the place in "the old play he was revising" where the roan Barbary story is given. Quite apart from the validity or otherwise of the "old play" hypothesis, Shakespeare is here emphasizing Bolingbroke's grandeur, not Richard's pathos, and to mention that the splendid horse was stolen would surely have detracted from that grandeur. The horse may derive from Daniel's "white courser" (see the quotation in note to l. 18 below): for its further significance, see note on v. v. 77–90.

9. *know*] Subject of the verb is the horse; it instinctively "sympathized" (cf. note to v. i. 46) with its rider.

13. *young and old*] Cf. III. ii. 119 and note.

15–16.] "You would have thought from the crowds of faces in the windows that the walls were hung with painted cloths which cried all together . . ." Then follow the actual words spoken by the crowds. *Painted imagery* refers to "the painted cloths that were hung in the streets, in the pageants that were exhibited in [Shakespeare's] own time: in which the figures sometimes had labels issuing from their mouths, containing sentences of gratulation" (Malone). Wilson connects the image with the mention in Froissart (VI. 380) of how, during another episode (Bolingbroke's coronation procession), the streets were "hanged as he passed by".

18–20.] The description of Bolingbroke's behaviour here is linked with I. iv. 24–36. The detail about his bowing may derive from Daniel, where Isabel describes Bolingbroke under the impression that he is Richard, *C.W.*, II, st. 74: ". . . yonder that is hee, / Mounted on that white courser all in white, / There where the thronging troupes of people bee, / I know him by his seate, he sits s'vpright: / Lo, now he bows: deare Lord with what sweet grace". Daniel himself may be drawing on Froissart's description (VI. 361) of Bolingbroke's reception by

Bare-headed, lower than his proud steed's neck,
Bespake them thus, "I thank you, countrymen".   20
And thus still doing, thus he pass'd along.
Duch. Alack, poor Richard! where rode he the whilst?
York. As in a theatre the eyes of men,
After a well-grac'd actor leaves the stage,
Are idly bent on him that enters next,   25
Thinking his prattle to be tedious;
Even so, or with much more contempt, men's eyes
Did scowl on Richard. No man cried "God save him!"
No joyful tongue gave him his welcome home,
But dust was thrown upon his sacred head;   30
Which with such gentle sorrow he shook off,
His face still combating with tears and smiles,
The badges of his grief and patience,
That had not God for some strong purpose steel'd

---

22. Alack] *Qq*; Alas *F*.   rode] *Q1*; rides *Q2–5, F*.   28. Richard] *F*; gentle
Richard *Qq*.

---

the Londoners on his first arrival in
their city (an earlier incident than
that being described here) where
occurs the phrase: ". . . and alwayes
as he rode he enclyned his heed to the
people on every syde." One would
feel more confidence in Wilson's claim
for a direct debt to Froissart on Shakespeare's part if the detail were less
easy to invent: Montaigne (II. xvii)
discusses royal bowing, and Hayward
(p. 77) may or may not be imitating
Shakespeare here and at I. iv. 24 ff
when he writes of Bolingbroke on his
first landing in England as "not negli-
gent to uncouer the head, to bowe the
body, to stretch forth the hand to
euery meane person, and to use all
other complements of popular be-
hauiour".

27. *Even*] Needs to be pronounced
e'en; perhaps another expansion of
what was originally a Shakespearian
contraction; cf. I. iii. 208.

28. *Richard*] The extra-metrical
gentle in the Qq seems to have intruded from l. 31; it may be either a compositor's error, or a memorial anti-

cipation by a scribe who knew the
play: cf. II. i. 254 and note, and
Introduction, p. xix.

31. *gentle*] noble and magnani-
mous: a word with a much stronger
and wider connotation then than now.

32.] Cf. III. ii. 9. Weeping and
smiling together are so common in
Shakespeare (Malone cites parallels in
five plays) that it seems unlikely that
there is any connection with Créton,
p. 237/421, where Isabel's return to
France causes "many a tear and
smile", or with *Traïson*, p. 63/214,
where Richard's face as he arrives at
the Tower is "so covered with tears
that they scarcely knew him". For the
medieval French taste for this item of
description, see J. Huizinga, *The Wan-
ing of the Middle Ages*, 1924, pp. 283–4.

33. *badges*] outward insignia.

34–6.] The same sentiment, that
Richard's lot is so pitiful that the
hard-hearted would have sympathized with him and his followers, is twice
found in Créton (pp. 116/340, 157/
370). A commonplace almost bound
to be used in such a passage as this.

The hearts of men, they must perforce have melted,   35
And barbarism itself have pitied him.
But heaven hath a hand in these events,
To whose high will we bound our calm contents.
To Bolingbroke are we sworn subjects now,
Whose state and honour I for aye allow.   40

Enter AUMERLE.

Duch. Here comes my son Aumerle.
York.   Aumerle that was,
But that is lost for being Richard's friend,
And, madam, you must call him Rutland now.
I am in parliament pledge for his truth
And lasting fealty to the new-made king.   45
Duch. Welcome, my son. Who are the violets now
That strew the green lap of the new-come spring?
Aum. Madam, I know not, nor I greatly care not;
God knows I had as lief be none as one.
York. Well, bear you well in this new spring of time,   50
Lest you be cropp'd before you come to prime.
What news from Oxford? Do these justs and triumphs
hold?
Aum. For aught I know, my lord, they do.
York. You will be there, I know.

39. subjects] *Q1–3, F;* subiect *Q4, 5.*   40. S.D.] *F; after l. 41 in Q4, 5; not in*
Q1–3.   46. are] *Q1–3, F;* art *Q4, 5.*   50. new spring] *Qq; hyphened in F.*
52. Do . . . hold] *Qq;* Hold those Iusts & Triumphs *F.*

38.] "To whose high will we limit ourselves, in peaceful happiness". *Calm contents* is the object of *bound*, and is used proleptically.

43. *Rutland*] Aumerle's loss of the ducal title of Aumerle because of his being appellant "in the last parlement against the duke of Gloucester" (see IV. i. 7 ff) is recorded by Hol., 513/2/1.

44.] The most convincing parallel with Hall is the use of the single word *pledge* here. Holinshed has (515/1/27): ". . . spitefullie reprouing his sonne of treason, for whom he was become suertie and mainpernour for his good

abearing in open parliament", while Hall (pp. 17–18) has: ". . . thou knowst wel inough that I am thy pledge borowe and mayneperner, body for body, and land for goodes in open parliament". But if Shakespeare had wished to gloss or translate Holinshed's *mainpernour* he might naturally have chosen *pledge* just as Hall himself glosses his own *mayneperner*.

46–7. *Who . . . spring*] i.e. "Who are the new favourites in the new court?"

52. *triumphs*] i.e. the Renaissance processional shows, named after the Roman triumphs, which they only generally resembled: cf. note on III. iv. 99.

Aum. If God prevent it not, I purpose so.   55
York. What seal is that that hangs without thy bosom?
        Yea, look'st thou pale? Let me see the writing.
Aum. My lord, 'tis nothing.
York.   No matter, then, who see it.
        I will be satisfied; let me see the writing.
Aum. I do beseech your grace to pardon me;   60
        It is a matter of small consequence,
        Which for some reasons I would not have seen.
York. Which for some reasons, sir, I mean to see.
        I fear, I fear ——
Duch.   What should you fear?
        'Tis nothing but some band that he is ent'red into   65
        For gay apparel 'gainst the triumph day.
York. Bound to himself? What doth he with a bond
        That he is bound to? Wife, thou art a fool.
        Boy, let me see the writing.

---

55. it] *Capell; not in Qq, F.*   58. see] *Qq;* sees *F.*   65. band] *Qq;* bond *F.*
66. 'gainst] *Q1;* against *Q2–5, F.*   day] *Q1; not in Q2–5, F.*

---

55. *prevent it . . . so*] Capell's conjecture restores the metre. H. F. Brooks
suggests that the compositor may have
skipped from the "t" of *prevent* to the
"t" of *it*, omitting the second word; or
that there has been memorial assimi-
lation to the parallel phrase in *R 3*, II.
iii. 26: "if God prevent not". (See
note on II. ii. 98–121 for the influence of *R 3*.) Memorial assimi-
lation to IV. i. 148 is also possible, if, as
Pope conjectured, that line originally
read: "*Prevent*, resist it, let it not be
so."
   56.] The seal would be on a narrow
strip hanging down below the edge of
the document.
   61–2.] Another coincidence with
Hall, amply accounted for by the
references to "seeing" in Hol., 515/1/
22: "the father espieing it, would
needs see what it was: and though the
sonne humblie denied to shew it, the
father being more earnest to see it, by
force tooke it out of his bosome"; cf.
Hall, p. 17: "The father espied it, and

demaunded what it was, his sonne
lowely and beningly [*sic*] answered,
that it myght not bee sene . . ."
   65. *band that*] The forms *bond* and
band (see I. i. 2) were interchangeable,
and Shakespeare might have written
both within three lines of each other
(see l. 67 below), with *bound* at l. 67
intervening to effect the change. For
band that H. F. Brooks conjectures
band, taking *band that* as a corruption
due to a transcriber's anticipation of
bond / *That* at ll. 67–8. This would
restore the metre to an alexandrine,
or, if *he is* is pronounced *he's*, to an
even smoother line.
   66. *'gainst*] in preparation for; cf.
III. iv. 28.
   66–8.] The Duchess suggests that
Aumerle has borrowed money to buy
clothes, and given his creditor an
I.O.U.; York says that in that case the
creditor would be in possession of the
bond: *Bound to himself?* = "Whoever
heard of a man giving I.O.U.s to
himself?"

Aum. I do beseech you, pardon me; I may not show it.   70
York. I will be satisfied; let me see it, I say.
                    [*He plucks it out of his bosom and reads it.*
    Treason, foul treason! Villain! Traitor! Slave!
Duch. What is the matter, my lord?
York. Ho, who is within there? Saddle my horse!
    God for his mercy! What treachery is here!   75
Duch. Why, what is it, my lord?
York. Give me my boots, I say! Saddle my horse!
    Now by mine honour, by my life, by my troth,
    I will appeach the villain.
Duch.   What is the matter?
York. Peace, foolish woman.   80
Duch. I will not peace. What is the matter, Aumerle?
Aum. Good mother, be content—it is no more
    Than my poor life must answer.
Duch.   Thy life answer!
York. Bring me my boots: I will unto the king.

                His man enters with his boots.

Duch. Strike him, Aumerle. Poor boy, thou art amaz'd.   85
    Hence, villain! never more come in my sight.
York. Give me my boots, I say.
Duch. Why, York, what wilt thou do?
    Wilt thou not hide the trespass of thine own?
    Have we more sons? Or are we like to have?   90
    Is not my teeming date drunk up with time?

71. S.D.] *Qq; Snatches it F.*   73. What is] *Qq; What's F.*   74. who is]
Qq; who's F.   75. God] *Qq; Heauen F.*   76. is it] *Qq; is't F.*   78. mine]
Qq; my *F.*   by my . . . by my] *Qq;* my . . . my *F.*   81. Aumerle] *Qq;* sonne *F.*
84. S.D.] *Qq; Enter Seruant with Boots. F.*   89. thou not] *Q1, F;* not thou
Q2-5.

70. *I do*] This may be extra-metrical, and caught by memorial error on
the part of a scribe from the near-
repetition in l. 60 above. "I do beseech" leading to a longer line occurs
at II. i. 141 and does not seem to be
suspect there.

79. *appeach*] inform against; cf. l. 102
below.

85–6.] The Duchess thinks Aumerle
is too stupefied (*amaz'd*) by the accusation to carry out her command to
strike the servant.

90.] In history, York had another
son, and Aumerle was only the step-
son of this Duchess; he was the son of
York's first wife, Isabella of Castile
and Leon.

91. *teeming date*] period of child-
bearing.

And wilt thou pluck my fair son from mine age
And rob me of a happy mother's name?
Is he not like thee? Is he not thine own?

York. Thou fond mad woman,   95
Wilt thou conceal this dark conspiracy?   '
A dozen of them here have ta'en the sacrament,
And interchangeably set down their hands
To kill the king at Oxford.

Duch.   He shall be none;
We'll keep him here, then what is that to him?   100

York. Away, fond woman! were he twenty times my son
I would appeach him.

Duch.   Had'st thou groan'd for him
As I have done, thou wouldst be more pitiful.
But now I know thy mind: thou dost suspect
That I have been disloyal to thy bed,   105
And that he is a bastard, not thy son.
Sweet York, sweet husband, be not of that mind;
He is as like thee as a man may be,
Not like to me, or any of my kin,
And yet I love him.

99–100. He . . . none / We'll . . . to him /] *As F;* He . . . heere / Then . . . to
him / *Qq.*   101. Away, fond] *Qq, F;* Away, / Fond *Steevens (1793).*   101-
2. Away . . . son / I . . . him] *As Qq;* Away . . . my / Son . . . him *F.*   102-
3. Hadst . . . him / As . . . done] *As Rowe (ed. 2);* Hadst . . . done / *Qq, F.*
103. wouldst] *Qq;* wouldest *F.*   108. a] *Q1 (Cap. and Hunt.), 2–5, F;* any *Q1
(Huth).*   109. to] *Q1, F;* not in *Q2–5.*   or] *Qq;* nor *F.* any] *Q1 (Cap. and
Hunt.), 2–5, F;* a *Q1 (Huth).*

95. *fond*] foolish.

97. *dozen*] Hol., 514/2/61 says that
an "indenture sextipartite" was made,
which would imply that only six persons "set down their hands", but says
that nine persons were present altogether; *Traïson* (p. 77/229) names
eleven persons as present.

98. *interchangeably*] reciprocally; cf.
I. i. 146.

99. *He . . . none*] He shall not be one
of them.

101. *Away! . . . woman*] Without
Away the line would be metrically
regular. In view of the similar phrases

in the same part of the scene ("Thou
fond mad woman", l. 95; "Make
way, unruly woman!", l. 110; the
extra-metrical "Away" at l. 117)
we may suspect memorial corruption
here, centring on these repeated
exclamations: see Introduction, p.
xix.

103. *thou wouldst*] Pronounced
"thou'dst"; see Introduction, p. xxviii.
The line is apparently parodied by
Mistress Wafer in *Westward Ho* (1604),
III. iii. 64–5: "I, I, I, if you had
groand fort as I haue done you wold
haue bin more natural."

York.   Make way, unruly woman!   [*Exit.*
Duch. After, Aumerle! Mount thee upon his horse,   111
      Spur post, and get before him to the king,
      And beg thy pardon ere he do accuse thee.
      I'll not be long behind—though I be old,
      I doubt not but to ride as fast as York;   115
      And never will I rise up from the ground
      Till Bolingbroke have pardoned thee. Away, be gone.
                                              [*Exeunt.*]

SCENE III.—[*Windsor Castle.*]

Enter BOLINGBROKE, PERCY, *and other* Lords.

Bol. Can no man tell me of my unthrifty son?

112. Spur] *F;* Spur, *Qq.*   117. S.D.] *Rowe (ed. 2); Exit F; not in Qq.*

Scene III

Location] Wright; not in Qq, F.   S.D.] *F; Enter the King with his nobles. Qq.*
1. *Bol.] F; King or King H in speech-prefixes throughout Qq.*   me] *Qq; not in F.*

111. *Mount . . . horse*] Shakespeare
increases the drama by suggesting
that Aumerle steals his father's horse,
unless the point is due to a hasty misreading of the passage from Holinshed
quoted in the next note.

111–15.] Cf. Holinshed: "Rutland
seeing in what danger he stood, tooke
his horsse, and rode another waie to
Windsore in post, so that he got
thither before his father". Hall's version (p. 18) is: "Aumerle seyng in
what case he stode toke his horse and
rode another way to Windsor, riding
in post thither (whiche his father being an old man could not do.)". This
may have given a hint to Shakespeare's imagination, as the Clarendon
editors suggest; but the Duchess's
comparison is between her own riding
and York's, not between Aumerle's
fast youthful riding and York's old
man's riding, as in Hall; it is the
"spurring post" (riding with relays of

post-horses) that gets Aumerle first to
Windsor, and Shakespeare was not
dependent upon Hall's suggestion for
the parents' age as compared with the
son's youth

Scene III

MATERIAL. Ll. 1–22: the tradition
of Hal's dissoluteness and high spirits
goes back almost to Henry V's reign.
The several elements of this passage—
beating the watch, robbing travellers,
absence from court, wantonness,
familiarity with taverns and stews—
are recorded in one form or another in
nearly all the 16th century historians
and were part of the general folk-
story of Hal. In these lines they are
sufficiently generalized to be adequately derived from what everybody
knew about Hal's youth. The idea in
ll. 11–12 may refer to an occasion
when Hal is supposed to have defied
the Lord Chief Justice on behalf of his

'Tis full three months since I did see him last.
If any plague hang over us, 'tis he.
I would to God, my lords, he might be found.
Inquire at London, 'mongst the taverns there,   5
For there, they say, he daily doth frequent
With unrestrained loose companions,
Even such, they say, as stand in narrow lanes
And beat our watch and rob our passengers,
While he, young wanton, and effeminate boy,   10

4. God] *Qq;* heauen *F.*   9. beat . . . rob] *Qq;* rob . . . beat *F.*   10. While]
Pope; Which *Qq, F.*   wanton,] *F;* wanton *Qq.*

arraigned companions; the first mention of this famous story appears in
T. Elyot's *The Governour*, 1531 (Everyman edn, pp. 139–40) and it is found
in many other places, including Hol.,
543/2/10 ff. (I am indebted for the
substance of this paragraph to Professor A. R. Humphreys, whose full
treatment of the matter in his Arden
edn of *Henry IV* should be consulted.)

The rest of the scene continues v. ii.
Indebtedness to Hall as well as to
Holinshed has again been suggested,
but there seems little or nothing in the
scene that cannot be read as Shakespeare's dramatization of Holinshed.
Wilson's point that Hall gives in
oratio recta some of the conversation
between Aumerle and Bolingbroke,
which Holinshed does not, does not
take account of the fact that Shakespeare's version of this conversation
owes nothing to those phrases in Hall's
account of it which differ from the
words used by Holinshed. The Duchess of York's part is again Shakespeare's invention.

1. *me*] Apparently omitted by F to
smoothe the metre.

unthrifty] profligate as well as prodigal (Wilson).

7. *companions*] Often used con-
temptuously; cf. *2 H 4*, II. iv. 116;
Jonson, *Every Man in his Humour*, IV. ii.
114; Chapman, *Bussy d'Ambois*, I. ii.
116.

9. *watch*] watchmen.

our passengers] passers-by on the
king's highway.

10–12. *While . . . crew*] Many editors
print the *Which* of Qq and F, perhaps
guided by Abbott's view (¶272) that
the relative is being loosely used ad-
verbially for "as to which" (like *The
which* at III. iii. 45). This seems unlikely. *Which* could be defended on the
grounds that the sentence could be
interpreted "All which conduct he,
young wanton fellow and unmanly
boy, undertakes as a matter affecting
his personal honour to support [so
dissolute a crew]"—the last phrase,
which wrecks the grammar, being
added as an afterthought by Shakespeare, who forgot that he had already
supplied a subject for "support" in the
relative (Wilson). H. F. Brooks suggests that *So dissolute a crew* might be a
marginal revision inserted in the
wrong place, after Shakespeare had
perceived that *watch* and *passengers*
might be taken as the antecedent of
Which, and that he intended to strike
out *and effeminate boy* as partially repeating *young wanton*. Thus the lines
might have been meant to go: "So
dissolute a crew, which he, young
wanton, / Takes on the point of
honour to support". Certainly Bolingbroke's half-line here looks more like
the result of some accident than of
calculation.

10. *wanton*] Probably a noun (Herford): cf.III. iii. 164.

Takes on the point of honour to support
So dissolute a crew.

Percy. My lord, some two days since I saw the prince,
And told him of those triumphs held at Oxford.

Bol. And what said the gallant?   15

Percy. His answer was, he would unto the stews,
And from the common'st creature pluck a glove,
And wear it as a favour; and with that
He would unhorse the lustiest challenger.

Bol. As dissolute as desperate! But yet   20
Through both I see some sparks of better hope,
Which elder years may happily bring forth.
But who comes here?

Enter AUMERLE *amazed.*

Aum.   Where is the king?

Bol.   What means
Our cousin, that he stares and looks so wildly?

Aum. God save your grace! I do beseech your Majesty   25
To have some conference with your grace alone.

Bol. Withdraw yourselves, and leave us here alone.
                              [*Exeunt Percy and Lords.*]
What is the matter with our cousin now?

Aum. For ever may my knees grow to the earth,
My tongue cleave to my roof within my mouth,   30
Unless a pardon ere I rise or speak.

Bol. Intended, or committed, was this fault?
If on the first, how heinous e'er it be,

11–12.] *As F;* Takes ... crew / *Qq.*   14. those] *Qq;* these *F.*   16. unto] *Q1,*
F; to *Q2–5.*   20. But] *Ed. (Brooks conj.); not in Qq, F.*   20–4.] *As Brooks conj.;*
... both / ... yeares / ... heere / ... King / ... wildly / *Qq;* ... both /
... dayes / ... heere / ... King / ... stares / ... wildely / *F.*   21. sparks]
Q1, F; sparkles *Q2–5.*   22. years] *Qq;* dayes *F.*   23. S.D.] *Qq; Enter*
Aumerle. F.   27. S.D.] *Capell; not in Qq, F.*

14. *triumphs*] See note on v. ii. 52.

20–4.] *But,* conjectured by H. F.
Brooks, makes possible the restoration
of the verse for ll. 21–4. The compositor, having three words ending
in "t" (*desperat, but, yet*) could mistake
the "t" of *desperat* for the "t" of *but,*
or fail to use the doublet *but yet* when

the single *yet* has the same meaning.

23. S.D. amazed] distraught.

30.] Noble cfs. Ps., cxxxvii. 6: "let
my tongue cleaue to the roof of my
mouth", and Job, xxix. 10.

33. *on the first*] = "If your fault
stands on the first condition, is of the
former nature" (Schmidt).

To win thy after-love I pardon thee.

Aum. Then give me leave that I may turn the key,   35
That no man enter till my tale be done.

Bol. Have thy desire.

> [*The Duke of York knocks at the door and crieth.*

York. My liege, beware; look to thyself;
Thou hast a traitor in thy presence there.

Bol. I'll make thee safe.   [*Draws his sword.*]

Aum.   Stay thy revengeful hand,   40
Thou hast no cause to fear.

York.   Open the door,
Secure, foolhardy king. Shall I, for love,
Speak treason to thy face? Open the door,
Or I will break it open.

Enter YORK.

Bol.   Uncle, speak,
Recover breath, tell us how near is danger   45
That we may arm us to encounter it.

York. Peruse this writing here, and thou shalt know
The treason that my haste forbids me show.

Aum. Remember, as thou read'st, thy promise pass'd;
I do repent me, read not my name there,   50
My heart is not confederate with my hand.   †

York. It was, villain, ere thy hand did set it down.
I tore it from the traitor's bosom, king;
Fear, and not love, begets his penitence.
Forget to pity him, lest thy pity prove   55
A serpent that will sting thee to the heart.

---

35. I] *Q2–5, F; not in Q1.*   37. S.D.] *Qq; Yorke within. F.*   40–5.] *As Brooks conj.; . . . safe / . . . feare / . . . King / . . . face / Open . . . open / . . . breath / . . . daunger / Qq, F.*   40. I'll] *Ed. (Brooks conj.); Vilain Ile Qq, F.*   S.D.] *Johnson (Drawing.); not in Qq, F.*   42. Secure, foolhardy] *F; secure foole, hardie Qq.*   44. S.D.] *F; not in Qq.* Uncle,] *Ed. (Brooks conj.); What is the matter vncle, Qq, F.*   48. treason] *Qq; reason F.*

40–45.] For the text and lineation, see Introduction, pp. xviii–xix.

40. *safe*] harmless.

42. *Secure*] over-confident, unsuspecting; cf. II. i. 266, III. ii. 34.

42–3. *Shall . . . treason*] "Must I be-

cause of my love and loyalty speak treason", i.e. by calling you "foolhardy".

52. *it*] Aumerle's signature on his portion of the indenture sextipartite.

56.] For the image, see III. ii. 131 and note.

Bol. O heinous, strong, and bold conspiracy!
    O loyal father of a treacherous son!
    Thou sheer, immaculate and silver fountain,   †
    From whence this stream, through muddy passages,   60
    Hath held his current and defil'd himself,
    Thy overflow of good converts to bad;
    And thy abundant goodness shall excuse
    This deadly blot in thy digressing son.
York. So shall my virtue be his vice's bawd,   65
    And he shall spend mine honour with his shame,
    As thriftless sons their scraping fathers' gold.
    Mine honour lives when his dishonour dies,
    Or my sham'd life in his dishonour lies;
    Thou kill'st me in his life—giving him breath,   70
    The traitor lives, the true man's put to death.
Duch. [*Within*] What ho, my liege, for God's sake, let me in!
Bol. What shrill-voic'd suppliant makes this eager cry?
Duch. A woman, and thine aunt, great king,—'tis I.
    Speak with me, pity me, open the door,   75
    A beggar begs that never begg'd before.
Bol. Our scene is alt'red from a serious thing,
    And now chang'd to "The Beggar and the King".
    My dangerous cousin, let your mother in;
    I know she's come to pray for your foul sin.   80
York. If thou do pardon, whosoever pray,
    More sins for this forgiveness prosper may.

---

61. held] *Q1, 2;* hald *Q3–5;* had *F.*   72. S.D.] *Wright; Dutchesse within. F*
(after l. 71); not in Qq.   God's] *Qq;* heauens *F.*   73. shrill-voic'd] *F;* shril
voice *Q1, 2; unhyphened in Q3–5.*   74. thine] *Qq;* thy *F.*   80. she's] *F;* she
is *Qq.*   81. pardon,] *F;* pardon *Qq.*

---

59. *sheer*] pure and translucent.

62. *converts*] changes; cf. v. i. 66.

64. *digressing*] transgressing, "deviating".

69.] "Or in his dishonour my life lies shamed".

78. *The Beggar . . . King*] Probably a reference to the ballad of King Cophetua and the Beggar-Maid; Percy (*Reliques*, 1st ser. Bk II, 6) printed such a ballad from Johnson's *Crown Garland of Goulden Roses* (1612), but Shakespeare is probably referring

here, and at *2 H 4*, v. iii. 101, *Rom.* II. i. 14, *LLL.*, I. ii. 105–10 and IV. i. 65–8, to an older form of the ballad; for full discussion, see Arden edn of *LLL.*, ed. David, pp. 66–7. John remarks: "Bolingbroke is merely struck by the farcical aptitude of the title; no reference to the subject [of the ballad] is thought of."

81. *pardon, . . . pray*] I follow the F punctuation; "whosoever pray" = "no matter who prays".

82. *for*] because of.

This fest'red joint cut off, the rest rest sound;
This, let alone, will all the rest confound.

Enter DUCHESS.

Duch. O king, believe not this hard-hearted man!   85
Love loving not itself none other can.
York. Thou frantic woman, what dost thou make here?
Shall thy old dugs once more a traitor rear?
Duch. Sweet York, be patient. Hear me, gentle liege.
Bol. Rise up, good aunt.
Duch.   Not yet, I thee beseech: 90
For ever will I walk upon my knees,
And never see day that the happy sees
Till thou give joy—until thou bid me joy,
By pardoning Rutland my transgressing boy.
Aum. Unto my mother's prayers I bend my knee.   95
York. Against them both my true joints bended be.
Ill may'st thou thrive if thou grant any grace!
Duch. Pleads he in earnest? Look upon his face.
His eyes do drop no tears, his prayers are in jest,
His words come from his mouth, ours from our breast;
He prays but faintly and would be denied,   101
We pray with heart and soul, and all beside;
His weary joints would gladly rise, I know;
Our knees still kneel till to the ground they grow;
His prayers are full of false hypocrisy,   105
Ours of true zeal and deep integrity;
Our prayers do outpray his—then let them have
That mercy which true prayer ought to have.

83. rest rest] *Qq;* rest rests *F.*   84. S.D.] *F; not in Qq.*   91. walk] *Qq;*
kneele *F.*   97.] *Not in F.*   100. come] *Q1, F;* do come *Q2–5.*   104. still]
Qq; shall *F.*   108. prayer] *Qq;* prayers *F.*

83.] Noble cfs. Matt., xviii. 8: "If
then thy hande or thy foote offend
thee, cut them off. . ."
84. *This . . . alone*] i.e. left untreated.
86.] "Love which does not love
itself [its own offspring] cannot love
another." The Duchess implies that
York does not really love Bolingbroke, as he professed to at l. 42
above, since it would appear that
he does not love even his own son.
91.] Wilson cfs. the Shakespearian
addition to *Sir Thomas More* (ed.
Brooke, *Shakespeare Apocrypha,* II. iv.
134–5): "your unreuerent knees, /
Make them your feet to kneele to be
forgyuen!"
102.] Noble cfs. Deut., iv. 29: "seeke
[God] with all thy heart, & with all
thy soule."

Bol. Good aunt, stand up.
Duch.   Nay, do not say "stand up";
   Say "pardon" first, and afterwards "stand up".   110
   And if I were thy nurse, thy tongue to teach,
   "Pardon" should be the first word of thy speech.
   I never long'd to hear a word till now;
   Say "pardon", king, let pity teach thee how;
   The word is short, but not so short as sweet;   115
   No word like "pardon" for kings' mouths so meet.
York. Speak it in French, king, say "pardonne moy".
Duch. Dost thou teach pardon pardon to destroy?
   Ah, my sour husband, my hard-hearted lord,
   That sets the word itself against the word!   120
   Speak "pardon" as 'tis current in our land,
   The chopping French we do not understand.
   Thine eye begins to speak, set thy tongue there;
   Or in thy piteous heart plant thou thine ear,
   That, hearing how our plaints and prayers do pierce,
   Pity may move thee "pardon" to rehearse.   126
Bol. Good aunt, stand up.
Duch.   I do not sue to stand.
   Pardon is all the suit I have in hand.
Bol. I pardon him, as God shall pardon me.
Duch. O happy vantage of a kneeling knee!   130
   Yet am I sick for fear—speak it again:

---

109. *Bol.*] Q2–5, F; *yorke* Q1.   110. *Say*] Qq; *But* F.   124. *thy*] Q1 (*Cap. and Hunt.*), 2–5, F; *this* Q1 (*Huth*).   129. *God*] Qq; *heauen* F.

111. *And if*] See note on IV. i. 49.

113. *long'd*] Referring to the "longings" before child-birth; cf. *Troil.*, III. iii. 237.

115. *short as sweet*] An echo of the common saying "short and sweet", recorded from 1552 by Tilley S396.

117. *pardonne moy*] = *pardonnez-moi*, a polite way of refusing a request, like "pardon me" in *Meas.*, IV. ii. 171. *Pardonne* (*pardon'ne* in F) is pronounced as three syllables; *moy* rhymes with *destroy*. Herford cfs. *Jew of Malta* (*Works of Marlowe*, ed. Brooke, l. 1965).

120. *sets*] See note on IV. i. 270.

122. *chopping*] changing the meanings of words. The modern *chopping and changing* was current early in the 16th century.

123. *to speak*] i.e. to express (the emotion of) pity. The line plays on two connotations of *speak*, the usual one and its figurative application to "speaking" looks of eye or countenance.

125. *pierce*] Pronounced to rhyme with "rehearse" in the next line; see Kökeritz, p. 474.

126. *rehearse*] speak.

130. *vantage*] advantage.

Twice saying "pardon" doth not pardon twain,
But makes one pardon strong.

Bol.   With all my heart

I pardon him.

Duch.   A god on earth thou art.

Bol. But for our trusty brother-in-law and the abbot,   135

133-4. With . . . heart / I . . . him] *As Pope;* I pardon him with al my heart /
Qq, F.   135. and the] *Qq;* the *F.*

132-3.] To paraphrase, "To say
pardon twice does not divide pardon
into two (and thus weaken or negative it), but makes one pardon strong
by doubling it." *Twain* must =
"divide in twain", a rare usage not
found elsewhere in Shakespeare. The
Duchess seems to be implying dis-
agreement with the notion that if you
affirm twice you thereby deny: a
notion perhaps developed as a corollary of the idea that if you deny twice
you thereby affirm, as in Weever's
Faunus and Melliflora (1600), ed.
Davenport, ll. 370-1: "But some said
nothing, these gave full consent, /
And some said twice No, which
affirmes content."

133-4.] Pope's re-arrangement is
needed to preserve the rhyme, which
Shakespeare probably meant to keep
up until this phase of the scene concludes and Bolingbroke turns to
sterner business at l. 135.

134. *god on earth*] Cf. the lines from
the Shakespearian part of *Sir Thomas
More*: "[God] . . . hath not only lent
the king his figure, / His throne and
sword, but gyven him his owne name,/
Calls him a god on earth" (ed.
Brooke, *Shakespeare Apocrypha*, II. iv.
126-8); "A King is a mortal God on
earth" ("Essay of a King", printed
1642, included in Bacon's *Philosophical
Works*, ed. Robertson, 1905 edn, p.
809). Hart (p. 25) cites a number of
plays in which this or a similar phrase
is used. It reflects normal Tudor doctrine, and is found in Baldwin's dedication to *Mirror* (1559), p. 65: "God
. . . honoring & calling all kinges &
all officers vnder them by his owne

name, Gods. Ye be all Gods, as many
as haue in your charge any ministra-
cion of Iustice"; cf. Castiglione, *Courtier*, trans. Hoby (1561), Everyman
edn, p. 276. The scriptural warrant
for this, somewhat tortuously extracted
from Ps., lxxxii, John, x. 34-5, and
elsewhere, is discussed by Calvin in
his *Institutes*, trans. by Norton in 1561,
IV. 20. 4 (London edn of 1599, sig.
Sss1ᵛ) and was the basis of the doctrine that to rebel against a lawful
ruler is to rebel against God (on this,
see L. B. Campbell in her edn of
Mirror, pp. 52-3, and cf. Baldwin's
reflections on Jack Cade, *Mirror*, p.
178). It is not necessary with Zeeveld
(p. 324) to look for a far-fetched
parallel in Hall's account of an incident in Edward IV's reign (Hall,
p. 324), though Hol., 490/2/57 may
have given a hint to Shakespeare:
"Bushie . . . did not attribute to
[Richard] titles of honour, due and
accustomed, but inuented unused
termes and such strange names, as
were rather agreeable to the diuine
maiestie of God, than to any earthlie
potentate." The phrase *god on earth*, as
H. F. Brooks notes, is particularly appropriate here, because Bolingbroke is
being merciful, and the magistrate is
most god-like when most merciful: cf.
Mer. V., IV. i. 191-2: ". . . earthly
power doth then show likest God's /
When mercy seasons justice"; Bolingbroke in granting pardon is acting in
a most kingly way—on this topic and
its bearing on the interpretation of the
play, see Introduction, p. lxxiii.

135. *our . . . -law*] This was John
Holland, Earl of Huntingdon, hus-

With all the rest of that consorted crew,
Destruction straight shall dog them at the heels.
Good uncle, help to order several powers
To Oxford, or where'er these traitors are.
They shall not live within this world, I swear,   140
But I will have them, if I once know where.
Uncle, farewell; and cousin too, adieu:
Your mother well hath pray'd, and prove you true.
Duch. Come, my old son, I pray God make thee new. [*Exeunt.*

SCENE IV.—[*Windsor Castle.*]

Enter EXTON *and* Servants.

Exton. Didst thou not mark the king, what words he spake?
"Have I no friend will rid me of this living fear?"

142. too] *Q6; not in Q1–5, F.*   144. God] *Qq; heauen F.*   S.D.] *Exeunt.
Manet sir Pierce Exton, &c. Qq; Exeunt. Enter Exton and Seruants. F.*

Scene IV

SCENE IV] *Sc. continuous with previous sc. in F.   Location] Alexander; not in Qq, F.*
S.D.] *F (after* v. iii. 144*); Manet sir Pierce Exton, &c. Qq (after* v. iii. 144*).*

band of Bolingbroke's sister Elizabeth
and ringleader of the Oxford conspiracy. Shakespeare read about him
in Hol. 514/2/33 and 68, and brought
him in here for this brief mention because the information stuck in his
mind and to lend more verisimilitude
and historical colour to Bolingbroke's
threats against "all the rest"; for a
similar device, cf. III. i. 43 and note.
The line is very awkward, unless we
are to suppose *the* is elided in pronunciation; Shakespeare may originally
have omitted the *and* and inserted it
later to avoid giving the impression,
as F's version does, that "our . . .
brother-in-law" and the "abbot"
were the same person.

136. *consorted*] associated: cf. v. vi. 15.

137.] Cf. *R 3*, IV. i. 40: "Death and
destruction dogs thee at the heels".

138. *order . . . powers*] direct various
forces.

142.] Q6's emendation (traditionally accepted since Theobald) makes

a botched line worse; if it was ever
satisfactory, it seems now beyond
repair.

143. *prove . . . true*] As Wilson notes,
Aumerle died at Agincourt: see *H 5*,
IV. vi. 3–32.

144. *make . . . new*] Noble cfs. Bap-
tism service, Book of Common
Prayer: "grant that the Old Adam in
this child may be so buried, that the
new man may be raised up in him";
cf. also 2 Cor., v. 17, and see Tilley
M170.

Scene IV

MATERIAL. From Hol., 517/1/7 ff.
Craig, and Wilson (pp. li–lii), drew
attention to some of the suggested
links with Daniel, *C.W.*, III, st. 56;
Daniel may contribute two words *fear*
(l. 2) and *wisht* (but see note on l. 7);
coincidence is not ruled out.

2. *rid . . . fear*] Mostly echoed from
Holinshed but possibly one word from
Daniel; both Daniel and Holinshed

Was it not so?

Ser.   These were his very words.

Exton. "Have I no friend?" quoth he. He spake it twice,
And urg'd it twice together, did he not?   5

Ser. He did.

Exton. And, speaking it, he wishtly look'd on me,
As who should say "I would thou wert the man
That would divorce this terror from my heart",
Meaning the king at Pomfret. Come, let's go.   10
I am the king's friend, and will rid his foe.   [*Exeunt.*

3. *Ser.*] *F; Man Qq.*   These] *Qq;* Those *F.*   4. friend] *Q1, 3–5, F;* friends
Q2.   7. wishtly] *Q1, 2;* wistly *Q3–5, F.*   6. *Ser.*] *F; Man Qq.*   11. S.D.]
Q4, 5; Exit. F; not in Q1–3.

speak of Bolingbroke's desiring to be
rid: of *fear* (Daniel), of *danger* (Holinshed); *living* seems to be a compression
of the conceit about "life" and
"death" in the second excerpt from
Holinshed quoted below: (i) Hol.,
516/2/51: "And immediately after
[the Oxford conspiracy], king Henrie,
to rid himself of anie such like danger
... caused king Richard to die a violent death". (ii) Daniel, *C.W.*, III,
st. 56: "And wisht that some would so
his life esteeme / As rid him of these
feares wherein he stood". (iii) Hol.,
517/1/10: "Have I no faithfull freend
which will deliver me of him, whose
life will be my death, and whose
death will be the preservation of my
life?"

5. *urg'd ... together*] insisted on it
twice running; for *urge*, cf. III. i. 4,
IV. i. 271.

7. *wishtly ... me*] Wishtly = stead-
fastly, longingly, intently. It is only in
Daniel that Bolingbroke singles out
Exton with his eye, but *wishtly*, which
Wilson sees as an echo of Daniel's line
as quoted in note to l. 2 above, may be
an alteration of the better-known

word *wistly* under the influence of
wish (see *O.E.D.*, s.v. wishly). It may
even in this context be Q1's error for
wistly: Shakespeare uses *wistly* twice or
three times in his poems and always
in a context entailing one person
gazing intently or desirously at another (cf. *Ven.*, 343–4, where Q12
prints *wishtly* for the original's *wistly*;
Lucr., l. 1355; *Pilgr.*, vi. 11–12); cf.
also this from Ro: Ba:, *Life of Sir T.
More*, ed. Hitchcock and Hallett,
E.E.T.S. (1951), p. 263: "He turned
hym to Queen Anne, who stood by,
wistlie looking vpon her, sayd 'Thou
art the cause of this mans death.' "
Here the variants in the MSS are
wishly, *wystly*, and *wisly*. In *O.E.D.*,
s.v. wistly, nearly all the citations are
associated with the act of looking, and
cf. *Edward III*, II. ii. 89–90. It may
therefore be that the whole line, its
wishes and looks, owes little to Daniel
and more to a common usage which
Shakespeare adopted before *R 2*.

11. *rid ... foe*] i.e. "rid him of his
foe". *Rid*, as in l. 2 above, may be an
echo of either Holinshed or Daniel or
both.

SCENE V.—[*A prison at Pomfret Castle.*]

Enter RICHARD *alone.*

Rich. I have been studying how I may compare
    This prison where I live unto the world;   †
    And, for because the world is populous
    And here is not a creature but myself,
    I cannot do it. Yet I'll hammer it out.   5
    My brain I'll prove the female to my soul,
    My soul the father, and these two beget
    A generation of still-breeding thoughts,
    And these same thoughts people this little world,
    In humours like the people of this world;   10
    For no thought is contented. The better sort,
    As thoughts of things divine, are intermix'd
    With scruples, and do set the word itself

Scene v

SCENE v] *Scæna Quarta* F.   *Location*] Pope; *not in* Qq, F.   S.D.] Qq; *Enter Richard.* F.   1. I may] *Q1*; to Q2-5, F.   5. hammer it] *Qq*; hammer't F.   8. still-breeding] *Qq; unhyphened* F.   13-14. word . . . word] *Qq*; Faith . . . Faith F.

MATERIAL. Richard's soliloquy, ll. 1–66: Daniel (*C.W.*, III, st. 64–71), like Shakespeare, opens his description of Richard's death with a soliloquy by him. The substance of the two soliloquies does not at all correspond. Most of the incidents prior to the actual murder appear to be invented, but the appearance of a faithful groom may derive from a "germ" in Holinshed: his account of the loyalty of Richard's Gascon follower Jenico Dartois, who was imprisoned by Bolingbroke at Chester for refusing to put off Richard's badge (500/2/58). Possible sources of the "roan Barbary" episode are discussed in the note to ll. 77-90. From ll. 95 ff the details all derive from Hol., 517/1/20 ff.

3. *for because*] because.

5. *hammer it out*] work hard at it, puzzle it out; cf. *Gent.*, I. iii. 17-18.

9. *this little world*] The tenor of Richard's argument suggests that he is referring to the prison and not to the human microcosm (Richard himself). He wishes to compare the prison to the great world, but this is difficult because there are no people in the prison as there are in the world (ll. 1–5); so, with brain and soul as male and female, he will engender thoughts which will perform the function, essential to the maintaining of an analogy between prison and world, of peopling the prison (ll. 6–9); the analogy is completed, and the prison becomes proleptically *this little world*.

10. *humours*] temperaments.

13–14.] As is the case at v. i. 25, the repetition of a previous passage (v. iii. 120) is marked by irregular metre. F's version, although possibly due to a consultation of the prompt-book motivated by the irregularity, does not mend it, and certainly weakens the precision of what Richard says.

Against the word,
As thus: "Come, little ones"; and then again,   15
"It is as hard to come as for a camel
To thread the postern of a small needle's eye".
Thoughts tending to ambition, they do plot
Unlikely wonders: how these vain weak nails
May tear a passage thorough the flinty ribs   20
Of this hard world, my ragged prison walls;
And for they cannot, die in their own pride.
Thoughts tending to content flatter themselves
That they are not the first of fortune's slaves,

14–15.] *As Capell;* Against . . . againe / *Qq, F.*   14. the] *Q1, F;* thy *Q2–5.*
17. postern] *Q1, 2, F;* small posterne *Q3–5.*   small] *Qq; not in F.*   20.
thorough] *Qq* (thorow)*; through F.*

15–17.] Richard's two texts are found together in Matt., xix (14, 24), Mark, x (14, 25), Luke, xviii (16, 25). The famous cruces of the second—the possible meanings of *camel* and *needle*—may have been in Shakespeare's mind. *Postern* (small gate) seems to suggest the interpretation by which *needle* means the small entrance for pedestrians in a city-gate, while *thread* hints at the opposite interpretation by which *camel* means "cable-rope" (from Gk. κάμιλος). Both interpretations were available to Shakespeare, and perhaps he compromised between them in his choice of words. Thus W. L. Edgerton (*M.L.N.,* LXVI [1951], 550) cites Erasmus' *Paraphrases*, prescribed reading in Elizabethan churches, for the "gate" interpretation, while the "cable-rope" interpretation is found in the gloss of the Genevan Bible and in Beza's note to Matt., xix. 24 in the Tomson Revised Genevan N.T. (see Noble, p. 96). T. Lupset in his *A Treatise of Dieying Well* (1534 and later editions), like Shakespeare neatly suggests both when he writes: "For as harde a thynge it is to pluck through the smale nedels eie a greatte caboull rope, as to brynge a riche man in at heauens wycket" (*Works,* ed. Gee, p. 286). The verbal echoes are probably co-incidental, but Shakespeare might have remembered Lupset's treatise when he came to write Richard's dying words.

17. *needle*] Pronounced as one syllable, *neeld* or *neele;* cf. *MND.,* III. ii. 204, *John,* v. ii. 157.

19–21.] Richard's thought is reminiscent of the proverb that "Hunger breaks down stone walls" (Tilley H811), which also lies behind the description of Famine in Sackville's Induction to *Mirror,* p. 310, ll. 358–9: "Great was her force whom stonewall could not stay, / Her tearyng nayles snatching at all she saw" (and cf. *ibid.* p. 129, "Owen Glendower", l. 229: "Then hunger gnew, that doth the stone wall brast".) Shakespeare might have made the connexion between Richard and the image and proverb of Hunger because of his knowledge (derived from Holinshed) that one version of Richard's death was that he died by starvation—see note on l. 106 below. (I am indebted for the substance of this note to H. F. Brooks.)

20. *thorough*] See note on III. ii. 170.

21. *ragged*] rugged.

22. *for*] because.

in . . . pride] in their prime; Kittredge cfs. *1 H 6,* IV. vii. 15–16: ". . . there died, / My Icarus, my blossom, in his pride."

Nor shall not be the last—like silly beggars   25
Who, sitting in the stocks, refuge their shame,
That many have and others must sit there;
And in this thought they find a kind of ease,
Bearing their own misfortunes on the back
Of such as have before indur'd the like.   30
Thus play I in one person many people,
And none contented. Sometimes am I king,
Then treasons make me wish myself a beggar,
And so I am. Then crushing penury
Persuades me I was better when a king;   35
Then am I king'd again, and by and by
Think that I am unking'd by Bolingbroke,
And straight am nothing. But whate'er I be,
Nor I, nor any man that but man is,   †
With nothing shall be pleas'd, till he be eas'd   40
With being nothing.

                    [*The music plays.*
          Music do I hear?
Ha, ha! keep time—how sour sweet music is
When time is broke and no proportion kept!
So is it in the music of men's lives.
And here have I the daintiness of ear   45
To check time broke in a disordered string;
But for the concord of my state and time,

27. many have] *Q1, 3–5, F;* haue many *Q2.*   sit] *Q3–5, F;* set *Q1, 2.*
29. misfortunes] *Qq;* misfortune *F.*   31. person] *Q1;* prison *Q2–5, F.*
32. king] *Q1, F;* a King *Q2–5.*   33. treasons make] *Qq;* treason makes *F.*
36. king'd] *Q1, F;* king *Q2;* a king *Q3–5.*   38. be] *Qq;* am *F.*   41. S.D.]
Q1–3, F (after l. 38 in F); Musicke playes Q4; Musicks plaies Q5.   45. ear] *Q1–4,*
F (eare)*; care Q5.*   46. check] *Qq;* heare *F.*   a] *Q1, F; not in Q2–5.*

25. *silly*] simple-minded.
26–7. *refuge . . . That*] "Seek protection for the shamefulness of their condition in the thought that . . ."
Refuge is not found as a verb elsewhere in Shakespeare.
27. *sit*] See I. ii. 47 and note.
36. *king'd*] Cf. *John,* II. i. 371 and *H 5,* II. iv. 26 for other examples with somewhat different meanings.
37. *unking'd*] Cf. IV. i. 220 and note.
39–40.] In meaning, a tangle

which awaits elucidation; the line could mean "Nor I, nor any man . . . shall be pleased with anything until he is eased . . ." or "Nor I, nor any man . . . shall be pleased with [having or being given] nothing until he is eased. . ."
41. *With . . . nothing*] i.e. by dying.
42. *Ha, ha!*] Exclamation of annoyance or rebuke; cf. *Meas.,* II. iv. 42.
46. *check*] rebuke.
string] string instrument.

Had not an ear to hear my true time broke:
I wasted time, and now doth time waste me;
For now hath time made me his numb'ring clock;   50
My thoughts are minutes, and with sighs they jar
Their watches on unto mine eyes, the outward watch,
Whereto my finger, like a dial's point,
Is pointing still, in cleansing them from tears.
Now sir, the sound that tells what hour it is   55
Are clamorous groans which strike upon my heart,
Which is the bell—so sighs, and tears, and groans,
Show minutes, times, and hours. But my time
Runs posting on in Bolingbroke's proud joy,
While I stand fooling here, his Jack of the clock.   60
This music mads me. Let it sound no more;
For though it have holp mad men to their wits,
In me it seems it will make wise men mad.
Yet blessing on his heart that gives it me,

50. me] *Q1,F; not in Q2–5.* 56. which] *Qq;* that *F.* 58. times, and hours] *Qq;* hours, and times *F.* 60. of the] *Qq;* o' th' *F.* 62. have] *Q1–4, F;* hath *Q5.*

50. *numb'ring clock*] i.e. the clock by which Time "tells" the hours.

51–2.] The basic idea behind *My thoughts are minutes* seems to be: "A man reckons up and measures his existence by thoughts; but a clock's unit of measurement is the minute. Since I have become just like a clock, what would be thoughts, if I were still a man, have become minutes." Then Richard may be understood to ask himself "What does a clock do with its minutes?" and to reply "It registers them on its dial. *And with sighs . . . outward watch* renders this reply. It describes the process whereby the pendulum's sounds—they are also the man's sighs—(*with sighs they jar*) and the pendulum's movement (*jar . . . on unto*) translate what in a clock are the abstract units of measurement, the intervals of time (*their watches*), and in a man would be the periods of wakefulness and thoughtful vigils (*their watches* again: there is a quibble on the word like that at II. i. 78) on to the *outward watch*, viz., what in a clock is its

dial, and in a thoughtful vigilant man his eyes keeping outward watch. For *jar*, which can mean both the tick of a clock and a musical discord, cf. *Wint.*, I. ii. 43.

53–4. *dial's point*] Richard compares his finger, constantly wiping away tears from the clockface-eye, to the hand of a clock. *Them* in l. 54 refers to "mine eyes" not to "watches".

58. *times, and hours*] F's order is more logical; *times* = "whole period" (of life) as in "my time" in l. 58 below.

58–9. *But . . . joy*] i.e. "But my time, the time of Richard II, now hastens on in the proud joyful time of Bolingbroke"—like a traveller who has moved into a fresh landscape.

60. *Jack . . . clock*] The mannikin that strikes the quarters on some clocks; cf. *R 3,* IV. ii. 113–20.

62. *holp*] past participle of *help.* Belief in the restorative power of music was widespread, and was connected with the belief that music had a special hold over the passions; see *Lr.,* IV. vii. 25 ff. See also p. lxxxiii, n. 1.

> For 'tis a sign of love; and love to Richard   65
> Is a strange brooch in this all-hating world.

Enter a Groom of the Stable.

Groom. Hail, royal prince!
Rich.   Thanks, noble peer;
> The cheapest of us is ten groats too dear.
> What art thou? and how comest thou hither,
> Where no man never comes, but that sad dog   70
> That brings me food to make misfortune live?
Groom. I was a poor groom of thy stable, king,
> When thou wert king; who, travelling towards York,
> With much ado at length have gotten leave
> To look upon my sometimes royal master's face.   75
> O, how it ern'd my heart when I beheld

66. S.D.] *Qq; Enter Groome. F.*   70. never] *Q1–4;* euer *Q5, F.*   76. ern'd]
Qq; yern'd *F.*

66. *strange brooch*] i.e. something
noticeable and valuable. The connotation here derives from the phrase
"brooch and gem", used to indicate a
remarkable and outstanding person,
as in *Ham.,* IV. vii. 94–5: "He is the
brooch indeed / And gem of all the
nation"; Jonson, *Staple of News,* III. ii.
265: "the very broch o' the bench,
gem o' the City." The phrase and its
special meaning may have arisen from
the fact that brooches were worn pro-
minently in the hat, and were either
jewelled (hence valuable) or badges
indicating the wearer's trade. The
latter seems faintly hinted at in the
word *sign* at l. 65, and may in its turn
connect with the loyalty of Jenico
Dartois to Richard's badge (see note
on material).
67–8. *royal . . . dear*] i.e. "You have
priced me, the cheaper of us, ten
groats too high: I am at least no
dearer than you, my equal (peer)."
The joke proceeds from the *royal*'s or
rial's being worth 10s. and a *noble*
6s. 8d., i.e. ten groats less, the groat
being worth 4d. Cf. *1 H 4,* II. iv. 278 ff.
Tollet (in Johnson-Steevens Variorum

edn) quotes from Hearne, *Discourse
of Antiquities* . . ."Mr John Blower in a
sermon before her majesty [Elizabeth
I], first said, 'My *royal* queen', and a
little after: 'My *noble* queen'. Upon
which says the queen: 'What am I
ten groats worse than I was?' "
69.] An irregular short line, possibly allowing for a pause while
Richard scrutinizes the groom. H. F.
Brooks cites the Q1 of *R 3,* I. iv. 85:
"In Gods name what are you, and
how came you hither?", which D. L.
Patrick (*Textual History of Richard III,*
p. 50) showed to be a conflation of
I. iv. 85, as correctly given in F: "What
would'st thou Fellow? And how
cammst thou hither", with I. iv. 159:
"In Gods name what art thou?" This
is a memorial error. It is possible that
the line here in *R 2* is a similar memorial conflation derived from the two
lines in *R 3,* the transcriber being
prompted to it by similar phraseology
in the line that he has damaged.
75. *sometimes . . . master*] "my master,
formerly royal" or "my royal former
master"; cf. I. ii. 54 and note.
76. *ern'd*] grieved.

In London streets that coronation day
When Bolingbroke rode on roan Barbary—
That horse that thou so often hast bestrid,
That horse that I so carefully have dress'd!   80
Rich. Rode he on Barbary? Tell me, gentle friend,
    How went he under him?
Groom. So proudly as if he disdain'd the ground.
Rich. So proud that Bolingbroke was on his back!
    That jade hath eat bread from my royal hand;   85
    This hand hath made him proud with clapping him.
    Would he not stumble? would he not fall down,
    Since pride must have a fall, and break the neck

---

79. bestrid] *F;* bestride *Qq.*   83. he] *Qq;* he had *F.*

77–90.] The groom is describing Bolingbroke's coronation procession on 13 October 1399, not the processional rides into London reported by York in v. ii. 1–40. Neither in Holinshed nor in Froissart's much more lavish account (VI. 380–2) is there any mention of Bolingbroke's horse having originally been Richard's; some of the sources, including *Traïson,* state that Bolingbroke went on foot to be crowned. Shakespeare probably invented the whole episode, but may have been inspired to do so by Daniel's information that when Richard rode to London after his capture in Wales he was "Most meanely mounted on a simple steed"; Daniel derived this from Stow, *Chronicles* (1580), p. 538, which describes how Bolingbroke made Richard mount a "little nagge not worth forty franks", and Stow in his turn took the incident from Créton, p. 172/375. The passage in Daniel together with Daniel's mention of Bolingbroke's "white courser" (see note on v. ii. 18–20) may have led Shakespeare to imagine a situation in which Bolingbroke's splendid horse was originally Richard's, that monarch being well-known for his love of fine horses (see Webb's edition of Créton, note on pp. 99–100). Steevens' suggestion that the incident derives from Froissart's story (VI. 369) of how a greyhound of Richard's left the fallen king to fawn upon Bolingbroke in the base court of Flint Castle does not seem very plausible; nor is the incident to be connected with Stow's account (following Créton's) of how Sir T. Percy, Richard's steward who deserted to Bolingbroke, carried off the king's clothes and jewels and "many a good horse of foreign breed", since Percy was immediately despoiled of these by the Welsh before he reached Bolingbroke, as both Stow and Créton report. Hayward (1599) says that "All [Richard's] treasure and Iewels, with his horses, and al his fardage came to the Dukes hands" (p. 85). Hayward may be relying on this incident in Shakespeare, on a misreading of Stow, or on a source as yet untraced; if the last, Shakespeare may have had access to it too.

81. *Barbary*] Here, and at l. 78, used as though it were the name of an individual horse; Barbary or "Barb" was also the generic name for a breed of horses, much fancied in Shakespeare's own time: see Sieveking in *Shakespeare's England,* II. 408.

88. *pride . . . fall*] The only Shakespearian use of the proverb (see Tilley P581) which derives from Prov., xvi. 18.

Of that proud man that did usurp his back?
Forgiveness, horse! why do I rail on thee,   90
Since thou, created to be aw'd by man,
Wast born to bear? I was not made a horse,
And yet I bear a burthen like an ass,
Spurr'd, gall'd, and tir'd by jauncing Bolingbroke.

Enter one to Richard with meat.

Keeper. Fellow, give place; here is no longer stay.   95
Rich. If thou love me, 'tis time thou wert away.
Groom. What my tongue dares not, that my heart shall say.
                                                    [*Exit Groom.*

Keeper. My lord, will't please you to fall to?
Rich. Taste of it first as thou art wont to do.
Keeper. My lord, I dare not. Sir Pierce of Exton, who   100
        lately came from the king, commands the contrary.
Rich. The devil take Henry of Lancaster, and thee!
        Patience is stale, and I am weary of it. [*Strikes the Keeper.*]
Keeper. Help, help, help!

The murderers rush in.

Rich. How now! what means death in this rude assault?   105

94. Spurr'd, gall'd] *Qq*; Spur-gall'd *F*.   S.D.] *Qq*; *Enter Keeper with a Dish. F.*
97. S.D.] *Qq*; *Exit. F.*   99. art] *Q1–4*; wert *Q5, F.*   100–1.] *As Collier*;
... Exton / ... contrary *Qq, F.*   101. lately] *Qq, F*; late *Pope.*   103. S.D.]
Rowe (Beats ...); not in Qq, F.   104. S.D.] *Qq; Enter Exton and Seruants. F.*
105. what ... death] *Qq, F;* what mean'st thou *Vaughan conj.*

94. *jauncing*] moving up and down
with the horse's motion. There seems
no reason to suppose with *O.E.D.* that
the verb is transitive here. Cf. *Rom.*,
II. v. 52.
    S.D. meat] food.
    99. *Taste ... first*] The king's food
was "assayed" by the royal taster as a
precaution against poison. Holinshed
speaks of Richard's being "serued
without courtesie or assaie".
    100–1.] "This can only be printed
as prose," says Wilson, who detects
the two blank verse lines into which
"who lately" intrudes. Some kind of
verse could be reconstructed by

eliminating "My lord" (as caught
from l. 98 above), accepting Pope's
late for *lately*, and dividing the lines as
Qq, F.
    103. S.D.] According to Holinshed,
Richard struck the keeper on the
head with a carving-knife; Rowe's
"Beats ..." gives the wrong impression.
    105.] Meaning obscure. Kittredge
suggests "What does Death mean by
assailing me so violently?" but *means*
might be the second pers. sing. pres.
(cf. IV. i. 270, V. iii. 120). Vaughan's
conjecture is the most plausible attempt at emendation.

Villain, thy own hand yields thy death's instrument.
Go thou and fill another room in hell.

> [*Here Exton strikes him down.*

That hand shall burn in never-quenching fire
That staggers thus my person. Exton, thy fierce hand
Hath with the king's blood stain'd the king's own land.
Mount, mount, my soul! thy seat is up on high,   111
Whilst my gross flesh sinks downward, here to die.

> [*Dies.*]

Exton. As full of valour as of royal blood.
Both have I spill'd; O would the deed were good!
For now the devil that told me I did well   115
Says that this deed is chronicled in hell.
This dead king to the living king I'll bear.
Take hence the rest, and give them burial here. [*Exeunt.*]

---

106. thy own] *Q1–4;* thine own *Q5, F.*   107. S.D.] *Qq; Exton strikes him
downe. F.*   112. S.D.] *Rowe; not in Qq, F.*   118. S.D.] *Rowe; Exit F; not
in Qq.*

106.] Richard wrung the "bill" out
of the hands of one of the eight murderers and slew four of them with it,
according to Holinshed. This was
derived from Hall, who copied it from
Traïson; it is not accepted by modern
historians, who hold that Richard
starved, or was smothered, or both
(Steel, pp. 286–7).

108–12.] Richard's dying words are
not reported by Holinshed, who says
"Sir Piers . . . rid him out of life,
without giving him respit once to
cal to God for mercie of his passed
offenses." In Daniel's *C.W.,* III, st. 79

ff, no dying words are reported, but in
later editions of *C.W.* he revised this
under Shakespeare's influence.

114–18.] Exton's guilt of conscience
is related by Hol., 517/1/46. Mal-
travers, one of the murderers in
Edward II, and Lapoole, Gloucester's
murderer in *Woodstock* (v. i. 35 ff),
also suffer from conscience. Hall (p.
14) gives a more vivid account of
Exton's remorse than does Holinshed,
but Shakespeare had already created
other guilt-haunted characters like
Exton—the second Murderers in *2 H6,*
III. ii. 2–3, and in *R 3,* I. iv. 266–76.

SCENE VI.—[*Windsor Castle.*]

Flourish. Enter BOLINGBROKE, YORK, *with other* Lords *and*
Attendants.

Bol. Kind uncle York, the latest news we hear,
Is that the rebels have consum'd with fire
Our town of Ciceter in Gloucestershire,
But whether they be ta'en or slain we hear not.

Enter NORTHUMBERLAND.

Welcome, my lord; what is the news?   5
North. First, to thy sacred state wish I all happiness.
The next news is, I have to London sent
The heads of Salisbury, Spencer, Blunt and Kent:
The manner of their taking may appear
At large discoursed in this paper here.   10
Bol. We thank thee, gentle Percy, for thy pains,
And to thy worth will add right worthy gains.

Enter FITZWATER.

Fitz. My lord, I have from Oxford sent to London
The heads of Broccas and Sir Bennet Seely,

Scene VI

SCENE VI] *Scæna Quinta F.   Location.*] *Wright; not in Qq, F.   S.D.*] *F; Enter*
Bullingbrooke with the duke of Yorke. Qq.   1. *Bol.*] *F; King. in speech-prefixes*
throughout Qq.   3. *of*] *Q1-4, F; not in Q5.*   8. Salisbury, Spencer, Blunt] *F;*
Oxford, Salisbury, Blunt *Q1;* Oxford, Salisbury *Q2-5.*   12. S.D.] *Q6; Enter*
Lord Fitzwaters. Qq; Enter Fitz-waters. F.

MATERIAL. All the names and
details about the plot, the Abbot's
death and Carlisle's imprisonment
derive from Holinshed's long account,
which is very greatly compressed. The
entry of Exton with the coffin was
suggested by Holinshed's account of
the showing of the embalmed coffined
corpse in all towns between Pontefract and London where the bearers
rested at night (517/1/53 ff). The presentation of it to Bolingbroke seems to
be invention, suggested by Holinshed's
statement that Bolingbroke was pre-

sent at a requiem mass for Richard at
Westminster. Bolingbroke's disavowal
of the murder, not in Holinshed, is
discussed in note to l. 34.

3. *Ciceter*] Cirencester. The name
was pronounced roughly as Q1 spells
it, but is now said to be locally rendered "Zirenzester" or "Cirenzester":
see letters in *Sunday Times,* 10 Oct.
1954.

8. *Spencer*] See Introduction, pp.
xvi and xxi.

10. *At . . . discoursed*] Recounted in
full.

Two of the dangerous consorted traitors   15
That sought at Oxford thy dire overthrow.
Bol. Thy pains, Fitzwater, shall not be forgot;
    Right noble is thy merit, well I wot.   †

Enter PERCY *and the* BISHOP *of* CARLISLE.

Percy. The grand conspirator, Abbot of Westminster,
    With clog of conscience and sour melancholy   20
    Hath yielded up his body to the grave.
    But here is Carlisle living, to abide
    Thy kingly doom and sentence of his pride.
Bol. Carlisle, this is your doom:
    Choose out some secret place, some reverend room,   25
    More than thou hast, and with it joy thy life.
    So as thou liv'st in peace, die free from strife;
    For though mine enemy thou hast ever been,
    High sparks of honour in thee have I seen.

18. S.D.] *Rowe; Enter H. Percie. Qq (Henry . . . Q3–5); Enter Percy and Carlile.* F.
22. living,] *Qq;* liuing *F.*   25. secret] *Qq,* F; sacred *Vaughan conj.*   reverend]
Q4, 5, F; reverent *Q1–3.*

15. *consorted*] associated; cf. v. iii.
136.
20. *clog*] burden; cf. "clogging",
I. iii. 200. A metaphor from the wood-
en weight used to keep animals from
straying: see Jonson, *Poetaster*, IV. ii.
56: "[a] husband, [is] like your clog to
your *marmaset*".
25–6.] *Reverent*, which Q1 prints
here, was sometimes equivalent to
mod. *reverent*, respectful, and sometimes to mod. *reverend*, worthy of respect. J. C. Maxwell notes (in his
Arden edn of *Tit.*, note on II. iii. 296)
that on occasions the two forms are
carefully distinguished in sense
though not necessarily in spelling (e.g.
1 H 6, III. i. 49–50). Here "worthy of
respect" seems to be the meaning, and
reverend is the correct modern form.
The meaning of the whole sentence is
still far from clear: it might be
"Choose some secret place more
worthy of respect than that you now
have," the latter being a prison-cell.

Shakespeare is departing from Holinshed, who says that, although the
"King of his mercifull clemencie pardoned him", Carlisle died "more
through feare than force of sicknesse". Bolingbroke's conduct to him
may be a further attempt to sketch his
magnanimity, as already displayed in
his pardon to Aumerle. Bolingbroke
may be awarding the Bishop not
merely forgiveness but another
"place" or office, as Vaughan suggests by his conjecture *sacred* for
secret. Joy (= enjoy) *thy life* might be
faintly ironic: "Make the best you can
of *that*" or imply "You may live; I'm
not going to execute you." Neither of
these interpretations of *joy* would support Vaughan, but the word could be
taken more positively: "Take pleasure in life (i.e. with your new place)."
Reading *sacred* for *secret*, the lines
would then imply: "Choose out
another ecclesiastical office in addition to those you've already got, and

Enter EXTON *with the coffin.*

Exton. Great king, within this coffin I present   30
    Thy buried fear. Herein all breathless lies
    The mightiest of thy greatest enemies,
    Richard of Burdeaux, by me hither brought.
Bol. Exton, I thank thee not, for thou hast wrought
    A deed of slander with thy fatal hand   35
    Upon my head and all this famous land.
Exton. From your own mouth, my lord, did I this deed
Bol. They love not poison that do poison need,   †
    Nor do I thee. Though I did wish him dead,
    I hate the murtherer, love him murthered.   40
    The guilt of conscience take thou for thy labour,
    But neither my good word nor princely favour;

---

29. S.D.] *Qq*; *Enter Exton with a Coffin. F.*   35. slander] *Q1*; slaughter *Q2–5, F.*

enjoy yourself—I am a Merciful King."

34.] Bolingbroke's disavowal: a sentence in Holinshed runs (516/2/51) ". . . king Henrie . . . caused king Richard to die of a violent death, that no man should afterwards faine him-selfe to represent his person, though some haue said, he was not priuie to that wicked offense." Here it is not clear whether "he was not priuie . . . offense" means that Richard was not privy to that wicked offence of repre-senting his person (the reference is to the clerk Maudelyn's impersonation of Richard during the Oxford con-spiracy), or Henry was not privy to the offence of causing Richard's death. If Shakespeare read it as the latter, Bolingbroke's disavowal may owe something to the passage. Hayward (pp. 133–4) makes Bolingbroke dis-miss Exton without reward, and may be indebted to Shakespeare, but the disavowal of the man who undertakes to serve another by a crime is the classical turn to such an episode, a commonplace—witness the story of Pompey's murderer whom Caesar "abhorred . . . as detestable" (Plu-tarch, *Lives*, trans. North, Temple

Classics edn, VI. 335), Henry II's remorse for the murder of Becket, where the knights, like Exton, take a hint from their master (Hol., pp. 79–83), or the story of Edricus who mur-dered Edmund Ironside and was "headed" by Canute, and the similar tale of Sigbert (*Parts Added to the Mirror for Magistrates*, pp. 485, 460–2). Shakespeare himself had developed the theme in John's repudiation of Hubert before he learns that Hubert has not really murdered Arthur (*John*, IV. ii. 203–48). The point is considered at length by E. Daunce, *A Briefe Dis-course* (1590), pp. 20 ff, who cites many examples, including King David, Canute, and Cesare Borgia.

38.] Tilley K64 cfs. the proverbial expression "to love the treason and hate the traitor", to approve the end and not the means. Cf. the Duke's banishment of the Doctor, Dekker's *1 Honest Whore*, IV. iv. 48–50: "I banish thee for euer from my court. / This principle is olde but true as fate, / Kings may loue treason, but the traitor hate." Hayward (p. 134) comments on the unfavourable reception of Exton's crime: "so odious are vices euen when they are profitayble".

With Cain go wander thorough shades of night,
And never show thy head by day nor light.
Lords, I protest my soul is full of woe   45
That blood should sprinkle me to make me grow.
Come mourn with me for what I do lament,
And put on sullen black incontinent.
I'll make a voyage to the Holy Land,
To wash this blood off from my guilty hand.   50
March sadly after; grace my mournings here
In weeping after this untimely bier.   [*Exeunt.*

FINIS

43. thorough shades] *Wright;* through shades *Q1;* through the shade *Q2–5, F.*
47. what] *Qq;* that *F.*   51. mournings] *Qq;* mourning *F.*   52. S.D.] *F; not in Qq.*

43–4.] The line recalls that used by Mowbray of his own exile at I. iii. 177; cf. Pucelle's curse, *1 H 6*, v. iv. 87–90, and for the general sentiments, Daniel's own curse on Exton, *C.W.,* III, st. 81: "... leaue thee wretch vnto blacke infamie, / To darke eternall horror, and disgrace, / The hatefull skorne to all posterity, / The out-cast of the world, last of thy race, / Of whose curst seed, nature did then deny / To bring forth more."

43. *thorough*] Cf. III. ii. 170, v. v. 20.

45.] Cf. *True Tragedy of Richard III* (1594), M.S.R., l. 52: "Blood sprinkled, springs: blood spilt, craues due reuenge", the closest of several parallels in *R 2* to a play that Shakespeare may have drawn upon when writing *R 3*: see Wilson in *Shakespeare Quarterly*, III (1952), 299–306.

48. *incontinent*] immediately.

49.] This looks forward to Bolingbroke's intention to go on a crusade proclaimed in *1 H 4*, I. i. 18–28. The association of this design with remorse for Richard's murder is Shakespeare's invention. Bolingbroke's behaviour here foreshadows the religious gravity characteristic of the Henry of *H 4*.

Appendix I

HOLINSHED

(from *The Historie of England,* second edition, 1587[1])

THE QUARREL BETWEEN THOMAS MOWBRAY AND HENRY BOLINGBROKE

... in this parlement holden at Shrewsburie, Henrie duke of Hereford accused Thomas Mowbraie duke of Norfolke, of certeine words which he should utter in talke had betwixt them, as they rode togither latelie before betwixt London and Brainford, sounding highlie to the kings dishonor. And for further proofe thereof, he presented a supplication to the king, wherein he appealed the duke of Norfolke in field of battell, for a traitor, false and disloiall to the king, and enimie unto the realme. This supplication was red before both the dukes, in presence of the king: which doone, the duke of Norfolke tooke upon him to answer it, declaring that whatsoever the duke of Hereford had said against him other than well, he lied falselie like an untrue knight as he was. And when the king asked of the duke of Hereford what he said to it: he taking his hood off his head, said; My souereigne lord, even as the supplication which I tooke you importeth, right so I saie for truth, that Thomas Mowbraie duke of Norfolke is a traitour, false and disloiall to your roiall maiestie, your crowne, and to all the states of your realme.

Then the duke of Norfolke being asked what he said to this, he answered: Right deere lord, with your favour that I make answer unto your coosine here, I saie (your reverence saved) that Henrie of Lancaster duke of Hereford, like a false and disloiall traitor as he is, dooth lie, in that he hath or shall say of me otherwise than well. No more said the king, we have heard inough: and herewith commanded the duke of Surrie for that turne marshall of England, to arrest in his name the two dukes ...

... there was a daie appointed about six weeks after, for the king to come unto Windsor, to heare and to take some order betwixt the two dukes, which had thus appealed ech other. There was a great

1. Reprinted from the copy in the White Collection, King's College Library, Newcastle upon Tyne. The original is in black-letter; "u" (for "v") has been modernized, and marginal references omitted.

scaffold erected within the castell of Windsor for the king to sit with
the lords and prelats of his realme: and so at the daie appointed, he
with the said lords and prelats being come thither and set in their
places, the duke of Hereford appellant, and the duke of Norfolke
defendant, were sent for to come & appeare before the king, sitting
there in his seat of iustice ... withall the king commanded the dukes
of Aumarle and Surrie, the one being constable, and the other
marshall, to go unto the two dukes, appellant and defendant,
requiring them on his behalfe, to grow to some agreement: and for
his part, he would be readie to pardon all that had beene said or
doone amisse betwixt them, touching anie harme or dishonor to
him or his realme: but they answered both assuredlie, that it was
not possible to have any peace or agreement made betwixt them.

When he heard what they had answered, he commanded that
they should be brought foorthwith before his presence, to heare
what they would say... When they were come before the king and
lords, the king spake himselfe to them, willing them to agree, and
make peace togither: for it is (said he) the best waie ye can take.
The duke of Norfolke with due reverence hereunto answered it
could not be so brought to passe, his honor saved. Then the king
asked of the duke of Hereford, what it was that he demanded of the
duke of Norfolke, and what is the matter that ye can not make
peace togither, and become friends?

Then stood foorth a knight; who asking and obteining licence to
speake for the duke of Hereford, said; Right deare and sovereigne
lord, here is Henrie of Lancaster duke of Hereford and earle of
Derbie, who saith, and I for him likewise say, that Thomas Mowbraie duke of Norfolke is a false and disloiall traitor to you and your
roiall maiestie, and to your whole realme: and likewise the duke of
Hereford saith and I for him, that Thomas Mowbraie duke of Norfolke hath received eight thousand nobles to pay the souldiers that
keepe your towne of Calis, which he hath not doone as he ought:
and furthermore the said duke of Norfolke hath beene the occasion
of all the treason that hath been contrived in your realme for the
space of these eighteene yeares, & by his false suggestions and
malicious counsell, he hath caused to die and to be murdered your
right deere uncle, the duke of Glocester, sonne to king Edward.
Moreover, the duke of Hereford saith, and I for him, that he will
prove this with his bodie against the bodie of the said duke of Norfolke within lists. The king herewith waxed angrie, and asked the
duke of Hereford, if these were his woords, who answered: Right
deere lord, they are my woords; and hereof I require right, and the
battell against him.

There was a knight also that asked licence to speake for the duke of Norfolke, and obteining it, began to answer thus: Right deere sovereigne lord, here is Thomas Mowbraie duke of Norfolke, who answereth and saith, and I for him, that all which Henrie of Lancaster hath said and declared (saving the reverence due to the king and his councell) is a lie; and the said Henrie of Lancaster hath falselie and wickedlie lied as a false and disloiall knight, and both hath beene, and is a traitor against you, your crowne, roiall maiestic, & realme. . .

The king then demanded the duke of Norfolke, if these were his woords, and whether he had anie more to saie. The duke of Norfolke then answered for himselfe: Right deere sir, true it is, that I have received so much gold to paie your people of the towne of Calis; which I have doone, and I doo avouch that your towne of Calis is as well kept at your commandement as ever it was at anie time before, and that there never hath beene by anie of Calis anie complaint made unto you of me. Right deere and my sovereigne lord, for the voiage that I made into France, about your marriage, I never received either gold or silver of you, nor yet for the voiage that the duke of Aumarle & I made into Almane, where we spent great treasure: Marie true it is, that once I laid an ambush to have slaine the duke of Lancaster, that there sitteth: but neverthelesse he hath pardoned me thereof, and there was good peace made betwixt us, for the which I yeeld him hartie thankes. This is that which I have to answer, and I am readie to defend my selfe against my adversarie; I beseech you therefore of right, and to have the battell against him in upright iudgement.

After this, when the king had communed with his councell a little, he commanded the two dukes to stand foorth, that their answers might be heard. The K. then caused them once againe to be asked, if they would agree and make peace togither, but they both flatlie answered that they would not: and withall the duke of Hereford cast downe his gage, and the duke of Norfolke tooke it up. The king perceiving this demeanor betwixt them, sware by saint John Baptist, that he would never seeke to make peace betwixt them againe. And therefore sir John Bushie in name of the king & his councell declared, that the king and his councell had commanded and ordeined, that they should have a daie of battell appointed them at Coventrie. Here writers disagree about the daie that was appointed: for some saie, it was upon a mondaie in August; other upon saint Lamberts daie, being the seventeenth of September, other on the eleventh of September . . .

At the time appointed the king came to Coventrie, where the

two dukes were readie. . . The king caused a sumptuous scaffold or theater, and roiall listes there to be erected and prepared. [*Holinshed then reports that the two dukes took leave of the king, Bolingbroke on the Sunday, and Mowbray early on Monday morning.*]

The duke of Aumarle that daie, being high constable of England, and the duke of Surrie marshall, placed themselves betwixt them, well armed and appointed. . . About the hour of prime came to the barriers of the listes, the duke of Hereford, mounted on a white courser, barded with greene & blew velvet imbrodered sumptuously with swans and antelops of goldsmiths woorke, armed at all points. The constable and marshall came to the barriers, demanding of him what he was, he answered; I am Henrie of Lancaster duke of Hereford, which am come hither to doo mine indevor against Thomas Mowbraie duke of Norfolke, as a traitor untrue to God, the king, his realme, and me. Then incontinentlie he sware upon the holie evangelists, that his quarrell was true and iust, and upon that point he required to enter the lists. Then he put up his sword, which before he held naked in his hand, and putting downe his visor, made a crosse on his horsse, and with speare in hand, entered into the lists, and descended from his horsse, and set him downe in a chaire of greene velvet, at the one end of the lists, and there reposed himselfe, abiding the comming of his adversarie.

Soone after him, entred into the field with great triumph, king Richard. . . The king had there above ten thousand men in armour, least some fraie or tumult might rise amongst his nobles, by quarelling or partaking. When the king was set in his seat, which was richlie hanged and adorned; a king at armes made open proclamation, prohibiting all men in the name of the king, and of the high constable and marshall, to enterprise or attempt to approche or touch any part of the lists upon paine of death, except such as were appointed to order or marshall the field. The proclamation ended, an other herald cried; Behold here Henrie of Lancaster duke of Hereford appellant, which is entred into the lists roiall to doo his devoir against Thomas Mowbraie duke of Norfolke defendant, upon paine to be found false and recreant.

The duke of Norfolke hovered on horssebacke at the entrie of the lists, his horsse being barded with crimosen velvet, imbrodered richlie with lions of silver and mulberie trees; and when he had made his oth before the constable and marshall that his quarrell was iust and true, he entred the field manfullie, saieng alowd: God aid him that hath the right, and then he departed from his horsse, & sate him downe in his chaire which was of crimosen velvet, courtined about with white and red damaske. The lord marshall viewed their speares, to see that they were of equall length, and delivered the one speare himselfe to the duke of Hereford, and sent the other unto the duke of Norfolke by a knight. Then the herald proclaimed that the traverses & chaires of the champions should be removed, commanding them on the kings behalfe to mount on horssebacke, and addresse themselves to the battell and combat.

The duke of Hereford was quicklie horssed, and closed his bavier, and cast his speare into the rest, and when the trumpet sounded set forward couragiouslie towards his enimie six or seven pases. The duke of Norfolke was not fullie set forward, when the king cast downe his warder, and the heralds cried, Ho, ho. Then the king caused their speares to be taken from them, and commanded them to repaire againe to their chaires, where they remained two long houres, while the king and his councell deliberatlie consulted. . . [*Finally, Sir John Bushie reads the sentences of exile.*]

When these iudgements were once read, the king called before him both the parties, and made them to sweare that the one should never come in place where the other was, willinglie; nor keepe any companie to gither in any forren region; which oth they both received humblie, and so went their waies. The duke of Norfolke departed sorowfullie out of the relme into Almanie, and at the last came to Venice, where he for thought and melancholie deceassed: for he was in hope (as writers record) that he should have beene borne out in the matter by the king, which when it fell out otherwise, it greeved him not a little. The duke of Hereford tooke his leave of the king at Eltham, who there released foure yeares of his banishment: so he tooke his iornie over into Calis, and from thence went into France, where he remained.

A wonder it was to see what number of people ran after him in everie towne and street where he came, before he tooke the sea, lamenting and bewailing his departure, as who would saie, that when he departed, the onelie shield, defense and comfort of the commonwealth was vaded and gone. [*Holinshed then has a paragraph on Bolingbroke in France, his proposed marriage to the French king's cousin, and how Richard very heinously and revengefully intervened to prevent it.*]

RICHARD'S HARD DEALING AND THE DEATH OF JOHN
OF GAUNT: THE DUKE OF YORK'S DISTRESS

. . . to content the kings mind, manie blanke charters were devised, and brought into the citie, which manie of the substantiall and wealthie citizens were faine to seale, to their great charge, as in the end appeared. And the like charters were sent abroad into all shires within the realme, whereby great grudge and murmuring arose among the people. . .

In this meane time, the duke of Lancaster departed out of this life at the bishop of Elies place in Holborne, and lieth buried in the cathedrall church of saint Paule in London, on the northside of the high altar, by the ladie Blanch his first wife. The death of this duke gave occasion of increasing more hatred in the people of this realme toward the king, for he seized into his hands all the goods that belonged to him, and also received all the rents and revenues of his lands which ought to have descended unto the duke of Hereford by lawfull inheritance, in revoking his letters patents, which he had granted to him before, by vertue whereof he might make his attorneis generall to sue liverie for him, of any maner of inheritances or possessions that might from thencefoorth fall unto him, and that his homage might be respited, with making reasonable fine: whereby it was evident, that the king meant his utter undoing.

This hard dealing was much misliked of all the nobilitie, and cried out against of the meaner sort: but namelie the duke of York was therewith sore mooved, who before this time, had borne things with so patient a mind as he could, though the same touched him verie neere, as the death of his brother the duke of Glocester, the banishment of his nephue the said duke of Hereford, and other mo iniuries in great number, which for the slipperie youth of the king, he passed over for the time, and did forget aswell as he might. But now perceiving that neither law, iustice nor equitie could take place, where the kings wilfull will was bent upon any wrongfull purpose, he considered that the glorie of the publike wealth of his countrie must needs decaie, by reason of the king his lack of wit, and want of such as would (without flatterie) admonish him of his dutie: and therefore he thought it the part of a wise man to get him in time to a resting place, and to leave the following of such an unadvised capteine, as with a leden sword would cut his own throat.

Hereupon he with the duke of Aumarle his sonne went to his house at Langlie, reioising that nothing had mishappened in the common-wealth through his devise or consent. The common brute ran, that the king had set to farme the realme of England, unto sir William Scroope earle of Wiltshire, and then treasuror of England, to sir John Bushie, sir John Bagot, and sir Henrie Greene knights. [*In the remainder of this paragraph and the next two paragraphs further details of the king's fiscal exactions are given: these are attributed to his being* "destitute of treasure to furnish such a princelie port as he mainteined".]

HENRY BOLINGBROKE'S RETURN TO ENGLAND UNDER ARMS

Richard is in Ireland; letters are sent by divers of the nobility, magistrates and rulers in England to Bolingbroke "requiring him with all convenient speed to conveie himselfe into England, promising him all their aid, power and assistance, if he expelling K. Richard, as a man not meet for the office he bare, would take upon him the scepter, rule and diademe of his native land and region".

[*Details are given of the way Bolingbroke responds, goes to Brittany, prepares a fleet. Holinshed is uncertain whether he landed at Plymouth, or remained at sea, trying to judge the state of opinion in England.*]

When the lord governor Edmund duke of Yorke was advertised, that the duke of Lancaster kept still the sea, and was readie to arrive (but where he ment first to set foot on land, there was not any that understood the certeintie) he sent for the lord chancellor Edmund Stafford bishop of Excester, and for [*Scroope, Bushie, Bagot, Greene*] of these he required to know what they thought good to be doone in this matter, concerning the duke of Lancaster, being on the seas. Their advise was, to depart from London, unto S. Albons, and there to gather an armie to resist the duke in his landing, but to how small purpose their counsell served, the conclusion thereof plainlie declared, for the most part that were called, when they came thither, boldlie protested, that they would not fight against the duke of Lancaster, whome they knew to be evill dealt withall.

The lord treasuror, Bushie, Bagot, and Greene, perceiving that the commons would cleave unto, and take part with the duke, slipped awaie, leaving the lord governour of the realme, and the lord chancellor to make what shift they could for themselves: Bagot got him to Chester, and so escaped into Ireland; the other fled to the castell of Bristow, in hope there to be in safetie. The duke of Lancaster, after that he had coasted alongst the shore a certeine time, & had got some intelligence how the peoples minds were affected towards him, landed about the beginning of Iulie in Yorkshire, at a place sometime called Ravenspur, betwixt Hull and Bridlington. . . [*Names of the persons who flocked to his standard are given; York's army proves unwilling to fight Bolingbroke, and York eventually meets and communes with Bolingbroke at Berkeley; no details of their conversation are given. York and Bolingbroke proceed to Bristol, where* Scroope, Greene *and* Bushie *are* "taken and brought foorth bound as prisoners into the campe, before the duke of Lancaster. On the morow next insuing, they were arraigned before the constable and marshall, and found giltie of treason, for misgoverning the king and realme, and forthwith had their heads smit off."]

THE DEFECTION OF THE WELSH

Tempests prevent Richard hearing what is occurring in England; when he hears the news, after six weeks, Aumerle dissuades him from setting sail until all his fleet is ready, but he sends Salisbury over to gather forces in Wales and Cheshire, who within four days gets together forty thousand men.

But when they missed the king, there was a brute spred amongst them, that the king was suerlie dead, which wrought such an impression, and evill disposition in the minds of the Welshmen and others, that for anie persuasion which the earle of Salisburie might use, they would not go foorth with him, till they saw the king: onelie they were contented to staie fourteene daies to see if he should come or not; but when he came not within that tearme, they would no longer abide, but scaled & departed awaie; wheras if the king had come before their breaking up, no doubt, but they would have put the duke of Hereford in adventure of a field: so that the kings lingering of time before his comming over, gave opportunitie to the duke to bring things to passe as he could have wished, and tooke from the king all occasion to recover afterwards anie forces sufficient to resist him.

RICHARD'S ARRIVAL IN ENGLAND

At length, about eighteene daies after that the king had sent from him the earle of Salisburie, he tooke the sea, togither with the dukes of Aumarle, Excester, Surrie, and diverse others of the nobilitie, with the bishops of London, Lincolne, and Carleill. They landed neere the castell of Barclowlie in Wales [*and after hearing particulars of the forces arrayed against them went to join up with Salisbury at Conway.*]

He therefore taking with him such Cheshire men as he had with him at that present (in whom all his trust was reposed) he doubted not to revenge himselfe of his adversaries, & so at the first he passed with a good courage: but when he understood as he went thus forward, that all the castels, even from the borders of Scotland unto Bristow were delivered unto the duke of Lancaster, and that likewise the nobles and commons, as well of the south parts, as the north, were fullie bent to take part with the same duke against him; and further, hearing how his trustie councellors had lost their heads at Bristow, he became so greatlie discomforted, that sorowfullie lamenting his miserable state, he utterlie despaired of his owne safetie, and calling his armie togither, which was not small, licenced everie man to depart to his home.

The souldiers being well bent to fight in his defense, besought him to be of good cheere, promising with an oth to stand with him against the duke, and all his partakers unto death: but this could

not incourage him at all, so that in the night next insuing, he stole
from his armie, and with the dukes of Excester and Surrie, the
bishop of Carleill, and sir Stephan Scroope, and about halfe a
score others, he got him to the castell of Conwaie, where he found
the earle of Salisburie, determining there to hold himselfe, till he
might see the world at some better staie; for what counsell to take
to remedie the mischeefe thus pressing upon him he wist not. On
the one part he knew his title iust, true, and infallible; and his conscience cleane, pure, and without spot of envie or malice: he had
also no small affiance in the Welshmen, and Cheshire men. On the
other side, he saw the puissance of his adversaries, the sudden departing of them whom he most trusted, and all things turned upside
downe: he evidentlie saw, and manifestlie perceived, that he was
forsaken of them, by whom in time he might have beene aided
and relieved, where now it was too late, and too farre overpassed.
[*Holinshed then follows with a paragraph of moralization on the way in
which God has unexpectedly reversed the situations of Richard and Bolingbroke. Next, he recounts the desertion of the king's household officers.*]

THE CAPTURE OF RICHARD

*Bolingbroke's journey from Bristol to Chester by way of Berkeley and
Gloucester is described. . . Negotiations are set on foot between Richard (still
at Conway) and Bolingbroke (now at Chester), Northumberland being
Bolingbroke's emissary. Northumberland interviews Richard at Conway,
having on his way seized Flint Castle, and promises that if the king will call a
parliament to punish the murderers of Gloucester and will*"pardon the duke
of Hereford of all things wherin he had offended him" *the duke will
come on his knees to crave Richard's forgiveness. Richard believes Northumberland on the latter's oath, but on his way towards a meeting with Bolingbroke falls into an ambush already prepared and is forced by Northumberland
to go to Flint Castle. Bolingbroke, having learnt of the success of the plan,
musters his army before the Castle.*
The king that was walking aloft on the braies of the wals, to behold the comming of the duke a farre off, might see, that the archbishop and the other [i.e. *Aumerle, Worcester, and diverse other*] were
come, and (as he tooke it) to talke with him: whereupon he forthwith came downe unto them, and beholding that they did their due
reverence to him on their knees, he tooke them up, and drawing the
archbishop aside from the residue, talked with him a good while,
and as it was reported, the archbishop willed him to be of good comfort, for he should be assured not have anie hurt, as touching his
person; but he prophesied not as a prelat, but as a Pilat. For, was it
no hurt (thinke you) to his person, to be spoiled of his roialtie, to be

deposed from his crowne, to be translated from principalitie to prison, & to fall from honor into horror. All which befell him to his extreame hart greefe (no doubt:) which to increase, meanes alas there were manie; but to diminish, helps (God wot) but a few. So that he might have said with the forlorne man in the mercilesse seas of his miseries,

> Ut fera nimboso tumuerunt æquora vento,
> In mediis lacera nave relinquor aquis.

[*A paragraph follows discussing the position of the Archbishop and what the king said, or did not say, to him, and another describing how Bolingbroke's army surrounded the castle* "even downe to the sea".] . . . the duke came downe to the castell himselfe, and entred the same all armed, his bassenet onelie excepted, and being within the first gate, he staied there, till the king came foorth of the inner part of the castell unto him.

The king accompanied with the bishop of Carleill, the earle of Salisburie, and sir Stephan Scroope knight, who bare the sword before him, and a few other, came foorth into the utter ward, and sate downe in a place prepared for him. Foorthwith as the duke got sight of the king, he shewed a reverend dutie as became him, in bowing his knee, and comming forward, did so like wise the second and third time, till the king tooke him by the hand, and lift him up, saieng; Deere cousine, ye are welcome. The duke humblie thanking him said; My souereigne lord and king, the cause of my comming at this present, is (your honor saved) to have againe restitution of my person, my lands and heritage, through your favourable licence. The king herunto answered: Deere cousine, I am readie to accomplish your will, so that ye may inioy all that is yours, without exception.

Meeting thus togither, they came foorth of the castell, and the king there called for wine, and after they had dronke, they mounted on horssebacke, and rode that night to Flint [*and so through many places to London*] . . . neither was the king permitted all this while to change his apparell, but rode still through all these townes simplie clothed in one sute of raiment, and yet he was in his time exceeding sumptuous in apparell, in so much as he had one cote, which he caused to be made for him of gold and stone, valued at 30000 marks: & so he was brought the next waie to Westminster.

THE RECEPTION IN LONDON

As for the duke, he was received with all the ioy and pompe that might be of the Londoners, and was lodged in the bishops palace, by Paules church. It was a wonder to see what great concursse of

people, & what number of horsses came to him on the waie as he
thus passed the countries, till his comming to London, where (upon
his approch to the citie) the maior rode foorth to receive him, and
a great number of other citizens. Also the cleargie met him with
procession, and such ioy appeared in the countenances of the
people, uttering the same also with words, as the like not lightlie
beene seene. For in everie towne and village where he passed, children reioised, women clapped their hands, and men cried out for
ioy. But to speake of the great numbers of people that flocked togither in the fields and streets of London at his comming, I here
omit; neither will I speake of the presents, welcommings, lauds,
and gratfications made to him by the citizens and communaltie.

But now to the purpose. The next day after his comming to
London, the king from Westminster was had to the Tower, and
there committed to safe custodie. Manie evill disposed persons,
assembling themselves togither in great numbers, intended to have
met with him, and to have taken him from such as had the con-
veieng of him, that they might have slaine him. But the maior and
aldermen gathered to them the worshipfull commoners and grave
citizens, by whose policie, and not without much adoo, the other
were revoked from their evill purpose . . .

BOLINGBROKE'S ELECTION AND RICHARD'S ABDICATION
(*For the precise order of events see* IV. i *note on material.*)

[*In Parliament*] manie heinous points of misgovernance and
iniurious dealings in the administration of his kinglie office, were
laid to the charge of this noble prince king Richard, the which . . .
were ingrossed up in 33 solemne articles, heinous to the eares of all
men, and to some almost incredible . . . [*Here follow the articles.*]

[*Various persons who have access to Richard advise him to abdicate voluntarily, and*] . . . the king being now in the hands of his enimies, and
utterlie despairing of all comfort, was easilie persuaded to renounce
his crowne and princelie preheminence, so that in hope of life onelie, he agreed to all things that were of him demanded. And so (as
it should seeme by the copie of an instrument hereafter following)
he renounced and voluntarilie was deposed from his roiall crowne
and kinglie dignitie. . . [*Here follows the report of the commissioners sent
by Parliament to Richard, in which is contained Richard's written instrument of resignation. This reads in part as follows:*]

I Richard . . . acquit and assoile . . . all my liege men, both
spirituall and secular, . . . from their oth of fealtie and homage . . .
and from all manner bonds of allegiance, regalitie and lordship .
and them, their heires, and successors for evermore, from the same

bonds and oths I release, deliver, and acquit, and set them for free, dissolved and acquit. . . And also I resigne all my kinglie dignitie, maiestie and crowne, with all the lordships, power and privileges . . . and all other lordships . . . of what name, title, qualitie, or condition soever they be. . . And I renounce all right, and all maner of title of possession, which I ever had or have in the same lordships and possessions. . . And also I renounce the name, worship and regalitie and kinglie highnesse, clearelie, freelie, singularlie and wholie, in the most best maner and forme that I may, and with deed and word I leave off and resigne them, and go from them for evermore. . .

[*The lords and commons agree to the renunciation, the 33 articles had been drawn up and were ready to be read, but* "the reading of those articles at that season was deferred"; *certain persons are appointed to publish the* "open sentence of the deposing of king Richard", *which document then follows in full. The homage and fealty is to be formally disannulled by the commissioners, and immediately afterwards Bolingbroke* "laieth challenge or claime to the crowne". *The lords agree and the commons acclaim him; the Archbishop of Canterbury places him in the throne, and then delivers a sermon, which Holinshed prints in full, on the text* Vir dominabitur in populo, *1 Kings, chap. xi.*

Various other actions of the Parliament are reported, and it is related how representatives of the various estates go to Richard to signify their renunciation of the oaths of fealty and homage made to him]—Which renuntiation to the deposed king, was a redoubling of his greefe, in so much as thereby it came to his mind, how in former times he was acknowledged and taken for their liege lord and sovereigne, who now (whether in contempt or in malice, God knoweth) to his face forsware him to be their king. So that in his hevines he might verie well have said with a greeved plaintife,

> Heu quantæ sortes miseris mortalibus instant!
> Ah chari quoties oblivia nominis opto!
> O qui me fluctus, quis me telluris hiatus
> Pertæsum tetricæ vitæ deglutiat ore
> Chasmatico?

ON RICHARD'S CHARACTER AND FATE

His chance verelie was greatlie infortunate, which fell into such calamitie, that he tooke it for the best waie he could devise to renounce his kingdome, for the which mortall men are accustomed to hazard all they have. . . He was prodigall, ambitious, and much given to the pleasure of the bodie. He kept the greatest port, and mainteined the most plentifull house that ever any king in England did either before his time or since. For there resorted dailie to his court above ten thousand persons that had meat and drinke there allowed them ... in gorgious and costlie apparell they exceeded all measure, not one of them that kept within the bounds of his degree. Yeomen and groomes were clothed in silkes, with cloth of grain and skarlet ... and also other people abroad in the towns and countries, had their garments cut far otherwise than had beene accustomed before his daies, with imbroderies, rich furres, and goldsmiths worke, and every daie there was devising of new fashions, to the great hinderance and decaie of the common-welth.

[*There were abuses in the church.*] Furthermore, there reigned abundantlie the filthie sinne of leacherie and fornication, with abhomiable adulterie, speciallie in the king, but most cheefelie in the perlacie [*These sins so* "infected" *the kingdom that prince and people were justly punished by the wrath of God*].

... he was a prince the most unthankfullie used of his subiects, of any one of whom ye shall lightlie read. For although (thorough the frailtie of youth) he demeaned himselfe more dissolutelie than seemed convenient for his roiall estate, & made choise of such councellors as were not favoured of the people, whereby he was the lesse favoured himselfe: yet in no kings daies were the commons in greater wealth, if they could have perceived their happie state: neither in any other time were the nobles and gentlemen more cherished, nor churchmen lesse wronged. But such was their ingratitude towards their bountifull and loving sovereigne, that those whom he had cheeflie advanced, were readiest to controll him; for that they might not rule all things at their will, and remove from him such as they misliked, and place in their roomes whom they thought good, and that rather by strong hand, than by gentle and courteous meanes, which stirred such malice betwixt him and them, till at length it could not be asswaged without perill of destruction to them both.

The duke of Glocester cheefe instrument of this mischeefe, to what end he came ye have heard. And although his nephue the duke of Hereford tooke upon him to revenge his death, yet wanted he moderation and loialtie in his dooings, for the which both he himselfe and his lineall race were scourged afterwards, as a dire punishment unto rebellious subiects: so as deserved vengeance seemed not to staie long for his ambitious crueltie, that thought it not inough to drive king Richard to resigne his crowne and regall dignitie over unto him, except he also should take from him his guiltlesse life. What unnaturalnesse, or rather what tigerlike crueltie was this, not to be content with his principalitie? not to be con-

tent with his treasure? not to be content with his deprivation? not
to be content with his imprisonment? but being so neerelie knit in
consanguinitie, which ought to have moved them like lambs to
have loved each other, woolvishlie to lie in wait for the distressed
creatures life, and ravenouslie to thirst after his bloud, the spilling
whereof should have touched his conscience so, as that death ought
rather to have beene adventured for his safetie, than so savagelie to
have sought his life after the losse of his roialtie.

BAGOT'S INFORMING AND THE SUBSEQUENT
CHALLENGES IN PARLIAMENT

[*Parliament, 16 October:*] Sir John Bagot knight then prisoner in
the Tower, disclosed manie secrets . . . and further what great
affection Richard bare to the duke of Aumarle, insomuch that he
heard him say, that if he should renounce the governement of the
kingdome, he wished to leave it to the said duke. . . [*He further reported part of an alleged conversation with Mowbray, quoted in part in note
to* I. i. *132–4, as well as further alleged remarks of Aumerle showing his
complicity in Gloucester's murder and wish for Bolingbroke's death. Other
evidence, not mentioned by Shakespeare, is adduced; Aumerle denies everything.*]

[*Parliament, 18 October:*] The lord Fitzwater herewith rose up,
and said to the king, that where the duke of Aumarle excuseth himselfe of the duke of Glocesters death, I say (quoth he) that he was
the verie cause of his death, and so he appealed him of treason,
offering by throwing downe his hood as a gage to prove it with his
bodie. There were twentie other lords also that threw downe their
hoods, as pledges to prove the like matter against the duke of
Aumarle. The duke of Aumarle threw downe his hood to trie it
against the lord Fitzwater, as against him that lied falselie . . .
the duke of Surrie stood up also against the lord Fitzwater [*affirming that those who in Richard's parliament condemned Gloucester and his
associates were constrained to do so.*] . . . Moreover, where it was
alledged that the duke of Aumarle should send two of his servants to Calis, to murther the duke of Glocester, the said duke
of Aumarle said, that if the duke of Norfolke affirme it, he lied
falselie, and that he would prove with his bodie, throwing downe an
other hood which he had borowed . . . the king licenced the duke of
Norfolke to returne, that he might arraigne his appeale. . .

[*Parliament, 27 October:*] After [*much other business*] came the lord
Fitzwater, and praied to have day and place to arreigne his
appeale against the earl of Rutland [i.e. *Aumerle, whom Holinshed*

has already reported to have been deprived of his dukedom in the same sitting of Parliament]. The king said he would send for the duke of Norffolke to returne home, and then upon his returne he said he would proceed in that matter. . . [*Holinshed then turns to other matters, which fill his next column, at the foot of which he writes:*] This yeare Thomas Mowbraie duke of Norffolke died in exile at Venice, whose death might have been worthilie be wailed of all the realme, if he had not been consenting to the death of the duke of Glocester. [*cf. the previous report of his death, page 185 above.*] The same yeare deceassed the duchesse of Glocester, thorough sorrow (as was thought) which she conceived for the losse of hir sonne and heire the lord Humfrie [*see* II. ii. 97].

THE BISHOP OF CARLISLE'S SPEECH

[*In Parliament, 22 October:*] On wednesdaie following, request was made by the commons, that sith king Richard had resigned . . . he might have iudgement decreed against him, so as the realme were not troubled by him, and that the cause of his deposing might be published . . . which demand was granted. Whereupon the bishop of Carleill, a man both learned, wise, and stout of stomach, boldlie shewed foorth his opinion concerning that demand; affirming that there was none amongst them woorthie or meet to give iudgement upon so noble a prince as king Richard was, whom they had taken for their sovereigne and liege lord, by the space of two & twentie yeares and more; And I assure you (said he) there is not so ranke a traitor, nor so errant a theef, nor yet so cruell a murtherer apprehended or deteined in prison for his offense, but he shall be brought before the iustice to heare his iudgement; and will ye proceed to the iudgement of an anointed king, hearing neither his answer nor excuse? I say, that the duke of Lancaster whom ye call king, hath more trespassed to K. Richard & his realme, than king Richard hath doone either to him, or us: for it is manifest & well knowne, that the duke was banished the realme by K. Richard and his councell, and by the iudgement of his owne father, for the space of ten yeares, for what cause ye know, and yet without licence of king Richard, he is returned againe into the realme, and (that is woorse) hath taken upon him the name, title, & preheminence of king. And therfore I say, that you have doone manifest wrong, to proceed in anie thing against king Richard, without calling him openlie to his answer and defense. As soone as the bishop had ended this tale, he was attached by the earle marshall, and committed to ward in the abbeie of saint Albons.

THE ABBOT OF WESTMINSTER'S CONSPIRACY AND
AUMERLE'S PART IN IT

Its origins and the persons concerned are described—see note on IV. i. 152–3.
Holinshed continues:

The abbat highlie feasted these lords, his speciall friends, and
when they had well dined, they withdrew into a secret chamber ...
at length by the advise of the earle of Huntington . . . it was
devised, that they should take upon them a solemne iusts to be
enterprised . . . at Oxford, to the which triumph K. Henrie
should be desired, & when he should be most busilie marking
the martiall pastime, he suddenlie should be slaine and des-
troied. . . . Herupon was an indenture sextipartite made, sealed
with their seales, and signed with their hands, in the which each
stood bound to other, to do their whole indevour for the accomplish-
ing of their purposed exploit. Moreover, they sware on the holie
evangelists to be true and secret to each other, even to the houre and
point of death ...

... by [*the earl of Rutland's*] follie their practised conspiracie was
brought to light and disclosed to king Henrie. For this earle of Rutland departing before from Westminster to see his father the duke of
Yorke, as he sat at dinner, had his counterpane of the indenture of
the confederacie in his bosome.

The father espieng it, would needs see what it was: and though
the sonne humblie denied to shew it, the father being more earnest
to see it, by force tooke it out of his bosome; and perceiving the
contents thereof, in a great rage caused his horsses to be sadled out
of hand, and spitefullie reprooving his sonne of treason, for whom
he was become suertie and mainpernour for his good abearing in
open parlement, he incontinentlie mounted on horssebacke to ride
towards Windsore to the king, to declare unto him the malicious
intent of his complices. The earle of Rutland seeing in what danger
he stood, tooke his horsse, and rode another waie to Windsore in
post, so that he got thither before his father, and when he was
alighted at the castell gate, he caused the gates to be shut, saieng that
he must needs deliver the keies to the king. When he came before
the kings presence, he kneeled down on his knees, beseeching him of
mercie and forgivenesse, and declaring the whole matter unto him
in order as everie thing had passed, obtained pardon. Therewith
came his father, and being let in, delivered the indenture which he
had taken from his sonne, unto the king, who thereby perceiving
his sonnes words to be true, changed his purpose for his going to
Oxenford, and dispatched messengers foorth. . . [*Holinshed then
relates at great length the suppression of the conspiracy: the deaths of the*

Abbot ("through melancholy and palsy") *and the Bishop of Carlisle* ("more through feare than force of sicknesse") *are recorded in the conclusion.*]

THE DEATH OF RICHARD

[*Holinshed first discusses whether Richard* "died of forced famine" *or* "was so beaten out of hart, that wilfullie he starved himselfe, and so died in Pomfret castell".]

One writer which seemeth to have great knowledge of king Richards dooings, saith, that king Henrie, sitting on a daie at his table, sore sighing, said; Have I no faithfull freend which will deliver me of him, whose life will be my death, and whose death will be the preservation of my life? This saieng was much noted of them which were present, and especiallie of one called sir Piers of Exton. This knight incontinentlie departed from the court, with eight strong persons in his companie, and came to Pomfret, commanding the esquier that was accustomed to sew and take the assaie before king Richard, to doo so no more, saieng: Let him eat now, for he shall not long eat. King Richard sat downe to dinner, and was served without courtesie or assaie, whereupon much marvelling at the sudden change, he demanded of the esquier whie he did not his dutie; Sir (said he) I am otherwise commanded by sir Piers of Exton, which is newlie come from K. Henrie. When king Richard heard that word, he tooke the kerving knife in his hand, and strake the esquier on the head, saieng The divell take Henrie of Lancaster and thee togither. And with that word, sir Piers entred the chamber, well armed, with eight tall men likewise armed, everie of them having a bill in his hand.

King Richard perceiving this, put the table from him, & steping to the formost man, wrung the bill out of his hands, & so valiantlie defended himselfe, that he slue foure of those that thus came to assaile him. Sir Piers being halfe dismaied herewith, lept into the chaire where king Richard was woont to sit, while the other foure persons fought with him, and chased him about the chamber. And in conclusion, as king Richard traversed his ground, from one side of the chamber to an other, & comming by the chaire, where sir Piers stood, he was felled with a stroke of a pollax which sir Piers gave him upon the head, and therewith rid him out of life, without giving him respit once to call to God for mercie of his passed offenses. It is said, that sir Piers of Exton, after he had thus slaine him, wept right bitterlie, as one striken with the pricke of a giltie conscience, for murthering him, whome he had so long time obeied as king...

Appendix II

DANIEL

(from *The First Fowre Bookes of the ciuile warres betweene the two houses of Lancaster and Yorke*, first edition, 1595[1])

Book II, stanzas 66–98

66

Straight towards London in this heate of pride
The *Duke* sets forward as they had decreed,
With whom the *Captiue King* constraind must ride,
Most meanely mounted on a simple steed:
Degraded of all grace and ease beside,
Thereby neglect of all respect to breed;
For th'ouer-spreading pompe of prouder might
Must darken weaknes and debase his sight.

67

Approaching nere the Citty he was met
With all the sumptuous shewes ioy could deuise,
Where new-desire to please did not forget
To passe the vsuall pompe of former guise;
Striuing applause as out of prison let,
Runnes on beyond all bounds to nouelties:
And voice and hands and knees and all do now
A straung deformed forme of welcome show.

68

And manifold confusion running greetes
Shootes, cries, claps hands, thrusts, striues and presses nere:
Houses impou'risht were t'inrich the streetes,
And streetes left naked that vnhappy were
Plac'd from the sight where ioy with wonder meets,
Where all of all degrees striue to appeare:
Where diuers-speaking zeale, one murmur findes
In vndistinguisht voice to tell their mindes.

69

He that in glorie of his fortune sate,
Admiring what he thought could neuer be,

1. Reprinted from the copy in King's College Library, Newcastle upon Tyne. Long "s" has been modernized.

Did feele his bloud within salute his state,
And lift up his reioicing soule to see
So manie hands and harts congratulate
Th' aduancement of his long-desir'd degree:
When prodigall of thankes in passing by
He resalutes them all with cheereful eie.

70

Behind him all aloofe came pensiue on
The vnregarded king, that drooping went
Alone, and but for spight scarce lookt vpon,
Iudge if he did more enuy or lament:
O what a wondrous worke this daie is done,
Which th' image of both fortunes doth present,
In th' one to show the best of glories face,
In th' other worse then worst of all disgrace.

71

Now *Isabell* the young afflicted Queene,
Whose yeares had neuer shew'd her but delights,
Nor louely eies before had euer seene
Other then smiling ioies and ioyfull sights:
Borne great, matcht great, liu'd great and euer beene
Partaker of the worlds best benefits,
Had plac'd her selfe, hearing her Lord should passe
That way where shee vnseene in secret was.

72

Sicke of delay and longing to behold
Her long mist loue in fearfull ieoperdies,
To whom although it had in sort beene told
Of their proceeding, and of his surprize,
Yet thinking they would neuer be so bold
To lead their Lord in any shamefull wise,
But rather would conduct him as their king,
As seeking but the states reordering.

73

And forth shee looks: and notes the formost traine
And grieues to view some there she wisht not there,
Seeing the chiefe not come, staies, lookes againe,
And yet she sees not him that should appeare:

Then backe she stands, and then desires as[1] faine
Againe to looke to see if he were nere,
At length a glittring troupe farre off shee spies,
Percieues the thronge and heares the shoots & cries.

74

Lo yonder now at length he comes (saith shee)
Looke my good women where he is in sight:
Do you not see him? yonder that is hee
Mounted on that white courser all in white,
There where the thronging troupes of people bee,
I know him by his seate, he sits s'vpright:
Lo, now he bows: deare Lord with what sweet grace:
How long haue I longd to behold that face?

75

O what delight my hart takes by mine eie?
I doubt me when he comes but something neare
I shall set wide the window: what care I
Who doth see me, so him I may see cleare?
Thus doth false ioy delude her wrongfully
Sweete lady in the thing she held so deare;
For nearer come, shee findes shee had mistooke,
And him she markt was *Henrie Bullingbrooke*.

76

Then *Enuie* takes the place in her sweet eies,
Where sorrow had prepard her selfe a seat,
And words of wrath from whĕce complaints should rise,
Proceed from egar lookes, and browes that threat:
Traytor saith shee: i'st thou that in this wise
To braue thy Lord and king art made so great?
And haue mine eies done vnto me this wrong
To looke on thee? for this staid I so long?

77

O haue they grac'd a periur'd rebell so?
Well for their error I will weepe them out,
And hate the tongue defilde that praisde my fo,
And loath the minde that gaue me not to doubt:
O haue I added shame vnto my woe?
Ile looke no more; *Ladies* looke you about,

1. "was" (1595) corr. 1609.

And tell me if my Lord bee in this traine,
Least my betraying eies should erre againe.

78
And in this passion turnes her selfe away:
The rest looke all, and carefull note each wight;
Whilst she impatient of the least delay
Demaunds againe, and what not yet in sight?
Where is my Lord? what gone some other way?
I muse at this, O God graunt all go right.
Then to the window goes againe at last
And sees the chiefest traine of all was past.

79
And sees not him her soule desir'd to see,
And yet hope spent makes her not leaue to looke,
At last her loue-quicke eies which ready be,
Fastens on one whom though shee neuer tooke
Could be her Lord: yet that sad cheere which he
Then shew'd, his habit and his wofull looke,
The grace he doth in base attire retaine,
Causd her she could not from his sight refraine.

80
What might he be she said that thus alone
Rides pensiue in this vniuersall ioy:
Some I perceiue as well as we doe mone,
All are not pleasd with euery thing this day,
It maie be he laments the wronge is done
Vnto my Lord, and grieues as well he may,
Then he is some of ours, and we of right
Must pitty him, that pitties our sad plight.

81
But stay, ist not my Lord himselfe I see?
In truth if twere not for his base araie,
I verily should thinke that it were he;
And yet his basenes doth a grace bewray:
Yet God forbid, let me deceiued be;
O be it not my Lord although it may:
And let desire make vowes against desire,
And let my sight approue my sight a liar.

82

Let me not see him, but himselfe, a king;
For so he left me, so he did remoue:
This is not he, this feeles some other thing,
A passion of dislike or els of loue:
O yes tis he, that princely face doth bring
The euidence of maiestie to proue:
That face I haue conferr'd which now I see
With that within my hart, and they agree.

83

Thus as shee stoode assur'd and yet in doubt,
Wishing to see, what seene she grieud to see,
Hauing beliefe, yet faine would be without;
Knowing, yet striuing not to know twas he:
Her hart relenting, yet her hart so stout
As would not yeeld to thinke what was, could be:
Till quite condemnd by open proofe of sight
Shee must confesse or else denie the light.

84

For whether loue in him did sympathize
Or chance so wrought to manifest her doubt,
Euen iust before, where she thus secret pries,[1]
He staies and with cleare face lookes all about:
When she: tis ô too true, I know his eies
Alas it is my owne deare Lord, cries out:
And with that crie sinkes downe vpon the flore,
Abundant griefe lackt words to vtter more.

85

Sorrow keepes full possession in her soule,
Lockes him within, laies vp the key of breath,
Raignes all alone a *Lord* without controule
So long till greater horror threatneth:
And euen in daunger brought, to loose the whole
H'is forst come forth or else to stay with death,
Opens a sigh and lets in sence againe,
And sence at lēgth giues words leaue to complaine.

---

1. "prize" (1595) corr. 1609.

86

Then like a torrent had beene stopt before,
Teares, sighes, and words, doubled togither flow,
Confusdly striuing whether should do more,
The true intelligence of griefe to show:
Sighes hindred words, words perisht in their store,
Both intermixt in one together grow:
One would do all, the other more then's part
Being both sent equall agents from the hart.

87

At length when past the first of sorrowes worst,
When calm'd confusion better forme affords
Her hart commands her words should passe[1] out first,
And then her sighes should interpoint her words;
The whiles her eies out into teares should burst,
This order with her sorrow she accords,
Which orderles all forme of order brake,
So then began her words and thus she spake.

88

O dost thou thus returne againe to mee?
Are these the triumphs for thy victories?
Is this the glory thou dost bring with thee,
From that vnhappy Irish enterprise?
O haue I made so many vowes to see
Thy safe returne, and see thee in this wise?
Is this the lookt for comfort thou dost bring,
To come a captiue that wentst out a king?

89

And yet deare Lord though thy vngratefull land
Hath left thee thus, yet I will take thy part,
I doo remaine the same vnder thy hand,
Thou still dost rule the kingdome of my hart;
If all be lost, that gouernment doth stand
And that shall neuer from thy rule depart:
And so thou be, I care not how thou be,
Let greatnes goe, so it goe without thee.

1. "past" (1595).

90

And welcome come, how so vnfortunate,
I will applaud what others do dispise,
I loue thee for thy selfe not for thy state,
More then thy selfe is what without thee, lies:
Let that more go, if it be in thy fate,
And hauing but thy selfe it will suffize:
I married was not to thy crowne but thee,
And thou without a crowne all one to mee.

91

But what doe I heere lurking idlie mone
And waile apart, and in a single part
Make seuerall griefe which should be both in one,
The touch being equall of each others hart?
Ah no sweete Lord thou must not mone alone,
For without me thou art not all thou art,
Nor my teares without thine are fullie teares,
For thus vnioyn'd, sorrow but halfe appeares.

92

Ioine then our plaints & make our griefe ful griefe,
Our state being one, ô lets not part our care,
Sorrow hath only this poore bare reliefe,
To be bemon'd of such as wofull are:
O should I rob thy griefe and be the thiefe
To steale a priuate part, and seuerall share,
Defrauding sorrow of her perfect due?
No no my Lord I come to helpe thee rue.

93

Then forth shee goes a close concealed way
As grieuing to be seene not as shee was;
Labors t'attaine his presence all shee maie,
Which with most hard a doe was brought to passe:
For that night vnderstanding where he laie
With earnest treating she procur'd her passe
To come to him. Rigor could not deny
Those teares, so poore a suite or put her by.

94

Entring the chamber where he was alone
As one whose former fortune was his shame,
Loathing th'obraiding eie of anie one
That knew him once and knowes him not the same:
When hauing giuen expresse commaund that none
Should presse to him, yet hearing some that came
Turnes angerly about his grieued eies;
When lo his sweete afflicted Queene he spies.

95

Straight cleeres his brow & with a borrowed smile
What my dere Queene, ô welcome deare he saies?
And striuing his owne passion to beguile
And hide the sorrow which his eie betraies,
Could speake no more but wrings her hands the while,
And then (sweet lady) and againe he staies:
Th'excesse of ioy and sorrow both affords
Affliction none, or but poore niggard words.

96

Shee that was come with a resolued hart
And with a mouth full stoor'd, with words wel chose,
Thinking this comfort will I first impart
Vnto my Lord, and thus my speech dispose:
Then thus ile say, thus looke, and with this art
Hide mine owne sorrow to relieue his woes,
When being come all this prou'd nought but winde,
Teares, lookes, and sighes doe only tell her minde.

97

Thus both stood silent and confused so,
Their eies relating how their harts did morne
Both bigge with sorrow, and both great with woe
In labour with what was not to be borne:
This mightie burthen wherewithall they goe
Dies vndeliuered, perishes vnborne;
Sorrow makes silence her best oratore
Where words may make it lesse not shew it more.

98

But he whom longer time had learn'd the art
T'indure affliction as a vsuall touch:
Straines forth his wordes, and throwes dismay apart
To raise vp her, whose passions now were such
As quite opprest her ouerchardged hart,
Too small a vessell to containe so much,
And cheeres and mones, and fained hopes doth frame
As if himselfe belieu'd, or hop'd the same.

Appendix III

JOHN ELIOT

(from *Ortho-Epia Gallica*, 1593)

O Fruitfull France! most happie Land, happie and happie
    thrice!
O pearle of rich *European* bounds! O earthly Paradise!
All haile sweet soile! O France the mother of many conquering
    knights,
Who planted once their glorious standards like triumphing wights
Upon the banks of *Euphrates* where *Titan* day-torch bright
Riseth, and bloodie swords unsheathed where Phoebus drounds
    his light,
The mother of many Artist-hands whose workmanship most rare
Dimmes Natures workes, and with her fairest flowers doth
    compare.
The nurse of many learned wits who fetch their skill diuine
From *Rome* from *Greece* from Aegypt farre, and ore the learnedst
    shine,
As doth the glymmering-Crimsin-dye over the darkest gray:
Titan ore starres, or Phoebus flowers ore marigolds in May.
Thy flouds are Ocean seas, thy Townes to Prouinces arise,
Whose ciuill gouernment their walls hath raised to loftie skies;
Thy soile is fertill-temperate-sweete, no plague thine aire doth
    trouble.
Bastillyons fower borne in thy bounds: two Seas and mountaines
    double.

Appendix IV

SYLVESTER'S DU BARTAS

(from *Deuine Weekes and Workes*, 1605)

All-haile (deere ALBION) *Europes* Pearle of price,
The Worlds rich Garden, Earths rare Paradice:
Thrice-happy Mother, which aye bringest-forth
Such Chiualry as daunteth all the Earth,
(Planting the Trophies of thy glorious Armes   5
By Sea and Land, where euer *Titan* warmes):
Such Artizans as doo wel-neere Eclipse
Faire Natures praise in peere-less Workmanships:
Such happy Wits, as *Egipt*, *Greece*, and *Rome*
(At least) haue equal'd, if not ouer-come;   10
And shine among their (Modern) learned Fellowes,
As Gold doth glister among paler Yellowes:
Or as *Apollo* th'other *Planets* passes
Or as His Flower excels the Medow-grasses.
    Thy Riuers, Seas; thy Cities, Shires doo seem;   15
Ciuil in manners, as in Buildings trim:
Fenc'd from the World (as better-worth then That)
With triple Wall (of Water, Wood, and Brasse)
Which neuer Stranger yet had power to passe
(Saue when the Heau'ns haue for thy haynous Sinne   20
By some of Thine, with *false Keyes* let them in.

ADDITIONAL NOTES
TO TEXT AND COMMENTARY

p. 25, I. iii. 61.] A reference to the white falcon badge of Lancaster, suggests M. Maclagan, 'Genealogy and Heraldry . . .' in *English Historical Scholarship*, ed. L. Fox (Dugdale Society, 1956), p. 31.

p. 26, I. iii. 81. *casque*] helmet.

p. 38, I. iii. 294–9.] Compare also Ovid, *Metamorphoses*, VIII. 788–98, and for a probable indebtedness to Chaucer, see *Wife of Bath's Tale*, D. 1139–40: "Taak fyr, and ber it to the derkeste hous / Bitwix this and the mount of Kaukasous . . ." (cited by N. Coghill, 'Shakespeare's Reading in Chaucer' in *Elizabethan . . . Studies Presented to F. P. Wilson* [1959], pp. 94–5).

p. 50, II. i. 40–68.] In an important article in *S.P.*, LIII (1956), 114–40, 'Britain among the Fortunate Isles', Josephine Waters Bennett has thrown fresh light on this speech by tracing further the complex of ideas that, regarding Britain as geographically isolated from the rest of the world, associated it with the Isles of the Blest, with Eden, and with the Elysian Fields, by reason of its mild climate, its fertility, and the establishment in it of a reformed church, which had transformed it into a type of the Christian as well as of the classical Paradise. These ideas were eagerly adopted by many Elizabethan and later poets; they probably influenced Spenser's conception of fairyland as well as much in Gaunt's speech. Of the many post-Shakespearian allusions to them, Sir Edward Coke's speech at Norwich in 1606 after the discovery of the Gunpowder Plot may be cited: "this sea-environed island, the beauty and wonder of the world; this so famous and far-renowned Great Britain's monarchy . . . This so well-planted, pleasant, fruitful world, accounted Eden's Paradise, should have been made a place disconsolate [by the Plot]. Then, in our congregations, the songs of Sion had no more been sung. . ." (quoted by C. D. Brower, *The Lion and the Throne: the Life of Sir Edward Coke*, 1957, p. 249).

p. 51, II. i. 45.] Compare also the anonymous *Locrine* (? 1591), M.S.R., ll. 1407 ff: "If all the braue nation of the *Troglodites* . . . / If all the hostes of the Barbarian lands, / Should dare to enter this our little worlde . . ." For Giordano Bruno's use of the phrase *penitus toto divisos orbe Britannos* in his *Eroici Furori* (1585) see E. Wind, *Pagan Mysteries in the Renaissance* (1958), p. 182. Later, Ben Jonson celebrated the notion in three of his court masques: *The King's Entertainment* (1604), ll. 45–50, *The Masque of Blacknesse* (1608), l. 248, and *Love Freed from Ignorance and Folly* (1616), ll. 160–298 (line-references to the editions by Herford and Simpson, *Ben Jonson*, VIII).

p. 53, II. i. 55.] For the sentiments compare *True Tragedy of Richard III*, M.S.R., ll. 2196 ff: "Then happie England mongst thy neighbor Iles, / For peace and plentie still attends on thee. . . / The Turke admires to heare here government, / And babes in *Iury* sound her princely name. . . / The Turke hath sworne neuer to lift his hand, / To wrong the Princesse of this blessed land."

p. 59, II. i. 129. *Whom . . . befall*] whom may happiness await.

p. 60, II. i. 164. *tender*] careful, scrupulous (*O.E.D.* tender *adj.* 9b); cf. l. 207 below.

p. 61, II. i. 168. *my . . . disgrace*] The Petworth copy reads *his owne disgrace*. J. G. McManaway (*Shakespeare Survey*, XI [1957], 151) considers that the alteration found in the other three copies is a "patent error".

p. 65, II. i. 250. *wot*] know.

p. 71, II. ii. 22. *shapes*] pictures, or imaginary forms (*O.E.D.*, Shape *sb.* 1d, 5c).

p. 74, II. ii. 62–6.] Compare also Spenser, *Daphnaida*, ll. 29–34: "There came into my mind a troublous thought, / Which dayly doth my weaker wit possess; / Ne lets it rest, vntill it forth haue brought / Her long borne Infant, fruit of heauinesse."

p. 77, II. ii. 105. *sister*] For a similar speech-mistake supposed to be caused by distraction ("Countess" for "Emperor") cf. *Edward III*, II. ii. 35–7.

p. 82, II. iii. 59. *wot*] know.

p. 82, II. iii. 65.] Compare also Webster's use of the phrase "smile me a thanke", *Devils' Law-Case*, I. ii. 187.

p. 85, II. iii. 133. *challenge*] lay claim to, urge as my right.

p. 86, II. iii. 151. *issue*] outcome.

p. 97, III. ii. 60–3.] Cf. *The Wars of Cyrus* (printed 1594, Illinois Studies XXVIII [1942] edn., ll. 701 ff): "The lives of kings are garded by the gods / Nor are they in the hands of mortall men. / Assyrian, though thy sword were at my breast / The gealous angell that attends on us / Would snatch it from thy hands and fling it downe." (I owe this reference to Dr. G. K. Hunter.)

p. 103, III. ii. 179. *prevent . . . wail*] remove [or forestall] the causes for grieving (Deighton).

p. 105, III. ii. 204. *Beshrew thee*] = "I curse you, wish you ill" (*O.E.D.*, Beshrew 3b).

p. 105, III. ii. 212. *ear the land*] Cf. *Arden of Feversham* (1592), III. iv. 24.

p. 106, III. iii. 11–13.] For the sentiments compare *Edward II*, IV. vi. 93.

p. 108, III. iii. 30. *belike*] probably, possibly.

p. 108, III. iii. 52. *tottered*] Compare *Edward II*, II. ii. 21: "this tottered ensign".

p. 112, III. iii. 119. *prince and just*] Sisson's conjecture (*New Readings in Shakespeare*, 1956, II. 24) is adopted. He rightly says that the Folio emendation, adopted by most editors, is awkward and artificial, and suggests that the compositor of Q1 misread the sign for an ampersand as *es* and read *princes*, spelling it *princesse*; later Quartos and the Folio emended variously but failed to restore the original.

p. 114, III. iii. 174.] Richard is probably using a proverbial phrase, which increases the effect of mechanical weariness shot through with irony; cf. Dekker, *Shoemaker's Holiday*, IV. ii. 63: "Hereof am I sure, I shall liue till I die, / Although I neuer with a woman lie".

p. 116, III. iii. 203.] Compare Heywood, *If You Know not Me* (1605; Shakespeare Society edn, p. 20): "Wishes and tears have both one property: / They show their love that want the remedy."

p. 132, IV. i. 129. *forfend*] forbid.

p. 132, IV. i. 131. *obscene*] foul.

p. 136, IV. i. 185. *owes*] possesses.

p. 146, v. i. 11.] Shakespeare also may have had in mind the Ovidian tag "Iam seges est, ubi Troia fuit" (*Heroides*, I. 53); compare Marston, *Malcontent* (1604), II. v: "I ha seene Oxen plow up Altars: *Et nunc seges ubi Sion fuit*" (*Plays of Marston*, ed. Wood, I. 173).

p. 147. v. i. 30–3.] For the situation and metaphor compare *Edward II*, III. ii, 28–31: "This haught resolve becomes your majesty, / Not to be tied to their affection, / As though your highness were a schoolboy still, / And must be aw'd and govern'd like a child."

p. 150, v. i. 70. *part . . . part*] "part from [her], for you must depart".

p. 162, v. iii. 51.] This distinction between "heart" and "hand" here and at v. i. 82 is traditional: compare Dekker, *Shoemaker's Holiday*, III. iv. 40–1: "*Iane.* So, now part. / *Hamond.* With hands I may, but neuer with my heart"; Heylyn, *Cyprianus Anglicus* (1671), sig. Ggg 3ᵛ: "all the Members . . . Subscribed; every mans heart going together with his hand".

p. 163, v. iii. 59.] Heywood (*If You Know not Me*, Shakespeare Society edn, p. 55) describes the English Bible as a "fountain, clear, immaculate", and the fountain/stream metaphor as applied to parents and children here (and compare *Macb.*, II. iii. 96, *Oth.*, IV. ii. 60) may derive from Proverbs, v. 15–18.

p. 169, v. v. 2.] This line, says W. D. Smith ('Stage Settings in Shakespeare's Drama', *M.P.*, L (1952–3), 35) is "typical, for every time a character is in what is supposed to be prison the dialogue says so"; compare *1H6*, II. v. 57, *John*, IV. i. 17, *Meas.*, II. iii. 5.

p. 171, v. v. 39–40.] W. B. C. Watkins (*Shakespeare and Spenser*, 1950, p. 286) takes the lines in the former sense, and calls attention to the Spenserian structural balance and the *ease/please* internal rhyme: see *Faerie Queene*, I. ix. st. 40: "Sleepe after toyle, port after stormie seas, / Ease after warre, death after life does greatly please."

p. 178, v. vi. 18. *wot*] know.

p. 179, v. vi. 38.] Compare Nashe, *Pasquil of England*, sig. A4 (McKerrow, *Works of Nashe*, I. 63): "them that hauing somwhat to doe with a confection of poyson, reioyce when they finde it, yet they hate the malice of it, and throw it out of the doores when their turne is serued".